OXFORD CLASSICAL MONOGRAPHS

Published under the supervision of a Committee of the
Faculty of Literae Humaniores in the University of Oxford

The aim of the Oxford Classical Monographs series (which replaces the Oxford Classical and Philosophical Monographs) is to publish books based on the best theses on Greek and Latin literature, ancient history, and ancient philosophy examined by the Faculty Board of Literae Humaniores.

Powers of Expression, Expressions of Power

Speech Presentation and Latin Literature

ANDREW LAIRD

OXFORD
UNIVERSITY PRESS

OXFORD
UNIVERSITY PRESS

Great Clarendon Street, Oxford OX2 6DP

Oxford University Press is a department of the University of Oxford
and furthers the University's aim of excellence in research, scholarship,
and education by publishing worldwide in

Oxford New York

Athens Auckland Bangkok Bogotá Bombay Buenos Aires Calcutta
Cape Town Chennai Dar es Salaam Delhi Florence Hong Kong Istanbul
Karachi Kuala Lumpur Madras Melbourne Mexico City Mumbai
Nairobi Paris São Paulo Singapore Taipei Tokyo Toronto Warsaw

and associated companies in Berlin Ibadan

Oxford is a registered trade mark of Oxford University Press

Published in the United States
by Oxford University Press Inc., New York

© Andrew Laird 1999

British Library Cataloguing in Publication Data

Data available

Library of Congress Cataloging in Publication Data

Powers of expression, expressions of power: speech presentation
and Latin literature / Andrew Laird.
Includes bibliographical references.
1. Latin literature—History and criticism. 2. Speech in
literature. 3. Power (Social sciences) in literature. 4. Oral
communication in literature. 5. Latin language—Spoken Latin.
6. Language and culture—Rome. 7. Rome—In literature.
8. Rhetoric, Ancient.
PA6029.S62L35 1999 870.9′355—dc21 98-52497
ISBN 0-19-815276-0

1 3 5 7 9 10 8 6 4 2

Typeset in Imprint
by Joshua Associates Ltd., Oxford
Printed in Great Britain on acid-free paper by
Biddles Ltd., Guildford and King's Lynn

namque ferunt fama Hippolytum, postquam arte novercae
occiderit patriasque explerit sanguine poenas
turbatis distractus equis, ad sidera rursus
aetheria et superas caeli venisse sub auras,
Paeoniis revocatum herbis et amore Dianae.

(Virgil, Aeneid 7. 765–9)

Acknowledgements

First and foremost, I would like to thank Don Fowler for his generosity in providing all kinds of assistance, intellectual and practical, and for endeavouring (sympathetically) to purge this book of excessive idealism and eccentricity. I owe a great deal to him as a mentor and friend. A doctorate provided a major point of departure for the research presented here, so this is a fitting place to express my gratitude to Donald Russell who first supervised my D.Phil. thesis. None of my work will ever do justice to the outstanding guidance I received—and continue to receive—from him. Denis Feeney and Oliver Lyne, my thesis examiners, prompted me to plan the shape and nature of the study which follows.

David Cram, Irene de Jong, Monica Gale, Bruce Gibson, Christina Kraus, David Levene, Penny Murray, Keith Percival, Trevor Saunders, Michael Stokes, Ralph Walker, Andrea Wilson Nightingale, and Tony Woodman kindly read drafts of particular chapters, making valuable suggestions and criticisms; Adriana Cavarero read everything except Chapter 4—which was itself added at her prompting. Anthony Maude was patient enough to proof-read the whole manuscript. I have benefited from conversations with Alessandro Barchiesi, John Bramble, Pepe Clemente, Michael Comber, Mark Edwards, Tony Free, Michael Gilsenan, Ahuvia Kahane, Javed Majeed, David Norbrook, Jonathan Powell, Keith Sidwell, Michael Silk, Lambert Stepanich, and Greg Woolf. Oliver Taplin has been an enduring source of stimulus and morale: his impact on this endeavour is greater than he would realize.

I began the preparatory reading for this book as a Fellow by Examination at Magdalen College Oxford between 1989 and 1992. I am deeply grateful to the President and Fellows of Magdalen for electing me to a position which allowed me to pester, on a daily basis, leading authorities in a variety of disciplines. I should also thank St Hugh's College, Oxford for awarding me a Gateway Scholarship. Support from my students and colleagues in the

University of Warwick has made the completion of this project as pleasurable as it could be. Families are even more important institutions than universities: this is one place to thank my parents and my brother, Stephen, for their entertaining and useful advice, encouragement, and help.

David Nicholls will long be recognized for his significant contributions to Caribbean politics and history, political theory and political theology. His wisdom and kindness were conveyed by a sense of humour and a special presence which inspired everyone who met him. This book is dedicated to all the memories of David—of his ponchos, cigars, and disconcertingly erudite parrot, as well as of his writing and thought—and dedicated also to the future of the David Nicholls Memorial Trust. It is a very small way of acknowledging a very big influence.

A.L.

Oxford 1998

Contents

Introduction

It is characteristic of philosophical writing that it must con-
tinually confront the question of representation.

(Walter Benjamin, *The Origin of German Tragic Drama*)

We are aware of three types of poetic expression. In the first,
only the poet speaks—this is the case in three books of the
Georgics. The second type is dramatic in which the poet never
speaks—this is the case in comedies and tragedies. The third
type is mixed, as is the case in the *Aeneid*. For there, the
characters who are introduced speak, as well as the poet.

('Servius', *Commentary on Virgil*[1])

Ismail Kadare is Albania's best known writer. His novel *The File on
H* (*Dosja H*) was first published in 1981. It is about the controversy
caused by two Irish-American scholars who travel to rural Albania
in the 1930s. Their purpose is to study contemporary oral poetry in
order to understand how Homer's epics came to be composed.
Their use of a tape-recorder—a device previously unknown in
Albania—to capture poetry and speech arouses particular suspicion
and fear. The Irishmen, suspected of espionage, are themselves
spied upon. A local governor receives frequent reports, which
aspire to be comprehensive, from a man named Dull, the informer
responsible for trailing the scholars:

That was the tenor of the first part of the conversation, Dull reported,
saying that he had not managed to work out whether the monk Dushan
already knew the hermit, or whether this was his first visit to the cave. But
the spy was now going to relate the second part of the conversation, in no
way comparable to the foregoing, and begged the governor to forgive him

---

[1] See Ch. 2 nn. 16 and 48 for remarks on the context and significance of these
comments from the Servian corpus on Virgil, *Eclogues* 3.1.

for reproducing excerpts in direct speech, a form which in his view would give a more faithful rendering of what was actually said.

'So now he's going to write dialogue!' the governor exclaimed. 'Not what you'd call an uninventive fellow!'[2]

The File on H is concerned, in various ways, with the difficulties inherent in reportage: as messages move from speech to the written word, from oral poetry to literature, from one language to another, from an author to a reader. The excerpt quoted here highlights a specific problem which has immense implications. Direct discourse is not as straightfoward as it seems—for the spy it is a means of conveying what was said as closely as possible; for the governor it is a characteristic of literary invention.

Problems of this kind are not only apparent to readers of Albanian novels. On 7 September 1994, the *Daily Telegraph* newspaper ran a headline story about a dispute between John Major, then British Prime Minister, and Ian Paisley, head of the Democratic Ulster Unionist Party. This feature offered two competing accounts of a meeting between Paisley and Major. One account is attributed to Paisley himself:

Mr Paisley's account of his meeting with Mr Major:
❝When we entered the room Mr Major said to me: "Except you now give me a categorical assurance that you believe me, I will not talk with you."
I told Mr Major: "When you hear my submission, you will know what my position is."
Mr Major: "I will not listen to your submission, except you right now give me a categorical assurance that you believe my word."
Mr Paisley: "You are the first Prime Minister that ever asked a political opponent in this room, or outside this room, that if he doesn't swear he believes in your truthfulness, then you will not listen to him."
He said: "Get out of this room and never come back until you are prepared to say that I speak the truth and do not tell lies." ❞

The newspaper affects to reproduce Paisley's actual words in direct discourse. Unusually large quotation marks in bold type are supposed to emphasize that *all* the words quoted here are straight from the old warhorse's mouth. Paisley himself uses direct discourse *within* his own account of the conversation that took place. So Paisley's account is both rendered by direct discourse, and, in turn, happens to contain embedded direct discourse—as Paisley

[2] Kadare (1997), 127.

seeks to repeat, verbatim, his own very words and the very words of the Prime Minister. The second account of the same event—attributed to Sir Patrick Mayhew—runs as follows:

Sir Patrick Mayhew's account:
Sir Patrick said Mr Major saw no purpose in answering Mr Paisley's questions if he declined to accept the word of the British Prime Minister [that there had been no secret deal with the IRA]. The Prime Minister invited the DUP leader from the outset to say whether he accepted his word:
'Dr Paisley declined to answer that question. The Prime Minister reiterated it. Dr Paisley said that would become clear in the course of a submission he wished to make.
The Prime Minister heard the submission and reiterated the question.
The answer was not forthcoming so the Prime Minister said he saw no purpose whatsoever in answering the questions Dr Paisley had put.'

The early part of this second account is given by the *Daily Telegraph* in indirect discourse. The first distended quotation marks, which signal the direct discourse attributed to Mayhew, come halfway down this column. But Mayhew himself uses indirect discourse to recount what was said by Major and Paisley. Different forms of speech presentation are used for, and used by, the two witnesses.

The two accounts stand side by side in a box on the page of the newspaper. They are presented without explicit verbal comment. It would appear that we are not being inclined to prefer either of them as the control, as the true account from which the other deviates. However, the use of direct and indirect discourse does affect us in certain ways. The use of direct discourse for Paisley gives us the sense of having direct access, a window, not to his conversation with Major, but to what Paisley told the paper about the conversation. Almost because these *are* his actual words, we are not so inclined to believe their content: we judge them as we might judge Paisley himself. The indirect discourse reporting Mayhew's utterance is explicitly a version of it rather than a reproduction of it, just as Mayhew's own account of the conversation between Major and Paisley is an epitome, not a word by word rendition of it. For instance, we would never claim Mayhew was lying in saying 'Dr Paisley said that would become clear in the course of a submission he wished to make', if Dr Paisley had actually said, as he claims to have done:

'When you hear my submission, you will know what my position is.'

Indirect discourse gives room for manoeuvre to the person reporting the words of others. The use of the word 'invited' in the first
paragraph of that second account is an interesting example:

The Prime Minister invited the DUP leader from the outset to say whether
he accepted his word.

'Invite' is a curious performative word to find in this sort of
exchange. How often do we *invite* people to say whether or not
they believe us? One cannot say the use of the word 'invite' is an out
and out lie, but the word 'invite' functions rhetorically to make
Major's insistence look mild. The quoted words which follow
(attributed to Mayhew) indicate that Major began the exchange
with a question. Here is a discrepancy with the Paisley account.
According to the Paisley version, Major began the exchange not
with an invitation, nor with a question, but with a blunt assertion:

Except you now give me a categorical assurance that you believe me, I will
not talk with you.

Some other speech act verbs follow in Mayhew's quoted account:
'Dr Paisley *declined* to answer', 'The Prime Minister *reiterated*',
and again 'The Prime Minister reiterated'. These are ingenious.
They look neutral, but are they? The effect of distance and
objectivity is sustained all the way through. It is only in the last
sentence that Mayhew creeps, almost unnoticed, out of the closet,
and ever so discreetly emits a judgement on the event, a judgement
dressed in the ministerial grey of bland, disinterested description:

The answer was not forthcoming, so the Prime Minister said he saw no
purpose whatsoever in answering the questions Dr Paisley had put.

The word 'so' is significant here. It looks like an innocent connective,
but the words 'then' or 'and' would not incline us to buy into the
rationale of the Prime Minster's behaviour in quite the same way.
The word 'so' carries the innuendo of 'so for good reason', just as
Mayhew's use of the definite article ('*the* answer') delicately but
firmly conveys 'The *right* answer'. In these respects, indirect discourse appears to allow Mayhew's account more scope for manoeuvre and manipulation. Indirect discourse allows one to gloss
other people's words without being held liable for misquoting them.
It also looks more sober and restrained: opinion can be disguised as

fact. Paisley's account, on the other hand, exploits the drama of a direct speech rendition—even at the risk of misquoting, and thus being exposed to accusations of misrepresenting, what was said.

Both accounts of the conversation are partial, both accounts are rhetorically coloured; some of the partiality and rhetorical colouring has come from the ways in which direct discourse, indirect discourse, and even performative verbs (like 'invite') are deployed. These modes of speech presentation are deployed on more than one level. They operate within the accounts by Paisley and Mayhew themselves, and they are also used—by the *Daily Telegraph*—to render those very accounts in the first place.

The effects of such modes of discourse being used to construct characters' words, whether spoken or thought, is the subject of this book. The range of texts to be covered is principally drawn from Roman literature. But as these excerpts from *The File on H* and from the newspaper story indicate, this subject has applications for the study of many other kinds of spoken or written expression—in historical, cultural, linguistic, and social scientific investigations. The study of speech presentation is important for two major reasons. First, it can throw light on the themes and stylistic features of particular texts. Second, functions of speech presentation bear on broader concerns including form and content, representation, genre, ideology, and intertextuality. Insofar as it covers issues of wide theoretical interest, this book is addressed not only to readers of ancient literature—Greek as well as Latin—but also to those in other disciplines who are concerned with theories of discourse and narrative. To that end, all the significant passages discussed have been translated. The translations, unless indicated, are my own.

The opening chapter on speech and symbolic power shows how connections between reported discourse and power can be seen as a model for theories of *discourse* in its broader senses. This will be illustrated by examples from a range of authors including Homer, Horace, Suetonius, and Augustine. The relationship between a text and reader offers some important insights, if it is considered in conjunction with the connections between speakers and addressees, as they are presented in the texts we read. Conceiving of texts as utterances affirms the ideological dimension of intertextuality. The final part of the chapter will outline the connections between intertextuality and speech presentation. The second chapter will then consider the specific importance of speech presentation for the theory of narrative. The realization that narrative itself is a kind of discourse or speech will remain important for understanding the account of speech and poetry in Plato's *Republic*. This discussion will provide a synchronic account of some ancient and modern reflections on narrative: Plato's emphasis on the primary place of speech presentation stands as a useful critique of modern narratological theory.

Once the centrality of speech presentation has been established, the third chapter will explain the functions of 'speech modes'—all the various means by which characters' spoken or thought discourse can be presented in a text. Definition of these speech modes is not always a straightforward business. Moreover, different definitions have different implications for the identity of literary narrative, and for the problem of whether there is such a thing as 'literary language'. These questions remain prominent in the fourth chapter, which is devoted to historical narrative. This examination of discourses within historiography as well as the discourse of historiography itself will show how speech presentation can reveal something about the nature of historical representation. Most exemplary passages will be taken from works of Tacitus, but the chapter will conclude with a fresh consideration of the 'reliability' of the speeches recounted in Thucydides' *History of the Peloponnesian War*.

Some insights from these more theoretical essays are then directly applied to Latin narrative texts in the remaining part of this book. Some detailed discussion of linguistic features of particular passages is unavoidable, but the general tenor of my observations should be clear to non-Latinate readers. The fifth and sixth chapters survey speech presentation in Virgil's *Aeneid* and Petronius' *Satyricon* respectively. The discussion of Virgil bears directly on questions which have long been regarded as central to study of the *Aeneid*: these include divine and political authority, characterization, emulation of Homer, and the use of epic conventions. Some issues raised (e.g. the role of speech and silence in the poem) have a more general importance and applicability.

Whilst the *Aeneid* has always enjoyed exceptional prominence, the *Satyricon* is a rare example of Roman prose fiction. But even if prose fiction was a relatively marginal kind of writing in the ancient world, its importance for the history of narrative form has been amply demonstrated. The *Satyricon* not only pioneers a particular kind of sustained first-person narration. It is also celebrated for appearing to portray a real society, by seeming to caricature the colloquial language of its members. Study of speech presentation in a document like this inevitably raises larger questions about taste and ideology.

Specific techniques of reporting discourse are characteristic of recognized genres. Furthermore, speech presentation can expose striking differences of style between authors working in the same genre, even when they treat similar or virtually identical subjects. The final chapter will home in even more intensely on particular texts in order to illustrate this. It will offer a comparative analysis of speech presentation in scenes which involve the dictation and delivery of messages in epic poetry. As well as reviewing the practices of ancient poets including Homer, Virgil, Ovid, Statius, and Valerius Flaccus, I shall consider significant variations on the form in two later European epics: the *De Partu Virginis* of Iacopo Sannazaro and John Milton's *Paradise Lost*. Other motifs or contexts could be examined profitably, but scenes involving messengers or angels are especially useful because they are bound to employ reported discourse with a considerable degree of complexity. This analysis will involve many of the broader issues discussed earlier: notably ideology, intertextuality, and narratival representation.

But most importantly, the messenger scene itself can be seen as an *allegory* of both discursive representation and of textual interpretation. Readings from a variety of sources—including Plato's *Cratylus*, Coluccio Salutati's *De Laboribus Herculis*, and Umberto Eco's *Theory of Semiotics*—will inform my approach to the examination of this convention. Thus, the final chapter will be a reconfiguration, as well as an application, of the arguments previously presented.

Overall, this study moves gradually from general questions of theory in the earlier chapters to specific critical observations in the later ones. However, theoretical assertions have little value if they are not derived from—or demonstrated by—actual examples. Thus even the early chapters are organized around some key passages of ancient literature which signpost or even shape their arguments. Conversely, close readings of texts are of little use in a project like this unless they raise wider questions: inevitably the later chapters will engage with theoretical issues as well. It has not been easy to arrange this subject matter into the sequence just described. It was especially hard to decide which of the first three chapters should introduce the rest of the material offered here. I have tried to turn that authorial dilemma to the readers' advantage. Readers should be able to make sense of any one of those first three chapters, without needing to know the other two. Again, each of the last four chapters is self-standing. However, those chapters employ some abbreviations which, for convenient reference, are explained over-leaf. (These basic terms are given full discussion in Chapter 3.) Given that the importance of speech presentation cannot easily be conveyed in a linear manner, each chapter may be regarded as presenting the same state of affairs from a different perspective.

The presentation of characters' words or discourses has often been discussed as an aspect of narrative. But this has not been considered in connection with the awkward fact that words or discourses are also the medium of narrative itself. What narrative often 'represents' is actually made of the same material as the means it uses to 'represent'. That is a basic concern of this book. The realization that narrative and characters' discourse are made of the same stuff opens up several new lines of enquiry. Putting speech presentation at the centre stage does more than offer fresh insights on characterization, genre, ideology, representation and other issues. It also shows, in new ways, how these issues are intimately and inextricably connected.

Abbreviations

The following abbreviations will be used occasionally:

AND   angled narration of dialogue
DD   direct discourse
FDD   free direct discourse
FID   free indirect discourse
ID   indirect discourse
MID   mimetic indirect discourse
RSA   record of a speech act

These terms are discussed in full in Chapter 3.

I

Speech and Symbolic Power:
Discourse, Ideology, and Intertextuality

Speech is a great prince

(Gorgias of Leontini,
Helen)

In the first book of Homer's *Odyssey*, Penelope asks the bard Phemius not to sing about the Greeks' return from Troy. She says the subject is too depressing for her because she misses her husband Odysseus. This is the response of her son, Telemachus:

'Mother, why do you begrudge the loyal minstrel giving pleasure in whatever way his spirit moves him. It is not minstrels that are responsible, but Zeus who is to blame, who gives to men that live by toil to each one as he will . . . For yourself, let your heart and soul endure to listen; for Odysseus is not the only one who lost in Troy the day of his return: many others perished as well. But go to your quarters, and busy yourself with your own work, the loom and the spindle, and ask your handmaidens to get on with theirs. But speech (μῦθος) shall be for men, for all, but most of all for me; for mine is the authority (κράτος) in the house.'

(*Odyssey* 1. 346–9, 353–9)

Penelope respects Telemachus' claim to authority:

She then, seized with wonder, went back to her chamber, for she laid to heart the wise speech (μῦθον πεπνυμένον) of her son.

(*Odyssey* 1. 360–1)

This whole passage points to a relation between speech and power which is an inevitable feature of human communication.[1]

[1] Verses 356–9, deemed an interpolation by Aristarchus, are not to be found in all ancient editions. This does not adversely affect the tenor of my discussion here. In fact, aspects of the controversy about the inclusion of these verses highlight the importance of speech and power for philological interpretation. The recent commentary of Heubeck *et al.* (1988) ad loc. agrees with Aristarchus' verdict and describes Telemachus' claim that speech is not women's business as 'outrageous'

Telemachus here uses speech to assert his right to speak. Penelope acknowledges her subordinate role by silently obeying, and by not speaking in her turn—not even to say that she has heard, agrees and will comply. This passage also suggests that the relation between speech and power has something to do with truth. It is not just that Telemachus gets his way; he is shown to be right about the way things should be: Penelope laid to heart 'the wise speech' of her son.[2] This view of the way things should be can easily become—or become confused with—a view of the way things are. Power shapes and determines knowledge of the truth. It can consititute *authority* in the sense of 'the correct source of information' as well as in the sense of 'the powers that be'.

Speech, power, and claims to knowledge are connected in certain ways by the words of the characters in this passage. These notions might be connected in certain other ways by considering the discourse of the narrator here, in relation not only to the characters, but in relation also to various audiences and readers. In representing this episode, the narrative may be endorsing, opposing, or simply conveying the prevalent assumptions of these various communities of readers and listeners. The interaction between speech (or, in its broadest sense, 'discourse'), power, and knowledge is the field of ideology.[3] Ideas and beliefs about power and knowledge are apprehended through discourses.

and 'quite contrary to Homeric custom as we see it'. This impressionistic reaction does not offer adequate grounds for excision. Women *do* speak in Homer: but Telemachus might be opining on the way he thinks things ought to be, and not on Homer's poems. Anyway, the motives Heubeck *et al.* (1988) ascribe for an interpolation—of showing Telemachus' newly found assertiveness and of explaining Penelope's withdrawal—offer equally good grounds for regarding these verses as authentic.

[2] The narrator *more or less* makes it clear that Telemachus is right, because 'she laid to heart the wise judgement of her son' could be read as Penelope's own estimation of Telemachus' words. However, whether or not the narrator endorses it, Telemachus' opinion is validated to some extent by Penelope's acceptance of it. A subsequent utterance from Telemachus to Penelope at 21. 350–3 is interesting in this regard. The verses are a virtual repetition of the formula here with a significant difference: 'The *bow* shall be for men, but most of all for me, for mine is the authority in the house'!

[3] I define ideology as the (examination of) ways in which ideas, beliefs, and discourses are connected with power structures and power relations in society. The term 'ideology' has been fraught with controversy since it was first coined by Destutt de Tracy in *Éléments d'idéologie* (1801–5). Bullock and Stallybrass (1977), 298–9 and R. Williams (1988), 153–7 provide summaries of prevalent definitions. J. B. Thompson (1984) and Eagleton (1991) are more extensive discussions. Eagleton

I.I THEORIES OF DISCOURSE AND SPEECH PRESENTATION

The word 'discourse' has a long history and a broad spread of applications. Deriving from the Latin *discursus* ('running to and fro'), the word in English has at different times connoted reasoning, talk, conversation, narration, and—a sense which is still widely current—a spoken or written treatise on a particular subject.[4] In Anglo-American linguistics, 'discourse' has come to be a technical term for a continuous stretch of (mostly spoken) language longer than a sentence: a series of utterances which make up a 'speech event' like a sermon, lecture, or conversation.[5] Generally, discourses are understood as actually occurring instances of linguistic expression. The area of linguistics known as 'discourse analysis' is devoted to examples of everyday communication.[6] A great deal of discourse analysis adopts a socio-linguistic perspective, in considering the purpose or function of the discourse examined. Such examination of the relations between linguistic and non-linguistic behaviour highlights the potential of discourse analysis for investigating ideology. For example, the discussion of the newspaper article in the Introduction, though it is not 'discourse analysis' in the technical linguistic sense, at least shows that the scrutiny of linguistic features of a text, in conjunction with a sense of some of the text's functions can raise broader issues. One can obtain some impression of just how manifold these issues can be by considering the countless specific types of discourse available for examination: from education, the mass media, advertising, and so on.

A sense of the real potency of discourse for forming society, the personality, and even the unconscious may best be acquired by

(1994) is an anthology of writing on the theory of ideology from the Enlightenment to the present day.

[4] The *Oxford Latin Dictionary* article on *discursus* gives three broad senses for the word: (1) 'running off in different directions', (2) 'action of running this way and that', (3) 'bustling activity'. The major senses of 'discourse' given by the *Oxford English Dictionary* are mentioned in the main text here.

[5] Crystal (1985) at 96 provides useful definitions of 'discourse' and 'discourse analysis' in linguistics, and further bibliography. Benveniste (1971) has been a major influence on conceptions of discourse in the humanities and social sciences; Macdonell (1986) examines the role of discourse in cultural and literary theory.

[6] Brown and Yule (1983) is a standard account. For another view of 'discourse analysis' in relation to ideology, see J. B. Thompson (1984) and Eagleton (1991), 193–220.

thinking about the various relations discourses can have to the world.[7] The philosopher J. L. Austin drew a distinction between 'constative utterances' which more or less truthfully *describe* a state of affairs, and 'performative utterances' which aim to *bring about* a certain state of affairs.[8] Austin's speech act theory, which sees language as largely performative can apply to extended discourses, as well as to the shorter sentences it was designed to analyse. Discourses too can inform, clarify, confuse, warn, persuade, endorse, prohibit, praise, blame, welcome, exclude, entertain, or intimidate. Any one kind of discourse is likely to do a number of such things at once—some explicitly, others implicitly. Again, a discourse will accomplish different things for different sets of listeners or readers, and different things again for the agency that has produced or disseminated it. The very existence of a discourse determines, and is determined by, a complex of social exchanges.

There are parallels between the modern studies of discourse and the traditional domain of rhetoric. Indeed, the two have been held to be identical.[9] Rhetoricians, whether in antiquity or later ages, were not only concerned with the theory of composing political, forensic, or epideictic speeches. They were also concerned with the study of all kinds of previously existing discourses: drama, narrative poetry, history, philosophy, as well as oratory. The purpose of such study was to recognize and imitate techniques of persuasion and argumentation, figures of speech, and features of style. Rhetoric—which has always incorporated literary criticism—was a creative activity which acknowledged the affective capacity of discourses it reviewed. In defending eloquence from the charge that it is affected and superfluous to the ordinary demands of linguistic communication, Quintilian effectively distinguishes between the performative and constative roles of discourse:[10]

---

[7] The work of Jacques Lacan has been very much concerned with the role of discourse in understanding and conceiving the unconscious. See Lacan (1966). Wright (1986), 151–65 is a clear introduction to Lacanian psychoanalysis and its importance for textual interpretation. Crapanzano (1992) extends Lacan's thought to representation of the self in ethnology and philosophy.

[8] See J. L. Austin (1971) on performatives and constatives. J. L. Austin (1962) and Searle (1979; 1980) provide standard discussions. Ohman (1971), Petrey (1990) and Pratt (1977) consider implications of speech act theory for theory of literature in different ways. See also Derrida (1967). Cohen (1994) and Kahane (1996) apply speech act theory to particular ancient texts.

[9] Eagleton (1983), 206. See also Leith and Myerson (1989).

[10] I am grateful to Ahuvia Kahane for alerting me to this passage.

Nam mihi aliam quandam videtur habere naturam sermo vulgaris, aliam viri eloquentis oratio; cui si res modo indicare satis esset, nihil ultra verborum proprietatem elaboraret; sed cum debeat delectare, movere in plurimas animum audientis species impellere, utetur his quoque adiutoriis, quae sunt ab eadem nobis concessa natura.

(Institutio Oratoria 12. 10. 43)

For common language seems to me to have one kind of nature, the speech of an eloquent man has another. If it was sufficient for him merely to convey the facts, he might not engage in any elaboration beyond the customary range of what words mean. But since he has to delight, move the mind of his hearer, and induce all sorts of impressions, he is bound to employ those additional aids which are granted to us by that nature already mentioned.

The very conception of discourse here supports the claims of today's speech act theory. Contemporary disciplines and systems of thought have come to consider discourses in terms of the ways in which they represent, enforce, or undermine political, social, and psychological structures. A deliberate preoccupation with these issues has spread from philosophy, literary studies, and linguistics into history, politics, the social sciences, psychology, and many other fields which endeavour to give accounts of the world. The role of discourse theory in enlarging, even constituting, feminism as a system of critique has been especially remarkable.[11]

A direct and detailed treatment of these broad theories of discourse and their applications is beyond the scope of this study. However, speech is the issue in this book—and these general theories of discourse derive from the specific example of speech. The simple idea of somebody engaged in the act of speaking is not merely a vehicle or microcosm of these theories: it is the basis for them. Just as discourse constitutes social hierarchy and human identity, so speech makes up the organization of a narrative and shapes the identity of characters. The relations I shall discuss between speech and power in narrative texts are part and parcel of the relations between discourse and domination in every area of human activity. Thus the recurrence of the word 'discourse' in labelling speech modes ('direct discourse', 'free indirect discourse', etc.) discussed throughout this book felicitously evokes the larger significances of the term.

[11] See e.g. Courtivron and Marks (1980), Kristeva (1984), Moi (1985) and (1986*b*).

It may look as if I am drawing specious analogies in order to make speech presentation appear to be a grander business than it really is. But these analogies or identifications are not of my own invention. Pioneering work by the Bakhtin Circle in the 1920s heralded the importance of discourse theory and ideology for history, literature, and the social sciences in later decades: some studies were specifically devoted to the study of speech modes in narrative texts.[12] I do not aim to reproduce or directly apply the insights of those studies here—though I will mention them at certain points in this book, as their importance for the subject of speech presentation is considerable.

1.2 SPEECH AS AN INDEX OF POWER

Examples of speech being used to assert or display power are ubiquitous. Telemachus' silencing of Penelope in the *Odyssey* naturally has parallels elsewhere in Homer. I will discuss briefly here an example which has gained the particular attention of scholars. This is the episode involving Thersites, in the second book of the *Iliad*.[13] The character of Thersites is introduced as follows:

> Now the others sat down and stayed disciplined in their places. But one man still railed on, Thersites of measureless speech, who knew in his mind many disordered words (ἔπεα), recklessly, and not according to good order, to strive against kings, saying whatever he thought would raise a laugh among the Argives.
>
> (*Iliad* 2. 210–15)

The details of Thersites' unattractive character and physical ugliness given by the narrator (216–23), are followed by a rendering of Thersites' rebuke of Agamemnon in front of the Greek soldiers (225–42). Odysseus' verbal retort (246–64) makes scant reference to

---

[12] Bakhtin (1981; 1986), Bakhtin and Medvedev (1978), Voloshinov (1973); see also Todorov (1984).

[13] Thalmann (1988) offers a stimulating account of the political and ideological implications of the Thersites episode. Postlethwaite (1988) compares the heated exchange of speeches between Agamemnon and Achilles over the surrender of Chryses (earlier in *Iliad* 1. 106–92: see the two notes below) and views Thersites' speech as a comment on that quarrel, concluding that Thersites provides a 'value-judgment on the central theme of the poem, the quarrel and *menis*'. There are various discussions of the language used of and by the characters involved in R. P. Martin (1989). My account does not seek to compete with these treatments: it merely aims to highlight some basic issues relevant to my concerns.

what Thersites has said. It is more concerned with the fact that
Thersites has spoken in the first place:[14]

Thersites, of reckless speech, although you are a clear speaker, restrain
yourself and do not try to strive against kings. For I say that there is no
mortal worse than you, of all who came to Ilios with the sons of Atreus. So
you should not put the names of kings in your mouth as you talk and cast
reproaches on them, watching for a return home.

(*Iliad* 2. 246–51)

Odysseus concludes his words with a speech act: an announcement
and promise (or threat) which assert and demonstrate verbally his
proper right to speak:[15]

I will tell you this and it will certainly be fulfilled, if I find you playing the
fool like this again, then no longer should the head of Odysseus rest on his
shoulders, no longer may I be called father to Telemachus if I do not take
you, strip off your clothing, and the cloak and tunic which hide your shame,
and send you off to the swift ships, beaten out of the assembly with
shameful blows.

(*Iliad* 2. 257–64)

A physical action then reinforces the speech act: Odysseus strikes
Thersites with his gold sceptre. But this is emphatically not a
fulfilment of the threat in 261–4: Thersites has no opportunity to
'play the fool' a further time. Although this actualized assault of
Thersites is cruel, it is not as severe as the threat of stripping him
naked: the exposure of genitals is especially shameful in epic.[16] The
purpose of Odysseus' violence here is to show the validity of his
threat *as* a threat—to show that what he says can be fulfilled. Thus a
contrast is drawn with the inefficacy of Thersites' words which (as
is now clear) are futile in urging his fellow soldiers to return home.
    Odysseus' authority, in the fullest sense of the word, is endorsed
by the rank and file:

But the men, sorrowful though they were, laughed merrily at Thersites,
and thus one would speak with a glance at his neighbour: 'Well now!

---

[14] Note the slight echo of Agamemnon's opening statement to Achilles in *Iliad*
1. 131–2: 'Godlike Achilles, although you are noble (ἀγαθός περ ἐών), do not seek to
trick me with your wit.'
[15] Agamemnon's remarks at the end of his verbal contest with Achilles in *Iliad*
1. 181–7 have some similarities to Odysseus' threat here. These also come at the
close of the final speech of an exchange. The issue at stake is very much one of
authority.   [16] See Kirk (1985), 143 on 2. 261–4.

Odysseus has accomplished thousands of good deeds, leading in good counsels and setting battle in array, but this is by far the best deed that he has accomplished among the Argives, to keep this abusive babbler out of the assembly. Never again will his proud spirit set him to contest with kings with words of reviling.'

(Iliad 2. 270–7)

Discussions of this episode do not always spell out a rather important detail which shows how intimately Odysseus' physical action is connected with his speech act. The sceptre with which Odysseus hits Thersites is an emblem of power: of kings (cf. 1. 279, 2. 86) and priests (1. 15, 1. 28).[17] More specifically it is an emblem of the power to *speak* in Homer's poetry. Achilles throws a sceptre down to the earth when he finishes an angry speech (1. 245); Odysseus, right after his silencing of Thersites, is again described as holding a sceptre (2. 279) as he addresses the multitude. This detail might serve to show that normal conditions of debate have been restored after some disruption.[18]

This episode offers comments from characters which specifically address the relation between speech and power. Members of subordinate groups do speak, but this is not the way most characters seem to want it—even characters who are members of the lower orders themselves. In whatever ideological frames such a sociology of speech was conceived or understood by its audiences, Homer's portrayal of a correlation between social status and the right to speak may have affected subsequent representations. The *Iliad* and *Odyssey* had a pervasive influence on virtually all forms of ancient narrative. In particular, a discreet encoding of the relationship between speech and power in the narrative form of Virgil's *Aeneid* seems to bear this out. That will be discussed in detail in Chapter 5. The specific episode involving Thersites has of course its own legacy for later cultural history and political theory.[19]

My next example, from Horace's *Satire* 1. 6, is very different.[20] It

---

[17] Compare Hesiod *Theogony* 30 and see West (1966) ad loc., 163–4.

[18] As Kirk (1985) on 278–82 suggests at 145.

[19] Notably Estienne de la Boëtie's anti-monarchist tract *Discours de la servitude volontaire* and Johannes Spondaeus' standard edition of Homer (Basle 1583) take up some implications of this episode for statecraft. For discussion of these and related texts in the English Renaissance see Norbrook (1994), at 144 f. Lowrie (1991) specifically studies the legacy of Thersites.

[20] My comments here were prompted by Duncan Kennedy's analysis of this passage in a paper he gave to the Bristol Classical Seminar in 1989.

presents a more complex set of connections between the status of two speakers and what they are inclined or entitled to say. In this satire, the poet recalls his first meeting with Maecenas who came to be his patron:

> nulla etenim mihi te fors obtulit; optimus olim
> Vergilius, post hunc Varius, dixere quid essem.
> ut veni coram, singultim pauca locutus,
> infans namque pudor prohibebat plura profari,
> non ego me claro natum patre, non ego circum
> me Satureiano vectari rura caballo,
> sed quod eram narro. respondes, ut tuus est mos,
> pauca: abeo, et revocas nono post mense iubesque
> esse in amicorum numero.

(Satires 1. 6. 54–62)

Certainly no chance occurrence put me in your way: some time ago the admirable Virgil, and, after him, Varius told you what I was. When I first came face to face with you, I stuttered out a few words; for speechless shame was stopping me from saying more. I could not recount that I was born of a famous father, I could not recount that I rode around country estates on a Saturian steed, but I recount what I was. You reply, as is your manner, in a few words: I depart, and you call me back after nine months and order me to be in the number of your friends.

The complex nature of the power relation between the poet and his patron is strikingly epitomized by the apparent oxymoron in the last two verses of this passage: *iubesque esse in amicorum numero* 'you *order* me to be in the number of your friends.'[21] Shortly before this excerpt, the poet has twice with the same words emphasized his humble origin as 'a son of a freedman father' (*libertino patre natum* 45, 46). The preoccupation with his origin is expressed here in 55: Virgil and Varius told Maecenas *what*—not *who*—Horace was.[22] That preoccupation pervades the account of the conversation: 'I recounted what I was' (60). Evidently it is the shame or modesty (*pudor*) the poet feels about his status which makes him tongue-tied in the company of a famous and important nobleman.

---

[21] However, Appendix 3 '*Iubere* and Literary Requests' in P. White (1993), 266–8 is salutary at 267: 'But what is more important about the use of *iubere* is that (as with "tell" and "bid" in English) the nuance of command which it conveys is significantly weaker than in other Latin verbs meaning "order" or "command".' Even so, it is still Maecenas who has the power to initiate the friendship.

[22] See the commentary of Lejay (1911) ad loc., 187–8.

Maecenas also speaks 'in a few words'. However, it is emphasized that he is laconic because of his personal inclination (*ut tuus est mos*)—not because of any unease arising from social constraint or inhibition. There is possibly some contrivance here: if Maecenas had in fact been as garrulous as a Homeric hero and Horace had made this clear, the effect would have been much less flattering. Horace says that he departed after hearing Maecenas' words without replying in turn. This reported exchange of words is obviously very different in style from those in the extracts from Homer I have already considered, but the right or inclination to speak is no less clearly an index of power and status. In this passage, exchange of speech is shown to follow certain unstated, perhaps instinctively held, rules of social behaviour; whilst in the passages from Homer, Telemachus and Odysseus explicitly point to such rules, rather as if they were prescriptive laws.

Horace's account places less emphasis on the content of the conversation than it does on the fact that the conversation occurred. No direct or indirect discourse is used; there are only simple records of minimal speech acts. Indeed, Horace elaborates more about what he could not say than what he did say to Maecenas. Nonetheless, there are other ways in which the poet reproduces this exchange quite vividly, even without reference to its verbal content. The alliteration of *p-*, *pr-*, and *pl-* sounds in *pudor prohibebat plura profari* (57) obviously mimics the sound of what the phrase describes: faltering, stuttered speech as a result of social unease. The words *sed quod eram narro* ('I recount what I was') (60) which conclude the description of the poet's part of the conversation come before the caesura—the natural break in a line of hexameter verse. Thus the account of Maecenas' reply (*respondes, ut tuus est mos*) comes in more emphatically than it might otherwise, and helps convey the intrusion of another speaker's utterance.[23] There is also an elision between *pauca* (61)—the last of the five words describing that utterance of Maecenas—and *abeo* (I depart). That elision could suggest the abruptness of Horace's withdrawal after Maecenas has spoken.

These devices draw attention to the *event* of the conversation, as

[23] However Winbolt (1903)—a manual of verse composition—notes at 31: 'In the Latin hexameter, breaks in sense seem naturally to coincide with strong caesuras. Hence the $2\frac{1}{2}$ pause, being near the middle of the line is a favourite pause . . . it seldom has any specific or descriptive meaning . . . Special uses are (i) *speech endings*, and (ii) *speech introductions* . . .' [my emphases].

well as enhancing a sense of the different behaviour of the two speakers as a result of their unequal status. However, there is a further complexity. The satire in general, and the part I have quoted in particular, is not just *about* Maecenas: it is addressed *to* Maecenas. In his present discourse the poet is no longer tongue-tied: he now displays himself as articulate and expressive of his ideas, experiences, and reflections, as he communicates with his patron. There is no inconsistency here: the passage quoted draws a clear contrast between who the poet is 'now' and what he was before. But the change is still immense. If we cease to conceive of Horace's discourse as an inert poem, as a 'closed' work of satire, then Maecenas' silence, or rather, Horace's dramatized loquacity becomes far more astonishing.

Consideration of this text shows two things. First, speech as a token or currency of power cannot adequately be understood in terms of a crude binary system of ownership versus deprivation. Speech, as Horace shows here, is related to power, but the economics of that relation will not be simple. The well-known complexities of the hierarchy between poets and patrons raised here clearly indicate this.[24] Other kinds of hierarchy have their own kinds of complexities—and likewise determine, or are determined by, complex relations between speech and power. In spite of the wishful sentiments of characters like Telemachus and Odysseus, it is rarely the case (even in Homer) that superior people have all the discourse and inferior people have none.[25]

Second, a full account of relationships between speakers cannot be given without considering the text which presents those speakers as a speech (or discourse) in itself.[26] This is more obvious in reviewing the excerpt from Horace's *Satire* 1. 5: the poet is presenting his past relationship with Maecenas in the episode he recounts, but we also learn something about his current relationship with Maecenas by looking at his style of recounting it. The

---

[24] West and Woodman (1984) (particularly Duquesnay's discussion, 19–58), Gold (1987) and P. White (1993) deal with the problem of patronage.

[25] The examination of the *Aeneid* in Ch. 5 will consider questions of this nature in greater depth.

[26] The difficult business of establishing how far a poet who mentions his patron is subordinate to that patron in fact depends considerably on analysis of discourses of the poems the poet himself produced. Thus P. White (1993) concedes at 206, that his thorough study of poetry in Augustan society, which draws from all kinds of discursive evidence, can only offer 'tentative conclusions'.

importance of considering a text like the *Iliad* as discourse is just as great. Our estimations of how the relation between speech and power is portrayed there, and our estimations of the validity of that portrayal actually depend on what we think Homer's audiences or readers are like.[27] A more thorough investigation of texts themselves as discourses will follow shortly.

It has often been remarked that the study of ideology is itself ideological. My review of these texts from Homer and Horace certainly bears this out. We cannot regard them as vehicles of ideology, nor even as disinterested presentations of competing ideological systems, without placing ourselves as audience (or our conceptions of other audiences) in some ideological relation to those texts. This chain of reasoning is closely related to the problems raised by speech presentation itself. In simple terms, nobody can report what someone does or says without saying something himself or herself (and thereby saying something *about* himself or herself). Nor can other speakers present that report in turn without saying something about themselves either.[28] In presenting this chain of reasoning, I am bound to acknowledge that I can make no claims for the neutrality of the arguments that I will offer here. In order to avoid being hoist by my own petard for failing to reveal the partiality of my own conclusions about speech and power in ancient texts, I will briefly give an explicit statement of my own position.

In studying ancient literature, I am often concerned with social and historical issues in my endeavours to produce images or reconstructions of the past. In my view, some claims about relations between speech and power make an important contribution to our understanding of that past. There are also more personal reasons for my seeking to make conjectures from texts about actual social behaviour and attitudes to the right to speak in the ancient world. I am anxious to show that the presentation and allocation of

---

[27] Compare these remarks on the *Iliad* from Thalmann (1988) at 28: 'Its text should be seen neither as neutral ground for the play of rival ideologies nor as the ideological weapon of a dominant class. It is deeply involved in ideology, but in a complex way that is reflected, in part, by the failure of the Thersites scene to attain genuine closure.'

[28] Voloshinov (1973), 115: 'Reported speech is speech within speech, utterance within utterance, and at the same time also *speech about speech, utterance about utterance*.'

characters' discourse in a text are not only of interest as features of form: they also raise questions of a political nature. In alerting readers to these political questions, I also hope to bring those who have been mainly concerned with literary studies into contact with insights from other disciplines, particularly ethnography.[29]

Social scientists have addressed the problems involved in making conjectures about social behaviour from discursive accounts. Investigation of speech and authority in existing societies is a common theme.[30] Such investigation also poses problems of ethnographic method: there are difficulties raised by 'muted groups' (like women or children) whose symbolic weight in a society cannot easily be assessed by the ethnographer simply because such groups 'do not speak'.[31] On a second level, the potency of the form and rhetoric of narratives which are available to the ethnographer is a related issue, and a prominent one. A social scientist's data may be circumscribed by customary procedures of muting and silencing in the society under scrutiny. But the social scientist's data, unlike that of the historian of antiquity, is always available in unlimited quantity. What is to be done with that data then becomes a more conspicuous problem. Here is one account of the difficulties notions of 'data' and of 'what really happened' raised for a social anthropologist:

[29] This is not to overlook the fact that ethnography and other forms of social-scientific writing have themselves, no less than other 'disciplines', been influenced, even shaped, by methods drawn from various fields of enquiry including literary criticism and literary theory. See (e.g.) Geertz (1973) and the other works cited in note 33 below.

[30] Consider these observations drawn from fieldwork in Algeria from Bourdieu (1979), 102 n. 6: 'Of a man who takes little thought for his honour, the Kabyles say: "He is a Negro". Negroes do not have and do not need honour. They were kept out of public affairs; though they might take part in collective work, they were not entitled to speak in assembly meetings; in some places they were not even allowed to attend. A tribe which listened to the opinions of a Negro would have covered itself with shame in the eyes of other tribes.' See also Bourdieu (1977), (1991) and (1992). Free (1996) presents a useful critical overview of Bourdieu's anthropology.

[31] Ardener (1989), 73–85 and 128–30 introduced the notion of 'muted groups'. The extent to which this kind of subject matter hampers (or determines?) the production of ethnographic writing is conveyed by this account of North Lebanese society in Gilsenan (1989) at 215: 'the *fellahin* in the village ("peasant" stratum in the status honour idiom) . . . cannot and dare not speak. Speech, public and challenging would bring violent retribution by these superior forces whose violence is often seen as part of their very nature as much as of the nature of the hierarchical order in practice . . . In the discourse of power they have neither the right nor the capacity to "speak". They have no "word", and no words can properly be spoken by or of them (in that sense my writing here would seem unthinkable to someone local in the village—how do you write about peasants?)'

I suspect that the whole discourse of evidence as distinct from mere anecdote, that powerful tool of the scientist against the non-professsional in the defence of boundaries and practices, also made me nervous. For a long time I thus did not wish to take any cognizance of the fact that one crucial element in my fieldwork was that I was being told stories; that . . . manner and matter were indistinguishable, the what and the how were one question. The vividness of the tellings and retellings successfully performed one of their critical functions—to blind the listener, or at least this listener, to the fact that it was these accounts and reports and reminiscences that constituted 'the event' of which they were apparently just the vehicle.[32]

And third, on the level of the ethnographic text itself, there is the problem of the ethnographer's rhetoric which Geertz and others have considered: ethnography also performs the action of telling a story.[33] The mediation of 'data' by the ethnographer must be determined by his or her own ethnicity, gender, class background and beliefs. How and to what extent should these issues of 'reflexivity' be taken into account? So there are (at least) three levels of aporia which are clearly interrelated. However, these difficulties have not brought disciplines like social anthropology to an end. They are more likely to produce a stimulating dialectic between ethnographic theory and ethnographic practice. Another important consideration can be brought into play. The peoples, societies, and cultures scrutinized by the ethnographer cannot be regarded as comparable to flora, fauna, artworks, or written texts which are surveyed by other kinds of specialist. We interact with these peoples and societies in many other complex ways.[34]

Responses to aporias facing contemporary ethnographers cannot be brought to bear *tout court* on the problems involved in studying ancient texts. The authors and cultures which produced those texts cannot be interrogated or consulted. Ancient historians who regard at least some ancient texts as discourses of evidence, would certainly see problems with making inferences about social practices from portrayals of—or hints about—the relation between speech and hierarchy in historiography which is manifestly literary

[32] These remarks are also from Gilsenan (1989), 193.
[33] See Geertz (1973; 1988), Clifford and Marcus (1986). Silverman (1990) is a useful account of Geertz's writing. Free (1996) attacks Bourdieu's own 'intellectualism'.
[34] Balandier (1955) and Asad (1973) consider, in different ways, the relationship between colonial politics and anthropology.

and rhetorical. A more orthodox procedure would be to turn to any specific testimonies on the relationship between speech and power that can be found in historical writing.

However, historical testimony is unlikely to present a straight-forward picture. A brief chapter in Suetonius' biography of the emperor Augustus which discusses freedom of speech in the senate can serve as an example. Attempting to make sense of this chapter shows the kind of problems posed by historical 'sources' where these issues are concerned:

In senatu verba facienti dictum est: 'Non intellexi,' et ab alio: 'Contra dicerem tibi, si locum haberem'. Interdum ob immodicas disceptantium altercationes e curia per iram se proripienti quidam ingesserunt licere oportere senatoribus de re p. loqui. Antistius Labeo senatus lectione, cum virum legeret, M. Lepidum hostem olim eius et tunc exulantem legit interrogatusque ab eo an essent alii digniores, suum quemque iudicium habere respondit. nec ideo libertas aut contumacia fraudi cuiquam fuit.

(*Divus Augustus* 2. 54)

As Augustus was speaking in the senate someone said to him: 'I did not understand', and someone else said: 'I would contradict you if I had the opportunity.' Several times when he was rushing from the senate house in anger at the excessive bickering of the disputants, some shouted after him that senators ought to have the right of speaking about public affairs. At the selection of senators, when each member chose another, Antistius Labeo named Marcus Lepidus, an old enemy of the emperor who was at the time in banishment: and when Augustus asked him whether there were not others more deserving of the honour, Labeo replied that every man had his own opinion. Yet for all that, none of this freedom of speech or insolence brought harm to anyone.

The last sentence implies that (in the narrator's view) senators enjoyed freedom of speech with impunity—yet in some examples provided of this permissiveness, the senators complain that they are not allowed to say what they please and get a hearing. It is also hinted that Labeo's answer to Augustus' question is insolent—yet for Labeo to claim that each man holds his own opinion is far less insulting than a direct retort to the effect that no others deserved the honour he wished to confer on Lepidus. Altogether we are left with a rather confusing impression: again we see that speech and power are connected, but again our idea of the situation portrayed depends on our response to the discourse portraying it. Other kinds of evidential discourse possibly available to the historian are equally problematic. Records of procedure in political or judicial assemblies, for example, which might be used to determine who had the right to speak and when, may well give accounts of theory rather than practice. And accounts of what was supposed to happen in the guise of what did happen are still bound to inscribe prejudices, and to present puzzles and ambiguities.[35]

The realization that historical texts require, at least for my purposes, more open-ended interpretation has some welcome consequences. There might be grounds for drawing tentative conclusions from non-historical writing about speech and power in ancient societies. Literary as well as historical texts provide useful resources for investigating anthropological or cultural categories. Often for the study of Greek and Roman societies, the presentations of basic concepts in literature can be as important as those in 'factual' discourses. In this respect, classicists have been practising forms of 'new historicism' long before the term was ever coined.[36] Moreover it is worth emphasising that the *form* of a text, no less than its content, is inevitably conditioned by the society that produced it—conversely the form of a society is constituted by the texts through which that society is perceived.[37] The ascription of speech to some characters and not to others is really a formal feature commonly present in all kinds of texts—but which is especially prominent in narratives. The ascription of speech to certain characters obviously leads to the determination of social hierarchies which are conjured up by narratives. Even if some narratives are fictional, I would maintain that the mechanisms of the hierarchies we apprehend through them are worth investigating. There are at least some impressive precedents for making extensions from the realm of myth and poetry to the world outside.[38]

In short, studying speech and power in all kinds of ancient texts

[35] Even such records which might be in documentary form (as opposed to that of formal historical narrative) will include some facts and exclude others; they thus can be shown to have their own rhetoric and partiality. See H. White (1981), and the opening discussion in Ch. 4.

[36] For accounts and examples of new historicism (a term coined by Stephen Greenblatt) see Veeser (1989) and (1994).

[37] Few literary theorists have really taken into serious consideration this way in which the form of a text is related to the society that produces it. The work of Bakhtin and Voloshinov is a notable exception: see again (e.g.) Bakhtin and Medvedev (1978) and Voloshinov (1973).

[38] Dodds (1973) and G. Thomson (1941), 199–346 are commendable examples of this tendency in classical scholarship.

can be useful. No text or discourse will ever represent a state of affairs neutrally. However comprehensive or disinterested a writer or speaker sets out to be, the inevitable determinations of omissions, closure, provenance, and genre will mean that the account produced will be angled, selective, partial, and ideological. Thus, attributing a kind of historical significance to a text's explicit and implicit constructions of the relationships between speech and power can be justified. This is simply because they *are* constructions: they could never faithfully represent a state of things outside the text. Textual constructions of relationships between speech and power configure aspirations which could not ever be directly expressed. Conjectures about these aspirations are of historical interest to the same degree that conjectures about the rhetorical slants or implicit biases of any ancient work might be of historical interest.

It might already be clear that connections between speech and power are also to be found in texts which do not attribute words or thoughts to any characters presented in them. These connections consist in the relations between texts and their readers or audiences: relations which take on an ideological form—as the examples discussed above have shown. This is most easily seen if one considers texts as discourses, or, to put it more accurately, if one can show how texts *are* discourses. Before proceeding with this, it is necessary to give an account of how I will be using the terms 'speech' and 'text'. I use 'speech' to stand for spoken discourse. A 'text' is generally regarded as something written or printed, or as written discourse. Here—so far at least—the word 'text' is mostly used in its traditional sense, to denote what is, effectively, a published work or an excerpt from a published work.[39] However, in linguistics, in some literary theories (including those which do not presuppose the notion of literature), and in social science, that conception of text has often been deliberately expanded to denote (like 'discourse') a continuous stretch of language, spoken or written.[40] A small

---

[39] The notion of 'publication' is far from unproblematic: McGann (1991) considers the effect of the circumstances of publication on literary works. A further set of questions are raised by consideration of ancient texts: the nature of 'publication' in antiquity means that the kind of closure presupposed by the philologist would not apply to texts in the climate of their production. On ancient book production see Blanck (1992); on closure, see D. P. Fowler (1989), and Roberts, Dunn, and Fowler (1997) on closure and the ancient book in general. The entries in the *Oxford Classical Dictionary* (1996—3rd edn.) by Maehler and Hines, respectively, on 'Books, Greek and Roman' and 'Books, poetic' are also useful.

[40] See e.g. Bakhtin's essay 'The problem of the text in linguistics, philology and

distinction between this expanded notion of 'text' and discourse, however, has on the whole escaped notice. A text, in this broader sense, is actually discourse which is held up for scrutiny. Once discourse is examined or quoted (as an object of attention or source) in forms of writing like literary criticism, historiography or ethnography, it is inevitably framed and possibly aestheticized.

In calling attention to the status of *texts as discourses*, my purpose is to consider, in the manner of ancient rhetoricians, their affective power. I hope to highlight their capacity to move hearers as speech acts, to demonstrate their affinity with reported discourse, and to emphasize their important ideological dimensions.[41] To conceive of *discourses as texts*, on the other hand, would be to downplay or ignore all these issues. However, even in this study, which is more or less devoted to the notions of speech, text, and discourse, there is bound to be slippage in my own use of these terms. The important thing though, here and throughout, is to understand that even ancient literary texts, as discourses, have much in common with spoken utterances.[42] The discussion to follow will present three fundamental features of this community which turn out to be closely related: the question of the addressee, the role of indexicals, and the nature of intertextuality. Ideology is important for understanding all of these.

1.3 TEXTS AS DISCOURSES: ADDRESSEE AND SUPERADDRESSEE

Texts, like spoken discourses, have addressees: these addressees may be readers or hearers. They may be individual or collective (or both), present or absent (or both), factual or fictional (or both). Power relations inevitably obtain between the 'speaker' of a text

the human sciences: an experiment in philosophical analysis' in Bakhtin (1986), 103–31. The versatility of the word 'text' is shown by the designations 'narrator text' and 'character text' for narrator's discourse and character's discourse in Bal (1985) and De Jong (1987a). Engler (1991) gives an account of how conceptions can vary from insistence on the fixed authority of the text (e.g. Hirsch (1967)) to the substitution of 'contexts' in Fish (1980), where texts are conceived as constructions of 'interpretative communities'.

[41] R. Fowler (1981; 1986) and also Verdonk (1991) employ comparable approaches.

[42] Of course neither ancient nor modern literary texts are the *same* as spoken utterances in the realm of everyday experience: a principle difference is that literature is 'reusable'—something I shall mention later on. See the bibliography in n. 39 above.

and its addressees, whoever they may be and however they are conceived. It is obvious and inescapable that the longer the 'speaker' of a text speaks, the longer its 'addressee' is silent. This must set up a power relation of a kind, even if it does not appear to be very spectacular.

In sustained narratives for example, there is an inevitable dramatization of the relationship between narrator and reader—as speaker and addressee respectively—which develops as the narration proceeds. Indeed, factual narratives, no less than fictional ones, progressively construct and characterize their addressees. At the same time, an inequality may be discerned between speaker and addressee which consists in the domineering tone of the text as discourse: the discourse constitutes a speaker who remains speaker, while the addressee has no discourse and remains subordinated as the addressee. However, this interpretation of the power relation between the narrator as speaker and the reader as addressee could be reversed. Power does not only consist in the ability or propensity to speak: silence too can on occasions be an emblem of power. The speaker of a text need not only be seen as wielding a sceptre: he could be attempting to win the attention of an addressee who occupies a superior position.

A relation between speech and power is easily identifiable in texts where (for instance) the speaker is generally characterized in a subordinate role—perhaps as a poet singing for a patron, or hymning a deity. A love elegy by Ovid addressed to the poet's mistress (*Amores* I. 10) is a pertinent example. The poem provides a whole series of objections to the principle of men giving gifts to mistresses. The vehement tone of these objections gradually diminishes in the closing verses:

> nec tamen indignum est a divite praemia posci:
>   munera poscenti quod dare possit habet;
> carpite de plenis pendentis vitibus uvas,
>   praebeat Alcinoi poma benignus ager.
> officium pauper numerat studiumque fidemque;
>   quod quis habet, dominae conferat omne suae.
> est quoque carminibus meritas celebrare puellas
>   dos mea: quam volui, nota fit arte mea.
> scindentur vestes, gemmae frangentur et aurum;
>   carmina quam tribuent, fama perennis erit.
>
>   (*Amores* I. 10. 53–62)

It is not unacceptable to demand gifts from a rich man: he has whatever he can give to someone demanding presents; you must all pick the grapes hanging from well-laden vines, let the bountiful estate of Alcinous display its fruits. A poor man counts out devotion, enthusiasm, and faithfulness; let each man pass on to his mistress all that he has. It is my gift to celebrate deserving girls with my poems: the woman I wanted to celebrate is being made well known through my art. Clothes will be torn, jewels and gold will shatter; but it will be an everlasting fame which songs will confer.

However, the final couplet presents a complete *volte face* :

> nec dare, sed pretium posci dedignor et odi
> quod nego poscenti, desine velle, dabo.
>   (*Amores* 1. 10. 63–4)

It is not the giving, but the demanding of a fee that I despise and hate; cease to want what I refuse to someone demanding it, and I will give it to you.

The whole argument of the poem has normally been regarded as pointedly academic—conducted for its own sake in a realm remote from any realistic situation.[43]

However, if we conceive of this text as a plain discourse from speaker to addressee we are more liable to discern the communicative, dramatic function of this elegy. The speaker shifts his ground, not merely because he is rehearsing literary conventions as a poetic *tour de force*. The speaker also could be reneging because the addressee might be somehow in his hearing. The course and tone of his utterance could be increasingly conditioned either by the dramatization of her presence or even by the imagination of it. Whatever conjectures can be made about the precise nature of the mistress's emotions (e.g. anger, hurt, etc.) or behaviour (e.g. seductive gestures, attempts to depart), the idea of her presence might be modulating the nature of the utterance as it proceeds. Thus, a power relation is inescapably built into this discourse. The silent addressee seems to have the upper hand and to be compelling the speaker to give more and more ground. Again, a power relation is encoded in the opposition between speech and silence, although we have to accept that the interpretation offered here can just as easily be reversed. Verses 61–4 at least, could show that the discourse of the poet could also be regarded as a sign of power:

[43] Barsby (1973), 119 remarks: 'Ovid is merely adopting his usual *persona*; but even so he presents a convincing picture'. At 127: 'Ovid has taken a stock theme and treated it with amused detachment.'

the mistress may wield power over him in life, but it is only his poetry which can enable her to achieve literary immortality.

Amores 1. 10 also makes more prominent a complexity—which I have not yet indicated—involved in considering texts as discourses. Dramatically the speaker in Ovid's elegy has only one addressee: the mistress who is, or has been, demanding presents from him. However, if this discourse is regarded as a poetic text, the speaker has readers or audience as a further addressee, in addition to the petulant mistress. This distinction between the addressee (here, the mistress) who is explicitly called on by the speaker and the 'super-addressee' who is not so manifestly called on by the speaker (here, the reader or audience of *Amores* 1. 10) has been set out by Mikhail Bakhtin:

Any utterance always has an addressee (of various sorts, with varying degrees of proximity, concreteness, awareness, and so forth), whose responsive understanding the author of the speech work seeks and surpasses. This is the second party . . . [after the speaker]. But in addition to this addressee (the second party), the author of the utterance, with a greater or lesser awareness, presupposes a higher superaddressee (*third*), whose absolutely just responsive understanding is presumed, either in some metaphysical distance or in distant historical time (the loophole addressee). In various ages and with various understandings of the world, this superaddressee and his ideally true responsive understanding assume variously ideological expressions (God, absolute truth, the court of dispassionate human conscience, the people, the court of history, science, and so forth) . . . The aforementioned third party is not any mystical or metaphysical being (although, given a certain undertanding of the world, he can be expressed as such)—he is a constitutive aspect of the whole utterance, who, under deeper analysis can be revealed in it.[44]

In fact, a superaddressee is rather obviously presupposed by the speaker in Ovid's poem. First, the use of the plural form of the

---

[44] Bakhtin (1986), 126. Sharrock (1994) applies to Ovid's didactic poetry a distinction between 'Reader' and 'reader'. These terms roughly correspond to Bakhtin's 'addressee' and 'superaddressee' respectively. Sharrock's distinction is explained thus at 7: 'The convention of the didactic addressee allows the teacher to criticise within the bounds of literary tact, and allows the reader both to identify with the disciple and to distance himself. Ovid stands at the end of a sophisticated didactic tradition of reader/addressee interrelations, and his addressee is an unusually subtle creation. I shall frequently refer to the Reader, by which I mean the notional addressee. I use the term 'Reader' in preference to 'addressee' in order to encourage the potential slippage between Reader and reader, which I am suggesting, while at the same time retaining the difference by the use of the upper case R.'

imperative at several points in the poem (e.g. verse 55 *carpite* 'you must all pick' in the first passage quoted) suggests this text is addressed to others, in addition to the single mistress, present in the poem's story. (In literary historical terms, these shifts between singular and plural forms in the second person may be explained by the generic influence of declamatory literature on this kind of poem.[45]) And second, the speaker's references to his poems and their enduring quality (59–62) reminds us that poems—including this one—have further audiences and addressees. Signals like these indicate the existence of the superaddressee. But we do not have to depend on them to assert it.

The superaddressee is a constituent of discourse. Of course, any construction of a superaddresee is performed by a reader. But the superaddressee is above any notion of 'implied reader' or 'reader in the text'. Contrast Conte's attempt to use a dyadic relation of author and 'reader-addressee':

I could define my operative notion as the idea not of a *reader-interpreter* (which seems to have become prevalent in contemporary hermeneutics), but of a *reader-addressee*. This reader-addressee is a form of the text, it is the figure of the recipient as anticipated by the text. To this prefiguration of the reader, all future, virtual readers must adapt themselves.

The author conceives the form of the reader as a communicative function, foreseeing it and articulating his discourse so as to entwine the reader's actions with the literary act. In short the text's form and intentionality determine the reader's form. This is a model of directed reception, for this kind of reader's form is defined precisely by a structure of constraints: strategies, conventions, codifications, expressive norms, selections of contents, all organised within a competence. This competence is the force that makes sure that a text's score is correctly performed.[46]

It was suggested earlier that sustained narratives progressively construct and characterize their readers or addressees, rather on the lines that Conte is here suggesting for his 'reader-addressee'. As a 'form of the text', the submissive 'reader-addressee' is rather like a character in the story, whose profile is developed more precisely as the narrative continues. The opening of F. Scott Fitzgerald's short story 'The Lees of Happiness' illustrates the extremes to which a text can take characterization of the 'reader-addressee':

[45] See McKeown (1989), 281 ad loc.
[46] Conte (1994), p. xx.

If you should look through the files of old magazines for the first years of the present century you would find, sandwiched in between the stories of Richard Harding Davies and Frank Norris and others long since dead, the work of one Jeffrey Curtain: a novel or two, and three or four dozen short stories. You could if you were interested, follow them along until say, 1908, when they suddenly disappeared.

When you had read them all you would have been quite sure that there were no masterpieces—here were passably amusing stories, a bit out of date now, but doubtless the sort that would then have whiled away a dreary half-hour in a dental office. The man who did them was of good intelligence, talented, glib, probably young. In the samples of his work you found there would have been nothing to stir you to more than a faint interest in the whims of life—no deep interior laughs, no sense of futility, or hint of tragedy.[47]

In ancient literature, equivalently developed profiles of the addressee are found in *ekphrases* (rhetorical descriptions) of works of visual art. The reader-addressee is often thus apostrophized in the second person and characterized by the speaking narrator as a viewer and judge of the artefact described.[48] But the 'reader-addressee', as a form of the text, cannot help becoming an object of scrutiny—just as much as any characters or items presented or addressed by that text. If the 'reader-addressee' is an object of scrutiny, a further scrutinizing party must be posited. It is precisely this party which is the superaddressee.

A further consideration is very important. Bakhtin also pointed out that the superaddressee assumes 'variously ideological expressions'. Identification of the superaddressee with God is not a surprising example for Bakhtin to provide, given that the super-addressee's ideal response necessarily subsumes and reflects upon that of the addressee directly hailed by the text. The superaddressee 'understands' as well as hears the speaker—to an even greater degree than the speaker may expect to be understood. The discourse of Augustine's *Confessions* illustrates this forcefully:

quo deus veniat in me, deus, qui fecit caelum et terram? itane, domine deus meus, est quicquam in me, quod capiat te? an vero caelum et terra, quae fecisiti et in quibus me fecisti, capiunt te? an quia sine te non esset quidquid est, fit, ut quidquid est capiat te? quoniam itaque et ego sum, quid peto, ut venias in me, qui non essem, nisi esses in me?

(*Confessions* 1. 2)

---

[47] Fitzgerald (1994), 155. Sterne's *Tristram Shandy* is replete with this kind of device, often working in very complex ways. Sterne (1980), 330–2 is discussed in Engler (1991), 180–1.   [48] Cf. Bartsch (1989).

Where may God come into me, God who made heaven and earth? Is it so
my lord God, and is there anything in me which may receive you? Indeed
can heaven and earth which you made, and in which you made me, receive
you? Or since whatever is could not exist without you, must it follow that
whatever exists could receive you? Since therefore I also exist, why do I
seek that you come into me when I would not exist if you were not in me?

The entire text is 'spoken' to God as the primary addressee:
everything the narrator recounts is recounted to God himself who
is regularly apostrophized in the second person. With this passage,
we readers can configure ourselves as superaddressees: we witness
the rhetorical effect (not least upon ourselves) of the narrator's
frequent apostrophes, exhortations, and imprecations to the primary addressee.

But, as we see in this excerpt from the *Confessions*, God is
conceived as being all-knowing and omnipresent. Thus defined,
God becomes superaddressee, above and beyond his role in the
discourse as primary addressee. Our understanding of the *Confessions* as discourse is fundamentally formed by whatever conception
we have of its superaddressee. That conception could, for instance,
consist of God and ourselves, God but not ourselves, or ourselves
but not God. Thus our ideological situation determines just how we
understand the actual *linguistic* constitution of this text. In fact, our
understanding of how all texts are constituted as discourses is no
less ideologically determined—even when, unlike Augustine's
Confessions, they may not so explicitly raise issues of ideological
interest. This ideological determination will be missed if we ignore
or suppress the superaddressee's constitutive role in an utterance.
For better or worse, this is what Conte's remarks quoted above
would incline us to do. They hold that the prefiguration of the
reader as anticipated by the text (i.e the 'reader-addressee') is
something to which 'all future, virtual readers [i.e. the super-
addressees] must adapt themselves'. [49]

The construction of the reader-addressee—no less than the
construction of the primary addressee (like Ovid's mistress or
Augustine's God) is of course a legitimate and necessary exercise.
But the construction of the reader-addressee will be flawed, if we do

[49] Sharrock (1994), 21 has a more supple view of this adaptation: 'The reader is
and is not the Reader. The act of reading this text necesssarily involves both
identification with and separation from the aspiring lover to whom it is notionally
addressed.'

not consider the steps that were taken to achieve it. The presupposition of the superaddressee as we 'adapt ourselves' to the figure of the
reader-addressee is precisely what should be examined—if we are to
grasp the precious historical quality of a text as discourse. Bakhtin
makes it clear that texts have always had superaddressees. This
must apply to ancient texts even at the time of their production:

> The author can never turn over his whole self and his speech work to the
> complete and *final* will of addressees who are on hand or nearby (after all,
> even the closest descendants can be mistaken), and always presupposes
> (with a greater or lesser degree of awareness) some higher instancing of
> responsive understanding that can distance itself in various directions.
> Each dialogue takes place as if against the background of the responsive
> understanding of an invisibly present third party who stands above all the
> participants in the dialogue.[50]

There is a space between the field of the primary addressee (a
projection of the form of a text) and the field of the superaddressee
(an equally inevitable projection, whose shape we ourselves determine). That space is the terrain we should explore if we want to
appreciate that text's affective quality. Consideration of what I shall
call 'indexicals' should contribute to this appreciation. Indexicals
can also help to reveal the possible ideological determinations of a
text.

1.4 TEXTS AS DISCOURSE: INDEXICALS AND TRANSFORMATION

Indexicals are signals in written texts or spoken utterances which
point to the position or identity of their speakers and addressees.
Indexicals are by no means confined to 'first person' texts in which
the speaker is named or openly characterized. Indexical phrases like
'the first years of the present century' and 'a bit out of date now'
(from the F. Scott Fitzgerald passage quoted above) are useful
illustrations of this. Some examples from Virgil's *Aeneid* can show
that epic—still often regarded as an 'objective' form of narration—
establishes a realm common to narrator and primary addressee.[51]
The third word of the poem is a *personal* indexical:

[50] Bakhtin (1986), 126–7.
[51] Advocates of the 'objectivity' of Homeric epic include Auerbach (1953), 3;
H. Fraenkel (1955), 4; and Griffin (1986), 40 who cautiously states 'in a general way

Arma virumque *cano* . . .
(*Aeneid* 1. 1)

I sing of weapons and of the man . . .

The first person singular verb *cano* signals the presence of a single narrator by indicating that he (?) can sing. The following indexical is primarily spatial:

Tu quoque *litoribus nostris* Aeneia nutrix
aeternam moriens famam, Caieta, dedisti
(*Aeneid* 7. 1)

You too, nurse of Aeneas, in dying brought eternal fame to *our shores*

At the risk of sounding pedantic, one might point out that there is no other firm evidence in the *Aeneid* that the speaker's voice belongs to an Italian. In this verse, the word *nostris* ('our') could also include, and thus help define, the poem's addressees. The indexical is also temporal: signalling a *time* in which a Latin speaker and his primary addressees could be so defined.[52]

   This apostrophe to a member of a specific Roman family is an example of an indexical which is more obviously temporal:

genus unde *tibi, Romane Cluenti*
(*Aeneid* 5. 123)

from there comes *your* family, *Roman Cluentius*

The utterance of the poem (at least at this point) can be located in a time when the name Cluentius would be meaningful. These verses might be taken to present a different kind of temporal indexical:

vix illum lecti bis sex cervice subirent,
qualia *nunc* hominum producit corpora tellus
(*Aeneid* 12. 899–900)

Scarcely a dozen selected men of such physique as the earth produces *now* could have borne that [stone] on their shoulders

every reader is aware that the Homeric style is impersonal'. De Jong (1987*a*), 15–20 is an excellent account of 'Objectivity' in classical scholarship.

[52] The position of these verses at the opening of *Aeneid* 7 is significant. They mark a contrast between the second half of the poem (made more explicit in 7. 37–45—discussed in part below) and the first which presented Italy as the 'Lavinian shore' in *Aen* 1. 2–3.

The word *nunc* ('now') suggests that speaker and addressee occupy a realm which is remote from the world of the events described in the story.

Taken alone, such indexicals help us assemble a modest profile for *both* the speaker-narrator of this text *and* its primary addressee.[53] This is what I call the 'field of the primary addressee'. The indexicals also make clear the extent to which that field is derived from the form of the text itself. At the end of the previous subsection, I suggested it was necessary to explore the 'space' between the field of the primary addressee and the field of the superaddressee in order to understand a text's quality as an utterance, and to appreciate the ideological determination it has for us.

I also remarked that we ourselves are entirely responsible for shaping the field of a text's superaddressee. Generally we construct the superaddressees of the *Aeneid* as ourselves—that is to say we see ourselves as readers who are 'informed', 'disinterested', 'modern', 'competent', or whatever. (This epistemological complacency would obviously be of interest to the theorist of ideology—such a construction of superaddressees unfortunately leads to a frequent *mis*construction of the field of the primary addressee.) Accepting that construction of the field of the superaddressee is a matter of opinion rather than the simple truth has an important implication. Descriptions of the field of the primary addressee in a text which rely on inferences beyond those which can be made from indexicals are really descriptions of *ourselves*, or of matters of interest to us.[54]

---

[53] The apocryphal verses (given in the *praefatio* of the Servian corpus and Donatus *Vita* 42) supposed to precede *Aeneid* 1. 1 provide a cluster of indexicals: *Ille ego qui quondam gracili modulatus avena | carmen, et egressus silvis vicina coegi | ut quamvis avido parerent arva colono | gratum opus agricolis, at nunc horrentia Martis:* 'I am the man who once composed poetry in a pastoral strain, and who then came out of the woods and compelled the neighbouring fields to obey the most exacting tiller. That work delighted farmers, but now I sing of Mars' bristling weapons.' The status of these verses could be of fundamental importance for both literary and ideological interpretations of the whole poem: its speaker would not only acquire a definite spatial and temporal position—he (after *ille* it would be a 'he') could also be characterized as singer of the *Georgics* and *Eclogues*. Thus he could be more readily identified with constructions of Virgil as the poet in history. However, R. G. Austin (1968) presents strong arguments against these verses which the defence of them in Koster (1988) does not really meet: Reynolds and Wilson (1974), 182 note that 'the frequency with which *arma virumque cano* is scrawled on the walls of Pompeii helps to prove that this, and not *ille ego quondam* is the true beginning of the *Aeneid*.'

[54] See (e.g.) Rabinow (1986); and the discussion of Augustan ideology in D. Kennedy (1992): '*no* statement (not even made by Augustus himself) can be

The notion that we might really be describing ourselves when we seek to describe texts—or even other cultures—is now an acceptable commonplace. The appeal of this commonplace, however, can occasionally be weakened by the indirect moral and political consequences of a widely shared reluctance to postulate any external position of certainty.[55]

The role of indexicals is best demonstrated by an exemplary account, of their transformation in a cluster of ancient literary texts. The purpose here is not to give an account of the comings and goings between these texts and the world of *Realien* which brought them about.[56] However, this account, which owes something to Jean Pierre Faye's application of speech act theory to modern historiography, shows that at least positing an underlying historical reality can enhance our understanding of those texts as discourses, and of the connections between them.[57] I shall examine the

categorically "Augustan" or "Anti-Augustan"; the traces of its constituent discourses were—and still are—open to appropriation in the opposite interest. The degree to which a voice is heard as conflicting or supportive is a function of the audience's or—critic's—ideology, a function, therefore of *reception*.'

[55] Of course such reluctance is neither intrinsically indefensible, nor *per se* morally or politically irresponsible. But such a stance can lead to theorizing which risks obscuring the relevance of political action, and even the clarity of political thought. See e.g. Derrida (1988) on Paul de Man's activities in occupied Brussels (though I agree with D. Simpson (1989) that the controversy should not discredit deconstruction). Foucault's behaviour on a Dutch television debate with Noam Chomsky, recorded in Rabinow (1984), 3–7 shows how Foucault's obscurantism, however intellectually genuine, might debilitate activism: 'The interviewer asks each man why he is interested in politics . . . Given modern technology and science, Chomsky argues, the means are currently available to overcome the alienation and drudgery of labour. The real problem we must confront, therefore is a political one: how to bring about the just society in which creativity and reason would reign. . . . Foucault, typically, refuses to answer why he is interested in politics. He finds this both trivial and self-evident. Instead he shifts the "why" question to a "how" question—how am I interested in politics?'! Foucault is not necessarily wrong here—it is just that his response is less *useful* than Chomsky's. Some connections between ethics and epistemology will be considered in Ch. 4, and in my Conclusions and Envoi.

[56] There are profound problems with the division between 'what happened' (events) and the discourse which presents what happened (narrative). These will be discussed in the following chapter, and again in Ch. 4.

[57] The methods in Faye (1972) have the advantage of being demonstrated in practice, by particular analyses of the narratives of National Socialism. Faye's conception of extended discourses impacting on the historical circumstances which generated them ('positions') is now generally accepted: his 'topography' of positions is produced by study of the ways political groups use or appropriate what I call indexicals in their narratives and propaganda. For a presentation and critique of Faye (notably for disregarding the audiences of the narratives he examines), see J. B. Thompson (1984), 205–31.

recurrence of an indexical motif through some Roman poems: chiefly Virgil's fourth *Eclogue* and an excerpt from the *Aeneid*. An elegy by Propertius will serve as an accessory to this examination. Virgil's eclogue begins thus:

> Sicelides Musae, paulo maiora canamus.
> non omnis arbusta iuvant humilesque myricae;
> si canimus silvas, silvae sint consule dignae.
> Ultima Cumaei venit iam carminis aetas;
> magnus ab integro saeclorum nascitur ordo.
> iam redit et Virgo, redeunt Saturnia regna,
> iam nova progenies caelo demittitur alto.
> tu modo nascenti puero, quo ferrea primum
> desinet ac toto surget gens aurea mundo,
> casta fave Lucina: tuus iam regnat Apollo.
> teque adeo decus hoc aevi, te consule, inibit,
> Pollio et incipient magni procedere menses . . .
>   (*Eclogue* 4. 1–12)

Muses of Sicily, let us sing of rather greater things. The forest and humble tamarisks do not serve everyone; if we sing of the woods, let the woods be worthy of a consul. The last epoch of Cumaean prophecy is now coming. The grand order is being born anew. Now also Virgo is returning, the Saturnian kingdoms are returning, now a new progeny is being sent down from high heaven. Chaste Lucina, do you only grant favour on this boy who is now being born, under whose guidance the iron race will cease, and a golden race rise over the whole world: now your own Apollo is reigning. This glorious age will come in, while you are consul Pollio, and the great months will begin to proceed . . .

The expression *paulo maiora canamus* ('let us sing of rather greater things') serves as a personal indexical of the speaker: it intimates his involvement with other poems in the collection.[58] The deictic force of the threefold repetition of *iam* ('now') might well appear to be rooted to the events that are about to be unfolded by the poem and thus indicate nothing about the temporal location of the speaker. Modern editions of this text reinforce such a suggestion with a paragraph indentation in the fourth verse: the first three verses are set apart as a kind of proem in which the speaker introduces himself and invokes the Muses. The 'argument proper' is thus supposed to get underway in the verses that follow.[59]

---

[58] On the arrangement of the poems, see Coleman (1977), 14–21.

[59] Cf. Coleman (1977) (who indents the fourth verse of the text) at 153: 'Structurally the poem divides after the three-line prologue into three major

However the fourth *iam*, (10) changes things. It is part of a second invocation—to Lucina, the goddess of childbirth. The existence of this, and then of a third apostrophe to Pollio show that the poem's speaker is very much present and dramatically involved in the events as he unfolds them. The present moment of the situation described is also the present moment of the discourse describing it. In other words the poem from verse 4 does, after all, provide us with temporal indexicals for both the speaker and the primary addressee. The speaker (with the addressee) is speaking in (or shortly before) the consulship of Pollio. He is actually witnessing the arrival of the epoch of Cumaean song; he is actually witnessing the grand order of ages being born, and everything else described.

The speaker of the *Aeneid* also witnesses a grand order of things being born, as he too moves on to a greater theme, after he too has invoked a Muse:

> tu vatem, tu, diva, mone. dicam horrida bella,
> dicam acies actosque animis in funera reges,
> Tyrrhenamque manum totamque sub arma coactam
> Hesperiam. maior rerum mihi nascitur ordo,
> maius opus moveo.
>
> (*Aeneid* 7. 41–5)

You goddess, you advise this prophet. I shall speak of gruesome wars, I shall speak of battle lines and kings driven to carnage by their impulses—of the Etruscan band and all Hesperia driven to arms. For me a greater order of things is being born—a greater work I set in motion.

The birth of the 'greater order of things' (*maior rerum ordo*) fanfared in this passage is somewhat contrary to the birth of the 'order of ages' (*saeclorum ordo*) advertised in the *Eclogue*. That was characterized, at least in part, as an era of progress towards peace.[60] The grander order of things in this excerpt from the *Aeneid* involves bloodshed and war: this is the nature of the greater work which the speaker here is commencing. The motifs from *Eclogue* 4 (*maiora canamus*; *magnus . . . nascitur ordo*) have been adopted, but

---

sections . . .'. Thematic groupings of four verses and three verses are found at the beginning and ending of this poem which is dominated by the number seven. Note also that *Ultima* 'last' (4. 4) is the first word of the prophecy proper.

[60] Cf. *Eclogue* 4. 17: *pacatumque reget patriis virtutibus orbem*, 'he will guide a world made peaceful with his father's virtues'.

their significance has been adjusted, if not perverted. The motifs also have a mild indexical function in their new form and context: the word *mihi* ('for me') indicates their relation to the speaker. It is the speaker's own view that the order of things now emerging is something grander than what has so far been recounted in this text. In sum, *nascitur ordo* retains its eulogizing force. A formula of praise which the *Eclogue* speaker applied to his poetic celebration of the birth and golden age inaugurated by Pollio's consulship is applied by the speaker of the *Aeneid* to a narrative of conflict. It may already be tempting to detect some kind of significance generated by this 'appropriation'.

However, it remains to look at Propertius' elegy:

> me iuvet hesternis positum languere corollis,
> quem tetigit iactu certus ad ossa deus;
> Actia Vergilium custodis litora Phoebi,
> Caesaris et fortis dicere posse ratis,
> qui nunc Aeneae Troiani suscitat arma
> iactaque Lavinis moenia litoribus.
> cedite Romani scriptores, cedite Grai!
> nescio quid maius nascitur Iliade.
> tu canis umbrosi subter pineta Galaesi
> Thyrsin et attritis Daphnin harundinibus,
> utque decem possint corrumpere mala puellas
> missus et impressis haedus ab uberibus.
> felix, qui vilis pomis mercaris amores!
> huic licet ingratae Tityrus ipse canat.
> felix intactum Corydon qui temptat Alexin
> agricolae domini carpere delicias!
> quamvis ille sua lassus requiescat avena,
> laudatur facilis inter Hamadryadas.
> (*Elegies* 2. 34. 59–76)

Let it please me, whom Cupid sure in aim has struck to the bone, languidly to recline on yesterday's garlands; and let Virgil tell of the Actian shores guarded by Phoebus and Caesar's brave ships, Virgil who now rouses Trojan Aeneas' arms and the walls founded on the Lavinian shores. Give way Roman writers! Give way, Greeks! Something greater than the *Iliad* is being born. You sing under the pines of shady Galaesus about Thyrsis and about Daphnis with his worn pipes, of how ten apples can seduce girls, and of a young goat sent from the teats it has pressed. Happy, you who can buy love with cheap fruit!—though Tityrus himself sings to an ungrateful girl.

Happy Corydon who seeks to pick up Alexis still untouched, the favourite of his farmer master! Although he rests, weary from his piping, he is praised among the easy Hamadryads.

Here too the word *nascitur* has an indexical function, situating temporally the speaker and the primary addressee. The field of the primary addressee is coeval with the time in which Virgil's *Aeneid* is being produced. And here too, *maius nascitur* is eulogistic. Clearly it celebrates, as well as announces, the arrival of the epic. This part of the elegy is important for two reasons.

First, it connects, quite independently, Virgil's *Aeneid* with the *Eclogues*, by going on to refer explicitly to the contents of those pastoral poems (67–76). Thus in this context, *maius nascitur* evokes the *Eclogues* as well as the *Aeneid*, even before the *Eclogues* are epitomized in the verses immediately following. (In a similar fashion, Propertius' panorama of the *Eclogues* evokes the *Georgics*, before the *Georgics*, in their turn, are overtly mentioned, in 77–8.)[61] Secondly, verse 66 highlights a shift, from the opening of *Eclogue* 4 to the *Aeneid* passage, in the way each text stands in relation to the material it presents. In Propertius' elegy, *nascitur* conveys the birth of poetic discourse, of something greater than the *Iliad*. The production of Virgil's poem about historical events is *itself* a historical event.

The speaker in the *Aeneid*, in the passage quoted previously, identifies his own utterance with the birth of the *ordo rerum*. That 'order of events' is something for which he as speaker is responsible, in the sense that he is responsible for *constituting* them. The repetition of *dicam* ('I shall speak of')—and the *mihi* already noted—make this very clear. And as the significance of that 'order of events' (the *narrative*) which that utterance is supposed to convey becomes greater (*maior*), so that utterance itself also becomes greater (*maius opus moveo*). For the speaker in *Eclogue* 4 on the other hand, *saeclorum nascitur ordo* is an event which is *not* constituted by his words: the birth of an order of ages is, as it were, outside of him. Along with the return of Virgo and the Saturnian

---

[61] The evocations are (i) the river Galaesus in 67 found in *Georgics* 4. 126 and *not* mentioned in the *Eclogues*; (ii) the structure *felix qui* ('Happy you who . . .') in 7 and *felix . . . qui* ('Happy [Corydon] who . . .') in 73: cf. *felix qui potuit rerum cognoscere causas* ('Happy he who has been able to know the causes of things') in *Georgics* 2. 490 and *fortunatus et ille deos qui novit agrestis* ('Happy he who has known the gods of farming') in *Georgics* 2. 493.

kingdoms, it is one of the 'rather greater things' he apologizes (1–3) for singing about in his bucolic medium. The *ordo* is conceived by this speaker of the *Eclogue* as the referent of his utterance, not merely as the signified element.

Distinct meanings of the Latin word *ordo* fit in either situation: *ordo* can signify the order or arrangement of a speech, as well as an order of events.[62] In simple terms, the notion of *ordo* being born is a theme in the content of the *Eclogue*; whilst for the *Aeneid* it refers to a change in the design or form of the epic.[63] If such a distinction holds between the text of *Eclogue* 4 and *Aeneid* 7, the respective fields of the primary addressees of these texts must also be distinct, even in relation to these highly similar indexical phrases. The primary addressee of *Eclogue* 4 is inclined, by and with the speaker, to regard the birth of a new (eventually peaceful) order as something which is already there to be described—something known not only to the speaker but also the Muses, Lucina, and Pollio—about which that addressee is now being informed. The primary addressee of the *Aeneid* passage is inclined, by and with the speaker, to regard the birth of a new (violent) order as something conjured up by the speaker himself: perception or praise of that order is an act of the speaker's will, no longer an inevitability.

The earliest known rendering into Greek of *Eclogue* 4. 5 (which may be by Eusebius) is of great interest here. It occurs in Constantine's *Oration to the Saints* (possibly delivered in 324 at Antioch).[64] The Latin verse *magnus ab integro saeclorum nascitur ordo* becomes:

Αὖθις ἄρ' αἰώνων ἱερὸς στίχος ὄρνυται ἡμῖν

Again a holy verse of the ages is born to us

Yet these words would more nicely translate *mihi nascitur ordo* from *Aeneid* 7, as I have understood it. The word στίχος, used as an equivalent of *ordo* here, normally means a line of verse. The sense of

---

[62] See the *OLD* on *ordo* at 1266–7: originally a weaving term for thread on the loom, the senses of the word range from physical formations (s.v. 1–3); social rank (4–5); a line or sequence, temporal or logical (6–8); steps or stages in an argument or process (9); and the connected sequence of a narrative or discourse.

[63] In narratological terms, the notion of *ordo* being born would be an element of the *story* in the *Eclogue*; and part of the *narrative* of the *Aeneid*. (A critical account of the narratological distinction between narrative and story will be set out in the next chapter.)

[64] Constantine, *Oration* 19; see Winkelmann (1975). I am grateful to Mark Edwards for alerting me to the existence of this passage—a discussion of the Oration will be found in Edwards (1999).

ordo as 'discursive arrangement' from *Aeneid* 7. 44 seems to have contaminated this translation of *ordo* as 'order of events' from *Eclogue* 4.

In conclusion, an underlying 'relation of positions' (in Faye's sense) may be discerned between the first passage of Virgil (*Eclogue* 4) and the second (*Aeneid* 7). That underlying relation of positions, which generates the change in narrative function of the surface indexical phrase, can itself be regarded as being in a state of change, or motion. These exemplary passages of Virgil can be understood if we see these indexicals operating in succession: *nascitur ordo* has shifted, from predicating a state of affairs conveyed by the narrative discourse of poetry, to predicating the narrative discourse of poetry itself. Conjectures can still be made about the significance of the change of position noted here for literary history, or even for the chronicling of the political sympathies of Virgil and his audience. But this treatment has at least shown that sense can be made of a set of verbal resemblances between texts which would otherwise appear to be random and impossible to explain.

1.5 TEXTS AS DISCOURSES: INTERTEXTUALITY

Intertextuality can be discerned in every written text and every spoken utterance. Intertextuality—though it has been most commonly scrutinized by literary theorists and literary critics—is an inevitable property of all kinds of discourse: it is what enables texts to have any meaning at all. Consideration of intertextuality, no less than addressees, superaddressees, and indexicals is vital for an understanding of texts as discourses. Intertextuality, far from segregating literary texts (like those considered in the previous section) from other kinds of discourse, in fact unites them with all other kinds of discourse. Julia Kristeva who coined the term 'intertextuality', attributed the original idea to Bakhtin, and explained it as follows:

Each word (text) is an intersection of word[s] (texts) where at least one other word (text) can be read . . . any text is a mosaic of quotations; any text is the absorption and transformation of another. The notion of *intertextuality* replaces that of intersubjectivity, and poetic language is read as at least *double*.[65]

---

[65] Kristeva (1981), 66, a translation from Kristeva (1969).

This notion of intertextuality does not involve aesthetic evaluation or source criticism. Intertextuality is an inevitable property of every text, because every text functions in terms of other texts. Bakhtin's formulation of intertextuality (as 'dialogism') makes it perfectly clear that *any* discourse stands in an intertextual or dialogical relation to other discourses:

The dialogical relation is obviously a characteristic phenomenon of all discourse. It is the natural aim of all living discourse. Discourse comes upon the discourse of the other on all the roads that lead to its object, and it cannot but enter into intense and lively interaction with it. Only the mythical and totally alone Adam, approaching a virgin and still unspoken world with the very first discourse, could really avoid altogether this mutual reorientation with respect to the difference of the other, that occurs on the way to the object.[66]

The intertextuality of discourse is not solely a concern for Bakhtin and his successors. In a sociolinguistic study of repetition and dialogue in everyday conversation ('involvement strategies'), Deborah Tannen remarks that 'the meanings of individual words ... and the combinations into which we can put them are given to us by previous speakers, traces of whose voices and contexts cling inevitably to them'.[67]

It is a matter of some irony that the technical term 'intertextuality' has itself been subjected to a degree of transformation and appropriation.[68] Kristeva's concept has 'nothing to do with matters of influence by one writer upon another, or with the sources of a literary work'.[69] Nonetheless, it has been adapted (with varying degrees of self-consciousness) by a number of critics, of Latin

[66] The translation here is from Todorov (1984), 62. A translation of the essay 'Discourse in the Novel' from which this passage is excerpted can be found in Bakhtin (1981), 259–422.

[67] Tannen (1989), 100. Tannen notes at 213 : 'Even seemingly made-up words must be patterned on familiar phonological and morphological configurations to have meaning at all. For example, the playful neologisms of Lewis Carroll's "Jabberwocky" are traceable to familiar words and set in regular syntactic frames. "'Twas brillig" suggests a scene-setting description of weather reminiscent of "brilliant;" "slithy toves" suggests creatures ("toves," resembling "toads"?) characterized by the adjective "slithy" which blends "sliding," "slimy," "blithe," and so on.'

[68] Van Erp Taalman Kip (1994) opens with a detailed account of how the idea of intertextuality has developed.

[69] I am quoting from Roudiez's account of the term in a glossary from Kristeva (1981), 15.

literature in particular. Gian Biagio Conte applied his own version
of intertextuality to his influential discussions of allusion and poetic
memory.[70] He professed both a debt to Kristeva and a departure
from her conception:

The term 'intertextuality' is now widely accepted not least because of its
opposition to 'intersubjectivity.' The term was coined by the Tel Quel
group and was associated with Kristeva's work. Although these scholars
often extend the ideological import of the notion too far for the concrete
needs of the philologist, who is a less abstract analyst of texts, we should
probably accept the term and redefine it. I consider it equivalent to the less
technical poetic memory—a strategic working equivalence suited to our
needs.[71]

There is some justification for Conte's appropriation of the term
'intertextuality' into his area of expertise: the traditional terminology of 'allusion' and its cognates in discussions of resonances
between texts has its drawbacks. The simple positing of a subject
to the verb 'allude' can allow us to slide into making unjustified
assertions about a writer's intentions and motives.[72] Of course more
ludicrous claims can be made in the business of literary interpretation: a complaint about insights couched in intentionalist terms is
often only a complaint about a minor matter of protocol.[73] But the
crucial point about theory of intertextuality is that resemblances or
resonances between texts or discourses only exist in the eyes of the
beholder. Intertexts are only there because readers see them.

Yet critics who still insist that relationships between texts or
discourses have some kind of 'official' or objective status have
hijacked the term 'intertextuality', simply in order to purge the
notion of allusion of intentionalist accretions. They soon run into

---

[70] Conte (1986). Farrell (1991), Lyne (1994), Schrijvers (1995), and Smolenaars
(1995), Gale (forthcoming) are examples of Latinists applying customized theories
of intertextuality in Conte's wake. The treatment of repetition in Latin poetry in
Wills (1996) contains an important chapter at 15–41 on allusion which considers the
whole question of how 'allusive markers' come to exist and be perceived; see also
Nosarti (1996). Hinds (1998) cautiously defends the notion of allusion: see
especially 17–51. D. P. Fowler (1998) provides a survey of these questions with
further bibliography in an issue of *Materiali e Dicussione* devoted to intertextuality
in Latin literature. Fowler recognizes the ideological dimension of intertextuality,
argued here. The importance of speech presentation for intertextuality (discussed
in the next section and further in Ch. 4.1) merits further exploration.

[71] Conte (1986), 29 n. 11.

[72] See Lyne (1994) for a clear statement of this case.

[73] J. G. F. Powell (1997), 304 argues this engagingly.

trouble and often give themselves up.[74] One scholar has offered a clear and honest articulation of the dilemma which confronts those who operate with Conte's brand of intertextualism:

I should conclude by admitting that avoidance of the Intentionalists' evasion leads to no objective and ever-applicable *Methode*. We still have to use our judgment, knowledge and instinct. Inevitably, subjectivity cannot be completely expelled. When is an intertext readable and identifiable enough to constitute an intertext? This is a problem that the theoreticians seem to me to evade.[75]

That problem is simply alien to the theory of intertextuality I shall outline here. An intertext is constituted by whoever sees it; it does not make sense to talk about whether it is 'readable and identifiable enough'.[76] In my own view, the very detection of an intertext—no matter how palpable, demonstrable and well attested—is in the end ideologically determined.[77] Thus, if we are capable of identifying an intertext, we ought always to be capable of saying what (we think) it is doing there.

An objection to my presentation of intertextuality might be that it makes the notion so accommodating and inflated that it comes to be meaningless. If intertextuality is a characteristic of all utterances, texts and narratives, and if it only exists in the eye of the beholder, how do we manage to talk about specific examples of intertextuality? It is partly this which has prompted the kind of defence of allusion offered by Stephen Hinds: as Hinds puts it, allusion is an easier tool 'to think with'.[78] But this sort of response

[74] Farrell (1991), 23 and 64 f. who shows how often—and how far—Conte himself resorts to intentionalism, in a chapter 'On Vergilian Intertextuality', admits that his own position is 'on some level concerned with a poet's intentions'.

[75] Lyne (1994), 200 (cf. 189). Hinds (1998) shows at 47 (and 47 n. 57) that he is trying to get beyond this aporia in a similar way.

[76] The discussion of 'External markers' in Wills (1996), 30–1 might seem to threaten my position here: he notes that poetry can contain 'overt mentions of similarity, concealment, variation, antiquity, recurrrence or memory'.

[77] Monica Gale's forthcoming study of relations between Virgil's *Georgics* and Lucretius argues that, if a certain sort of readership is presupposed, some intertexts are simply more prominent and readily identifiable than others. In my view, such an approach concedes too much validity to certain reading conventions which are purely disciplinary. (Compare my comments about the role of reading communities in determining the nature of history writing in the opening section of Ch. 4.)

[78] Hinds (1998), 51. It is significant that Hinds's conception of intertextualism is post-Contean: he makes no mention of Bakhtin or Kristeva. This might explain why the ideological dimension of intertextuality does not really feature in his study.

takes no real account of ideology. The examples we talk about are the examples we, as a circumscribed community of readers, are conditioned to see. Instances of irony, parody, or stylization in texts or utterances—which are manifestations of intertextuality—are notorious for not being evident to everyone. Such qualities are not part of the 'matrix' of a text. They are actualized only by readers or hearers with a certain competence.

The principle applies, for instance, to the 'presence' of Homer in Virgil's *Aeneid*, which is generally considered to be so self-evident as to be beyond question. However, at no point does the *Aeneid* explicitly mention Homer, the *Iliad* or the *Odyssey*.[79] This is important: to 'see' a Homeric intertext in Virgil is an act of *interpretation*, not plain description. It may indeed be the case that Virgil's imitation of Homer is presupposed by his ancient emulators or noted by ancient critics.[80] But that observation obscures the basic point. The basic point is that apprehension of the importance of Homer in Virgil cannot be an inevitable or even the 'proper' response to reading Virgil. Our identification of Homer as a key intertext for 'understanding' Virgil leads us to assume that any sensible, informed reader would have to share that apprehension.

That identification of the intertext, as well as the assumption of its universal validity, is ideological. We ascribe to our beliefs the status of knowledge of objective truth. Medieval readers availing themselves of other 'facts' and giving priority to other intertexts—principally from Christian scripture—clearly did the same. It could be objected that it is a matter of *truth*, not opinion, that medieval readers simply know less (about Virgil, his culture, pertinent literary history, etc.) than modern readers, and that it is also *true* that their readings are less informed than ours, and therefore demonstrably less valid. This objection only serves to clarify the real basis of the debate. The view that matters of chronology and

---

[79] Again, contrast the approach in Gale's forthcoming study of Lucretius and the *Georgics* in which 'direct quotation' of a text is privileged as the most indisputable form of intertextuality. But even if Virgil may seem (to some readers) to 'quote' Homer, perhaps no verdict can be completely decisive unless Homer is named. Apparent quotation of Homer in Virgil is *not* tantamount to mentioning Homer.

[80] Ancient commentators can be remarkably non-committal about identification of Homer as a model for Virgil's epic. For example the biographer Donatus says: *novissime Aeneidem incohavit, argumentum varium et multiplex et quasi amborum Homeri carminum instar* . . . (21), 'Last of all Virgil began the *Aeneid*, a varied story which had many features but which was also occupying the place of both Homer's poems . . .'.

literary history are more important than revelation through scripture may have a strong appeal in the current intellectual climate, but it is a view which is nonetheless ideological. The suspension of a sense of chronology is in fact quite routine in various scholarly contexts.[81]

In my view, the principle ideological dimension of intertextuality is actualized between texts and audiences or readers. This is actually a different position from that of Bakhtin and Kristeva which is more structuralist: for them, ideological concerns, at least primarily, obtain between the *systems* of the texts themselves.[82] The passages examined in the previous section show that intertextuality facilitates scrutiny of ideological transformation or conflict. This is the case if one conceives (as I have) texts as affective discourses or speech acts, which appear to constitute and impact on a network of social exchanges. Either way, I hope to have shown that ideology is of fundamental importance for an understanding of how intertextuality (as opposed to allusion) really operates. It ought to be clear now that attempts to 'purify intertextuality of its ideological overtones . . . to make it a more neutral instrument suited to philological analysis' actually end up doing philologists a disservice.[83]

Any endeavour to apprehend intertextuality without ideology will result in a Gordian knot of methodological quandaries. It

---

[81] Some examples: (i) historians examine events 'in the light of' their consequences more often than they examine past events for and in themselves. Nicholls (1989), 14–15 thus makes a strong case for 'writing history backwards'. (ii) In many disciplines, past cultural categories are more often than not interpreted in terms of those currently prevailing—although this process can be challenged e.g. Crapanzano (1986) and (1992). (iii) Classicists (and Latinists especially) often study ancient authors through the filter of their successors: it is notorious that Apollonius of Rhodes until relatively recently tended to be approached 'through' Virgil. Compare D. P. Fowler (1998).

[82] Frow (1986), 169 usefully summarizes his own version of the structuralist position: 'It is in the articulation of different modes of language, different registers that the reality effects and the fiction effects of the literary text are generated. This articulation involves relations of dominance and subordination between registers, and this clash of language is a clash of realities—that is, of moral universes. The text can be defined as the process of these relations of discursive contradiction; and it is here that ideological value is confirmed or challenged, and textual historicity generated.' The notion of language constructing a reality or even a 'moral universe' will be taken up again, as part of the discussion of narrative as representation in Ch. 2 and in the opening of Ch. 5, as well as in the Conclusions to this study. See also Laird (1993*a*), 148–56 on 'story worlds'.

[83] Conte (1986), 29 n. 11, in praise of Genette (1982*b*). My objection to this is consistent with my view on the comments in Conte (1994), quoted earlier.

cannot be untied by appeals to problematic notions of aesthetic evaluation and authorial intention.

1.6 INTERTEXTUALITY AND SPEECH PRESENTATION

It should now be clear that connections between speech and power can be found in texts whether or not they attribute words or thoughts to any characters presented in them. The more we consider the issues involving addressees, indexicals, and intertextuality, the more evident it becomes that even the most literary of texts have things in common with all other kinds of discourse. These other kinds of discourse include, of course, speech presented in narrative, as well as actual spoken utterances. The realization of the parallel between discourse in general and discourse of characters presented in texts is central to this study as a whole. Intertextuality, which we have seen is a feature of all discourse (or 'texts'), has a special bearing on speech presentation.

Kristeva reformulated her own definition of intertextuality—as the 'transposition of one or more systems of signs into another, accompanied by a new articulation of the enunciative and denotative position'.[84] This is more than analogous to what happens when the words of a specific character are reported in a narrative. We shall see later that even the apparently straightforward use of direct discourse changes many of the original aspects and objects of the utterance which is being 'reproduced'. Intertextuality is in fact comparable to, if not ultimately identifiable with, speech presentation. Both are concerned with 'quotation', or the perception of a text changing tenor, owing to the intrusion of another voice or text.

But where intertextuality is concerned, no *explicit* indication is given in a text or utterance of the presence of an alien text or speaker. Intertextuality is always there but it can often only be discerned when a text deviates from its customary tenor, whether in parody, stylization, irony, or in some other kind of variation which may or may not be recognized in conventional terms as an echo or allusion. If we conceive of a scale to differentiate between

[84] See Kristeva (1974), 59–60. This actual quotation is from Roudiez's epitome in Kristeva (1981), 15.

the degrees of intrusion of an 'alien' discourse in a narrative text, intertextuality represents the most remote form, whilst direct discourse represents the closest and most immanent. In between these, come various hybridized forms such as focalization and various forms of indirect discourse. These three degrees of presence are successively exemplified in the opening of the *Aeneid*.

The most remote range of the scale is illustrated in the second word of the poem: *virum* ('man') is generally held to echo *andra* ('man'), the first word of the first verse of Homer's *Odyssey*. No explicit mention of Homer or of the *Odyssey*'s text is made by the speaker of the *Aeneid*, but Homer's discourse is an intertext because it is visible to readers of Virgil who know Homer. The middle range of the scale is exemplified a few verses later:

> id metuens veterisque memor Saturnia belli,
> prima quod ad Troiam pro caris gesserat Argis—
> necdum etiam causae irarum saevique dolores
> exciderant animo; manet alta mente repostum
> iudicium Paridis spretaeque iniuria formae
> et genus invisum et rapti Ganymedis honores
>
> (*Aeneid* 1. 23–8)

Juno was afraid of this, and mindful of the old war which she had first waged at Troy for the beloved Argives—not yet had the causes of her anger and the cruel grief left her heart; the judgement of Paris and the injustice of her slighted beauty remained, stored deep in her mind; as did the hateful race of the Trojans and the honours paid to Ganymede after he had been carried off.

Syntactically all these verses belong to the speaker of the poem, but there is a clear sense in which the voice and conceptual horizon of another speaker (Juno) are blended into them: 'the irruption of the unspecified *et genus invisum* "And the hateful race" reproduces in mimetic *oratio obliqua* the way Juno herself put the matter in her mind.'[85]

Finally, the nearest range of the scale, in which another speaker has the maximum possible intrusion in a monologic utterance, is demonstrated by the introduction of direct discourse:

---

[85] D. P. Fowler (1990), 48.

> cum Iuno aeternum servans sub pectore vulnus
> haec secum: 'mene incepto desistere victam
> nec posse Italia Teucrorum avertere regem!'
>
> (*Aeneid* 1. 36–8)

Juno, keeping an eternal wound under her breast, [said] this to herself: 'Am I to give up in defeat, unable to keep the king of the Trojans from Italy?'

The exact nature of that maximum possible intrusion is not in fact as clear-cut as it may seem: below and in subsequent chapters I shall try to show the extent to which even instances of direct discourse like this might be considered the property of the reporter (here the narrator) as much as of the speaker to whom they may be ascribed (here Juno). Leaving that question aside, it should now be obvious that intertextuality is intimately related to speech presentation. I should also point out that speech presentation, like intertextuality, is ideological: the relation between a narrator and the discourse of others he presents determines, and is determined by, the nature of the relation between a text and its reader or audience. The ideological nature of intertextuality, as we have already seen, is very similar: the relation between text and intertext similarly determines, and is determined by, the nature of the relation between that text and its reader or audience.

This chapter began with Penelope's distraught response to a recitation by the bard Phemius, related in Homer's *Odyssey*. Donatus' biography of Virgil includes a story about a recitation of the *Aeneid* by Virgil himself. This recitation had an even more devastating effect on Octavia, sister of the emperor Augustus:

> tres omnino libros recitavit, secundum, quartum et sextum, sed hunc notabili Octaviae adfectione, quae cum recitationi interesset, ad illos de filio suo versus: 'tu Marcellus eris', deficisse fertur et aegre focilata.
>
> (Donatus, *Vita* 32)

He recited three books in one sitting; the second, fourth, and the sixth—but that one prompted a remarkable reaction from Octavia. It is reported that when she was present at the recitation, those verses about her son—'You will be Marcellus'—caused her to faint, and she could only be revived with difficulty.

Here it is hard even to retain a theoretical distinction between the categories of speech presentation and intertextuality. The two simply collapse into each other. The account of Octavia's response is in indirect discourse, governed by *fertur* ('it is reported that'). This is to signal the presence of some other discourse in Donatus' text, either spoken or written, to which we have no access: its identity and content are irrecoverable.[86] And, embedded within this reported discourse, there is another text: the first three words of verse 6. 883 of the *Aeneid*. In that verse, Anchises hails Marcellus in a speech which is for the most part addressed to Aeneas. The embedding of the verse adds the complication—or revelation—that Virgil is really the speaker of these words, with Augustus and Octavia as the addressees. So, in this context, the words *tu Marcellus eris* ('You will be Marcellus') have an ambivalent function. On one level they are a 'quotation' from the *Aeneid* as a reusable text. On another they constitute a transformation of this text, by representing a speech act which occurred once and once only: Virgil's utterance of *tu Marcellus eris* which caused Octavia to faint. Donatus' account nicely illustrates the parallels and connections between speech presentation within a text and the affective power of poetic discourse itself.

---

[86] The consensus that Donatus' life is really by Suetonius of course changes nothing. On the authorship of the *Vita*, see Rostagni (1944), 68–9.

Platonic Formalism: Socrates and
the Narratologists

Plato was essentially a poet—the truth and splendour of his
imagery, and the melody of his language, are the most intense
that it is possible to conceive. He rejected the measure of the
epic, dramatic and lyrical forms, because he sought to kindle a
harmony in thoughts divested of shape and action, and he
forbore to invent any regular plan of rhythm which would
include under determinate forms, the varied pauses of his
style.

(Percy Bysshe Shelley, *A Defence of Poetry*[1])

The story of Virgil's *Aeneid* is well known. Ulysses' stratagem of
the wooden horse caused the city of Troy to fall to the Greeks,
prompting Aeneas to flee from Troy with his son, his father
Anchises, and his comrades. They travel to various places, including Carthage, where Aeneas has an ill-fated love affair with Dido.
The Trojans then sail to Italy and, after Aeneas' visit to the
underworld, arrive in Latium. The pact made with the Latins is
soon broken and a bitter war ensues. The outcome is determined by
single combat between Aeneas and Turnus, the leader of the
Rutuli. Turnus is defeated and killed.

That summary of the story, however, is not at all the same thing
as the *narrative* of the *Aeneid*. The actual narrative of the *Aeneid* is
doubtless less well known than the story. The narrative is in Latin
verse and runs for several thousand lines. It does not begin at the
beginning of the *story*—the chain of events the poem seeks to
recount. The *narrative* opens *in medias res* with the sea storm
which brings the Trojans to Carthage. The account of the fall of
Troy and of Aeneas' flight from the city is given subsequently as a
'flashback' in the second and third books of the poem. That account

---

[1] This text is from Brett-Smith (1972), 29.

(a whole sixth of the work) is not given in the third-person voice of the poet, but in the first person by Aeneas himself. This shows that there is a range of possibilities for narration: any character can be shown to know more or less about the events described than the audience or readers; time can speed up or slow down relative to the time events might actually take to occur; and events in the story can be presented at first hand or through the account of a character.

This range of possibilities available for narration is most easily understood in terms of the distinction indicated here: between 'story' as the totality of narrated events, and 'narrative' as the discourse that narrates them. The *events* of the *Aeneid*, abstracted from the narrative in which we find them, and reconstructed in their supposed original order can be designated by the word 'story'. The 'narrative' is the specific spoken or written text produced by Virgil which tells these events—it is what we actually read or hear. Henceforth, the words 'narrative' and 'story' will mainly be used in these technical senses. However, on certain occasions it is hard to avoid either of these words being used in a looser, colloquial way. The field of study called 'narratology' is generally devoted to the relation between narrative and story.[2]

The influence of Aristotle's *Poetics* must be in part responsible for a great divorce: the isolation of speech presentation from the understanding of narrative as a whole. Aristotle's analysis of speech presentation follows Plato's in showing how types of poetry are differentiated according to the speech modes a poet adopts:[3]

καὶ γὰρ ἐν τοῖς αὐτοῖς καὶ τὰ αὐτὰ μιμεῖσθαι ἔστιν ὁτὲ μὲν ἀπαγγέλλοντα, ἢ ἕτερόν τι γιγνόμενον ὥσπερ Ὅμηρος ποιεῖ ἢ ὡς τὸν αὐτὸν καὶ μὴ μεταβάλλοντα, ἢ πάντας ὡς πράττοντας καὶ ἐνεργοῦντας τοὺς μιμουμένους.

(*Poetics* 3 1448[a])

For one can represent the same objects in the same media (i) sometimes in narration and sometimes becoming someone else, as Homer does, or (ii) speaking in one's own person without change, or (iii) with all the people engaged in the *mimesis* actually doing things.

[2] The word *narratologie* was coined in Todorov (1969) which sought to give an account of the general science of narrative.

[3] See Lucas (1968), ad loc.; Halliwell (1987), 77–8 and Halliwell (1986), 128 n. 34 look at the precise ways in which Aristotle's use of terminology here differs from Plato's and at his shifting conception of epic as *mimesis*. Unlike Plato, Aristotle offers this basis for generic distinction in conjunction with two others in this context; the media of delivery (like metre) and the objects of delivery.

However, in contrast to Plato, Aristotle has no interest in distinctions between form and content, or between narrative and story. Aristotle's notion of *muthos* or 'plot-structure' covers both the narrative design of a poem and its subject matter.[4] Aristotle does not connect discourse in poetry with the discourse of poetry: the latter as *mimesis*, or representation is of a different order.[5] Plato's conception of poetry or narrative, as affective discourse, on the other hand, does connect the distinctions between narrative and story with speech presentation—and shows how speech presentation can be used to interpret those distinctions.

2.1 A CRITIQUE OF NARRATOLOGY

The distinction between narrative (*récit*) and story (*histoire*) was popularized by Gérard Genette in his influential book *Narrative Discourse*.[6] In fact Genette's distinction was based on one first conceived by the Russian formalist, Viktor Shklovsky in 1926.[7] Remarkably, Shklovsky's similar discrimination—between *fabula* and *syuzhet*—was itself inspired by the fictional narrator of Sterne's *Tristram Shandy* who supplies graphs to illustrate the flow of his own narrative.[8] It is not hard to see why classicists in particular have responded warmly to the narrative/story distinction.[9] In the

---

[4] Fusillo (1986) is an important examination of Aristotle's *muthos* in the light of narratology.

[5] Halliwell (1986), 24 remarks that Aristotle's 'structured *muthos* turns the gaze more inwardly than the Platonic view had allowed onto the intrinsic properties of the poetic work of art'.

[6] Genette (1980), 29.

[7] Shklovsky (1965), 57 is a translation of the relevant passsage: 'The idea of plot is too often confused with the description of events—with what I propose provisionally to call the story. The story is, in fact, only material for plot formulation. The plot of *Eugeny Onegin* is, therefore, not the romance of the hero with Tatyana, but the fashioning of the subject of this story as produced by the introduction of interrupting digressions.' This is discussed in Eichenbaum (1965), 122. Another English translation of Eichenbaum can be found in Matejka and Pomorska (1978), 3–37.

[8] The diagrams are in *Tristram Shandy*, vi, ch. 60 (Sterne (1997), 391–2), and reproduced in Shklovsky (1965), 55–6. Shklovsky, with characteristic thoroughness, notes at 57 that Sterne's diagrams 'are approximately accurate, but they do not call attention to the crosscurrent of motifs'.

[9] The application of narratological analysis to the *Iliad* in De Jong (1987a) has been a seminal influence. See also Winkler (1985) on Apuleius' *Metamorphoses*, Fantuzzi (1988) on Apollonius' *Argonautica*, and Hornblower (1994) on Thucydides.

field of classical literature, comparison of different narrative versions of mythological stories is a frequent activity. The narratologists' distinction is also useful for history—provided it is understood that the 'story' of the texts they deal with has nothing directly to do with whatever actually happened.[10] The story is merely something constructed from the narrative to facilitate a review of aspects of narration in the historical text under scrutiny. The word 'story' should not be taken to imply that the events it contains are necessarily fictitious. The realm of what actually happened is a different realm from that of the analysis of narrative and story which looks only at manners of discursive presentation.

However, consideration of historical texts highlights a general problem with this distinction which Genette himself has been forced to recognize.[11] Can a story really be conceived independently of its narrative? If it can, would not the story or 'totality of events', as Genette put it, have to be everything that ever happened at all or could happen?[12] Barbara Herrnstein Smith unfavourably likens the narratologists' conception of story to a Platonic Form. As soon as we try to approach this story we come up with a version of it—which can only be another *narrative*, embodying a particular point of view. '[Narratology]' she argues 'appears to be afflicted . . . with a number of dualistic concepts and models, the continuous generation of which betrays a lingering strain of naïve Platonism.'[13] She makes her case by reviewing instances of the Cinderella myth, mentioning 345 instances of the tale—any notion of a story constructed from these variant narratives is, as she puts it, 'a Platonic version: disembodied, untold, unheard, and so forth'.

Seymour Chatman vehemently opposes this with the argument that narrative in the general sense is something which operates beyond language:

Smith confuses the surface medium, language, with the deep structure of the text, which is a logical structure. Narrative subsists in an event chain, operating through time. Its logic is xRy where R is the temporal succession.[14]

---

[10] H. White (1987) considers the importance for historians of understanding narrative discourse. Hornblower (1994) also raises some crucial questions. See also Laird (1993*a*), 160–1 and 173–4. There will be further discussion of these issues in Ch. 4.

[11] See Genette (1991), 69 f. where he responds to Herrnstein Smith (1981).

[12] See Genette (1991), 73 n. 3.

[13] Herrnstein Smith (1981).   [14] Chatman (1981), 264.

48 *Platonic Formalism*

Chatman also specifically answers the charge of naïve Platonism:

I must ask in all reasonableness whether my book or books like Gérard Genette's *Narrative Discourse* . . . could possibly be described as 'spiritualist', 'contemptuous of sense knowledge and empirical studies,' or unduly marked by the belief in the possibility of 'absolute truth'. Structuralists are surely pragmatists to a fault. Aristotle, not Plato, is our mentor . . . Dualists we are, but dualists who burrow for the structures precisely for the sake of the precious surfaces, the better to appreciate them. Our intention, then, . . . is not Platonic but anti-Platonic.[15]

The repeated invocation of Plato and Platonism may seem extravagant or even misleading in this context: could we argue for or against 'the' story behind a narrative being 'perfect' in the sense that Plato's forms are often held to be perfect? However, in my view, there does appear to be an expression of that very narrative/story distinction in Plato. Although the text in which this occurs has been discussed by narratologists, it has never been considered in terms of the distinction which is so fundamental to their method.[16]

This Plato text, which is part of the celebrated argument about poetry in the third book of the *Republic*, not only contributes to our understanding of the debate outlined above. It can also enrich our conception of what narrative theory in general is, or what it ought to be. Socrates has been talking to Adeimantos about the role poetry has in education. He then moves on to another moral aspect of poetry:[17]

'So much for *what is said* (τὰ μὲν δὴ λόγων). We must next consider its *expression* (τὸ δὲ λέξεως). When that is done we shall have covered the whole subject of *what is to be said and how* (ἅ τε λεκτέον καὶ ὡς λεκτέον).'
'I don't understand what you are saying.'
'You ought to; but perhaps you'll know better if I put it like this. Isn't

---

[15] Chatman (1981), 259.
[16] Both De Jong (1987a), 1–7 and Fantuzzi (1988), 47 f. treat the passages from the *Republic* and *Poetics* in considerable detail for their own purposes. Fantuzzi relates the testimonies of Plato, Aristotle, 'Longinus', and Diomedes to those in the Greek scholia. Genette (1980), 162 f. and Genette (1992) provide more discussion of these Plato passages and their implications. The treatment in Lodge (1990), 28–9 is derived from Genette (1980), but again demonstrates the importance of Plato's observations. 'Servius' and Scaliger also mediated ancient and later receptions of this discussion: see n. 48 below.
[17] The translations from Plato here are, or are modelled on, those supplied by Russell and Winterbottom (1972), 51 f.

everything that poets or story tellers say a narrative of past or present or future?'

'Of course.'

(Republic 392c6–d4)

Only this far into the conversation several points can be raised. Socrates goes to some pains to bring out the contrast between the notion of what is said and the manner of saying it. The difference is first expressed as that between *logoi* and *lexis*; it is then put another way in the next part of the sentence: 'what is to be said and how' (*ha te lekteon kai hōs lekteon*). The distinction made at this transitional point in the dialogue is often regarded as a straightforward one between content and form.[18] The idea of 'content' will be reconsidered below. A working definition can be found in Barthes's account of how content and form are customarily understood:

As everyone knows, this dichotomy derives from the opposition in classical rhetoric between Res and Verba: Res (or the demonstrative materials of the discourse) depends on Inventio, or research into what one can say about a subject (Quaestio); on verba depends Elocutio (or the transformation of these materials into a verbal form) . . . The relationship of Content and Form is phenomenological: Form is taken to be the 'appearance' or 'dress' of Content, which is the 'reality' or 'substance' of Form. [19]

The words 'form' and 'content' convey something rather different from the divide given in Plato's Greek. The English words, though commonly paired, usually indicate two different or even opposing sorts of thing, whilst the two formulations Socrates makes here convey different aspects of the *same* sort of thing: speech.[20]

His distinction is no less clear just because of that: Adeimantos is surely being dense when he says he does not understand what Socrates is saying. Socrates laboured his distinction, but in doing so, he sticks to cognates of the Greek verb *legein* ('to speak')—in

---

[18] Compare e.g. Grube (1965), 50 f.; Vicaire (1960), 41 f.

[19] Barthes (1971), 3–4.

[20] Genette (1992), 8 n. 10 acknowledges this: 'Of course the terms *logos* and *lexis* do not a priori have this antithetical value; out of context, the most faithful translations would be "discourse" and "diction".' However he then says that 'it is Plato himself who constructs the opposition (392c) and glosses it as *ha lekteon* ("the matter of speech") and *hōs lekteon* ("the manner of speech")'. My argument is that there is no 'opposition' here. The very use of the same verbal expression (*lekteon*) in both parts of the gloss suggest that matter and manner are aspects of the same thing.

both of his pairings. When his companion fails to understand, Socrates refrains from using more distinguishable terms, and so retains the connection between them. Instead he will proceed on a different tack. This sentence in *Republic* 392c is of interest because Socrates' words call to mind the distinction outlined earlier: *logoi* would correspond to the story; *lexis* to the narrative.[21] If this is correct, the use of *logoi*, like the technical use of *story*, can be safely distinguished from any actual events which may have prompted the narrative from which the story is constructed.[22] What Socrates says next could well enhance our understanding of the narrative/story distinction:

ἆρ' οὐ πάντα ὅσα ὑπὸ μυθολόγων ἢ ποιητῶν λέγεται διήγησις οὖσα τυγχάνει ἢ γεγονότων ἢ ὄντων ἢ μελλόντων;

(*Republic* 392d2)

Isn't everything that is said by storytellers or poets a narrative of past or present or future?

This is the new tack, but the occurence of the word *legetai* shows that Socrates is still really talking about the same thing: speech. Everything, we are told, that poets or storytellers say is a narrative. The actual word *diegesis* has not occurred before now in this conversation. It would seem, nonetheless, that Socrates must have been discussing narrative in his previous sentence which we have already considered. But what is meant by poets and story-tellers producing 'a narrative (*diegesis*) of past and present and future'?

Regarding poetry as a narrative of things that have happened is acceptable. A narrative of the present (in certain senses) is also conceivable—but how can poetry be a narrative of the future? Yet Adeimantos, generally slow to understand what Socrates says is quick on the uptake here: poetry surely isn't anything else, he says.

---

[21] Bers (1997), 12–13 discussing 392d8–393c10 could support what follows: Bers compares *Apology* 17d–18a to argue that *lexis* denotes style in a more general sense. However his remark at 12 that Socrates 'subsequently analyses *lexis* as φωνή and σχῆμα' is not so convincing: Socrates smuggles in these terms to illustrate the argument—they are not part of it.

[22] The effect would be somewhat different if we had had something like, say, *praxis* or even *muthos* instead of *logoi*. I do not think Plato always wants to commit himself to the reality of objects of literary representation. This is clearly shown by the opening discussion of poetic fables in *Republic* 378 f. See also Gould's discussion in Barker and Warner (1992).

Perhaps he is ready to agree because Hesiod's famous verses bear on the discussion here:

> The eloquent daughters of Zeus plucked and gave me a staff
> a splendid branch of glowing bay.
> And they breathed divine song into me
> that I might tell of the past and of the future . . .
>
> (*Theogony* 29–32[23])

We can compare what is said of Calchas in *Iliad* 1. 70—'the best of diviners, who had knowledge of all things that were, and that were to be, and that had been before'. The observation that *diegesis* is of things past, present or future is not just flowery ornamention. In stating that poets and storytellers provide *diegesis*, Socrates effectively clarifies his distinction between *logoi* and *lexis* which is equivalent to the distinction between story and narrative held now. Socrates could merely have said at 392d: 'Everything that is said by poets or storytellers is a narrative' and no more. There would be no doubt that Adeimantos (as well as Plato's readers) would still have happily snapped this up: poetry is simply narrative. But it becomes clear in Socrates' next sentence that *diegesis* functions as a kind of technical term.

Socrates could also have said at 392d—going slightly further: 'Everything that is said by poets or storytellers is a narrative of things that have happened.' Then we would indeed have got the idea of the narrative being distinct from what it presented. But there would have been the strong possibility of a fatal misunderstanding. A narrative of past events (*diegesis gegonotōn*) is not at all the same as the expression of material (*lexis logōn*) i.e. the narrative of the story. On the basis of the earlier part of Socrates' conversation with Adeimantos, the last thing he wants us to believe is that poetry, at least as it has existed so far, always tells us what happened.

The best thing for Socrates to say at 392d is what he does say: 'Everything that is said by poets or storytellers is a narrative of things that have happened or are happening or are about to happen.' This presents us with something like the distinction between *lexis* and *logoi*—a differentiation between the narrative and what it narrates, namely the story. The past, present and future

---

[23] I am using the translation from Russell and Winterbottom (1972), 3. West (1966) ad loc. and Murray (1981) give standard discussions of the importance of this passage for our understanding of early Greek theories of poetry and inspiration.

events are those *conjured up* in the world of a poem, regardless of
whatever actually has happened or will happen. And by ingeniously
adopting such an expression familiar from Hesiod and others,
Socrates has got Adeimantos to understand what he means without
compromising at all on the subtlety of his first distinction. If we
need any further assurance that the distinction made between *lexis*
and *logoi* actually corresponds to that now made between narrative
and story, Socrates' second formulation provides it.

It is a happy coincidence that Barbara Herrnstein Smith turns
out to be right about the narrative/story distinction being Platonic,
in the sense that Plato's Socrates seems to articulate something very
much like it. A better impression of Plato's version of the distinction emerges as Socrates' argument proceeds:

'And they execute their narrative either *by simple narrative or by narrative
conveyed by mimesis* (ἀπλῇ διηγήσει ἢ διὰ μιμήσεως γιγνομένῃ), or both.'
    'I should like a clearer account of that too please.'
'I must be a ridiculously obscure teacher. I'll try to do what incompetent
speakers do and show you what I mean by taking a little bit and not the
whole topic. Tell me: you know the beginning of the *Iliad*, where the poet
says that Chryses asked Agamemnon to release his daughter, Agamemnon
was angry and, and, Chryses, unsuccessful, cursed the Achaeans to the god?'
    'I know.'
'Then you know that as far as the lines :
        And he begged all the Achaeans
        and especially the two Atreidae, the generals of the host,
the poet speaks in his own person and does not try to turn our attention in
another direction by pretending that someone else is speaking [i.e. by
employing direct discourse]. But from this point he speaks as though he
were Chryses himself and tries to make us think that it is not Homer
talking, but the old priest. And he does practically all the rest of the
narrative in this way, both the tale of Troy and the episodes in Ithaca and
the whole *Odyssey*.

                                                    (*Republic* 392d5–393b5)

It was noted earlier that part of the importance of this passage is
well known to current theorists of narrative. Here *mimesis* has a
restricted meaning—the poet's impersonation of his character's
actual words, using direct discourse. *Diegesis* (or 'simple narrative')
is the poet speaking in his own person, and this includes indirect
speech. Genette first showed how Plato's pairing of *mimesis* and
diegesis could be seen as a happier attempt at the pairing of

'showing' and 'telling' made previously by Anglo-American critics.[24] That dichotomy of 'showing'/'telling' (or 'scene'/'summary') has caused much grief for students of the novel. It could never be agreed which features of fictional description were which.[25] Socrates' formulation makes the matter far clearer: direct discourse (or *mimesis*) corresponds to 'showing'; all the rest is 'telling'. Thus 'telling' includes narrative of events, indirect discourse, and even descriptions or *ekphrases*—no matter how vivid they may be. A number of theorists have made the same general points.[26] But it is clear that many have taken their cue from Genette to do so, rather than consider this part of the *Republic* in its own right. Plato's text does a good deal more than provide an ancient authority for prevalent views on speech presentation and on the 'showing'/'telling dichotomy'. It throws into question the way narrative discourse, narrative, and story are customarily regarded.

Socrates underlines his distinction between *mimesis* (direct discourse) and *diegesis* (or narrative) to make sure Adeimantos has understood it:

'Now it is *narrative* (διήγησις) both when he makes the various *speeches* (ῥήσεις) and in the passages between the speeches.'
'Of course.'
'But when he makes a speech pretending to be someone else, are we not to say that he is assimilating his *expression* (λέξιν) as far as possible to the supposed speaker?'
'Certainly.'

---

[24] Genette (1980), 162 f.
[25] Hägg (1971), 87–111 deals with the showing/telling dichotomy in the Greek romances. The traditional discussions which have influenced Hägg are in the wake of Henry James's classic discussion 'The Art of Fiction' in James (1884). See Wellek and Warren (1949), ch. 16 'Nature and Modes of Narrative Fiction'; Liddell (1953); Friedman in Stevick (1967), 113; Booth (1965) *passim*. It is obviously tempting to compare close descriptions of things with the 'verbatim' rendering of speech: both slow down the progress of events in a story, and provide detailed information. Hence both have been described as 'showing'. But the former type of representation is really ἐναργεία ('vividness'): see Quintilian 8. 3. 61–71. No matter how extensive or vivid a description of something may be, selection is always involved. This notion of selection does not generally apply to direct discourse. Thus Plato is right to use *'mimesis'* to designate direct discourse alone. But selection applies to indirect discourse as much as it does to description and to narrative in general. On description, see (e.g.) Barthes (1982); Bartsch (1989); Bourassa (1992); D. P. Fowler (1991); Genette (1982a), 133–7; Hamon (1982); Lukács (1978), 110–48; Modiano (1992).
[26] De Jong (1987a), Lodge (1990).

'And to assimilate oneself *in voice and gesture* (κατὰ φωνὴν ἢ κατὰ σχῆμα) to another is to imitate him?'

'Yes.'

'So in this sort of thing Homer and the other poets are conveying their *narrative* (διήγησιν) by way of *imitation* (διὰ μιμήσεως)?'

'Yes.'

(*Republic* 393b7–c10)

All the way through this exchange Socrates uses the same word *diegesis* to stand for (i) narrative in general and (ii) more specifically to stand for what he sometimes calls *haplē diegesis*: 'single narrative', or narrative which does not contain speeches.[27]

This usage resembles the way in which modern theorists who use the word 'narrative' to denote narrative in a general sense as well as *narrative*-as-*récit*. This resemblance is a significant one for the use of the word *diegesis*, but it is not a correspondence. However, in the passage above, the word *lexis*, has a precise correspondence, already noted, to 'narrative' in the stronger, technical sense. Socrates' own notion of the narrative/story distinction allows him to demonstrate his idea of a narrative without *mimesis*, by presenting in another manner his chosen bit of the *Iliad*:

'Now if the poet never concealed himself, his whole poetry and narrative would be free of imitation. Don't say you don't understand again—I'll explain how it would be. If Homer, having said that Chryses came with his daughter's ransom to be a suppliant of the Achaeans, and particularly of the kings, had gone on not as Chryses but as Homer, it would have been single narrative not imitation. It would have gone something like this—I'll do it without metre, for I'm no poet. "The priest came and prayed that the gods might grant them to capture Troy and return home safely, if they accepted the ransom, respected the god, and freed his daughter. Most of them respected his words and were ready to agree, but Agamemnon was angry telling him to go away and never come back, lest his staff and the god's garlands might prove of no avail to him: before the daughter was freed, she would grow old in Argos with him. And he told the old man to be off and not stir up trouble, if he wanted to get home safely. Hearing this, Chryses was frightened and went silently away, but when he had left the camp he prayed long to Apollo, calling on him by his special names, reminding him and begging him, if he had ever given him before an acceptable gift in

---

[27] De Jong (1987*a*), 2–4 defines these terms usefully: ἁπλῆ διήγησις is 'single-layered [narrative], the opposite being διπλοῦς ("double-layered")' where the poet is speaking only as himself and is not to be identified with the character.

temple-building or sacrifice; in return for this, he prayed to him to avenge his tears on the Greeks with his arrows." . . . That is single narrative without imitation.'

(Republic 393d–394b1)

That 'single narrative without imitation' of course involves the transformation of Homer's direct discourse into indirect discourse of various kinds. The remarks about speech presentation in this passage will be discussed later, but the implications for the modern narratological distinction are my main concern here. Socrates' reformulation of *Iliad* 1. 17–42 is clearly a different *narrative* from that of *Iliad* 1. 17–42 itself. But does that narrative (or *lexis*) convey the same *story* (*logoi*) as that passage of the *Iliad* or a different one? Thinkers like Chatman who hold that narrative is something ultimately beyond language are bound to maintain that Socrates' reformulation is another version of the same *story*, that the same *story* underlies the tellings of both Homer and Socrates. The change in the presentation of characters' discourse from one account to the other does not constitute a change in the nature or sequence of events, provided that there is mention that the speech acts occurred in both *narratives*.

On the other hand those like Herrnstein Smith, who have a language oriented theory of narrative, would argue that a different *narrative* means a different *story*. They would warn us of the danger of this kind of example: because we, along with Socrates, know Homer's telling and know that it is the prior one, we are very liable indeed to think (mistakenly) that Homer's *story* is the same as the *story* Socrates is telling. A dualistic conception of *narrative* and *story* would lead to this error. What hints does Socrates give about how this retelling should be understood? By changing the *narrative* Socrates could be providing us with a different *story*. At the same time it is clear that there is nothing so hard and fast as a *res/verba* or content/form distinction here. As we have already seen, *logoi* and *lexis*, or the *what* and the *how* something is said, are aspects of the same sort of thing. The modern technical terms 'narrative' and 'story', on the other hand, suggest that rather different categories make up what is more loosely called 'narrative'.

In this retelling, Socrates offers an important advance on narratology, as it is classically formulated. He will explain that his retelling of the *Iliad* will have an *effect on the audience* very different from that of the original Homeric version. This is very important. The whole point of the discursus on amounts of *mimesis* and *diegesis* in poetry is a notorious prescription:

> 'I think I'm making clear to you what I couldn't before, namely that there is one kind of poetry and fable which entirely consists of imitation: this is tragedy and comedy, as you say; and there's another kind consisting of the poet's own report—you find this particularly in dithyrambs; while the mixture of the two exists in epic and in many other places, if you see what I mean.'
>
> 'Yes I understand now what you meant then.'
>
> 'Remember also what we said even before—that we've dealt with the question of *what* to say, but have still to consider how . . . Well what I meant was, that we must come to an understanding as to whether we allow our poets to *narrate* (διηγήσεις ποιεῖσθαι) by imitation, or partly by imitation (and if so, what parts), or not to imitate at all.'
>
> 'I foresee' says Adeimantos 'that you are asking whether we should admit tragedy and comedy into the city or not.'

(Republic 394b8–d6)

For Socrates, as for Genette, narrative (as *lexis*) and story (as *logoi*) are components of narrative discourse in general (*diegesis*). However Socrates does not need to conceive of narrative and story as being categorically distinct. He does not necessarily offer what Herrnstein Smith derogatorily referred to as 'a dualistic model'.[28] Socrates' readiness to legislate about *how* poets narrate actually suggests some agreement with her thesis: a change in the narrative will determine a change in the story—the difference is that the change resides in the pragmatics of telling. Certainly Herrnstein Smith's stronger thesis should be taken seriously. The summary of the *Aeneid* given at the opening of this chapter might be seen as a narrative, not just of the poem's story, but also of quite a different story. After all, that summary contained no reference to a number of events presented in the *Aeneid* itself. The encounter with Polyphemus, the funeral games for Anchises, and Aeneas' shield need not occur in the posited story of that summary if they were not mentioned in its narrative.

Herrnstein Smith highlighted the fact that there are 345 narrative variants of the Cinderella myth in order to argue against the existence of any underlying *story*. I have been more agnostic: I have provided another narrative in my summary of the *Aeneid* and just

---

[28] Herrnstein Smith (1981).

suggested that there could be two possible stories underlying it—
one is the story of the *Aeneid* itself, the other could be abstracted
from my summary alone. But the view Socrates has of how
narrative affects our access to the story is actually more refined
than either of these. This is because he is ingenious enough to
develop a different kind of empirical sample: a close retelling of a
part of the *Iliad* to which Socrates makes only two changes: prose is
used instead of verse and indirect discourse is used instead of direct
discourse. Although these changes are far from trivial, this kind of
retelling shows that a change of narrative (or *lexis*) need not entail a
change of the serial elements which constitute the story. But this
retelling still succeeds in showing how a change of narrative—even
on a stylistic level—entails a change of what that story *means* to its
audience—not least where its ethical effects are concerned.

This needs further illustration. It might help to consider a
different hypothetical example in order to show the full significance
of Socrates' retelling of the *Iliad*. Imagine encountering three
narratives of an air crash:

1. A first-hand account from the sole survivor
   (i.e. everything is in direct discourse);
2. A report which uses (1) as its only source, occasionally quoting
   from it, neither adding to nor taking away any of its elements,
   presenting them in the same order
   (some things are in direct discourse);
3. A slightly shorter report of what is in (1), also preserving all its
   elements and following the same order
   (with no direct discourse).

Narrative 3 is shorter than 2 because it contains no direct quotation
from the survivor's oral account (i.e. nothing is in direct discourse).

Here it is hard to see how we could even think of constructing
three different stories from these narratives, because all three
narratives present exactly the same sequence of events. That
sequence of events corresponds harmoniously with the serial
nature of the accounts in these three narratives. So much so, we
might be strongly tempted to say that there can be situations in
which we do find one self-same story underlying a number of
narrative versions. There might appear to be a case for cheerfully
reinstating the dichotomies that were questioned earlier: narrative
and story, *logoi* and *lexis*, form and content.

But in fact this case cannot be upheld. Narratives 1, 2, and 3 each give the story a different meaning. This is most clearly seen if we consider the different impact narrative 1 will have on its addressees compared to that of 2 and 3. First, there is a straightforward point about dramatic interest. As a first-hand account of an air crash by its sole survivor, 1 may prompt emotions (pity, vicarious fear, or relief) more directly than narratives 2 or 3. This would be all the more salient if 1 is an oral narrative and 2 and 3 are written ones. There is perhaps a lesser degree of difference between 2 and 3: 3 will have the least immediacy because it contains no quotation from the first-hand source; 2 by containing some quotation is almost bound to induce a greater degree of pathos than 3.

There is also a more subtle explanation for the different impact of these three narratives which is of greater theoretical interest. Narrative 1, told by the survivor, will endeavour to tell us about the air crash alone. Narratives 2 and 3 are both going to tell us about something else which 1 could not include. They will inevitably tell us about the survivor's narration. This is most obvious in the case of 2. Every time 2 quotes from 1, it signals the existence of the first-hand account being given. The survivor's telling which told the story in 1 becomes *part* of the story of 2. The signalling may be very mild: the narrator of 2 and narrator of 3 need not give us any information about the situation of the survivor's account or about the manner in which it is delivered. Plain expressions like 'according to the survivor', 'she said: "x"', 'she described it like this' are themselves enough to make the survivor's telling constitute a narrated event.

Thus the story presented by 1 (of an air crash) is clearly different from the story presented by 2 (of a survivor recounting an air crash). Narrative 3, which contains no direct discourse, could have two possible stories. If it presented the survivor's words using indirect discourse (3*a*) its story would be highly similar to that presented by 2. But 3*a* would not be the same as 2 because the survivor would be characterized in a different way, by not being quoted. If, on the other hand, 3 presented no spoken or thought discourse *of any kind*, not even propositions after expressions like 'according to the survivor' (3*b*), the survivor's account would have no part in the story. In this case, the story presented by narrative 3*b* would be more similar to the story presented by the survivor herself in 1. But it would not be the same. The very fact that 3*b* would be a third-person narrative, and 1 a first-hand, first-person narrative would make their respective stories different because a protagonist's presence would be consistently explicit in 1. In a sense, the stories would be 'about' different things: that of 3*b*, without any presented discourse, would be about the air crash; that of narrative 1 would be about personal experience of the air crash.

Narrative 1, told in the first person would implicitly make it very clear from the beginning that the survivor survived the crash simply because she is there to narrate it. This would not *necessarily* be so immediately clear from narratives of 2, 3*a* or 3*b*. For it to be clear they would have to refer proleptically to the passenger's survival, perhaps by using the word 'survivor' in the opening. Since narratives 2, 3*a*, and 3*b* are supposed to follow the order and elements of 1, they could not do this unless the narrator of 1 gave an explicit indication of her survival in her opening sentence.

This may seem to be a pedantic set of observations. After all, the gist of all three narratives is pretty similar. We could imagine a journalist or novelist first getting hold of the events of the air crash which he or she would then sculpt into a particular narrative form— presumably 1 or 2 would be the most likely choices. But the observations above show that the underlying story can change quite notably, even if the changes from one narrative to another are only of a stylistic nature. And the type of narrative style would in turn depend on who was the narrator: the survivor, the survivor's friend, the novelist, a journalist. In each case the narrative, the story, and the relation between the narrative and the story would all have a different identity. The nature of what a narrative is, what a story is, what the relation between them is cannot be fixed. It is reconstituted each time by the pragmatics of a particular telling. This applies to all narrative discourses—factual, fictional, literary, or historical. Just as a short utterance or speech cannot be given meaning without constructing a speaker, an addressee, a purpose, context, and so on, one cannot make sense of even the most formal aspects of a narrative without positing a narrator, addressees or readers, and conditions of performance.

Thus, we might now be able to see more clearly why Socrates' retelling of the *Iliad* has such important implications. Plato's presentation of the relation between narrative and story in terms of the function of *diegesis* in general, can be seen in terms of performance. The division between narrative and story is subordinated to

conditions of performance. As a result, he does not see narrative
and story as two static categories. They, and the *relation* between
them, will always be fluid and protean. And Socrates sees narrative
as affective discourse which works in a variety of contexts.
Although he is discussing the form and content of poetry, his
terminology in the original Greek is far from specialized. *Logoi* is
more usually translated 'words', 'speech'; *lexis* as 'phrasing',
'diction'. It was pointed out that both terms are related to the
verb *legein* to speak. I glossed them with the technical terms
'narrative' and 'story' here simply to highlight the technical
subtlety of Socrates' argument.

Overall Socrates' use of everyday terms for speech is enlightening, even if it seems confusing at first. It makes us aware that
narrative in all its apparitions, literary or non-literary, is made of
exactly the same sort of stuff as other kinds of discourse. This in
turn reveals something about speech presentation—discourse presented in a narrative. I will quote again a sentence from 393c:

> 'But when [Homer] makes a speech pretending to be someone else, are we
> not to say that he is assimilating his expression as far as possible to the
> supposed speaker? (ὅτι μάλιστα τὴν αὐτοῦ λέξιν ἑκάστῳ ὃν ἂν προείπῃ ὡς
> ἐροῦντα)'.

It is no accident that the same word—*lexis*—is used for both
Homer's discourse and for the diction of a supposed actual speaker.
A little further on, Socrates recommends the way a good poet
should narrate his poems:

> He will thus use the type of narrative discourse (διηγήσει) we outlined in
> relation to Homer's epic a little earlier: his *narrative* (λέξις) will have
> elements both of *speech and narrative in the other sense* (μιμήσεώς τε καὶ
> τῆς ἄλλης διηγήσεως) but with quite a small proportion of *speech* (μιμήσεως).
> (*Republic* 396e4–7)

The word *diegesis* is again used in a very supple way—it is almost
interchangeable with *lexis* in the first instance; but it is used
specifically for single narrative (i.e. narrative without quotation)
in the second. *Diegesis* can either be a part of *lexis*, or it can be *lexis*
itself, and as we saw earlier at 392d, it can be used to denote
everything poets and storytellers say.

This suppleness, I would hold, is helpful rather than infuriating.
The English word 'narrative', which also has a number of mean-

ings, has perhaps come to be taken too seriously. Its frequent occurrence can give a misleading impression of the centrality of narratology as a field of study. A problem with narratology is its tendency to consider narrative in isolation—independently of its discursive, rhetorical, social, or political contexts. But narratologists are often content to see this isolation of narrative as the definition of their disciplinary terrain.[29] It generally seems to be a question of one assertion against the other.

What Plato's discussion here seems to show is that it is impossible to isolate the notion of narrative anyway. Plato's terms are smudgy at the edges because the notions behind them overlap. Distinctions between the terms *logoi*, *lexis*, and *diegesis* cannot be made easily, even if Socrates exhibits a sense of a difference between *logoi* and *lexis*. For him, the point of acquiring this sense of the difference is not for literary theoretical purposes but for practical moral and political ends. For these practical ends, it seems that Socrates is most worried that Adeimantos understands the difference between *mimesis* and *diegesis*. I share Socrates' view of the primary importance of the *mimesis/diegesis* distinction. Exploration of that distinction and of its important implications for our understanding of narrative will be a major concern in this book.

Herrnstein Smith was anxious to show that the notion of story cannot be held *in vacuo*: any example of a pure story once presented or expressed will end up becoming a narrative. Plato's discussion only seems to hold to the notion of story so far as it is necessary—it is there perhaps, but it cannot be defined independently of any particular context. But Plato's discussion also goes one stage further: it appears that for him narrative cannot subsist *in vacuo* either. It is there when it is instantiated in different ways. It can be instantiated in poetry as a whole (that is the genres of poetry including drama as at 394), giving an account of past, present and future. Or it can be instantiated as narrative poetry. Or as *lexis*—poetry's manner of expression or diction. Or again as a kind of literary mode, a more specific type of *lexis*: expression not using direct discourse.

By preventing us from conceiving of narrative *in vacuo*, Plato allows us to conceive of the narrative/story distinction only as it

---

[29] Compare the opening of Barthes (1967) and my remarks in section (ii) below. Rimmon-Kenan (1983) opens her study by hailing the omnipresence of narrative. In contrast, the preface to Bal (1985) is admirably cautious.

operates in particular contexts. So we are saved from the theoretical pitfall of a possibly infinite regress which begins like this:

What is the narrative?
What is the story of that narrative?
What is the narrative of that story of the narrative?
What is the story of the narrative of that story of the narrative?

The distinction between narrative and story offered by Plato is practical rather than theoretical. It has as many *ad hoc* applications as there are narrative discourses. We do not have to conceive of it as a universal opposition.

This distinction, as I have remarked, is the founding principle of narratology. Narratology has been seen as a fragile dualism open to deconstruction: every 'story' turns out to be a—'narrative'. The critique of the distinction offered here has shown how it can be refined to bypass this deconstruction. The role that pragmatic aspects of narration (context, audience, genre, identity and purpose of narrator) can play in conceptions of that distinction must be recognized. Narratologists ought to consider those pragmatic aspects of narration, which they have always regarded as extraneous to their field, as central to it. Narrative itself, in the broader sense, cannot properly be understood, as long as people endeavour to think of it as independent of the pragmatic determinants, which are constructed at the point of a narrative's reception.

It is worth explicitly stating something about content which modifies the conventional definition given earlier and which, until now, I have only mildly implied. The pragmatic aspects of narration, which can be listed (probably not exhaustively) as context, performance, audience, genre, identity and purpose of narrator, also determine what is generally called 'content'. The 'content' or meaning of an an utterance like '27th of May 1963' will be understood in a variety of different ways—diary entry, public announcement, private thought, question, answer, correction to a mistaken answer—depending on those various determinants. In a similar way the 'content' of a narrative is affected by such determinants, which themselves are very much part of the elements of form (person, diction, style). If an account of the *Aeneid* was given a different 'form', as a result of having, say, a different narrator, a different content will be attached to it. Here this may seem to be a slight difference of degree, but it is an important one to recognize. Nor is the form of the poem we have a clear and unchanging entity (even if our Latin text is basically 'right'): a modern narratologist will not be seeing what an ancient Roman reader or a medieval allegorist would have seen.

It is necessary to labour this point about the chimerical nature of 'content' and 'form', and about the difference between them also being chimerical. This is because narratologists see their field of study as safely circumscribed. For a convenient illustration of this, one can quote Genette's later justification of the territory covered by his own book *Narrative Discourse*:

Narrative Discourse bears on the narrative and the narrating, not on the story, and the strengths and weaknesses, the graces or disgraces of heroes basically depend on neither the narrative nor the narrating but on the story—that is, the content or (and for once this word has to be used) the *diegesis*. To reproach *Narrative Discourse* for disregarding them is to reproach it for its choice of subject. I can, moreover, well imagine such a criticism: why do you speak to me of forms when only content interests me? But if the question is legitimate the answer is only too obvious: everyone busies himself with whatever arouses his interest.[30]

Consideration of Plato's anxiety about direct quotation provides a basis for opposing Genette's claim that 'the strengths and weaknesses, the graces or disgraces of heroes depend on neither the narrative nor the narrating but on the story.' Discussions of narratives to come later in this book will show how considering speech and thought presentation can lead to moral evaluation of characters or groups of characters.

The emphasis in the first section of this chapter has been on a critique of the narrative/story distinction drawn from Plato's discussion. Other important issues raised by this part of the *Republic*, which bear on later chapters, remain to be introduced. These include the issue of verse and prose in narrative; the importance of genre for regarding narrative as utterance and performance; narrative as expression; and narrative discourse as representation. A close reading of this part of the *Republic* best shows how these issues are essentially linked to those already raised, and to each other. Nonetheless, I will attempt, however speciously, to isolate them and offer some brief introductory discussion here.

---

[30] Genette (1988), 154.

2.2 VERSE AND PROSE IN NARRATIVE

Socrates draws attention to the fact that his version of the *Iliad* is in prose:

φράσω δὲ ἄνευ μέτρου· οὐ γάρ εἰμι ποιητικός   (*Republic* 393d8)
I'll speak without metre: for I am no poet.

This example of self-deprecating Socratic irony is followed with grave respect in Aristotle's *Poetics* (1447^b) which recalls this part of the *Republic*. Aristotle considers the importance of metre for the definition of poetry. He thinks poets are called 'makers' not because they make verses, but because they make imitations. (That is the point of Socrates' joke—if he thought poetry was only things in metre he would not discuss it in the way he does.) According to Aristotle, at least in the *Poetics*, Homer is a poet, and Empedocles, who writes scientific verse is not.[31] A further point can be made about the relation between verse and prose to the narrative/story distinction. The Russian formalists' version of that distinction, with *syuzhet* and *fabula* as the respective correspondents, was mentioned earlier. Ann Jefferson remarks that the relation between *fabula* (story) and *syuzhet* (narrative) is roughly analogous to the more celebrated distinction the formalists made between practical and poetic language:

The *syuzhet* creates a defamiliarising effect on the *fabula*: the devices of the *syuzhet* are not designed as instruments for conveying the *fabula*, but are foregrounded at the expense of the *fabula*. These devices [of the *syuzhet*] can vary enormously in nature and scope: from the overall presentation of narrative structure down to linguistic play.[32]

In this order of things, the *syuzhet* then is the poetic manner of presentation which dresses up or 'defamiliarizes' (in Russian formalist terms) the plain *fabula* even to the point of obscuring it altogether. This provides us with a new worry about the prose telling of the *Iliad* we get from Socrates—is it supposed to be the

---

[31] A note accompanies the translation of *Poetics* 1447^b in Russell and Winterbottom (1972), 91: 'The argument is no better here, given Aristotle's own commendation of Empedocles in *On the Poets* as Homeric and stylistically excellent, particularly in his use of metaphor.' This is useful, but too dismissive of Aristotle's distinction in the *Poetics* between *discursive* and *narrative* poetry. See Benveniste (1971), Genette (1988), 98–9 and Laird (1990).

[32] Jefferson (1986), 39.

actual story, the dowdy *fabula* that is really lurking behind Homer's adorning verse narrative or *syuzhet*? The reverse might strike a formalist as equally plausible: the prose version in Plato is more literary than Homer's and is actually the *syuzhet* of Homer's dowdy *fabula* because it 'defamiliarizes' the original well known verses. (The Russian formalists' notion of 'defamiliarization' (*ostraneniye*) as an attribute of literariness does not lack counterparts in ancient theories of discourse.[33])

Looking at the contexts of these versions could be one way of finding, not a solution to this conundrum, but a way around it. Both accounts are *diegesis* or narratives in the looser sense according to Socrates. His own narrative differs from Homer's in that it contains no direct discourse and can therefore be called *haplē diegesis* or 'single narrative'. They differ rather as narratives 2 and 3 of the air crash differ: they have a very similar gist but their particular stories can be conceived as distinct. This is because even the *story* behind Homer's narrative contains direct discourse and will thus be more affective. Direct discourse could be seen to belong to the level of story as well as to the level of narrative.[34] In theory, what Chryses says is heard by Agamemnon and other characters in Homer's story, just as much as it is heard by the audience of Homer's narrative. This sort of thing will be further explored in the next chapter. The main point is that both Socrates' version of the Chryses incident and Homer's can be regarded as narratives in the stricter technical sense. Each is a *syuzhet* with its respective *fabula*.

Or so it would seem in general. Unfortunately an impertinent remark from the talking cock who figures in Lucian's dialogue, *Dream* (or *Oneiros*) threatens this orderly picture. The cock in response to Micyllus' amazement at his ability to speak recalls the anomaly of the talking horse in *Iliad* 19. 407 ff.:

Micyllus, you strike me as utterly uneducated and you don't even seem to have read Homer's poems, in which Xanthus, the horse of Achilles, saying goodbye to neighing forever, stood still and talked in the middle of the

---

[33] The positive notion of defamiliarization is set out in Shklovsky (1965). Corresponding ideas have a complex tradition in ancient rhetoric and poetics going back to Bacchylides (*Paeans* fr.5 Snell-Maehler). Compare Isocrates *Euagoras* 8–10, Aristotle *Poetics* 1458ᵃ22, and *Rhetoric* 3. 1403ᵇ3. Conte (1986), 43 f. considers these passages.

[34] This is debatable: see Ch. 3 (esp. 90–4) on free direct discourse (FDD).

fighting, reciting whole epic verses, not speaking without metre as I am now (ἔπη ὅλα ῥαψῳδῶν, οὐχ ὥσπερ ἐγὼ νῦν ἄνευ τῶν μέτρων).[35]

(*Dream* 2)

We might compare Borges's retort to those who claim that Dante 'believed in' the Hell, Purgatory, and Paradise of his *Commedia*: Dante would not even have believed that Virgil could speak in vernacular tercets.[36] These lighter observations raise a serious question. Are we to believe that the personages in Homer's epics, and in other verse narratives like the *Commedia*, actually spoke to each other in metre in the heroic story world they inhabited? Or should Homer's presentation of the words of his characters in verse, in a verse narrative, lead us to believe that the supposed original utterances on the level of story must be different?[37] If we adopt the latter view, we might well be more inclined to consider the like-lihood of their only being one story underlying the narratives of the Chryses incident.

The two changes Socrates made to Homer's original narrative seem to be far more involved with each other than was first apparent. Socrates' object was to render a portion of the *Iliad* without using direct discourse. It appeared that his failure to put the new rendering in verse was an accidental consequence of changing the speech mode. In fact, the transformation from verse to prose has turned out to be as integrally involved with the 'fidelity' of speech presentation to character's supposed words, as the transformation from direct to indirect discourse. Metre and speech presentation have another thing in common. The presence, absence, or instance of a specific type of either speech presentation or metre can serve as a register of a narrative's genre.

2.3 GENRE, NARRATIVE AS UTTERANCE AND RECEPTION

Narratology has tended to ignore the importance of genre and conditions of reception. This may be the result of a vested interest, already noted, in demonstrating the ubiquity of narrative. If

---

[35] The disclaimer is reminiscent of Socrates' remark in *Republic* 393d, quoted above.

[36] 'The Divine Comedy' in Borges (1986), 6–25

[37] In Ch. 3 I will suggest that all examples of verse in direct discourse could be counted as 'free direct discourse'.

narrative can be shown to be ubiquitous, then the study of narrative will look more important. The opening of Roland Barthes's influential essay *Introduction to the Structural Analysis of Narratives* might have triggered off this tendency. There Barthes presented a conception of narrative as being 'international, transhistorical, transcultural . . . like life itself'. This was illustrated with a spectacular list of genres of many different orders: myth, legend, fable, tale, novella, epic, history, tragedy, drama, comedy, mime, painting, stained-glass windows, cinema, comics, news items, conversation, etc. All these genres were reduced to one central concern:

So what of narrative analysis, faced as it is with millions of narratives? Of necessity, it is condemned to a deductive procedure, obliged first to devise a hypothetical model of description (what American linguists call a 'theory') and then gradually to work down from this model towards the different narrative species which at once conform and depart from the model. It is only at the level of these conformities and departures that analysis will be able to come back to, but now equipped with a single descriptive tool, the plurality of narratives, to their historical, geographical and cultural diversity.[38]

The model of linguistic description referred to, apparently a Saussurean one, is less current now than it was when Barthes was writing in 1967. I have sought already to regard narratives as affective discourses and not to conceive them as texts that are studied, as it were, in formaldehyde.[39] The very idea of what a linguistic utterance or speech *is* cannot be understood without taking context into account. By the same token, narrative, whether as a general notion or in specific cases cannot be conceived without genre.

To illustrate this, if we took the *narrative/story* distinction as our 'hypothetical model of description' and tried to apply it to the first two forms of narrative in Barthes's catalogue—myth and legend—we would not have much success. Myths and legends are by nature mutable and have a number of possible incarnations. Could we ever find the *narrative* of Robin Hood or Hercules, let alone the *story*? The *mimesis/diegesis* distinction which is favoured in this study, is an excellent hypothetical model of description for most verbal narratives, but is of little use for describing stained-glass windows.

---

[38] Barthes (1967).
[39] Compare the attack on Saussurean linguisitics and the opposition to 'philologism' in Voloshinov (1973).

However, that *mimesis/diegesis* model when applied to verbal
narrative inevitably leads to consideration of genre. After his
presentation of the *Iliad*, Socrates shows how:

'There. That's single narrative without imitation . . . Understand that the
opposite happens when the poet removes the passages between the
speeches and leaves just the exchanges of conversation.'
  'I see, that's what we have in tragedies.'
  'Quite right. I think I'm making clear to you what I couldn't before,
namely, that there is one kind of poetry and fable which entirely consists of
direct speech: this is tragedy and comedy, as you say; and there's another
kind consisting of the poet's own report—you find this particularly in
dithyrambs; while the mixture of the two exists in epic and in many other
places, if you see what I mean.'

(*Republic* 394b–c)

In these lines, Plato's narrator has removed the 'passages between
the speeches'—this is the very practice Socrates the character is
here discussing.[40] Could this suggest that the *Republic* itself is akin
to drama?

   Ancient rhetoricians often demonstrate the devices they are
describing by employing them at the same time. 'Longinus' (17. 1)
for example says of rhetorical questions: 'What are we to say of
enquiries and questions? Should we not say that they increase the
realism and vigour of the writing . . .?' The end of Aristotle's
Rhetoric treats endings (3. 19. 5–6) and practises what it preaches.
But here Plato employs a form, which he has Socrates explicitly
condemn. In *Poetics* 1447[b]11, when Aristotle discusses genre, he
remarks that 'we have no common term to apply to the [prose]
mimes of Sophron and Xenarchus and to the Socratic dialogues'. In
this context Aristotle's point about the mimetic nature of Socratic
dialogues could either be ironic itself or it could merely show that
Aristotle has picked up an irony that is already inherent in the
Republic.[41] The fact that we hardly notice the fact that the *Republic*

---

[40] Plato's narrator in the *Republic* is in fact Socrates, who presents this particular
conversation between himself and Adeimantos.

[41] Rostagni (1926) suggests that Aristotle is pointedly exposing the *mimesis* in
Platonic dialogues in Aristotle *De poetis* fr. 72. See Fantuzzi (1988), 47 f. on the
omission of introductions to speeches in epic, and the treatment of 'Longinus' 27. 1
in the next chapter. Bers (1997), 4 sees little evidence to suggest that ancient prose
dialogues were performed—notwithstanding the suggestive testimonies assembled
in Ryle (1965), 21–32 to indicate that Plato or others might have recited his
dialogues.

itself is a narrative of a story could be seen to support the point Socrates is making about the power of direct speech.[42]

What is more certain is that Plato conceives narrative technique in terms of genre. Dramatic, epic, and dithyrambic genres are here distinguished according to the degree of *mimesis*, or direct speech, involved.[43] A sense of the importance of genre is not an optional appendage to understanding narrative—it is part and parcel of it. Socrates takes it for granted that genre and narrative technique are both bound up with the circumstances of performance. Someone asked nowadays about how dramatic genres are distinguished from narrative genres, would be likely to reply that the former are in general for reception by an audience, and that the latter, in general, are not. In the Roman as well as the Greek world, this means of discriminating between drama and narrative might have been less useful. If dramatic works were on occasions read silently, it is certainly no less conceivable that narrative works could also on occasions be declaimed.[44]

Socrates' method of assessing the relative proportions of 'single narrative' (*haplē diegesis*) and direct discourse (*mimesis*) provides one effective way of distinguishing not only drama from narrative, but also types of narrative from each other.[45] Even now, the names of some genres are derived from the original circumstances of a text's reception.[46] Reception can be understood in the broadest

[42] Gould (1992), 23 argues very much on these lines.
[43] A more specific version of these distinctions with respect to the *Eclogues* and Virgil's other works in 'Servius' is in some respects more practically correct than those provided by Socrates—dithyrambic poetry may not always confine itself to the poet's speech. Fantuzzi (1988), 48 n. 2 remarks that Plato here is making reference solely to narrative dithyrambs, keeping quiet about the 'dialogico-mimetic *arionei*' attested by Bacchylides and Pindar. Fantuzzi also refers to Gentili (1984–5).
[44] The vivid and dramatic quality a recitation from Homer may have had is described by Plato in the *Ion*. The direct speeches in epic poems would allow the rhapsode actually to take on a character's role and display his powers of impersonation. For ancient audiences this would have made a clear contrast with renditions of a poet who did not put his characters' words into direct speech. It would be a question of whether the rhapsode or *recitator* acted out the characters' parts or not. W. G. Rutherford (1905), 97–168 is an important chapter on reading καθ' ὑπόκρισιν which bases conjectures on evidence from scholia.
[45] Consider (for example) Trogus' comments on direct discourse in historiography discussed in Ch. 4.
[46] The extent to which Roman literature was encountered by public recitation rather than by silent reading of books is far from established: the evidence for *recitatio* having been the main means of access to literature is perhaps not as decisive

sense—ranging from theatrical production to the reading of written text, in silence or aloud, by individuals or groups. Conditions of, and reactions to, performance can be essential to the distinction between many generic forms.[47] For instance, *epithalamia* and *epinikia* are literary genres which were originally identified by their function in performance. Published sermons, lectures, diaries, etc. continue to reveal their original conditions of reception, long after they have solidified into literary prose. In Plato's *Laws*, this sort of development is described by the Athenian stranger, when he discusses the decline of generic decorum in music:

In those days our music was divided according to genres and forms (κατὰ εἴδη τε ἑαυτῆς ἄττα καὶ σχήματα). One kind of song was prayers to the gods—these were called *hymns*: another opposite to this was what might best be called dirges (θρήνους), then there were *paeans* and *dithyrambs*—these were concerned with the birth of Dionysus. They actually used the word 'laws' (νόμους). With these and other similar distinctions firmly established, it was impossible to use one type of song for the purposes of another.

(*Laws* 700a–b)

This impression of the close relation between narrative technique and genre, hinged on a construction of their original conditions of performance, had an extensive influence in antiquity.[48] Narratives

as it is taken to be. Here I have taken an agnostic line, but I feel it is important to consider what the implications for speech presentation would have been if recitation was a general and widespread practice. The difference between direct and indirect modes of speech presentation would have been much clearer if texts were read out loud. The significance of *recitatio* can be considered for our interpretation of some passages and authors, and for some stylistic practices such as apostrophe. Major treatments of *recitatio* and the evidence for it are Quinn (1982), Wiseman (1982*a*) and (1982*b*), and Vogt-Spira (1990). See also Jahn (1867); A. Hardie (1983), 74–102; Herington (1985), 41–57, 201–6; Rohde (1914), 326–7. Oliver (1989)—especially the chapter 'Narrative in Performance' 119 ff.—gives an account of the implications performance of poetry has for narrative form in our own era.

[47] Taplin (1986) and Taplin (1996) consider distinctions between Attic tragedy and comedy in terms of audience reception. A. Fowler (1982) cites many examples of genres whose literary form emerged from their social function e.g. French court drama and the country house poem. See also Dubrow (1982), 114–15.

[48] Aristotle *Poetics* 1448ᵃ19–28 seems to use speech presentation (along with metre and subject matter) as a basis for generic distinction. The 4th-cent. grammarian Diomedes also followed Plato's division of poetic genres and 'Servius' classified the *Eclogues* according to three genres based on speech presentation (Diomedes ed. Keil, 1. 482 and 'Servius' on *Eclogue* 3. 1—quoted earlier as the epigraph to my Introduction.) See Curtius (1979), 439 on these grammarians, and Rosenmeyer (1969), 4 f. and 13 f. (on the implications of the remarks of 'Servius' and Quintilian

are, after all actualized by their genres. The very existence of a narrative—like that of any other form of discourse—is determined by its genre: a complex of social exchanges and conditions of reception.

2.4 NARRATIVE AS EXPRESSION

If all narratives, including poetical or literary narratives, are forms of discourse (analogous to utterances), they must have 'speakers' and 'addressees' of some kind. An exploration of the effect of this realization on our understanding of speech presentation is a major concern of this whole study. Here I will look only at some of the ways in which Socrates presents narrative (chiefly, but not exclusively, poetical narrative) as the property and responsibility of a speaker.[49]

A view of narrative as the personal expression of the poet or storyteller pervades the whole discussion of literature in the third book of the *Republic*. Here are three examples. The discussion of *lexis* begins at 392d with the phrase: 'Everything that poets or storytellers *say* . . .'. When Socrates mentions the use of direct discourse to report Chryses' words in the *Iliad*, he puts it like this:

Homer *speaks* as though he were Chryses himself and *tries to make us think that it is not Homer talking* but the old priest . . .

Again in 393:

When he makes a speech *pretending to be someone else*, are we not to say he is assimilating his *lexis* as far as possible to the supposed speaker?

for criticizing pastoral poetry), Kayser (1906), Steinmetz (1964). Scaliger too used categories from speech to explain pastoral typology—see Padelford (1905) and also Grafton (1983) on Scaliger. A good treatment of ancient bases of classification in general is in Rosenmeyer (1985). Riffaterre (1972) attempts to analyse the modern genres. Genette (1992) is a study prompted by these questions.

[49] My remarks in this section and elsewhere have been influenced by the essay 'Literature as Discourse' in R. Fowler (1981) which states at 94: 'persona is commonly appealed to in criticism to excuse the "real author" from making political or ethical judgements'. (Wimsatt and Beardsley, 1946) yet as Goffman has shown (1969), the construction of a persona is an inevitable strategy (usually not conscious, in the management of one's public and 'private' presentation of 'self'. Similarly with fiction: the Crocean tradition of sceptical historiography (Croce 1941; Carr 1964), substituting for 'fact' in history the idea of a processing and ideologically dynamic dialectic between present and past, provides a definition of fiction which it is hard not to extend to the process of what is called 'narrative fiction'. These observations seem largely consistent with the interpretation of Socrates' views offered here.

Socrates' use of such terms to indicate the use of direct discourse in narrative has prompted two main responses in modern readers. The first is to assume that he is being deliberately uncharitable. Socrates knows perfectly well that the illusion of narratival representation depends on the suspension of disbelief, so that—at least temporarily—we allow ourselves to think it is the character not the poet who is speaking. By choosing to ignore this, Socrates is seen to indulge deliberately in a sort of philistinism: reminding us that characters generated by narratives are not real people. The second response is to assume that Socrates is ignorant: he does not know the difference between 'poet' and 'narrator' and calls both 'Homer'.[50] I shall discuss this second response first.

Socrates actually wants Adeimantos to remember constantly that *all* the diction of the *Iliad* is always 'Homer's'. He regards what a character 'says' as the property—and ultimate responsibility—of the author who produces the text in which that character appears. Socrates would say that it is T.S. Eliot who speaks these lines from the poem *Gerontion*:

> My house is a decayed house,
> And the Jew squats on the window sill, the owner,
> Spawned in some estaminet of Antwerp,
> Blistered in Brussels, patched and peeled in London.[51]

Now in one sense, this is obviously false. If I were to write a play in which a wicked character justifies his bad behaviour, I would not expect to be held personally responsible for that character's behaviour or its justifications. But Socrates' line of argument has more merit than may first be obvious. To ascribe the words quoted above to Eliot rather than to Gerontion, is not necessarily to confuse T. S. Eliot, the historical personage, with T. S. Eliot the body of texts. The use of the present tense in the phrase 'T. S. Eliot speaks these lines' refers to T. S. Eliot as a body of texts—which audiences can interpret and construct in various ways—and not to the body of T. S. Eliot mouldering in the grave. Plato's Socrates does not make such a confusion either. In quoting from Homer he

---

[50] Again, compare Gould (1992).

[51] These controversial verses highlight the moral issues that can be clouded by the prevalent positing of the notion of persona. For Socrates, the author of these verses would not be exculpated from anti-semitism. The debate should rather centre on how audiences construct both author and persona.

always uses this present tense as well ('Homer *says*', 'When Homer *makes* a speech' etc.).

The distinction between a poet (or body of texts) and a narrator is another matter.[52] That distinction is always there to be discerned. Some distinction between the presentation of another's words (e.g. as a narrator or character) and endorsement of them (e.g. as an author or poet) has to exist in any culture which talks about its own discourse. However, the degree to which in individual instances and genres, we allow this distinction to be invoked as a defence of sentiments expressed can vary within a culture, and from one culture to another. (There are, after all, numerous contexts in our culture in which the utterance of these verses from *Gerontion* would be utterly unacceptable.) It is unjust to accuse Socrates of not 'knowing' that poet and narrator are distinct in literature, when Socrates is really concerned with the propositions that literature can convey. After all, the 'Socratic Question' itself—the problem of whether we talk of Socrates' arguments or of Plato's in interpreting dialogues like the *Republic*—is a matter of modern controversy which revolves around this very issue.[53]

The first response, noted above, to Socrates' reluctance to submit to the illusion conjured by *mimesis* in narrative—that it indicates a kind of philistinism—also requires further examination. His view is far from philistine and can lead to more sensitive appreciation of all kinds of narrative. The tenth poem of Ovid's *Heroides* for example will have one kind of content if we 'realize' it is Ovid (or 'the poet') pretending to be Ariadne. It will have a different kind of content if we consider it as the disembodied utterance of an independent Ariadne.[54] However, it is often easier to evaluate a play or novel, or

[52] This conventional distinction certainly bears fruit for literary critics. For instance, much of the study of the *Satyricon* in Conte (1997) is derived from a claim first made in Conte (1986), 45: 'The literary nature of Petronius' *Satyricon* is already revealed between the "I" of the narrator and the "I" of the writer himself.' The tension between appreciation of a text as literature and consideration of the same text as discourse or utterance will emerge in Ch. 3; Ch. 5 will in part consider first-person narration in Petronius.

[53] It should never be forgotten that Socrates is the narrator of the *Republic*. Guthrie (1971) and Vlastos (1988) are influential discussions of the Socratic Question. See also Brickhouse and Smith (1994) and R. B. Rutherford (1995), 39–68; Corlett (1997) discusses the interpretation of Plato's dialogues, and has further bibliography.

[54] Spentzou (1997) has argued for this choice being available to readers of the

get a sense of overall design (including any 'moral' of the story) by considering the characters to be mouthpieces of an 'author'. Here, again, 'author' designates a principle of compositional unity or a body of texts, more than any flesh and blood individual.[55] Overall, Socrates is trying to show that a poet or a narrator is a speaker. The speeches quoted in direct discourse are themselves embedded in a larger speech which we call the narrative. Any narrative will be angled and partial. However, the prevalent tendency to conceive of narrators (especially unidentified third-person narrators) as independent from poets or authors can obscure this fact. It reinforces the rhetorical claims laid by or for such narrators to an authority they do not possess.

2.5 NARRATIVE AS REPRESENTATION

The theory of *mimesis* (in the more general sense as 'imitation' or 'representation') is the most celebrated aspect of Plato's treatment of poetry and storytelling in the *Republic*. It is part of a grander epistemological design which is not the chief object of this discussion. However, that epistemology, which is not always understood, does have a bearing on our understanding of the general nature of narrative. The popular view that literature or narrative 'copies life' could well be derived from the Platonic theory of poetry as imitation, but this popular view is not quite the same thing. The attention of modern theory of literature and narrative has generally turned to the ways in which the function of representation is determined by narrative construction.[56]

If a narrative text is being read, it is hard to imagine what particular types of reading do not lead to the construction of an

Heroides: consideration of the male author is not an inevitable reading strategy. A further published study is forthcoming.

[55] Compare Riffaterre (1983), 5: 'The author is not present in the text, but the reader readily imagines him and places him there, after the model of ordinary communication, where an encoder's existence is always evident. This image of an author is, therefore, nothing other than a rationalization. Not that it does not have its use: it serves a purpose to the limited extent that it enables us to complete the title and label and identify the text more quickly than we could by giving a synopsis of it . . . The rationalized author must also not be confused with the historical author, the living writer.' The relations between author and narrator in first-person and third-person narratives will be discussed again in Ch. 6.1.

[56] See (e.g) Todorov (1978) and Ricoeur (1991), 137–55.

imaginary universe from it. This construction is virtually inevitable for narrative texts of all kinds: factual, fictional, literary, historical. I argue this purely on the basis that all utterances, spoken or written, have a referential function. The process of constructing imaginary universes—which I call 'story worlds'[57]—from reading or hearing narratives is not particularly volitional or arbitrary. The 'story world' you construct from reading a *factual* account in a particular newspaper article will overlap with other 'story worlds' generated by other factual accounts you have heard or read. It is of course bound to be different from mine. But the different story worlds you and I construct from the newspaper article still have a great deal in common.

The process of constructing story worlds will admittedly involve extra-linguistic considerations (e.g. psychological, socio-historical factors). But even if we entertain a type of reading that expressly does not involve constructing a story world from a narrative—like structural or narratological analysis—extra-linguistic factors are still involved. For instance, the beholder or explicator of the deep structures in a text or in a tribe cannot disappear. It is important to understand that narrative discourse in general, more strictly, creates reality rather than imitates it. As Todorov has noted, 'only the perspective of construction allows us to understand correctly the textual function called representative.'[58] *All* narratives generate story worlds or 'create reality'. Creation of story worlds is the norm—not the result of a particular kind of reading or hearing.

In fact we have here what is more or less the view of narrative presented by Plato's Socrates. He takes all kinds of narrative into account. The pairing of poets and storytellers casts a wide net: today's journalists and historians (for example) could be included in it. On the macro-level, the Platonic notion of narrative as *mimesis* is not that narrative imitates what is really out there, but that it invents something which is not ultimately out there.[59] *Mimesis* in

[57] On 'story worlds' see Laird (1993a), 151–4, 160–1, 174.
[58] Todorov (1978), 175. Oliver (1989), 121 f. is a critique of Todorov's discussion.
[59] Plato again explores the notion of *mimesis* in the tenth book of the *Republic* (595–607). This contains discussion of *mimesis* in poetry with painting considered in a supporting role. There are numerous treatments of Plato's theory of *mimesis*. In particular, see Belfiore (1984a), Havelock (1963) and Moravcsik and Temko (1982).

general might be better translated by words like 'pretence', 'impersonation', or, at the mildest, 'version'. Although the terms 'imitation' or 'representation' are commonly used, they tend to imply that the objects of *mimesis* should be posited. And on the micro-level, we saw earlier how the Platonic notion of direct discourse as *mimesis* prompted grave doubts about whether we could safely conceive of a character's words as a faithful representation of whatever was supposed to have been said. These issues are of course connected, and they will be pursued further in the following chapter.

2.6 NARRATIVE AND SPEECH PRESENTATION IN PLATONIC DIALOGUE

The passages from the *Republic* reviewed so far give an adequate indication of the sophistication—and occasional deviousness—of Plato as a narrator.[60] Given my emphasis on the importance of speech presentation for Plato's theory of discourse, it remains to remark on his own practices of speech presentation, and to consider any theoretical significance they may have.[61] Plato recounts two fables in the *Republic* in indirect discourse, and attributes them to other sources: the myth of Gyges' ring (359d–360b) and the myth of Er (614b–621d). This practice seems to be in keeping with the prescriptions against direct discourse in 392–5. Although the myth of Er contains two samples of direct discourse—Er's own report of an interlocutor's words and the formulaic utterance of Lachesis' assistant—these are clearly 'embedded' within Socrates' indirect discourse narration.[62]

Questions of speech presentation bear on the narrative construction of two entire Platonic dialogues: the *Symposium* and the *Theaetetus*. The *Symposium* begins with a dramatized exchange of speeches between Apollodorus (who turns out to be the narrator of the dialogue) and a friend. Apollodorus begins his narration in his

---

[60] R. B. Rutherford (1995) looks at the rhetorical and artistic qualities of Plato's dialogues. See also Ferrari (1987), Nightingale (1995).

[61] Tarrant (1955) very briefly discusses Plato's use of indirect discourse—in the *Symposium, Phaedo, Republic, Parmenides,* and *Timaeus*; inexplicably the *Theaetetus* is omitted.

[62] Curiously both these examples of embedded direct discourse thematically bear on issues involving speech: 615d–e relates how judges interpret a wordless utterance (φθέγμα) and 617d–e is concerned with the words (λόγος) of Lachesis. Compare also *Phaedo* 108e–111e and *Charmides* 156e–57a.

third speeech to his companion, but he makes it clear that his account comes from another party, called Aristodemus. This is how Apollodorus characterizes his own narration and sets it into motion:

> Well, it was like this,—but I'd better try to narrate it all from the beginning, just as Aristodemus narrated it to me. He said that he met Socrates who was freshly bathed and wearing shoes—two things Socrates rarely did—and that he asked him where he was going as he had made himself look so fine. And he said that Socrates replied 'To dinner at Agathon's . . .'
>
> (*Symposium* 174a)

Apollodorus adheres to this technique all the way through the *Symposium*: The words of the company at Agathon's dinner party are reported (in direct discourse), but those reports are embedded in indirect discourse. The indirect discourse renders and constantly highlights Aristodemus' mediation of the story which Apollodorus claims to be reproducing.[63] So this pattern of narration more or less follows that adopted by Socrates in the myth of Er. Direct dicourse is eschewed on the primary level. Although the use of direct discourse embedded in an indirect discourse rendering allows the narrator to 'cheat' in following the *Republic*'s prescriptions, at all points Plato reminds his audience that they are not reading a dialogue, but a narrative of a dialogue.

In contrast to the *Symposium*, the *Theaetetus* is entirely presented in dramatic form.[64] The preliminary discussion (also in dramatic form) calls attention to this. Eucleides says Socrates gave him an account of his own conversation with Theaetetus, which he now claims to reproduce:[65]

> EUCLEIDES: Here's the book Terpsion. Look how I wrote down what they said: I portrayed Socrates, not repeating it to me in the way he did, but carrying on the discussion with the people he said he'd had it with—he said they were Theodorus, the geometrician, and Theaetetus. It was so as

---

[63] Dover (1980), 80 examines this feature of the *Symposium*.

[64] See Hirzel (1895) i. 212 f. and 544. Diogenes Laertes 3. 50 comments on this practice in Plato.

[65] This translation comes, almost wholly, from McDowell (1973). Campbell (1883) compares Cicero, *De Amicitia* 1. 3. The full passage is worth quoting: *Quasi enim ipsos induxi loquentes, ne inquam et inquit saepius interponeretur, atque ut tanquam a praesentibus coram haberi sermo videretur,* ('I have as it were brought the speakers on stage in person, avoiding a frequent insertion of "I said" and "he said", so that the conversation might seem to be held by people as if they were actually present.'). J. G. F. Powell (1990), 78 compares Cicero, *Tusculans* 1. 8 and notes that *induxi* ('I brought [the characters] on [stage]') is a theatrical word.

not to have the written account made tedious by bits of narration
between the speeches (ἵνα οὖν ἐν τῇ γραφῇ μὴ παρέχοιεν πράγματα αἱ
μεταξὺ τῶν λόγων διηγήσεις)—something about himself like 'And I said'
or 'And I remarked', whenever Socrates was speaking, or again, something about the person giving the answers: 'He concurred' or 'He didn't
agree'. That was why I cut out that kind of thing, and portrayed Socrates
as himself carrying on the discussion.

TERPSION: Nothing wrong with that, Eucleides.

(*Theaetetus* 143b)

These passages show that Plato's self-consciousness about speech
presentation is not confined to the discussion in the third book of
the *Republic*. They also prompt speculation about a more profound
relation between speech presentation and the nature of narrative
discourse.

The opening of Apollodorus' account in the *Symposium* appears
to suggest a correspondence between indirect discourse and *narrative* on the one hand, and between direct discourse and *story* on the
other. The idea that direct discourse 'tends to promise an accurate
report' is certainly widely held.[66] Indirect discourse calls attention
to the fact that the speeches (or story) it presents are mediated, if not
abbreviated, by the discourse presenting them. The excerpt quoted
from the *Theaetetus*, however, is salutary. It reminds us that direct
discourse, though it may correspond with the level of story, cannot
be equated with 'what was actually said': Eucleides makes it clear
that he *constructed* his dialogue in direct discourse from Socrates'
account.[67] The correspondence between direct discourse and story
is only theoretical. Direct discourse is also a form of narration.
These insights will be explored in the next two chapters: pragmatics of performance determine whether direct discourse should
be conceived as narrative ('form') in some circumstances, or as
story ('content') in others.

[66] Bers (1997),1.

[67] Ryle (1965) comments on the *Theaetetus* at 29: 'The slave does not read out a
reporter's story describing their conversation; he vocally re-enacts the conversation
itself . . . We, the audience, are listening, dramatically in Megara in 369, just to the
reciting-voice of the slave. But what he recites to us, like a delayed echo or a long-
preserved gramophone record . . . is not *oratio recta*. It is relayed or echoed *oratio
recta*.' Ryle's notion of 'the conversation itself' being conserved is clearly naïve. But
Ryle is right to detect that the central dialogue of the *Theaetetus* is not in a
straightforward form of direct discourse. It is what I term *free* direct discourse: an
account of this speech mode will be given in Ch. 3.

3

Speech Modes and Literary Language

There is no work by Plato and there never will be. The things said here belong to Socrates when he was young and in his prime. Farewell and obey me—as soon as you have read and reread this letter a number of times, burn it.

('Plato', *Second Letter*)

Alice was beginning to get very tired of sitting by her sister on the bank, and of having nothing to do: once or twice she had peeped into the book she was reading, but it had no pictures or conversations 'and what is the use of a book' thought Alice, 'without pictures or conversations?'

(Lewis Caroll, *Alice in Wonderland*)

This chapter has two principal aims. One is to give a full account of the forms in which spoken and thought discourse can be presented in narrative. These various forms of presenting discourse will be called 'speech modes'. The other aim is to show how speech presentation has a major role in determining the way a narrative represents—or constructs—a world. The notion of literary language is of central relevance to both these concerns.

3.1 NARRATIVE AND LITERATURE

The observations made in the previous chapter generally apply to literary and non-literary narratives alike. All narratives, whether factual or fictional, whether in writing or conversation, can be seen to have *stories*. All narratives inevitably generate 'story worlds' which intersect in various ways with the world we experience. Thus all narratives have a representational function, however we may conceive it. All narratives are constituted by a reception of some kind, whether they are heard, read, or constructed privately by an individual. However, there are some important issues, which still need to be raised, about the idea of literary narrative.

Most influential theories of narrative have evolved from consideration of literary narrative alone.[1] What is more, as Genette remarks, 'literary narratology has confined itself a little too blindly to the study of fictional narrative as if as a matter of course every literary narrative would always be pure fiction'.[2] The concentration on the terrain of fiction tends to be asserted rather than justified: if some of the procedures used to analyse fiction may be applied to non-fictional texts, then the reverse might apply too. Though it is speciously questioned by theorists of narrative, the distinction between fiction and non-fiction commonly emerges *de facto* in their work.

Narratologists in particular have been less prone to dwell on the fact that the texts they scrutinize are usually designated as 'literary'. At first sight, there might appear to be no need for them to discuss this: narratology deals with the relationship between *narrative* and *story* in a text. The question of whether a text is 'literary' or not is often a moot point. This involves enquiries of another kind—into aesthetic judgements, into fact and value distinctions, and into the cultural history of those judgements and distinctions. Such enquiries into the nature of literariness may not seem to be the business of the narratologist, who need not claim to be a literary critic. Yet the argument of the last chapter showed that a number of issues which appeared to be extraneous to narratology are in fact central to its field of enquiry.

The distinction between literary narrative and non-literary narrative is not at all of the same order as the distinction between fiction and non-fiction. The latter distinction appears to have clear pragmatic and epistemological foundations. The distinction between literary and non-literary narrative, on the other hand, rests on a variety of possible criteria. Epic is an example of a narrative genre, now widely regarded as 'literary', which was certainly not always received exclusively as 'literature' or poetry.

---

[1] Examples include Genette (1980), Bal (1985), Rimmon-Kenan (1983), Stanzel (1984) and Todorov (1978).

[2] Genette (1988), 15. The synthesis of contemporary approaches to narrative ('Anglo-American New Criticism, Russian Formalism, French Structuralism, the Tel-Aviv School of Poetics and the Phenomenology of Reading') in Rimmon-Kenan (1983) is significantly entitled *Narrative Fiction*. These schools of thought have all concentrated on literary, fictional narrative.

The major ancient narrative genres of epic and historiography were held to be closely related. Historians like Herodotus used Homer; there are numerous references to pre-existing historiographical and annalistic sources in the *Aeneid*.[3] The epics of Homer and Virgil have also been actively read as theology (Christian or pagan), cosmology, philosophy, political theory, military strategy, geography, and rhetoric.[4] Not all such academic or allegorical readings can be dismissed as fraudulent or misconceived. The passage of time also allows narratives to mutate from being non-literary to being literary. Conversely, a number of works conceived originally as poetry or literature have come to have other functions—for instance as factual sources. The theoretical endeavours of Foucault, de Certeau, and many others, have made commonplace the suspension or demolition of the notion of literature.[5]

Nonetheless it is striking that even the words 'literature' or 'literary' are used quite unselfconsciously in studies which claim to be made in the light of such theories. Most of the narratives treated in this book are called 'literary'. If this label affects our perception of those texts as *narratives* in any stricter sense, it is worth asking what, if anything, makes narratives literary; and whether such literary narratives are different from—or appreciated in a different way from—non-literary narratives.

3.2 NARRATIVE AND LITERARY LANGUAGE

It is now routine to account for the various senses of the word 'literature' by appealing to Wittgenstein's idea of definition by family resemblances. Notions like those behind the words 'literature' or 'game' have a variety of overlapping definitions, only some of which can be found in any actual instance.[6] However, one characteristic that might be a common marker of all texts deemed to be literary is the 'reusability' conferred on them by readers.

---

[3] On Homer and historiography see Strasburger (1972), Walbank (1960). For history in Virgil see Horsfall (1990) and V. Simpson (1975).

[4] Cf. Lamberton and Keaney (1992), Clarke (1981), Comparetti (1908), Hardie (1986).

[5] Foucault (1976), and in Rabinow (1984), 76–100; Foucault's historiography is discussed in H. White (1987), 104–41; De Certeau (1978) and (1983); Clifford (1986); Eagleton (1983), ch. 1.

[6] See e.g. Eagleton (1983). Van Peer (1991) criticizes Eagleton's 'verdict of aporia' and attempts to offer a descriptive definition of literature from the vantage point of pragmatics.

Certain texts (like the *Res Gestae* of Augustus) even if they were
once documents or speech acts with material causes and effects, can
still differ from other kinds of texts and utterances because they are
'reusable'.[7] In common with some other kinds of discourse (e.g
legal, magical and religious formulae), literary utterances can be
meaningfully reissued and reused, again and again. This reusability
of literary discourse is very much bound up with its 'defamiliarized'
quality and the aesthetic value attributed to it.

Alternatively, the nature of literature has been seen to consist in
its language—language which is defamiliarized and 'connotative'
(as opposed to the 'denotative' language of science). However much
the presence of literary language in a narrative may be a consequence of surrounding factors, it can at least be scrutinized in
isolation to some extent. And *narrative* (in the technical sense) is the
form of a text: in this respect, investigation of literary language
takes us to the heart of what makes narrative literary. The idea that
there are various formal, linguistic features in a text which demonstrate its literary quality has not gone unchallenged.[8] Arguments
serving to support this idea are frequently found to be circular: to
maintain that literary language is found in literary texts begs the
question 'What is literary?'

A new way through this impasse might be to define 'literary
language' itself by family resemblances: literary language consists
of a set of attributes, all of which can belong to other kinds of
discourse. Some of these attributes in combination, however,
could distinguish literary language from other kinds of language.
These include specific kinds of vocabulary and diction, specific
rhetorical figures (e.g. metaphor), specific types of acoustically
patterned discourse (e.g. an identifiable metre), specific accidental
forms (e.g. the French past historic tense), and specific forms of
syntax. Of these attributes, syntax seems to be the one most relevant
to narrative organization. There are, after all, numerous 'literary'
narratives which do not contain vocabulary and diction regarded as
literary, which do not contain rhetorical figures regarded as literary,

---

[7] The issue of 'reusability' is discussed at length in the chapter entitled 'Poetic
Memory: Its Historical and Systematic Features' in Conte (1986), 40 f.

[8] See Pratt (1977), R. Fowler (1981), and Banfield (1982). Enkvist (1991) has
considered literary communication in the light of discourse linguistics and makes
the obvious suggestion (at 23–4) that it is 'definable only in relative, social terms,
not in absolute linguistic or textual ones . . . Literature is what a certain social
group at a certain time choose to regard as literature.'

which do not contain verse forms which are regarded as literary, and
which do not contain accidental forms regarded as literary.

J. D. Salinger's *The Catcher in the Rye* affects what is called *skaz*:
it is a text which appears to follow the linguistic conventions of
colloquial speech (or at least of speech supposed to be colloquial in
New York forty or fifty years ago).[9] But the *syntax* in it does not
follow those conventions. Direct discourse is a feature of *skaz*
which is especially conspicuous in *The Catcher in the Rye*:

'Listen. How long you been going round with her, this sculpture babe?' I
asked him. I was really interested. 'Did you know her when you were at
Whooton?'
'*Hardly*. She just arrived in this country a few months ago.'
'She did? Where's she from?'
'She happens to be from Shanghai.'
'No kidding! She's Chinese, for Chrissake?'
'Obviously.'
'No kidding! Do you like that? Her being Chinese?'
'Obviously.'
'Why? I'd be interested to know—I really would.'
'I simply happen to find Eastern philosophy more satisfactory than
Western. Since you *ask*.'
'You do? Wuddaya mean "philosophy"? Ya mean sex and all? You mean
it's better in China? That what you mean?'
'Not necessarily in *China*, for God's sake. The *East*, I said. Must we go on
with this inane conversation?'[10]

Such a passage could never be a transcription of actual spoken
discourse. It affects to record *not* the conversation between Holden
Caulfield (the first-person narrator) and his friend, but Holden
Caulfield's *account* of that conversation. But if Holden Caulfield
existed as a speaker in real life, he would not reproduce the rapid
exchange of his own utterances with those of his interlocutor in this
manner. Unless his retelling was a highly self-conscious performance, declarative expressions ('I said', 'and then he said', etc.)
would be the norm.[11] It is only because J. D. Salinger has the

[9] *Skaz* or 'yarn' is the Russian name for a particular style of dramatic narrative
given in Tomashevsky in Lemon and Reis (1965), 67.
[10] Salinger (1958), 152; rev. edn. (1994), 132.
[11] Tannen (1989) provides several examples of accounts of conversations of this
kind which demonstrate this norm. Leith and Myerson (1989), 26 has a useful
illustration: 'My dad says—I said to my father one night, I said: "Dad I'm going
out to a party." He said. "If you're not home here at a certain time," he said, "I
shall be after you." . . .'

facility to use the conventions of quotation marks and line spacing that Holden Caulfield can recount the conversation as he does.[12] The existence of a passage like this cannot in itself prove the existence of literary narrative: the fact that passages like this may be found in non-literary texts could indicate that such syntax is a feature of *written* narrative as opposed to spoken narrative. However it can make us think about the reality of literary narrative as a possibility. The study of speech modes as a branch of syntax might be one way—perhaps the best way—of establishing a distinction between literary and non-literary narrative.

3.3 SYNTAX AND SPEECH PRESENTATION[13]

In contemporary linguistics, 'syntax' has been defined as follows:

A traditional term for the study of the RULES governing the way WORDS are combined to form sentences in a language. In this use, syntax is opposed to MORPHOLOGY.[14] An alternative definition (avoiding the concept of 'word') is the study of the interrelationships between ELEMENTS OF SENTENCE STRUCTURE, and of the rules governing the arrangements of sentences in sequences.[15]

This standard technical conception of syntax—confined to relations between abstracted categories of words—is similar to the

---

[12] Typographic conventions reveal an *author*—not just a narrator—at work. Compare my brief discussion of narrator and persona in the section on narrative as expression at Ch. 2.4.

[13] Here I am subordinating a number of linguistic issues to my chief concern: the role of speech presentation and representation in narrative discourse. Whilst the notes below will draw attention to some of the linguistic issues involved, I have pretty much excluded (i) detailed consideration of *discourse analysis* in the technical linguistic sense and (ii) recent post-Chomskian accounts of syntax. For an account of Chomsky's thinking, see Lyons (1977a).

[14] Since the 19th cent., *morphology* (probably a term imported from the natural sciences) has comprised not only inflection, but also word-formation; word-formation comprises both derivation (e.g. *per-spire*), and word compounding e.g. *poison-gas*. Keith Percival has informed me that in grammars of the classical languages written before 1800, word-formation tended to be treated unsystematically, but that in the late 19th and early 20th cent., the origin of inflection became a central issue and syntax was neglected: hence Voloshinov's attack on Saussure. This is implicit in his views discussed further on in this section.

[15] This definition is from Crystal (1985), 300. See also Lyons (1968), ch. 5; Radford (1981), ch. 3; Matthews (1981). The wider, alternative definition mentioned by Crystal emphasizes the relations between all sentence constituents of whatever size. This Chomskian version makes syntax effectively equivalent to grammar minus phonology.

conception of syntax long held by students of Greek and Latin language and literature. In 1895, Gildersleeve opened his study of Greek syntax with this crisp definition:

SYNTAX treats of the formation and combination of sentences.[16]

The technical linguistical conception of syntax (like Crystal's quoted above) may strike students of literature or of a particular language as being relatively narrow and unhelpful. Unlike practitioners of linguistics, those who study ancient languages are often influenced by the apparently self-evident distinction between 'Accidence' and 'Syntax' presented in traditional Latin and Greek grammar books.[17] That distinction is very similar to the opposition between morphology and syntax in the definition of syntax quoted above.[18] Syntax was once conceived as everything that was not 'accidence'.[19] Thus for many classicists, the semantic and pragmatic functions of the constructions they have learnt are automatically conjured up by the mention of 'syntax'.

According to the standard technical conception of syntax in linguistics, direct and indirect discourse have syntactic aspects only in that they bear on formal, abstract relations.[20] However,

---

[16] Gildersleeve (1980).

[17] For an account of 'accidence', see n. 19. Abbott and Mansfield divided Greek grammar thus. Gildersleeve and Lodge (1895) divided Latin grammar into two principal sections: 'Etymology' and 'Syntax', with a final, briefer section on 'Prosody'. Keith Percival pointed out to me that by 1895 this would have seemed old-fashioned: the term etymology in the sense of morphology has its origins in the Middle Ages. Goodwin (1894) divides Greek grammar thus: 'I Letters, Syllables, and Accents; II Inflection, III Formation of Words; IV Syntax; V Versification'. The part devoted to Syntax takes up nearly half the volume. Goodwin represents an advance on Gildersleeve and Lodge in that he assigns word-formation to a special section and renames 'accidence' inflection.

[18] Gildersleeve's definition of syntax differs from the one in Crystal (1985) only in explicitly mentioning sentence co-ordination and the formation of complex sentences (sentences containing subordinate clauses).

[19] The term 'accidence' has probably survived longer in Latin and Greek grammars than elsewhere. It derives from the Greek term παρεπόμενα (rendered *accidentia* by Roman grammarians), which referred to inflectional categories: number, case, tense, person, etc. Each part of speech had a different set of *accidentia* which had to be exhaustively enumerated. The Latin grammar of the humanist Guarino Veronese (c.1418) lists the accidents of the verb thus: *Accidentia verbi sunt octo: genus, tempus, modus, species, figura, coniugatio, persona, et numerus.* ('There are eight accidents of the verb: genus, tense, mode, species, figure, conjugation, person and number.') On medieval grammar, see Curtius (1979), 446 f. and *passim*.

[20] This is because speech presentation both reports the signified 'content' of an utterance and draws attention to the role of the reported utterance as a *sign*.

direct and indirect discourse also have *semantic* aspects in that they
they deal with the function of words as symbols, and the relation
between the sign and signified, and *pragmatic* aspects in that they
relate to the situation and circumstances of the utterance. In
addition, direct and indirect discourse have *poetic* aspects in as
much as they relate to style, larger themes, genre and so on.
Classicists among others, however, are likely to believe that all of
these aspects of direct and indirect discourse—except the poetic
ones—have something to do with 'syntax'. That belief is an
assumption based on a broad and unchallenged use of the word
'syntax'. However, such usage is not ridiculous. A term is still
needed for the nexus of semantic and pragmatic functions of
language that operate in a particular construction, such as a purpose
clause: a construction which, in stricter terms, is recognizable by its
syntactic aspects. The classicist's notion of syntax is a useful
shorthand; moreover, even within the field of linguistics, a broader
conception of syntax is now accepted. There is an increasing
acknowledgement that syntax and semantics—two major branches
of the subject—might be interdependent.[21]

This was anticipated by Valentin Voloshinov in his book *Marxism and the Philosophy of Language* written in the 1920s. At this time
syntax did not have the centre stage it now enjoys in post-
Chomskian linguistics.[22] After attempting to enlarge the role of
syntax, Voloshinov devoted the rest of his study to one of its special
problems. He deliberately chose a field 'which [had] become
bogged down in masses of meticulous and detailed—but utterly
pointless—classifications . . . because an apt posing of a problem can
make the phenomenon under scrutiny reveal the methodological
potentialities embedded in it'. The field of study Voloshinov chose
turns out to be that of speech presentation:[23]

[21] See e.g. Dik (1978). Pinkster (1990) is a good account of the syntax and
semantics of Latin.

[22] Voloshinov (1973), 109–10.

[23] What I call 'speech presentation', Voloshinov (with his translators) calls the
reporting of speech. I prefer to avoid using the notion of 'reporting' in relation to
speech presentation. This is because (i) 'reported discourse' is commonly used for
types of *indirect* discourse alone. The argument of this chapter will show that this
usage is misleading in giving the impression that direct discourse has more veridical
value than indirect discourse in not being 'reported'. (ii) Whether used of direct or
indirect discourse, the notion of reporting denies the current speaker's responsibility for forming the rendering of another's speech: an idea which is anyway
central to Voloshinov's perception. Tannen (1989), 101 prefers 'constructed

We believe that one such highly productive, 'pivotal' phenomenon is that of so-called *reported speech*, i.e. the syntactic patterns (direct discourse, indirect discourse, quasi-direct discourse) the modifications of those patterns and the variants of those modifications, which we find in a language for the reporting of other persons' utterances and for incorporating those utterances, as the utterances of others into a bound, monologic utterance.[24]

Voloshinov's 'syntax of the utterance', although it can be fully and usefully applied to dead languages, is rooted, not in textbook examples of linguistic forms, but in affective discourse as a living phenomenon.

In the rest of this chapter, the question of whether there are syntactic usages which distinguish literary narrative from other kinds of narrative will be discussed with specific reference to speech presentation. This is not only because of Voloshinov's identification of presented discourse as a 'pivotal phenomenon' which exposes the full role of syntax in language. It is also because presented discourse, as a linguistic feature, is obviously related to the referential nature of language and—by extension—to the representational function of narrative.

3.4 SPEECH MODES FOR PRESENTING DISCOURSE

A speaker or narrator has three major modes of presenting the discourse of persons or characters: quotation in direct discourse, a rendering in some kind of indirect discourse, or the simple mention that a speech act ocurred. These major modes are subdivided in different ways in different languages.[25] The different modes are enumerated in Table 3.1 and explained in greater detail in the text.

---

speech': 'I wish to question the conventional . . . literal conception of "reported speech" and claim instead that uttering dialogue in conversation is as much a creative act as is the creation of dialogue in fiction and drama.'

[24] Voloshinov (1973), 112.

[25] There is abundant discussion of the definition and functions of the speech modes in more specifically linguistic treatments of direct and indirect discourse. Those dealing with literary discourse include: Bers (1997)—a study of direct discourse in Attic drama and oratory, Banfield (1982), Coulmas (1986)—a useful anthology considering the reporting of speeches in a variety of languages, Fillmore (1981), Larson (1978), MacHale (1978) on free indirect discourse, Partee (1973), Calame (1986), Tannen (1986), Zwicky (1978). More general linguistic studies which have importance for the study of speech presentation are: Biber (1988), Hickmann (1982), Johnstone (1987), Lyons (1977*b*) (an important introductory

[*cont. on p. 89*]

TABLE 3.1: *Modes for presenting discourse ('Speech Modes')*

3.4.1 *Direct Modes*

(*a*) Direct Discourse (DD) or *oratio recta*. This is 'standard quotation'—
we are given an impression of hearing the original speaker's actual words.

> 'tune hinc spoliis indute meorum
> eripiare mihi? Pallas te hoc vulnere, Pallas
> immolat et poenam scelerato ex sanguine sumit.'
>
> (Virgil, *Aeneid* 12. 947–9)

'Are you to be snatched from my grasp, decked out in the spoils of loved
ones? Pallas makes a sacrifice of you with this wound and Pallas takes
retribution from your criminal blood.'

(*b*) Free Direct Discourse (FDD)—we are given a more approximate
impression of the words uttered or thought by the original speaker(s).

> 'tristius an miseris superest mare? linquite, terrae,
> spem pelagi sacrosque iterum seponite fluctus.'
> haec iterant segni flentes occumbere leto.
>
> (Valerius Flaccus, *Argonautica* 1. 631–3)

'Can a gloomier sea await us wretched men? Land-dwellers leave hope of
the sea and again shun the holy waves.' They repeat this, bewailing an idle
death.

3.4.2 *Indirect Modes*

(*a*) Indirect Discourse (ID) or *oratio obliqua*—we are given the explicit
impression that the words of the original speaker(s) have been modified by
the speaker or narrator presenting them.

> nuntius ingentis ignota in veste reportat
> advenisse viros.   (*Aeneid* 7. 167–8)

The messenger announced that huge men in strange garb had drawn
near.

(*b*) Free Indirect Discourse (FID)

> heu quid agat? quo nunc reginam ambire furentem
> audeat adfatu? quae prima exordia sumat?   (*Aeneid* 4. 283–4)

Alas what is he to do? With what address should he dare to approach the
queen in her rage? What should be his first words?

TABLE 3.1 (*cont.*)

3.4.3 *Records of Speech Acts (RSA)*

(*a*) 'Terse' RSA

Irim de caelo misit Saturnia Juno   (*Aeneid* 9. 2)

Saturnian Juno sent Iris down from heaven

(*b*) 'Expansive' or 'Informative' RSA

hic canit errantem lunam solisque labores,

unde hominum genus et pecudes, unde imber et ignes . . .   (*Aeneid* 1.742–3)

He sang of the wandering moon, the sun's tasks, of the origins of the human race and of beasts, of rain and fire . . .

The range of speech modes shown here does not quite match the categories in standard grammars of Latin, Greek, or English. Those categories (e.g. 'direct questions', 'indirect questions', 'indirect commands', etc.) are not so helpful for understanding the ways in which discourse is actually presented.[26]

3.4.1a *Direct Discourse*

The mode of direct discourse (DD) or *oratio recta* is familiar enough. The speaker's words, spoken or thought, are quoted. The narrator or current speaker gives the audience the impression that these words are a precise imitation of whatever the original speaker is supposed to have uttered. Direct discourse has always been regarded as possessing an important property which no other

---

work), Polanyi (1985), Romaine (1985). Crystal (1985) and the index of Lyons (1977*b*) are useful guides to the terminology in these works. Davidson (1969) offers a philosophical consideration of indirect discourse in English; see also Quine (1960) and (1966). My list of speech modes has obviously been developed with the Latin language (and literature) in mind—nonetheless it is very striking how similar the patterns of the relation between reporting and reported speech can be in a variety of languages. The third part of Voloshinov (1973), 109–61, is entirely devoted to reported speech (mostly indirect discourse). That study, on the boundary between linguistics and literary theory, is still pre-eminent in clarity and breadth.

[26] Hofmann and Szantyr (1965), Kühner and Stegmann (1912–14), and Madvig (1851) provide standard accounts of direct and indirect discourse in Latin. Ernout and Thomas (1951) is more discursive, and occasionally literary-historical. Rubio (1982) offers a more modern approach. There (257 f.), linguistic means of speech presentation in Latin are usefully compared to those in modern French and Spanish, and the problems posed for translation are considered.

style, mode or feature of narrative can match. When direct discourse is used, the time it takes to recount that speech on the narrative plane appears to become synchronized with the actual time it would take for that speech to be uttered in the world of the story. If 'narrative time' were ever equivalent to 'story time', it would have to be when direct discourse is presented. Of course direct discourse in a written narrative cannot reproduce the effect of a speech uttered in our world of experience: a precise timing for enunciation, pauses in or between enunciations and the timing for those, qualities of accent, tone and voice all defy notation.[27] Nor can they be comprehensively prescribed for oral narration. Nonetheless, utterances are the only things narrative can appear to imitate: utterances, like verbal forms of narrative, are made of language.

Direct discourse accomplishes more than a temporal synthesis of narrative and story: a voice other than the narrator's appears to take over and to confront us directly with the world of the story, and sometimes even to put us in it.

3.4.1b *Free Direct Discourse—Two Versions*

The rhetorician called 'Longinus' in *On the Sublime* identifies a device that modern theorists have also noticed:

Sometimes a writer, in the course of a narrative in the third person, makes a sudden change and speaks in the person of his character. This kind of thing is an outburst of emotion.

> Hector shouted aloud to the Trojans
> to rush for the ships, and leave the spoils of the dead.
> 'If I see anyone away from the ships of his own accord,
> I will have him killed on the spot'.   [*Iliad* 15. 346–9]

Here the poet has given the narrative to himself, as appropriate to him, and then suddenly and without warning has put the abrupt threat in the mouth of the angry prince. It would have been flat if he had added 'Hector said'. As it is, the change of construction is so sudden that it has outstripped its creator (νυνὶ δ' ἔφθακεν ἄφνω τὸν μεταβαίνοντα ἡ τοῦ λόγου μετάβασις).

Hence the use of this figure is appropriate when the urgency of the moment gives the writer no chance to delay, but forces on him an immediate change from one person to another. 'Ceyx was distressed at

---

[27] These issues bear on free direct discourse, discussed below.

this, and ordered the children to depart. "For I am unable to help you. Go therefore to some other country, so as to save yourselves without harming me." '   [Hecataeus fr. 30 Jacoby]

(*On the Sublime* 27. 1)

'Longinus' is speaking about general literary and rhetorical technique. In these reviews of passages from Homer and Hecataeus, there is a concern with how the manipulation of speech presentation operates as a figure, to enhance the effect of a narrative.[28] 'Longinus' observes that the omission of a declarative phrase like 'Hector said' causes a change of construction from indirect to direct discourse. This amounts to what has been called 'free direct speech':

Direct speech has two features which show evidence of the narrator's presence, namely the quotation marks and the introductory reporting clause [what I have just called the 'declarative phrase']. Accordingly, it is possible to remove either or both of these features, and produce a freer form, which has been called FREE DIRECT SPEECH: one where the characters apparently speak to us more immediately without the narrator as an intermediary.[29]

In my view, the term 'free direct discourse' (FDD) is better applied on occasions when we are unsure about how far a quoted speech corresponds to the speech we imagine was originally uttered. I certainly disagree with the claim that it is merely the absence of a declarative verb (a verb of 'saying' and 'thinking') that constitutes FDD.[30] Direct discourse with absence of a declarative phrase or absence of quotation marks is no more than direct discourse with that feature absent. 'Longinus' was illustrating a shift in speech mode, from indirect to direct discourse. The nature of Hector's utterance may have been presented indirectly first: now it is being quoted. A declarative phrase inserted *after* that shift has occurred would not have hampered that basic effect.

---

[28] Fantuzzi (1988), 54 f. examines this observation of 'Longinus' in conjunction with the scholia on the *Iliad* passage. He remarks (55 n. 20) that in modern editions of the *Iliad*, quotation marks are introduced earlier at 347; ἐπισσεύεσθαι and ἐᾶν are counted inside the direct speech as imperative infinitives. He notes that ancient sources were uncertain about the status of these words, but the prevalent opinion was that held by 'Longinus'. Bers (1997), 6 n. 11 has further discussion of this passage in 'Longinus'. The translation here is from Russell and Winterbottom (1972), 487.

[29] Leech and Short (1981), 322.

[30] I favour the term 'declarative verb' used by Genette and by linguists; the traditional *verbum dicendi* has its drawbacks, as Bers (1997), 6 n. 10 notes.

Here are two examples of what I would call FDD from English literary narrative. The first is from Dickens's *Bleak House*. In this excerpt, the novel's principal narrator is giving an account of an inquest. No graphic markers indicate direct discourse; *prima facie* then, the account is in the narrator's voice:

Now. Is there any other witness? No other witness.

Very well gentlemen! Here's a man unknown, proved to be in the habit of taking opium in large quantities . . . if you think it is a case of accidental death, you will find a verdict accordingly.

Verdict accordingly. Accidental death. No doubt. Gentlemen, you are discharged. Good afternoon.[31]

The second example is from Jane Austen's *Northanger Abbey*:

'I do not quite despair yet. I shall not give it up till a quarter after twelve. This is just the time of day for it to clear up, and I do think it looks a little lighter. There, it is twenty minutes after twelve, and now I *shall* give it up entirely . . .'

A critic remarks on that second passage:

Unblushingly, the novelist permits twenty minutes to elapse during the uttering of less than forty words. Quite clearly, the force of the quotation marks in this example is different from that in most direct speech: a protracted conversation, or at least a one-sided series of remarks has been telescoped into a single speech in the interests of narrative economy.[32]

This ruptures any comfortable illusion that direct discourse must always offer a temporal synthesis of narrative and story. The same could be said of the truncated monologue Dickens provides to narrate the inquest of Nemo. The effects of these passages are in some ways comparable.

In their study of style in English fiction, Leech and Short argue that the Dickens passage represents 'the most free form of all [modes of presenting discourse]'.[33] This is in no small part because of 'the lack of quotation marks and locutionary clauses'. In their view the narrator is not acting as an intermediary. We may compare the comment in 'Longinus' on Homer's rapid slide into Hector's direct discourse in *Iliad* 15. 346. But significantly, 'Longinus' is

---

[31] This example of FDD actually comes from Leech and Short (1981), 328—it just happens to conform to my idea of FDD as well as theirs!

[32] N. Page (1988), 32.

[33] Leech and Short (1981), 328.

speaking figuratively about Hector's order to hurry—'the act of overtaking outstrips the overtaker' is a literal rendering of the Greek words given above. Leech and Short, on the other hand clearly regard FDD as an indication that the narrator has actually lost control, rather than an indication that the intervention of a character is being simulated for rhetorical purposes. Presumably they would argue that the Jane Austen passage is less 'free' because of the presence of quotation marks. Moreover, they hold that presented utterances like those given above are somehow more liberated from the narrator's control than standard instances of direct discourse. Yet in many senses such utterances are less realistic—the 'telescoping' surely exposes the hidden grand design of the narrator as he is working his purpose out.

The misconception derives, I believe, from an aspiration to make FDD more parallel to free *indirect* discourse than it really is. It is mistakenly assumed that if FID is ostensibly a freer version of standard indirect discourse, FDD has to be freer than standard direct discourse in an analogous way. In my opinion, FDD can be so called because the narrator is 'free' from the constraint of quoting or constituting the precise words supposed to have been uttered by a character or characters. In classical narrative particularly, the following conditions for FDD can be identified:

1. Temporal telescoping. Direct discourse on the level of narrative can be longer (or occasionally) shorter in duration than we might expect an utterance to be on the level of story.

2. The ascription, and quotation, of shared direct discourse to a group of speakers. The convention is found in epic narrative, as the excerpt from Valerius Flaccus' *Argonautica* given above suggests; it occurs on a number of occasions in Homer and Lucan in particular.[34]

3. The ascription of direct discourse to a speaker (or speakers) which is uttered repeatedly. The same excerpt from Valerius Flaccus' *Argonautica* quoted above also happens to illustrate the condition of *iterative* FDD.

4. An apparently naturalistic quotation followed or preceded by the narrator remarking that this is *something like* what was originally said. If expressions like 'with such words' refer to the words of a

---

[34] De Jong (1987*b*) gives some examples from the *Iliad*; examples from Lucan *De Bello Civili* are: 1. 246 f., 2. 38–42, 2. 45–63, 2. 65–233, 3. 307–55, 5. 259–96, 5. 682–9, 8. 110–27, 9. 227–51, 9. 848–80. These are discussed in Laird (1992).

quoted speech, we are given the specific impression that the quoted words do not correspond at all precisely to whatever may have been said originally.[35]

5. Direct discourse in verse. Direct discourse in verse, whether as part of a verse narrative or embedded in a prose narrative (as in Menippean satire) could be considered FDD, given that actual speakers do not usually versify their utterances.[36] This recalls the question raised in the previous chapter about speeches in verse: would an ancient audience be any more inclined than we are to believe that in a heroic age people spoke to each other in Latin or Greek hexameters? Assuming that they would not, one could hold that *all* direct discourse in epic and other forms of verse narrative can count as FDD. On the other hand, epic poets and tragedians require audiences to suspend disbelief for their poems to work: the acceptance of speeches in verse is one example of such supension.[37]

Some speeches in real life can of course be made in verse. In conversation, an expression like 'What a tangled web we weave | when first we practice to deceive' can have an obvious pragmatic function. If an utterance containing or consisting of this quotation from Scott were to be (re)produced in a narrative, it would not be an automatic marker of FDD. In antiquity oracles were given in verse. Thus the presenting of verse oracles in direct discourse in ancient narrative is no more self-conciously literary or poetical than the oracle itself. The identification of FDD can have larger implications for the interpretation of a narrative in which it occurs. Conversely, broader interpretations of a narrative can determine the identification of FDD within it.

3.4.2a Indirect Discourse

The first indirect speech mode is standard indirect discourse (ID), traditionally labelled *oratio obliqua*. The original speaker's words (spoken or thought) are channelled through the voice of the narrator or presenter of the utterance. The audience of such a

---

[35] Hornblower (1987), 53 might confirm this supposition by considering the implications of an instance in Thucydides—a controversial one—when a formula like τοιαῦτα ('such words') is *not* used.

[36] Compare Ch. 2.2, on verse and prose in narrative.

[37] Lewis (1942) on the need for 'solemnity' to appreciate epic is pertinent. Compare Todorov (1984), 88 quoting Bakhtin: 'an absolute epic distance separates the epic world from contemporary reality'.

presentation hardly ever have the impression that they are hearing
what the original speaker said, because the narrator's presence is so
clearly accentuated by the syntax in a sentence in which ID
features. This is very much the case when we consider literature
in Latin—the accusative and infinitive construction generally used
is fairly unwieldy compared to those in English or Greek.[38] The
very use of this construction provides a constant reminder that the
discourse it constitutes is embedded.

However, there are types of ID in all three languages which come
closer to giving the illusion of precise imitation afforded by direct
discourse. The first we will call *mimetic indirect discourse* (MID).[39]
With this, the diction does seem to be more the property of the
original speaker than the narrator. Yet it is all held within the
confines of an ID clause. Jane Austen provides an example of this in
English:

> Mrs. Jennings however assured him directly, that she should not stand
> upon ceremony, for they were all cousins or something like it, and she
> should certainly wait on Mrs. John Dashwood very soon, and bring her
> sisters to see her.[40]

Here by the repetition of 'should', and the idiomatic 'cousins or
something like it', Jane Austen mimics Mrs Jennings without
actually quoting her. It is clear that the narrator is speaking all
the time, although there is an element of caricature of the supposed
original speaker. However, such caricaturing by no means has to be
always mocking or satirical. In Greek, this sort of effect is facilitated
by the fact that tenses feasibly used in a reported utterance do not
always change when the utterance is reported in indirect discourse.[41] But for Latin narrative, more vigilance is needed to
identify this kind of feature. The appearance of an oath, exclamation or other turn of phrase associated with direct utterances can

---

[38] The frequency of the accusative and infinitive diminished in post-classical
Latin, no doubt because of its unwieldy nature compared to the simpler *quod/quia*
type constructions. Ernout and Thomas (1951), 453 hold plausibly that even in the
classical period the traditional construction was confined to language that was
written and read.

[39] Neither MID nor FID are confined to fictional literature in Latin. Roman
historians are particularly fond of MID, as well as FID. Macaulay's practice was
similar. See my discussion of Runciman's use of FID in Ch. 4.

[40] *Sense and Sensibility*, 230 (Penguin edn.).

[41] See Rijksbaron (1994) and Bers (1997), 6–9.

often signal MID, e.g. *heu* or *immo vero*. The example from the *Aeneid* given above is an interesting one to consider:

> nuntius ingentis ignota in veste reportat
> advenisse viros.

> (*Aeneid* 7. 167–8)

The messenger announced that huge men in strange garb had drawn near.

This was classified above as standard ID. But it can be read as MID. The words could be seen to 'reproduce' a dramatically convincing sequence in the mesenger's original utterance: the size, the foreign dress and the arrival of the strangers are revealed in that order.[42] 'Servius' remarks on these verses:

INGENTES ex stupore nuntii laus ostenditur Troianorum. et bene novitatis ostendit opinionem: ingentes enim esse quos primum videmus opinamur.

'HUGE'—the amazement of the messenger conveys praise of the Trojans. And [that word] well illustrates an opinion prompted by a first impression: we tend to think of people as huge when we first see them.

This might support the idea that this instance of ID not only presents the messenger's utterance but also constructs it mimetically to some extent.[43] However, this example, even if it is of MID, serves to show that we can never actually reconstuct the original utterance of which we have only an impression. The messenger could be imagined to have announced the arrival in numerous ways.

3.4.2*b* Free Indirect Discourse

Another type of indirect discourse which comes near to giving the effect of direct speech has become more famous. This is free indirect discourse (FID). Bally's seminal study of 1912 has been succeeded by a vast number of treatments, including an important study by the film director Pasolini.[44] An example of FID in English comes from D. H. Lawrence:

---

[42] There is a change in *focalization* in this sentence, from the narrator to the messenger: it is worth considering this as a marker of MID.

[43] However, a cursory survey of occurrences of *ingens* in all its forms throughout the *Aeneid* shows that there is no preponderance of this adjective in speeches: so there is no overwhelming case for the diction here presenting the diction of the supposed original utterance.

[44] Bally (1912). Lips (1926) is another pioneering treatment. Pasolini's essay, originally published in 1972 and prompted by Herczeg (1963), is now translated as

She lifted her head and pondered. How could it be wrong to love him? Love was God's gift and yet it caused her shame. That was because of him, Paul Morel. [45]

There are still the customary alterations to any imagined original utterance that we find in conventional ID: changes of tense, mood and person. But the propositions recording the utterance (*How could it be wrong to love him?* etc.) are not hinged grammatically on a verb of saying and thinking.[46] They are quite independent and show a change of voice: the narrator does not have indisputable control, as he does with MID. Very often in Latin epic, deliberative questions in the third person of the present subjunctive signal FID. The sentiments of a character expressed in FID could be either spoken or thought—it is not usually revealed. Nor is it clear who is giving expression to these sentiments: the voices of narrator and character become synthesized, or at least confused.[47] In Latin poetic narrative, FID is usually involved in fright or flight

'Comments on Free Indirect Discourse' in Pasolini (1988), 79–101. This unjustifiably neglected discussion considers the full ideological implications of FID in Italian language and literature from Dante to the present, relating its apparitions and transformations to political and historical shifts in Italian society. Works cited in nn. 25 and 26 above include material on FID. For a general survey see MacHale (1978). For bibliography on FID in Latin, see Hofmann and Szantyr (1965), 362. There is a good account in Regula (1951). In this respect modern literatures have been better served. FID is a prominent speech mode in the novel; the number of works treating this aspect of the genre is vast. See especially Cohn (1978) for extensive treatment and bibliography, and N. Page (1988). Haig (1986) and S. Ullman (1957) discuss specific works. Two classic studies are Bakhtin (1973) on Dostoevsky, and Genette (1980) on Proust.

[45] *Sons and Lovers*, 211 (Penguin edn.).

[46] Ernout and Thomas (1951), 434–5: *A côté du style indirect proprement dit, rapportant à un verbe déclaratif une série de propositions dépendantes, il y a des exemples de style indirecte libre en proposition grammaticalement indépendente; mais les changements de temps de mode ou de personne que l'on observe alors montrent avec évidence que cette indépendence est purement extérieure: il y a en réalité dépendence dans la pensée de l'écrivain.* 'Dependence on the *voice* of the *narrator*' better expresses this basis on which tenses, moods and persons of verbs are determined for passages of FID, although even after this reformulation, the proposition is contestable. We shall see in the next subsection that a major problem with the FID is not so much who is speaking , as whether in some passages we actually have FID at all. For identification we have to rely on the general context of a passage, not just the linguistic forms the passage may contain.

[47] Incidentally, the situation in which FID is used in the Lawrence passage quoted here has striking parallels in Latin poetry. Scylla in Ovid's *Metamorphoses* 8. 25 f. and Medea in Valerius Flaccus' *Argonautica* 7. 336 f., are young girls in love questioning the legitimacy of their feelings. In all these passages, as often, FID opens out to a soliloquy in direct discourse.

situations, when a character is in a state of high emotion or agitation.[48] The example given earlier from the *Aeneid* 4 (in which the narrator presents Aeneas' agonizing about how to abandon Dido) illustrates these traits:

> heu quid agat? quo nunc reginam ambire furentem
> audeat adfatu? quae prima exordia sumat?
>
> > (*Aeneid* 4. 283–4)

Alas what is he to do? With what address should he dare to approach the queen in her rage? What should be his first words?

It is important to distinguish FID from 'focalization'. The latter term was coined by Genette when he drew a crucial distinction in narrative, between 'who speaks' and 'who sees'. This is an example of focalization:

> ardet abire fuga dulcisque relinquere terras
> attonitus tanto monitu imperioque deorum.
>
> > (*Aeneid* 4. 281–2)

He burns to flee away and leave the sweet lands, overwhelmed both by so mighty a warning and the gods' power.

These verses certainly do not present anything uttered by Aeneas, nor even necessarily an unvoiced thought. Yet they do tell us something about his attitudes. The lands of Carthage are *dulcis* ('sweet') really only to Aeneas. They are not sweet to us, nor to the poet-narrator, and certainly not to an audience of patriotic Romans. *Abire fuga* too is a rather embarrassing way of conceiving the last stage of Aeneas' great journey to Italy—but this is the way Aeneas *sees* it. It would be quite different for him to articulate in speech or thought '*ardeo abire fuga dulcisque relinquere terras*' ('I burn to flee away and leave the sweet lands'). Focalization ('seeing') can thus be distinguished from the reporting of spoken or thought discourse ('speaking'). So Aeneas' thoughts are not actually articulated, but rather discreetly conveyed by this focalization.[49]

---

[48] De Jong (1994) shows that examples of ID ('embedded focalization' in her terminology) are used in contexts in Homer's *Odyssey*—when characters are concealing their thoughts.

[49] I generally find it sufficient throughout to refer to such instances of 'deviant focalization' or 'focalization through a character' simply as 'focalization', since the identification of species of focalization is not an object of my enquiry. And I am sceptical about whether narrative can ever be in *any* sense 'unfocalized' (zero focalization) cf. Genette (1980), 188 f. and (1988), 73. D. P. Fowler (1990) and

It is worth emphasizing here that the 'thoughts' treated in this survey are only those which might be shown to involve presentation of characters' discourse. Focalization and 'exotopic' narration of thoughts—portrayal of a character's dispositions through imagery or other descriptive language—are not principle concerns here. In practice, there are always going to be instances of diction which are hard to categorize. The difference between focalization and speech presentation is not always so clear as I have made it seem— sometimes one can move into the other. There is no infallible criterion for identifying the presentation of discourse: the absence of a declarative verb often indicates little either way. The inter- pretation of ambiguous instances can depend on our interpretation of surrounding passages, and sometimes even of the entire works in which they appear.

3.4.3 *Records of Speech Acts*

There is one more general category of speech mode to consider. This is what I shall call 'the record of a speech act' (RSA).[50] We are given merely an indication that something was said or thought and we have much less information about the original utterance— though we may know its effect or the nature of its content. Ex- amples in English are:

> They agreed.
> She asked him to stay.
> He told them about the war.

The name I would give to this most remote way of presenting speakers' discourse is 'terse RSA'. The speeches or thoughts are mentioned mainly as events. In the terse kind of RSA, a good deal of the information about the utterance is provided by the verb alone. The verb does not even have to be a specifically declarative

---

(1991) have useful treatments of focalization in Latin literature. See also Laird (1997), 283–7.

[50] My category of RSA corresponds to what De Jong (1987*a*) refers to as 'speech act mention' and what Rimmon-Kenan (1983) calls 'diegetic summary'. Leech and Short (1981), 323–4 call it 'NRSA': 'narrative report of speech acts'. Since brief reports of speech acts are by no means exclusive to or typical of narrative discourse, my shortening of NRSA to RSA is meant to be more helpful. I prefer the term *record* of speech acts to the term *report* because it helps avoid ambiguity: all the speech modes, whether direct or indirect, are often said to 'report' discourse, so the use of 'report' as a noun is not always helpful.

one like 'say' or 'speak', as the use of *misit* ('sent') in the example in Table 3.1 from *Aeneid* 9. 2 shows.[51] A more informative type of RSA includes indirect commands or indirect questions. The rendering of Iopas' song in the *Aeneid* (part of which was reproduced in the table above) is a good example of this:

> Hic canit errantem lunam solisque labores,
> unde hominum genus et pecudes, unde imber et ignes
> Arcturum pluviasque Hyadas geminosque Triones,
> quid tantum Oceano properent se tingere soles
> hiberni, vel quae tardis mora noctibus obstet.
>
> (*Aeneid* 1. 742–6)

He sang of the wandering moon, the sun's tasks, the origins of the human race and of the animals, the causes of rain and fire, Arcturus, the rainy Hyades, the twin Triones; of why the winter suns so hurry to dip themselves in the Ocean, and of what delays the passage of slow nights.

The distinction to be made between ID and RSA as two types of speech mode is, in my view, an important one. Even informative RSA, as used here for Iopas, merely summarizes. It is not especially likely that the indirect questions Virgil uses to present Iopas' song are renderings of any actual questions which Iopas posed himself: they only serve to exemplify the subjects of his poem.[52] ID, on the other hand, is still a rendering of the imagined original, however brief, rather than a summary. The distinction is not without problems though: indirect questions and especially indirect commands are sometimes ID, sometimes what I call RSA. Then even within my finer subcategory of 'terse RSA' quite different things can go on: *iubet* ('orders') tells us a good deal more about a character's utterance than *loquitur* ('speaks').

This then, is the range of speech modes. In theory at least, soliloquies, exchanges of long speeches and rapid dialogue can all be presented in any of these modes or in any combination of

---

[51] It should be noted that even terse RSA can have quite striking positive effects—e.g. bathos in syncopated narration when an audience are deprived of a speech which may have been expected. A good example is the rendering of the final part of Anchises' exchange with Aeneas in Virgil, *Aeneid* 6. 888–891. MacHale (1978), 2258–9 in his scale of speech modes subcategorizes RSA in a similar way: terse RSA is called 'the diegetic summary'; expansive RSA is 'summary, less purely diegetic'.

[52] Such questions are to be found in philosophical poems e.g. Virgil, *Georgic* 1. 1 f., *Aetna* 1–4.

them. What I term 'angled narration of dialogue' (AND) alternates direct and indirect modes in the presentation of an exchange of speeches. The words of one speaker are spotlighted by being given in direct discourse; whilst the words of his interlocutor are presented by the narrator in indirect discourse. The words of the speaker who is quoted in direct discourse tend to have the most impact in these situations. For this reason I call it 'angled' narration of dialogue.

Certain speech modes and types of speech presentation will be employed in certain situations in narrative texts.[53] The dramatic facility of the direct modes tends to give most prominence to a speaker. The indirect modes, on the other hand have the usual effect of distancing the audience from whatever characters may have said, whilst rendering at least a part of it. In Latin narrative and poetry for instance, ID is used in certain kinds of situations. It provides the best ways in which to render rumours, for example, since these can never be presented *verbatim*. Fama or 'Rumour' though she is personified by Virgil, Statius, and Valerius Flaccus, is never given direct discourse.[54] ID can also be adopted to express the sentiments of a group of people speaking at once. (Another context in narrative which tends to favour indirect modes is a character repeating the same sentiment over and over again—possibly each time in a slightly different way. What can be called the *iterative* use of ID or RSA conveys this.)

Perhaps most importantly, different kinds of ID are used to present the thoughts and motivations of characters in a way that is far more revealing than soliloquy in direct discourse. This is because the narrator can explicitly interpret—as well as present—the character's thoughts, bringing certain things into focus to describe his or her behaviour.[55] RSA, on the other hand is found in many kinds of story situations. Needless to say, its occurrence is no rarity.

---

[53] On particular linguistic devices occurring in certain contexts see Todorov (1978) on the Russian formalists. For instance, soliloquies in ancient literature tend to be in direct discourse: see Otter (1914), Schadewaldt (1926) and the bibliography in Ch. 5 n. 3.

[54] See *Aeneid* 4. 190 f., Statius, *Thebaid* 2. 201, 11. 139, Valerius Flaccus, *Argonautica* 2. 115 f., and Ch. 7, on the messenger scene.

[55] See again De Jong (1994).

3.5 INDIRECT SPEECH MODES AND THE POSSIBILITY OF 'LITERARY' SYNTAX

After this survey of the speech modes that are to be found in narrative texts, we can now come to the question of whether they lead us to believe that there is such a thing as a syntax of presenting discourse which is conspicuously literary. The three major modes of presenting the discourse of persons or characters (DD, ID, and RSA) are common to all kinds of text and utterance, whether we deem them literary or non-literary discourse—just as those three major modes are common to most languages. But these modes have different syntactic subdivisions in the languages of Greek, Latin, French, and English. Do they have syntactic subdivisions in literary discourse which are distinct from the subdivisions they have in non-literary discourse? Do they show that there can be a special syntax for literature in the same way as there might be a special diction for poetry?

It was explained that my full list of speech modes was compiled from a survey of literary texts. However journalism uses MID, and even expansive RSA quite extensively.[56] Formal minutes (as we might find in Court circulars and Hansard) eschew direct discourse for the sake of conforming to traditional generic criteria. In spoken conversation, examples of MID are more unusual. Expansive RSA is more frequent, but usually occurs because it is manipulated to serve explicitly as part of the message of the current speaker, not the prior speaker whose utterance is rendered. Thus the report of an original statement like 'Tell her she's fired and has to go' can become more direct: 'He said that you're fired so you must leave now!'[57] Such a use of expansive RSA differs in effect from that in the Virgil passage quoted above which apparently presents the song of Iopas for its own sake.

---

[56] The front page of the *Independent* newspaper for 12 Dec. 1994 has this example: 'A senior member of the Saudi royal family has warned that continued campaigning from Britain by extreme Islamic opponents of the regime could call into question the "deep political and economical relationships between the two countries".' Here MID moves into DD.

[57] It might be argued that this sentence suggests MID: with a strong hint that the original utterance reported would be something like this: 'She's fired so she must leave now.' However the ID rendering I have given of this utterance is framed by 'that'. My classification of this sort of thing as RSA rests on the force of the declarative phrase ('he said that') in recording the utterance.

However, it should be noted that that particular instance of RSA in the *Aeneid* is not without its pragmatic aspects either, in both the *story* and the *narrative* of Virgil's epic. It helps provide a context for, and a complement to, Aeneas' lengthy narrative. The audience—the fictional audience of Dido's court in the *story*—are also prepared to hear a celebrated guest recount his experiences. For the audience of the epic *narrative* the rendering of Iopas' poem in a few verses RSA by Virgil will turn out to be a prelude to the major account given by Aeneas.

Theorists of narrative have acknowledged and given various names to the two sub-modes of MID and RSA. However those sub-modes have not prompted anything like as much scholarly interest as FID. This is partly because of the latter's stylistic and syntactic complexity, but chiefly because people see it as marking both narratival representation and 'literariness'. It could be held that the devices of MID and expansive RSA do this too. Rimmon-Kenan's elaboration of FID as a marker of representation and literariness could certainly, if we were to accept it, apply to those speech modes as well:

Whereas 'mimesis' names a relationship between literature and a certain version of reality, 'literariness' designates the specifically literary (non-referential) aspect of literature . . . And just as FID is often seen to index mimesis, so—at the other pole—it can be grasped as marking literariness. In a relatively weak sense, FID marks literariness simply by figuring more frequently and centrally in literature than in other forms of discourse. It is perhaps because of the difficulty a speaker would experience in trying to perform orally the co-presence of voices characterisitic of FID that the phenomenon seems more congenial to the silent register of writing . . . And although FID is by no means exclusively literary, it is at least characteristic enough of literature or fiction to have a fictional ring even when found in other types of discourse (Bronzwaer 1970, p. 49).[58]

This account has the advantage of being succinct whilst drawing from most major contributions to the subject. Although it is claimed FID figures 'more frequently and centrally in literature than in other forms of discourse', it may be retorted that statistical distribution does not make a case for FID constituting a distinctive literary syntax. Narrative of *all* kinds is bound to make frequent use of certain language forms—aorist tenses for example. But this does

---

[58] Rimmon-Kenan (1983), 115: the citation given is hers.

not make those forms a peculiar feature of literature. Moreover, what standard form of discourse do we use as a control for deciding that something like FID is especially germane to literature?

Bronzwaer, according to Rimmon-Kenan, has established that FID has 'a fictional ring even when found in other types of discourse'. But those other types of discourse in which he finds it turn out to be *non-fictional* rather than *non-literary*.[59] By Bronzwaer's own admission, only one of the passages 'outside fiction' he supplies contains an indubitable example of FID—and that is an excerpt from an essay, by Virginia Woolf on Jane Austen, which is patently *literary* on quite separate criteria. Even Bronzwaer's other passages (an article from *Encounter* and an excerpt from a book called *The Story of Mankind*) are from texts which are to some degree literary on other grounds. Rimmon-Kenan's deceptive slide from 'literature' to 'fiction' in the last sentence of that passage quoted has its origin here.

The apparent unutterability of FID in a living context would seem to make it the exclusive property of literary discourse. Voloshinov finds an example from Dostoevsky's *The Idiot* which makes a strong case for this unutterability:

And why did he [Prince Miškin] avoid going straight up to him and turn away as if he didn't notice anything, although their eyes had met. (Yes, their eyes had met! And they had looked at one another.) Didn't he himself, after all, want not long ago to take him by the arm and go with him *there*? Didn't he himself, after all, want to go to him tomorrow and say that he had been to see her? Didn't he himself, after all, renounce his demon on his way there, in mid-course, when suddenly joy flooded his soul? Or was there indeed something or other in Rogožin, that is in *today's* whole image of the man, in the sum total of his words, gestures, behaviour, looks, that might justify the prince's terrible forebodings and the infuriating insinuations of his demon? Something or other of the sort that makes itself felt but is difficult to analyse and relate, something impossible to pin down with sufficent reasons. But something nevertheless that produces, despite all the difficulty and the impossibility, a perfectly cogent and irresistible impression that unwittingly turns into the most absolute conviction. Conviction that what? (Oh, how the prince was tormented by the monstrosity, the

[59] This is what Bronzwaer (1970), 49 actually says: 'It is obvious that free indirect style is a characteristically *fictional* [my emphasis] technique, and that even those passages in which it is found outside fiction can more or less easily be shown to possess fictional features.'

'baseness' of that conviction, of 'that vile foreboding', and how he reproached himself!)[60]

Voloshinov then argues for the unutterability of this kind of presented discourse:

the very kind of development that quasi-direct discourse [i.e. FID] has undergone is bound up with the transposition of the larger prose genres into a silent register, i.e. for silent reading. Only this 'silencing' of prose could have made possible the multi-levelledness and voice-defying complexity of intonational structures that are so characteristic of modern literature.

In these circumstances, Voloshinov claims, 'acting out' the text is impossible: it would paradoxically require shifts and consistencies in the narratorial voice that could not be articulated. Whether or not Voloshinov is right (I suspect there are corresponding problems for the silent reader), he is making this point only for modern literature, and a specific kind of modern Russian literature at that. The problem of the silent register comes up only at the end of Voloshinov's discusion of FID. He cites some examples of FID which could be read aloud and which do not come from literature at all. More recently Anne Banfield has argued that FID is impossible to find in spoken language, and actually goes on to suggest that it proves that one can have a narrative without a narrator.[61] Genette objects vehemently to Banfield's Chomskian position principally on account of the instances of FID in 'autodiegetic' narrating.[62] Even so, in spite of his caustic attack on Banfield, Genette still sees the literary nature of FID as 'indisputable'.

But I would like to challenge the claim that FID is a marker of literariness or even of written language. It might even be *customary* in spoken discourse. I will reach this demonstration in stages. First, Genette accepts that FID can be found in what he calls 'autodiegetic' narration—narration in which the narrator has a starring role in his or her own narrative. He gives two examples, one from chapter 18 of Dickens's *Great Expectations* :

My dream was out; my wild fantasy was surpassed by sober reality; Miss Havisham was going to make my fortune on a grand scale.[63]

---

[60] Voloshinov (1973), 156.   [61] Banfield (1982).

[62] Genette (1988), 53–4: autodiegetic narration entails not only that a narrator exists, but also that he or she has a specific identity.

[63] Genette (1988), 54.

and the other from Balzac's *La Cousine Bette*:

I had said such things touching to him; that I was jealous by nature and an infidelity would kill me.[64]

Here are three more from Roman literature. (There are in fact numerous examples.[65]) The first is from Virgil's *Aeneid*. Aeneas is relating his response to his father's initial refusal to accompany him in the flight from Troy:[66]

> rursus in arma feror mortemque miserrimus opto.
> nam quod consilium aut quae iam fortuna dabatur?
>
> *(Aeneid* 2. 655–6)

Again I rushed to my arms and chose death in complete despair. What plan or fortune was now available?

If this were a third-person account, the second verse (656) taken alone would read without doubt as FID as it would blend the voices of character and narrator. But here character and narrator are the same person. In this context, in which Aeneas is telling his own story, verse 656 could either be a narratorial comment or a reformulation of the thoughts he had at the time. Secondly, there is an excerpt from Petronius' *Satyricon*. Encolpius the 'autodiegetic narrator' has suggested to his companion Ascyltos that they should escape a dinner party when the other guests are going to bathe. He and Ascyltos stumble into a fish pond as they are trying to leave. The doorman rescues them and they ask him to show them the way out:

> quid faciamus homines miserrimi et novi generis labyrintho inclusi, quibus lavari iam coeperat votum esse?
>
> *(Satyricon* 73. 1)

What are men as unlucky as us to do, trapped in a modern kind of labyrinth, now the idea of washing was starting to appeal?

---

[64] Genette (1988), 54: Balzac (1965), 244.

[65] Ovid's elegies are a rich hunting ground. Consider (e.g.) *Heroides* 10. 11–12: *nullus erat! referoque manus iterumque retempto, | perque torum moveo bracchia— nullus erat!* ('He was not there! I draw back my hands and try a second time, and move my arms over the couch: He was not there!')

[66] Compare Aeneas' comments on the loss of his wife in the account he gives of the fall of Troy to Dido's court in *Aeneid* 2. 738–40: *heu misero coniunx fatone erepta Creusa | substitit, erravitne via seu lapsa resedit, | incertum* . . . (Alas my wife Creusa torn from me by the cruelty of fate: it being uncertain whether she [has] stopped, lost her way, or sits down exhausted).

This sentence certainly prompts reflection. The use of the present subjunctive in this deliberative question makes it hard to determine whether these words belong to Encolpius as he is narrating or to Encolpius as he was experiencing these events. But then there is a shift of tense to the imperfect *coeperat*. This is curious. For the sentence to be located in the story time of events described we should expect a present tense. The move to the imperfect serves to ground what comes before in the current perception of Encolpius as he narrates. FID seems then to be the best diagnosis.

My third passage comes from Apuleius' *Metamorphoses*. It shows that an example of FID in Latin narrative can involve exclamation as well as a deliberative question or a *heu*: ('alas!'):

dii boni, quae facies rei! quod monstrum! quae fortunarum mearum repentina mutatio! quamquam enim iam in peculio Proserpinae et Orci familia numeratus, subito in contrariam faciem obstupefactus haesi. nec possum novae illius imaginis rationem idoneis verbis expedire.

(Metamorphoses 3. 9)

Great Gods, what an apparition! What a weird thing! What a sudden change in my fortunes! Although I was just now being inventoried among the property of Proserpina and the household of Orcus, suddenly facing a reversal of appearances, I became rooted to the spot dumbfounded. I cannot find the right words to give a rational account of that new vision.

All these examples have the major features of FID: no declarative verb, no necessary indication of whether the discourse presented was thought or spoken. As with FID in 'third-person' or hetero-diegetic narrative, it is not clear whether the discourse is the 'property' of character or narrator. Indeed it is difficult to distinguish the narrating 'I' from the 'I' of the experiencing subject in the story. These passages present an outline of *actual thoughts* experienced at the moment narrated. Even though explanations of this kind of device are theoretically complex, occurences of it in everyday conversation are clearly conceivable. Indeed the shifts of tense that make FID 'free' might well be more characteristic of living speech than of written prose.

Most theorists however, have not acknowledged the presence of FID in first-person forms, in literature or anywhere else. It is thus more important to ask whether FID in third-person forms be found in spoken discourse without possessing fictional or literary features. The examples from Virgil, D. H. Lawrence and Dostoevsky quoted above do not make this seem very likely. People cannot talk about the thoughts running through the heads of others with the confidence of literary narrators who render the thoughts of their characters. If a person did talk in the manner of a literary narrator about someone else's thoughts, we would probably assume that such a person was lying, joking, or mentally unbalanced. These assumptions reveal that it is constraints on our *social behaviour* as speakers, not rules of generative grammar, which stop us from using a syntactic device like FID in third-person forms in day to day speech. To demonstrate this, one only needs to identify everyday speech contexts for the use of FID in third-person forms, where these social constraints do not apply. These social constraints manifestly do not apply when people speak about those who cannot speak for themselves: small children, animals and so on. And in fact, children themselves use FID in this way very early, as documented instances of children constructing the discourse of animals, dolls, etc. can attest.[67] The social constraints which determine linguistic usage are usually derived from power relations and group interests.[68] Nobody would challenge a speaker's authority to 'speak for', or rather attribute spoken or thought discourse to, a 'muted group' by using FID in such a way.[69] On a grander scale, one can easily conceive of a political figure using FID to blend his own discourse with 'reported' spoken or thought discourse attributed to the voter, the members of public, or the nation.[70] In this way FID can be regarded as a means of manipulation. It is a speech mode which, in the realm of lived experience, could be used to present the discourse of those who cannot or will not speak for themselves.[71]

[67] Bretherton (1984) and Romaine (1985) provide examples of discourse in these contexts.

[68] See Chs. 1 and 5 for illustration of this principle.

[69] See Ardener (1989), 73–85, 129–30 for accounts of 'muted groups', and Goldschläger (1982).

[70] Here there might be an interesting analogy between speech presentation and the problems one might find with the notion of *political representation* as a whole; see Nicholls (1989), 26–8 Pitkin (1972) and Rousseau's classic critique of representation in *Du contrat social* 3. 15.

[71] These observations of social contexts for FID might complement the claims, made in Bakhtin (1981) and Voloshinov (1973), that the polyphony offered by FID in the novel is necessarily a 'liberating' form of language. Pasolini (1988) considers the political implications of authors 'reanimating' (*revivere*) characters in interior monologue—'a terrible thing happens: that person is united to the author by the substantive fact of belonging to his ideology'.

FID in narrative discourse can only present a dynamic inter-action between two or more voices if we conceive a narrator as being categorically different from a speaker who uses FID in real life. A speaker in real life is responsible for generating a polyphony all by himself. A fictional narrator can be conceived as being like such a speaker, who produces all the voices and quotations detectable in his discourse. Thus FID can no longer be called a marker of *mimesis* over any other feature of a narrative, any more than it can be called a marker of literariness: it is just another part of a narrator's rhetoric. This could well be why the ancient commentators and theorists see no need to discuss FID: 'Servius' for instance never comments on the many instances in Virgil, whilst focalizations *do* interest him.[72] The conception, which appears to be deeply rooted in ancient culture, of poetic or historical narrative as instantiations of the art of speaking could be taken to indicate that FID was understood as automatically belonging to the narrator.[73] It is an interesting fact, otherwise hard to account for, that FID in Latin poetic narrative is frequently to be found in the vicinity of narratorial apostrophes.

The widely held notion that FID is more suited to the silent register would collapse if we were to accept that *recitation* of long narrative texts was at all prominent in ancient culture.[74] The idea that FID is more suited to the silent register relies partly on a

[72] The important studies of Lazzarini (1984) and (1989) examine Servian poetics and attempt a reconstruction of their theoretical framework. For the tradition of 'Servius', see Murgia (1975), Zetzel (1981), 81–147. D. P. Fowler (1997) now provides a helpful introduction to 'Servius', with useful bibliography.

[73] My examination in Ch. 5 of Macrobius' comments on passages of FID in Virgil's *Aeneid* generally supports this. On the importance of rhetoric and oratory for ancient conceptions of poetic and historical narrative, see e.g. Russell (1967); (1981), 18–69; Woodman (1988).

[74] The extent to which Roman literature was encountered by public recitation rather than by silent reading of books is far from established: the evidence for *recitatio* having been the main means of access to literature is not as decisive as it is often taken to be. However, on occasions in this study, I feel it is important to consider what the implications for speech presentation would have been if recitation had been common practice. The difference between direct and indirect modes of speech presentation would obviously be much clearer if texts were read out loud. Major treatments of *recitatio* and the evidence for it include Quinn (1982), Wiseman (1982*a*; 1982*b*), and Vogt-Spira (1990). See also Jahn (1867), A. Hardie (1983), 74–102, Herington (1985), 41–57, 201–6, Rohde (1914), 326–7. Oliver (1989)—especially the chapter 'Narrative in Performance' 117–28—gives an account of the implications performance of poetry has for narrative form in our own era.

common myth that FID originated with the eighteenth-century novel. This misconception may have inhibited an active search for examples of FID in genres of current spoken discourse which could never be held to be literary. I have been seditious in seeking to show that the most exclusive, hallowed example of literary syntax is not particularly literary at all. And it was claimed at the opening of this section that what goes for FID goes for other speech modes like MID and expansive RSA. The same could surely be done with any other examples of syntax which people have believed to be exclusively or primarily literary. At this point the case for literary syntax in general does not appear to be a very strong one.

3.6 DIRECT SPEECH MODES AND THE POSSIBILITY OF A LITERARY SYNTAX

However there is a feature of syntax which remains to be discussed in greater detail. It can be argued that this feature of syntax might be primarily or even exclusively found in certain sorts of literary discourse. Yet it has been overlooked, because it appears on the surface to be quite unproblematic. I am referring to direct discourse. It was remarked earlier that direct discourse enables a narrative (of any kind) to imitate live utterances. A voice other than the narrator's appears to take over and to confront us directly with the world of the story, even to put us in it. We can feel that we hear the utterance as those present in the story hear it. In a strong sense, live utterances are the *only* things narrative can appear to imitate properly. We feel this because utterances, like verbal forms of narrative, are made of language.

The opinion that direct discourse offers a precise reproduction of a verbal communication, whilst indirect discourse is a form of paraphrase, is prominent and has been widely held for a long time. Researchers in linguistics, stylistics, and especially poetics have thus tended to set up a virtual opposition between direct and indirect discourse.[75] However, the view that direct discourse possesses 'literal fidelity' or 'documentary autonomy' (as Genette puts it)—and the opposition between direct and indirect discourse

---

[75] See esp. Banfield (1973), 19–20, 30; (1982), 23–63, cited in Sternberg (1991), 77. Compare Genette (1980), 172; Leech and Short (1981), 318 f., and Halliday (1985), 228 f. also countered in Sternberg (1991).

which follows from that view—can easily be challenged.[76] Meir Sternberg has spearheaded such a challenge:[77]

To put things in a nutshell, the direct form cannot reproduce where it (or we) would, because a number of original objects and aspects are unreproducible from the context of utterance through the turns of thought to the intonation of speech. Nor would it be reasonable to expect the reproduction for objects that do not, may not, or will not exist, as in modalized direct quotation: prospective ('I will tell him: " . . ."'), imperative ("Tell him: " . . ."'), hypothetical ('If I tell/told/had told him: " . . ."'), etc. Again discourse provides an entire set of anti-reproductive licenses and conventions, such as translational mimesis whereby Midianites (for example) speak pure biblical Hebrew, or interpretative paraphrase within quotes, or even intersemiotic transfer from non-verbal to verbal expression ('His eyes said: "Thanks"'). And life makes its own laws and loopholes: notably the faults of memory. Under such pressures from all quarters there is no way to maintain the bond between direct quotation and literal representation.[78]

Conversely, speech presentation in indirect discourse should not necessarily be regarded as paraphrase. Indirect discourse does not have to be regarded as a kind of interpretation of what we are supposed to posit as the 'content' of the actual utterance which it renders: 'Everyone agrees that indirectness not only can but may paraphrase; the only question is whether empirically it always does and formally must, to the exclusion of exact imagining.'[79] In my view, Sternberg's position is *generally* right. Effectively, it states that all direct discourse we encounter, whether it is embedded in spoken discourses or written texts, can only have the status of what I defined above as FDD.

However, there are two problems with this position. The first problem is a relatively trivial one. On this page I have just quoted Sternberg using direct discourse. When one written text like mine quotes from another written text like Sternberg's, we have quite a

[76] An irony could be discerned in my quotation in English direct discourse of these expressions from Genette. The simple fact that Genette writes in French means that even the phrases 'literal fidelity' and 'documentary autonomy' themselves do not have literal fidelity or documentary autonomy!
[77] Sternberg (1981), (1982a), (1982b) and (1985), 365–440 show various problems with the prevalent notion of 'directness'. Sternberg (1991) discusses the problems of 'directness' and 'indirectness'.
[78] Sternberg (1991), 77–8.
[79] Sternberg (1991), 78.

different set of circumstances from (i) when a speaker quotes another speaker in direct discourse (ii) when a speaker quotes from a written text in direct discourse (iii) when a written text quotes a speaker in direct discourse, and even from (iv) when an established written text quotes from an earlier written text in direct discourse but the writer of the later text (deliberately or accidentally) misquotes his source. Surely, when I quote from Sternberg's chapter here, it must be right to assume that there are more original objects and aspects which can be reproduced and fewer which cannot than there would be if I was attempting to transcribe in direct discourse a spoken utterance which I had heard in conversation.

This problem could be solved by positing a distinction between *quotation* of one written text in another, and direct discourse of the kind we encounter in circumstances (i)–(iv). *Quotation* in this specific sense, unlike direct discourse in general, is subject to correction like a set of printers' proofs: it can be right or wrong. Nonetheless, it cannot be claimed that *all*—or anything near to all— of the original objects and aspects of Sternberg's text can be reproduced in quotation: their registers and hues will change simply as a result of that text being *excerpted* and recontextualized. Even if I had quoted the *whole* of his text this would still be the case.[80]

The second problem with Sternberg's position will lead us to the central pivot of this chapter—the relation between literary syntax and narratival representation. Sternberg's sweeping dismissal of the belief in the literal fidelity of direct discourse is understandable. However his remark that it is 'a scholar's myth, an ivory tower delusion which has no leg to stand on in logic or in culture or in reality' is over-zealous, and actually points to an important oversight. Scholars and inhabitants of ivory towers often deal with literature—and it may be for this reason that an acceptance of the idea of the 'documentary autonomy' of direct discourse is still so

[80] McGann (1991), 205 (discussing the pragmatic significance of publication) illustrates this nicely: 'People tend not to realize that a certain way of reading is privileged when 'Ode on a Grecian Urn' is read in the *Norton Anthology of English Literature*, and that it is a way of reading which differs sharply from what is privileged in *Palgrave's Golden Treasury* or in the *Oxford Book of Romantic Verse*; and when the poem is (or was) read in other kinds of formats—for example in its first printing in the *Annals of the Fine Arts*—an entirely different field of reading is once again deployed.' *Mutatis mutandis* the same would apply to, say, Mynors's text of the *Aeneid* as it might appear in various commentaries.

widely held. In literary narrative, it might be felt, there is a clear boundary between direct discourse and all other speech modes (including even FDD). The use of direct discourse *constitutes* an utterance—it does not copy, inadequately render, or refer to an inaccessible, original utterance, as forms of indirect discourse and even free direct discourse do. In other words direct discourse gives us on the level of *narrative* or *récit* exactly what was said in the world of the *story* or *histoire*.

Unless a narrator uses a device like 'With words to that effect' which would mark FDD, readers usually see no need to question the quality or quantity of a quoted utterance. This could suggest that direct discourse is embedded in the fabric of literary texts quite differently from the way in which it is embedded in the fabric of non-literary discourse. To consider the way in which a direct quotation is embedded in the discourse surrounding it, is indubitably to consider a question of syntax. If the type of embedding can be shown to be different in literary texts, then we might have such a thing as literary syntax. That presents a very respectable case for its existence, resting on the presupposition that literary texts are to be treated in a specific way, not least that we often suspend disbelief and entertain the illusion that literature 'represents'.

There is a widely held conviction that direct discourse in literature is the real business, the point when narrative really does 'show' rather than 'tell'. This explains why the firm distinction made in, or read into, Plato's *Republic* between direct and indirect discourse has been so widely adopted. Or that might be putting the cart before the horse: that discussion in the third book of the *Republic* has had a huge influence on the development of poetics, traditional and modern, and could account for the special status of direct discourse as the hardcore essence of poetic *mimesis* (which Aristotle commends and Socrates deprecates). It might be worth looking at the relevant passage again. The crucial bit is at 393a:

You know that as far as the lines:
> And he begged all the Achaeans
> and especially the two Atreidae, the generals of the host,

the poet speaks in his own person and does not try to turn our attention in another direction by pretending that someone else is speaking. But from this point he speaks as though he were Chryses himself and tries to make us think that it is not Homer talking, but the old priest. And he does practically all the rest of the narrative in this way, both the tale of Troy and the episodes in Ithaca and the whole *Odyssey* . . . So in this sort of thing, Homer and other poets are conveying their narrative by way of *mimesis*.

It is well established that this use of the word *mimesis* is to be distinguished from its use elsewhere in the *Republic*, which covers visual artistic as well as poetic imitation in general. Nonetheless, I have a suspicion that the notion of visual imitation has contaminated the way the word is regarded here. People have long been tempted to see direct discourse in narrative relating to the utterance in the story as being rather like the uncomplicated relation Socrates conceives between a visual simulacrum and its object.[81] This pictorialism is nicely exposed by Rubio in the way he begins his chapter on speech presentation in Latin and Castilian Spanish: 'The concept of direct discourse is so *transparent* that it has never presented any problems of definition.'[82] He then goes straight on to deal with the varieties of indirect discourse. One could of course elaborate about how pervasive visualist accounts of language in general have been in the Western tradition, stretching from Plato's own discussion in the *Cratylus* where Socrates asserts that words, like images, have a connection of resemblance with their objects, to the picture theory of meaning in Wittgenstein's *Tractatus*.[83] Consideration of such visualist accounts would give deeper significance to the (programmatic?) opening of *Alice in Wonderland*—the second epigraph to this chapter. Speeches and 'pictures' or descriptions have been paralled in all sorts of intricate ways: as well as being regarded as the crowning jewels of narrative, each (distinctly or conjointly) has been regarded as detachable, if not undesirable.[84] No wonder then, that visualism has affected, or rather determined conceptions of what direct discourse is, and how it represents.

---

[81] Consider e.g. Livy 45. 25. 3: *non inseram simulacrum viri copiosi, quae dixerit referendo* ('I will not include here a *simulacrum* of this eloquent man by reporting what he said'). Brock (1995), 220 n. 2 remarks 'in other cases where he uses *simulacrum*, it refers either to statues, or to paintings and models (particularly those carried in triumphs) or to mock battles'. Brock's subsequent comment—that *simulacrum* must denote a paraphrase is more open to question. I suspect that Livy would have considered all direct or indirect discourse as a form of paraphrase.

[82] Rubio (1982), 257. The emphasis is mine.

[83] Wittgenstein (1961); Plato *Cratylus* 431–2. Mitchell (1986) and Hyman (1989) provide enlightening discussions. See also my remarks in the Conclusions and Envoi.

[84] For views on the role of description in ancient theory of discourse, see James and Webb (1991), Laird (1993*b*), Laird (1996), and Roberts (1989), 66–182; Genette (1982*a*), 133–7 is a modern theoretical account.

A visualist theory of direct discourse however is not what Plato's (perhaps unfortunate) use of the word *mimesis* in *Republic* 393 is driving at. A visualist theory suggests either that direct discourse is an object of apprehension (even Crystal says it refers to the 'use of actual utterance') or that it is an image of an utterance which obtains in a story world. But Plato's word *mimesis* designates an *activity* of imitating, which amounts to deception—it does not designate the end result, a work of imitation. Socrates is not saying that Chryses and his words were out there somewhere and that Homer is reproducing them. His whole point is that Homer is making it all up. It is therefore important to remember to translate ὥσπερ αὐτὸς ὢν ὁ Χρύσης λέγει carefully: not 'He speaks as Chryses' (which might look like an acceptable thing to do), but 'He speaks *as though* he were Chryses himself' (which is not an acceptable thing to do). This might be made more clear if we appreciate that Socrates conceives texts which present utterances as efficacious utterances themselves. He sees all texts—whether historical, literary or fictional—as being subject not only to refutation on veridical grounds, but as being subject to censorship if they say harmful things. Some modern theorists have argued in various ways for texts which have been conventionally designated literary to be treated as affective discourse.[85]

Is there such a thing as literary syntax? To answer this briefly, I will resort to another visual model, but this time one which is meant to be helpful: the picture of the two facial profiles, symmetrically opposite, which can also be a picture of a candlestick. There are two incompatible interpretations: if you ascribe aesthetic value to certain texts, then you can accept the existence of literary syntax. (A notion of art as illusion and the necessary suspension of disbelief may well be bound up with this persuasion.) If, on the other hand, you think we can only confidently discuss the characteristics which texts demonstrably possess as affective discourses, you have little need to accept the existence of literary syntax. Literary syntax is in the eye of the beholder, and the capacity to behold it is pragmatically—or ideologically—determined.

---

[85] Leith and Myerson (1989), R. Fowler (1981).

4

Fictions of Authority:
Discourse and Epistemology in
Historical Narrative

I do not know what meaning classical philology would have for
our age if not to have an untimely effect within it, that is, to act
against the age and so have an effect on the age to the
advantage, it is to be hoped, of a coming age.

(Friedrich Nietzsche, *On the Advantage and Disadvantage
of History for Life*)

The Formalists . . . believe that 'In the beginning was the
Word'. But we believe that in the beginning was the deed. The
word followed, as its phonetic shadow.

(Leon Trotsky, *The Formalist School of Poetry and Marxism*)

Divisions between historical narrative—along with other forms of
factual writing—and fictional narrative have never been hard and
fast. Greek and Roman historiography, for example, corresponds to
modern conceptions of *literary* writing. Ancient historians were
steeped in the principles of rhetoric, and applied techniques of
rhetorical invention to recount what could or might have happened.[1]
The tradition of sceptical historiography, which emerged in the
early part of the twentieth century, is in some ways comparable.
Benedetto Croce and R. G. Collingwood, in particular, presented
history writing as a process of selection and interpretation by a
historian who is entirely responsible for investing facts with their

---

[1] For ancient discussions see e.g. Polybius 1. 14. 1–9; 2. 56. 1–16; 8. 8. 3–11. 8;
12. 2. 1.–28. 10; 16. 14. 1–20. 9; 29. 12. 1–12; Cicero, *Ad Familares* 5. 12 and *De
Oratore* 2. 51–64; Dionysius, *Ad Pompeium* and *Thucydides*; Plutarch, *De Herodoti
Malignitate*; Lucian, *Quomodo Historia Conscribenda est*. Some further discussions
will be considered in this chapter. Important studies of the theory of ancient
historiography include Wiseman (1979), Fornara (1983), Woodman (1988), Moles
(1993), Hornblower and Spawforth (1994) and Marincola (1997).

significance.[2] 'Where there is no narrative, there is no history' wrote Croce, who also believed accounts of the past should serve under-standing of the present.[3] In the last three decades, philosophers and theorists of narrative and culture have been questioning distinctions between factual and fictional writing even more radically.

Some practising historians and ethnographers have welcomed the virtual evaporation of disciplinary boundaries. James Clifford, for instance, sought to herald a notion of ethnography as creative writing:

> To call ethnographies fictions may raise empiricist hackles. But the word as commonly used in recent textual theory has lost its connotation of falsehood, of something merely opposed to truth. It suggests the partiality of cultural and historical truths, the ways they are systematic and exclusive. Ethnographic writings can properly be called fictions in the sense of 'something made or fashioned', the principal burden of the word's Latin root *fingere*. But it is important to preserve the meaning not merely of making, but also of making up, of inventing things not actually real.[4]

Hayden White characterized a similar change in the perception of historical writing—a change in which he himself had a great part to play. He maintained that fictional and historical discourses have more in common if we look at the way they are put together formally (as sign systems) instead of looking at whatever realities are supposed to lie behind them.[5] Ideas of 'what happened' are

---

[2] See Croce (1951) and Collingwood (1946). Momigliano (1977), 345–64 is a useful assessment of Croce's contribution to historiography. Carr (1964) gives an accessible account of this sceptical tradition.

[3] Croce (1893), 38. This position is usefully discussed in H. White (1987), 218.

[4] Clifford (1986), 6.

[5] The preface to H. White (1987), p. x gives a more euphuistic account of his position: 'It was possible to believe that whereas writers of fictions invented everything in their narratives—characters, events, plots, motifs, themes, atmo-sphere, and so on—historians invented nothing but certain rhetorical flourishes or poetic effects to the end of gaining their readers' attention and sustaining their interest in the true story they had to tell. Recent theories of discourse, however, dissolve the distinction between realistic and fictional discourses based on the presumption of ontological differences between their respective referents, real and imaginary, in favor of stressing their common aspect as semiological apparatuses that produce meanings by the systematic substitution of signifieds (conceptual contents) for the extra-discursive entities that serve as their referents. In these semiological theories of discourse, narrative is revealed to be a particularly effective system of discursive meaning production by which individuals can be taught to live a distinctively "imaginary relation to their real conditions of existence," that is to say, an unreal but meaningful relation to the social formations in which they are indentured to live out their lives and realize their destinies as social subjects.'

renamed 'referents' or 'extra-discursive entities' and swept under the carpet as an incidental feature of discourse as 'semiological apparatus'.[6] We are thus left free to contemplate the way that narratives work on us, as they enforce upon us an imaginary conception of who we are, where we are, and how we got there. Academics like White and Clifford have magnified, as the object of their attention, the writer as beholder and diminished whatever it was, in history or ethnography, that was traditionally beheld. In 1986, White offered this account of historical interpretation:

> Historical interpretations . . . are not properly assessed by the criteria of truth and falsity which are honoured in the physical sciences. They are to be expressed in terms of their adequacy or inadequacy, with respect to their concomitance with the scholarly practices and standards prevailing among the community of professional historians. Interpretations which satisfy these standards may for practical purposes be regarded as true in a correspondence sense. This links historical truth to the conventions, rules and beliefs prevailing in a given society at a given time and place . . . rather than to some universal standard of veracity.

Such an account is persuasive. Examples to illustrate the ideological nature of history writing are legion. An account of historical truth which links it to 'conventions, rules and beliefs prevailing in a given society at a given time and place' is familiar: 'Grote's *History of Greece* has quite as much to tell us today about the thoughts of the English philosophical radicals of the 1840s as about Athenian democracy of the fifth century B.C.' wrote E. H. Carr in 1964.[7] A historian's interpretation itself could be scrutinized as a kind of ethnography.[8] However, that important realization does *not* require acquiescence to the prevalent academic order. Although White infelicitously gives the 'community' of professional scholars a sinister, singular form, a measure of pluralism within the academy is at least conceivable.[9] Besides there are many readers and writers

---

[6] See also Barthes (1986).

[7] Carr (1964), 37 quoted in R. Fowler (1981), 108.

[8] Not ethnography of the peoples and periods the historian discusses, but ethnography of the people and period to which the historian belongs. Ethnography is the usual name for a discourse which offers up for scrutiny the conventions and beliefs prevailing in a given society at a given time and place. Features of genuine ethnographic interest about a culture (or at least a section of it) can be inscribed in its history writing.

[9] Note the rhetorical force of words like 'scholarly', 'prevailing standards', 'professional historians', and 'community' as they accumulate to reassure us. We

of history who would be deeply suspicious of any model in which scholarly professionalism was the sole guarantee of intellectual validity.[10]

These concerns are as much ethical as they are epistemological. There are practical drawbacks in grounding the study of history on historians, or, for that matter, the study of ethnography on the ethnographer. Faced with the unattractive implications of this circularity, one may feel sympathy for Trotsky's brute assertion of the ontological priority of 'the deed' over the discourse which presents it, for the political motives of E. P. Thompson's defence of historiography as an empirical undertaking, or even for Momigliano's repeated insistence on 'the research of truth as the main task of the historian'.[11] However, there is little point in siding with those who claim to be privy to an objective, universal standard of veracity. This could involve, for instance, appeals to philosophical realism which might distinguish, on ontological grounds, the referents of a narrative conventionally designated fictional from those of a narrative that is conventionally designated factual.[12] However, philosophical realists themselves are only another 'community'. And distinguishing fact from fiction on this kind of basis is anyway unlikely to impress those who think that 'fact only has a linguistic existence'.[13]

As I have indicated, shoving a wedge between factual narrative and fictional narrative is not as easy as we might like it to be. One cannot simply argue that historical and ethnographic discourses are subject to refutation and that fictional or imaginative discourses are not. The difference between a narrative designated 'factual' and a

all like to think of our output as 'scholarly'. What historian would not consider himself or herself 'professional'? 'Community' is a rather benign word—more so than even 'institution' or 'society'—for the market-oriented scenario of Anglo-American higher education. The abbreviation of H. White (1986), 109 given above is from Woodman (1988), 200.

[10] The brief critique of pragmatism and 'interpretative communities' in Fish (1980) made in Eagleton (1983), 85–90 is well meant but misses the point: the models of Fish and White could, presumably, allow for readings from outside the academy—even if neither Fish nor White have remembered to state this. See n. 22 below for examples of interpretative communities 'fixing' the status of texts in the world at large.

[11] See Trotsky (1960), E. P. Thompson (1978), Momigliano (1984)—from which, at 49, I quote here—and Momigliano (1977), 365–74.

[12] These debates really go back to Kant's *Critique of Pure Reason*. For accounts of realism, see Putnam (1981; 1983). Goodman (1978) provides a defence of anti-realism.

[13] Barthes (1986) quoted as an epigraph to H. White (1987).

narrative designated 'fictional' is not innate, but culturally determined. We have to accept that a narrative can be read in a variety of
ways. This is why attempts to distinguish between fictional and
factual writing on a purely narratological basis will only have a
limited success. Any strategy one might want to identify as a
characteristic of historiography can be reproduced in fictional
narrative.[14]

The critique of narratology I offered in Chapter 2 was designed
to show that narratives, like other discourses, cannot properly be
understood in isolation from their speakers, addressees, and situations of performance. Speculation about the nature or function of
historical texts will accomplish little, if such factors—which bear on
texts in general—are disregarded. Historical texts, no less than any
other texts so far considered in this study, function in part as
affective discourses. Most debates about historiographical theory
have tended to concentrate either on referential aspects of narratives or on their rhetorical features.

The discussion to follow will deal with what falls between those
areas of concern. The approach here will be generally pragmatic.[15]
We have already seen that the idea of 'content' is at least partly
constituted by performance, by the relation—which can be conceived ideologically—between a text and its audience, or between a
discourse and its addressees. This will be shown for historical texts
principally by examination of the discourse presented within them:
speech presentation will be used as a kind of heuristic tool to
establish something about the nature of historical representation.[16]

---

[14] See 'Récit factuel, récit fictionnel' in Genette (1991) and Hornblower (1994).
Compare my remarks in Laird (1993a), 152–3, 174. However, contrast Riffaterre
(1990), 21: 'narrative verisimilitude tends to flaunt rather than mask its fictitious
nature'. Ricoeur (1988) is a study of time in narrative with important implications
for the theory of historical writing.

[15] On pragmatics and interpretation, see in Engler (1991), and the other essays in
Sell (1991).

[16] The status of historiography itself as discourse cannot be treated in full here.
Consider these comments from R. Fowler (1981), 109: 'The thesis of the relativity
of historical judgment might be illuminated by linguistics. In fact, *it is strictly
speaking a linguistic theory*. When Carr talks about the relation between "facts" and
"interpretation" (e.g., p. 29), arguing that facts become history only through the
mediation of interpretation, it is natural to remark that, if history is a kind of text or
discourse, the theory can be expressed in text-grammatical terms: propositions
(facts) cannot be communicated without modality (interpretation). As there is no
sentence which does not imply a speaker taking a certain stance, so there is no text
in which the content has not been filtered by an author who has selected and

A treatment of this brevity makes no pretence of dispelling all the aporias which beset historiographical theory, but the conclusions to be drawn from the study of specific texts should have wider implications.

4.1 THE RHETORIC OF SPEECH PRESENTATION

The rhetoricians' notion of *inventio*—recounting what could or might have happened—naturally applies to the presentation of speech in ancient historiography.[17] Indeed ancient notions of historiography as *inventio* could well have derived from the realization that speeches in historians are the product of rhetorical invention.[18] The adoption of an improved model of explanation for the behaviour of reported discourse in historical texts may enhance our understanding of the nature of ancient historiography. It is widely agreed that ancient historians enjoyed license, if not complete creative freedom in reporting speeches.

The only two orations in direct discourse in Tacitus' *Agricola* offer a convenient example of inventive speech presentation. Before the battle of Mons Graupius, the leader of each opposing army makes a speech of encouragement to his troops. These speeches are presented towards the climax of Tacitus' narrative, and form an obvious diptych. First, Calgacus, one of the British leaders, addresses his men in chapters 30–2. Then Agricola speaks to the Roman soldiers in chapters 33–4. Agricola's address is notably shorter than Calgacus'. That relative brevity has been seen as a significant indication of dignified Roman restraint.[19] But there are more specific ways in which this pairing of speeches is used to distinguish the characteristics of Romans and their enemies. This

expressed the propositions and so set himself in a certain belief posture towards them.' The apparently Derridean tenor of Fowler's discussion here has important implications for historiographical theory.

[17] For the term *inventio*, see Lausberg (1973), i. 235–67. Chausserie-Laprée (1969) is concerned with narrative techniques (including speech presentation) in Roman historiography; for Livy, see Bornecque (1933), Burck (1964) and Kohl (1872); for Tacitus, see R. Martin (1981), 214–35 and Walker (1952); for Quintus Curtius, see Helmreich (1927).

[18] See section 4.6 on Thucydides. Fornara (1983), 91–141 treats the theoretical foundations of historiography and the role of speeches (142–68). Woodman (1988), 87–94 (and *passim*) considers *inventio* in ancient historiography. Veyne (1984) is also important.

[19] Martin (1981), 44.

is how the reaction of the Britons to Calgacus' exhortation is described:

> excepere orationem alacres, ut barbaris moris, fremitu cantuque et clamoribus dissonis.
>
> (Tacitus, *Agricola* 33. 1)

They received the speech excitedly, as is the barbarian fashion—with singing, with uproar, and with cacophonous shouts.

And this is the response of the Romans to Agricola's words:

> et adloquente adhuc Agricola militum ardor eminebat, et finem orationis ingens alacritas consecuta est, statimque ad arma discursum.
>
> (*Agricola* 35. 1)

And whilst Agricola was still making his address, the enthusiasm of the soldiers was evident, and great excitement followed the end of the speech: immediately there was a rush to arms.

The verbal echo of *excepere orationem alacres* ('They received the speech excitedly') in *finem orationis ingens alacritas consecuta* ('great excitement followed the end of the speech') invites this comparison; but the comparison in fact reveals a mild contrast in the way the behaviour of each side is described. We are explicitly told that the Britons are barbarically obstreperous. But we are not told the same about the Romans. If they did exhibit great excitement and rushed to arms, there could well have been some concomitant hubbub; but Tacitus is anxious to highlight the rowdiness of the barbarians. The famous simile which opens the third book of the *Iliad* offers a similar kind of suggestive contrast:

> Now when they were marshalled, each side with their captains, the Trojans came on with clamour and with a cry like birds, as when the clamour of cranes goes up to heaven when they flee from wintry storms and endless rain, and with clamour fly toward the streams of Ocean, bearing slaughter and death to Pigmy men, and in the early dawn they offer evil battle. But the Achaeans came on in silence, breathing fury, resolved at heart to protect each other.
>
> (*Iliad* 3. 1–9)

The introductions to the speeches of Agricola and Calgacus in Tacitus' narrative, also differ in a subtle but significant way. The narrator first heralds Calgacus' speech like this:

Calgacus apud contractam multitudinem proelium poscentem in hunc
modum locutus fertur . . .

(Agricola 29. 4)

Before the assembled multitude demanding battle Calgacus is reported to
have spoken in this way . . .

The immediate lead-in to Agricola's speech is this:

Agricola quamquam laetum et vix munimentis coercitum militem accen-
dendum adhuc ratus, ita disseruit . . .

(Agricola 33. 1)

Agricola still thinking that his soldiery should be incited, even though they
were content and scarcely to be confined within the fortifications, delivered
these words . . .

A couple of formal features contribute to a sense of greater
authenticity being attached to what was said by Agricola as a
character than to what was said by Calgacus. One of these formal
features is the rendering of Agricola's *thoughts* before his speech
which helps us to understand his purpose in speaking these words.
The other effective formal feature is the use of *locutus fertur* ('he is
reported to have spoken') to introduce the reporting of Calgacus'
oration. No such expression introduces Agricola's words. Given
that these are the only two passages of direct discourse in the whole
of this text, and given that they are obviously set in parallel, this
distinction may be significant. To demonstrate this it will be
necessary to review the general function of *locutus fertur* type
expressions in Roman historiography.

An expression like *locutus fertur* might at first seem to have one
simple function—namely to indicate that our narrator is reporting a
speech not accurately, but from hearsay. That generally accepted
opinion can be challenged however. In Tacitus, *locutus fertur* is
only used for this apparent purpose in two other passages. On both
those occasions it also accompanies a verb of speaking and a
subsequent passage of direct discourse. In the first passage, exactly
the same sequence of words obtains as we find in the *Agricola* (*in
hunc modum locutus fertur*). This is in *Histories* 1. 15: the expression
introduces a speech from Galba to Piso. The second passage—
Annals 2. 40—precedes a short but significant piece of direct
discourse from Clemens to Tiberius. On the only two occasions
in which *fertur* ('he is reported') is found in Sallust, it is interesting

to note that it is in conjunction with *dixisse*. Instances in Livy of *fertur* in the sense of 'it is reported' are far more numerous and varied in context. In the later books of Livy, they occur in connection with the reporting of discourse as they do in Sallust and Tacitus. However, in books 1–4 of *Ab Urbe Condita*, the expression (along with *dicitur*, *traditur*, etc.) is used to enclose reporting of *events* in Livy's story: to indicate that those events are of doubtful probability because of their legendary nature.[20] If the same linguistic structure is used by Livy in later books in connection with the reporting of speech, the implication is that the reported words, whether presented in direct or indirect discourse, are of similarly doubtful reliability—either in their content or provenance. That implication would also seem to hold for the instances of *fertur* in Sallust and Tacitus.

However, there are literally countless examples of reported words of characters in Roman historiography which are obviously of doubtful authenticity and provenance, and which are *not* embedded in a *fertur* type of construction. For an obvious set of examples, one can point to the use of direct discourse without any such qualification in 'bedroom scenes' (like the account of the rape of Lucretia in Livy 1. 58 or Tacitus, *Annals* 14. 8—both quoted later) where no witnesses or reporters could have been present. Moreover the appearance of such formulae in Latin poetry has often been taken to imply that there *is* documentary evidence for a reported speech.[21] The use of an expression like *fertur locutus* to embed a reported utterance tells us almost nothing. The presence or absence of such an expression in connection with presentations of speech in historiography is really no criterion at all for the faithfulness of the rendering to anything that might have been originally uttered. It

---

[20] See Steele (1904).

[21] Cf. Thomas (1988) on Virgil, *Georgic* 4. 318: '*ut fama* a virtual footnote suggesting a prior version: . . . In fact [*sic*!] the story is almost certainly V's own invention, but the phrase by implying a tradition creates credibility.' Thomas refers to the discussion in Norden (1970) of such devices in his note to *Aeneid* 6. 14. Norden categorizes these types of phrase for Latin literature, along with their Greek roots, according to their varying degrees of '*diffidentia*'. However the function in a narrative for all these forms seems to me to be basically equivalent. See also Stinton (1976), although this article does not really discuss the implication of such expressions for questions of distancing, narrative voice etc. Horsfall (1990) examines these 'footnotes'—typical of epyllion narrative—in the *Aeneid* and the *Georgics*.

has everything to do with a historical narrator's rhetoric and virtually nothing to do with the truth of the case.

Even so, the *absence* of such an expression tells us even less. At least when an expression like *fertur locutus* precedes a speech, it induces in the reader or audience of a historical text an insecurity about that speech, a sense of its provisionality, relative to other speeches in the text which are not 'marked' in this manner. Though the sensation of that particular insecurity about certain speeches is palpable to modern readers of Roman historiography, it is really a fictional effect. That sensation is rather analogous to the experience of hearing a lie told by a character in a story which is itself untrue. No modern reader of Virgil's account of the fall of Troy believes the story is true. But every reader of that account acknowledges that Sinon is lying to the Trojans—whilst recognizing that on a pragmatic level the whole story of the *Aeneid* is a 'lie' insofar as it is a fiction.[22]

Modern readers of Roman historiography (who generally hold that speeches are invented) should therefore also accept that the ascription of dubious authenticity to some speeches by a historical narrator, though that authenticity obtains within the internal logic of the story, is actually an illusion.[23] Explicit reassurance can be offered to any who feel nervous about this simple principle. Comprehension of this principle is perfectly compatible with the view (i) that Roman history is not fiction and with the view (ii) that discourse reported in Roman historiography can be based on utterances which were actually issued in the real world of time and action (though speculations about those utterances tend to be perfectly useless).

The application of these observations to the diptych of orations in the *Agricola* ought now to be obvious. Differentiation between

[22] The essays in Gill and Wiseman (1993) consider various aspects of the relationship between lying and fictionality in antiquity and in contemporary culture. See also Feeney (1991), 225–32. Today's distinctions between 'lying' and 'fiction' clearly depend on communities 'fixing' interpretation: the scandal surrounding Asa Carter's *The Story of Little Tree*. The book was repackaged as 'fiction' in 1993, after it was discovered that this 'true story' of a Cherokee had in fact been written by a segregationist Klansman. See also Pratt (1986) on the controversy surrounding Donner (1982)—a partly plagiarized account of life among the Yanoama Indians.

[23] Cf. Morgan (1993), 187 on Polybius 2. 56. 11–12: 'it was within historiography itself that the contract of fictional complicity was first extended to narrative prose . . .'

them is in part achieved by a subtle narratorial assertion that Agricola's oration possesses a greater ontological stature than Calgacus'. That claim is implicit in the different ways the speeches are introduced: the phrase *locutus fertur* is perhaps too common in Livy and too rare in Tacitus to be insignificant or impotent in this context. The greater salience of Agricola's speech compared to Calgacus' then, like its brevity, like its internal form and structure, and like the characterized response of its hearers, is not a matter of historical fact. It is the result of rhetoric in historical narrative.

4.2 THE SIGNIFICANCE OF *IPSA VERBA*

Nonetheless, on certain occasions Roman historical narrators do seem to insist on the authentic status of words they report in direct discourse. This is signalled in various ways—sometimes by an appeal to the notion of *ipsa verba*. This expression—which is still current—is generally taken to mean the 'very words' of a speaker. Unfortunately, the idea of a speaker's 'very words' is not as simple as it may seem. A theoretical example can most usefully illustrate this. Consider the following reports of what was said by a certain Smith:

1. Smith liked it
2. Smith expressed pleasure at it
3. Smith said that he liked it
4. Smith said that it was good
5. Smith said 'It is good'
6. Smith said 'Bonum est'
7. Smith said 'bɔnəm 'est

If Smith actually made an exclamation in Latin, (1), (2), (3), and (4) present his utterance in various forms of ID and RSA and (5) would present it in FDD. (6) and (7) are both direct discourse renderings which are closer to the original exclamation: (7) differs from (6) only in using the International Phonetic Alphabet (IPA) transcription for the Latin expression. But even the IPA transcription does not convey the whole phonetic quality of Smith's enunciation: intonation, accent, pitch, and volume are all left out. At the same time, (7) conveys more than the sonic aspects of Smith's utterance: the function of words as units of sense is presupposed. This is shown by the fact that two words are physically discernible in the transcription because they are bounded by space: ʹbɔnəm and ʹest. It has long been acknowledged that it is far more difficult to identify *words* as units of sense in stretches of actual speech than in stretches of writing. There is frequent confusion between words as units of sound and words as units of sense. The fact that two quite different dimensions are in play makes discussion of a speaker's 'very words' problematic from the outset: speakers do not, strictly, speak in words.

This caveat should be borne in mind as we attempt one exemplary exploration of some specific appeals to the speaker's *ipsa verba*: in Tacitus, *Annals* 15.[24] This text offers three renditions of things said, two by Seneca and one by Subrius Flavus prior to their deaths. The first rendition is from the beginning of the account of Seneca's death:

ille interritus poscit testamenti tabulas; ac denegante centurione conversus ad amicos, quando meritis eorum referre gratiam prohiberetur, quod unum iam et tamen pulcherrimum habeat, imaginem vitae suae relinquere testatur, cuius si memores essent, bonarum artium famam fructum constantis amicitiae laturos. simul lacrimas eorum modo sermone, modo intentior in modum coercentis ad firmitudinem revocat, rogitans ubi praecepta sapientiae, ubi tot per annos meditata ratio adversum imminentia? cui enim ignaram fuisse saevitiam Neronis? neque aliud superesse post matrem fratremque interfectos quam ut educatoris praeceptorisque necem adiceret. *Vbi haec atque talia velut in commune* disseruit, complectitur uxorem . . .

(*Annals* 15. 62–63. 1)

Seneca, unafraid, demanded the tablets containing his will. But when the centurion refused, he turned to his friends, and adjured that since he was forbidden to show the gratitude he owed them, he had only one thing to leave them—in fact it was the finest thing: the model of his life. If they were mindful of this, they would possess a name for virtuous accomplishments as the reward for their constant friendship. He checked their tears with conversation at some moments—at others he was more intent on forcing them into a state of control. He kept on asking where the teachings of his philosophy had gone, and where their sense of reason had got to, which had been developed over so many years in view of impending evils. To whom

---

[24] There are numerous cases of Roman historians appealing to *ipsa verba*: the passage from *Annals* 15 was chosen simply because of the convenient density of such appeals in a reasonably short stretch of writing. It should become clear that, *mutatis mutandis*, the same conclusions could be drawn—though perhaps less transparently—from examinations of usage of *ipsa verba* in other Latin authors, as well as elsewhere in Tacitus.

had the cruelty of Nero not been known? Nothing else remained after the killing of his mother and brother apart from adding the murder of his guardian and teacher. When he had pronounced *this and words of this sort as if to everyone*, he embraced his wife . . .

The second rendition is at the end of the same account of Seneca's death:

et novissimo quoque momento suppeditante eloquentia advocatis scriptoribus pleraque tradidit, quae *in vulgus edita eius verbis* invertere supersedeo.

(*Annals* 15. 63. 3)

And [Seneca's] eloquence was on hand even at this very last moment: secretaries were called and he dictated a great deal of material to them, which, as it has been made *publicly available in his own words*, I think is needless to paraphrase.

The third rendition is that of Subrius Flavus' words to Nero, which are given after he admitted his role in the conspiracy against the emperor:

interrogatusque a Nerone quibus causis ad oblivionem sacramenti processisset, 'oderam te' inquit, 'nec quisquam tibi fidelior militum fuit, dum amari meruisti. odisse coepi, postquam parricida matris et uxoris, auriga et histrio et incendiarius extitisti.' *ipsa rettuli verba, quia non, ut Senecae, vulgata erant*, nec minus nosci decebat militaris viri sensus incomptos et validos.

(*Annals* 15. 67. 2)

And asked by Nero for what reasons he had been inclined to forget his military oath, he said 'I hated you—though none of your soldiers was more loyal to you than I, as long as you were worthy of adoration. I began to hate you after your parricide of your mother and wife and after you became actor, charioteer and arsonist.' I have rendered *his very words because, unlike Seneca's, they were not made public* though it was no less proper for the basic yet valid sentiments of a military man to be known.

These three passages, viewed in conjunction, might throw some light on what is meant, in this context, by a speaker's '*ipsa verba*'.

The diction of the narratorial comment on the rendering of Subrius Flavus' declaration picks up an earlier narratorial comment on the rendering (or lack of it) of Seneca's dictation to the *scriptores* at the end of 63. 1. Apparently, Tacitus claims he is providing Subrius Flavus' *ipsa verba* partly because they were not disseminated like Seneca's. Are we to surmise then—assuming the contrast is with the *pleraque* dictated in 15. 63—that Tacitus would actually have quoted the *ipsa verba* of the material transcribed by Seneca's secretaries if it had not been made publically available? It is hard to imagine the tempo of this narrative slowing down to accommodate a verbatim reproduction of Seneca's last ever treatise. But when the issue of that reproduction was first raised at 15. 63. 3, we were told that it was a paraphrase or adaptation (*invertere*) of Seneca's words that was being bypassed. If the rendering of Subrius Flavus' words is being contrasted with this instance of presenting discourse, it would seem that the expression *ipsa verba* denotes *the verbal content of the original utterance.*

There is of course another way of understanding the stated contrast between the reporting of Subrius Flavus' words and those of Seneca—and consequently another way of understanding what Tacitus means by *ipsa verba* in 15. 67. That is to see the contrast in 67 being made with Seneca's earlier remarks in 15. 62 as well as to those in 15. 63. The expresion *in commune* has after all been taken to mean that Seneca was addressing a broader audience than those present.[25]

To claim that the narrator contrasts the reporting of the soldier's words with this earlier passage holds up almost as well. Both characters condemn Nero's behaviour and both mention the matricide—but the reminder that Subrius Flavus is not a philosopher and the comment that sentiments are crude or basic (*incomptos*) specifically offer an inverted reflection of the reasoning and polished rhetoric in Seneca's address to his friends. The elegance of Seneca's piece which shines though the indirect discourse in which it is transmitted certainly casts into relief the direct quotation of Subrius Flavus' outburst: an exclamation followed by tumbling polysyndeton. If, then, the comparison with 15. 62 were to be a basis for the advertised contrast in 15. 67, another conception of *ipsa verba* could emerge—as *direct discourse rather than indirect discourse*, employed for the purpose of characterization.

Whilst the contrast between 15. 63 and 15. 67 is the principal one, a second pattern of contrast between 15. 62 and 15. 67 is also at work. Recognition of this will prevent us from coming to any decisive understanding of what is precisely meant by *ipsa verba*: two meanings stand in tension. Direct discourse (which is a form of

[25] Furneaux (1907), ad loc. The whole expression *velut in commune* which I translated 'as if to everyone' points to Seneca's superaddressee (see Ch. 1).

narration) and the exact content of an original utterance are not at
all the same thing, even if people do mistakenly equate them. To
iron out conundrums like this in Tacitus is like trying to untwist a
Mobius band: it cannot be done without changing the fundamental
nature of the object under examination. The systematic quality of
what is presented in the *Annals* often turns out to be an illusion; and
here, the impression of a rigorous sytem and rationale for presenting *ipsa verba* turns out to be a mirage. However, our problem with
understanding what the Romans meant by this notion is not
entirely due to the slippery nature of Tacitus' argumentation. All
Tacitus' text docs is exploit and work on our confusion about this
matter, just as it can where historical events are concerned.[26]

  The conjunction of three passages from *Annals* 15 gives little
ground for holding that the direct discourse in 15. 67 (or elsewhere)
has authentically reproduced an actual utterance. Nonetheless, that
veridical function of direct discourse has long been presumed by
readers in later times. Consider Furneaux's comment on the direct
discourse ascribed to Subrius Flavus in *Annals* 15. 67. 2:

Nipp[erdey] thinks that Tacitus must have derived [these words] from an
oral source; but they may have been contained in some private or otherwise
little known written narrative. The apparent differences in the version of
Dio may easily have arisen out of some negligence in Xiphilinus, not from
his having followed some other source than Tacitus.[27]

Such speculations need not be dismissed out of hand. However, it is
better first to examine the general nature of direct discourse in
historical writing. The question (i) 'Can such renderings of words
ever be veridical in the first place?' is far more problematic to
answer than (ii) 'What words did Tacitus base his renderings on?'
That second question is really about sources in particular cases,
though it may well only lead to speculative answers. But the first
question is central to an enquiry about the general nature of
historiography. That question—about whether renderings of
words in narrative can ever be veridical—hangs on the problem
of what 'words' are in the first place which was highlighted at the
beginning of this section. But at least it is possible to set about

---

[26] For accounts of Tacitus' enigmatic presentation of his subject matter see
Ryberg (1942), and Shatzman (1974), Martin and Woodman (1989), 30–3, Woodman (1995), Gibson (1999).

[27] Furneaux (1907), 405

answering it on a theoretical, linguistic level, without much need
for ancient data.

4.3 DIRECT DISCOURSE AND NARRATIVE
AUTHORITY: MODERN VIEWS

We are susceptible to the Roman historians' rhetoric of *ipsa verba*
because of a pervasive and deeply entrenched view about the nature
of direct discourse in factual narrative in general. The supposed
function of direct discourse is to be veridical. The presentation of
someone's words in direct discourse in a narrative has a special kind
of authority for us. The narrator, whether a journalist, novelist, or
historian, moves off stage and allows another speaker to take the
floor.[28] We feel we can trust a historian's quotation of the Gettys-
burg Address far more profoundly than, say, a description of the
events leading up to it, which is bound to be partial and subjective.
In narratological terms, direct discourse for once allows, at least in
theory, a convergence in pace, between the time the supposed
original event would have taken to happen and the time it takes to
narrate it. Direct discourse is like a tape playing. It is the essence of
verisimilitude—or so we think.

   This means that when we read or hear an account which contains
a direct rendering of someone's words, we are more liable to ask 'Is
that what he or she really said?' than we would if the words were
rendered indirectly. We ask this of utterances expressed by direct
discourse because we want to get the nuances right. We want to
make sure that the teller is not injecting too much interpretation or
sensation into his quotation: livening up someone's words is all too
tempting. Or we want to make sure that nobody has made a mistake.
As well as asking 'Is that what he or she really said?' we may also
want to ask 'Is that all he or she actually said?' 'What else did they
say?' I suspect that whenever the reliability of direct discourse
comes up as a problem for practising historians, it is seen as an
exceptional, local problem, specific to the period they are dealing
with—did it have tape-recorders, writing implements, astonishing
powers of memory?—or else as a problem specific to the historian

---

[28] I am developing Plato's figure here to remind readers of the fact that even
when a historian 'quotes' a 'source', the historian is still reponsible for the entire
content and diction of his narrative. This provides additional ammunition against
the objection anticipated in n. 34 below.

they are scrutinizing—is he generally reliable or is he susceptible to sensation and prone to hyperbole?

The opinion that direct discourse offers a precise reproduction of a verbal communication, whilst indirect discourse is a form of paraphrase, has been widely held for a long time. However, in the previous chapter I outlined Sternberg's opposition to this: in his view *indirect discourse* and direct discourse are equivalent in reporting and paraphrasing original utterances. I questioned the validity of this argument for the consideration of literary (fictional?) texts. In such texts direct discourse tends to *constitute* the speaker's utterance: it therefore can be contrasted with indirect discourse. But where factual or historical texts are concerned, there are more grounds for raising a question considered earlier: is it empirically true that indirect discourse always does and formally must paraphrase, to the exclusion of exact imagining?[29]

There is in fact an instance of indirect discourse involving exact imagining in Tacitus, *Histories* 3. 39. There the expression *ipsa verba* is actually used of a rendering of Vitellius' words in *indirect* discourse:

quin et audita est saevissima Vitellii vox qua se (ipsa enim verba referam) pavisse oculos spectata inimici morte iactavit.

(Tacitus, *Histories* 3. 39. 1)

A remarkably cruel comment of Vitellius had circulated in which he had boasted that he (and I will present here his actual words) had feasted his eyes on the sight of his enemy's death.

Much depends here on what Tacitus means by *verba*: the use here could imply that he has preserved the lexical elements but not the endings of the words. Again the currently prevalent notion of 'words'—which involves the conflation of words as both units of sense and units of sound—confuses the issue. Nonetheless, an example like this suggests that a position like Sternberg's is largely right, at least for those discourses which aspire to be factual or veridical. Our assessment of reports of speech in *direct* discourse in accounts purported to be factual should be made on exactly the same basis as our assessments of report of speech in indirect discourse.[30] Any rendering *at all* of an original utterance, whether

---

[29] This is a paraphrase of a point made in Sternberg (1991), 78 quoted in the previous chapter.

[30] Earlier English printing conventions which enclosed passages of ID in quotation marks strengthen the case against a categorical distinction between ID

in direct discourse or indirect discourse, can only be a version of
what was said, in which the role of the reporter is no less involved
and no less inevitable.

The notion that direct discourse in factual narrative takes us
closer to what was actually uttered than any form of indirect
discourse does not come from empirical evidence of reported
utterances in the real world. It actually comes from a longstanding
tradition in poetics and aesthetic theory which goes back to the
critique of the use of direct discourse in narrative in *Republic* 393a
(treated earlier in Chapter 2). This tradition can afford to give the
status of literal fidelity to direct discourse because, in literary or
fictional texts, the utterances of characters like Aeneas or Anna
Karenina are *constituted* in direct discourse, not reported from real
life, by the narrator. If the utterances of characters like these are
given in indirect discourse, we feel that the narrator's presence is
mediating, interfering with what was 'actually said'.

Ancient grammatical schemes of classification distinguished
between direct discourse (*oratio recta*) and forms of indirect
discourse (*oratio obliqua*). Modern linguistics and narratology
have generally adopted this distinction, which operates as a kind
of epistemological scale. There is an ascendance in degrees of
veracity from the murky unreliability of indirect discourse to the
clear certainty of direct discourse. The usefulness of this epistemological scheme even for the study of fictional texts can certainly be
questioned, although that is not a concern here. More importantly,
the readings of the passages from Tacitus given earlier have shown
that this scheme, in which direct discourse is privileged by being
equated with truthful rendition or at least with an attempt at it, is
less than useful for the study of Roman historical texts. The
problem is partly that the notion of truth in a rendition of an
utterance in a historical text is a different matter: one is not just
dealing with truth in the internal logic of a narrative, but truth in

and DD. Consider this excerpt from *Tom Jones*, bk. 5, ch. 2 (Penguin edn. 203–4):
'Hence likewise he advised him, "to foresee, with equal certainty the greater evils
which were yet behind, and which were as sure as this, of overtaking him in his
state of reprobacy. These are," said he, "to be averted by such a thorough and
sincere repentance . . .".' Note how here the quotation encloses a passage of ID
which shifts to DD. The comments in Parkes (1992), 91, and at 229 on an edition of
Tom Jones printed in 1749 are useful: he notes the original punctuation of such
speeches had 'elocutionary qualities' which distinguish them (in the style of
dramatic scripts) from the main narrative.

relation to what may actually have occurred. For the latter, our examples indicate that the stylistic selection of direct or indirect discourse by a historical narrator has little significance.

Nonetheless, the influence of the grammarians' distinction between direct and indirect discourse has been extremely pervasive in the study of ancient historiography. When scholars discuss speech in Greek or Roman historiography, they are often dealing only with set-piece orations in direct discourse (*rheseis*) to the exclusion of other modes of presenting discourse. And the extensive interest in the fidelity of these *rheseis* to whatever was actually said clearly reveals allegiance to the epistemological scale I have just described. The longstanding fascination with the relation between the two surviving presentations of a speech the emperor Claudius made to the senate—one in Tacitus, *Annals* 11. 24, the other an inscription on the Lyons tablet—illustrates this well.[31] I have two points to make in response to existing discussions of these texts.[32] The first is to suggest that if Tacitus' rendering of Claudius' speech about the Gallic senators had been in indirect discourse, everyone would have been happier: its divergences in content and expression from the inscription would have been less notable and certainly more acceptable to modern eyes.[33] The second is to question the constant assumption that the tablet is necessarily the 'control' or primary account. Indeed the words on the tablet are constantly equated with what Claudius really uttered. The tablet is constantly referred to as the original text of the speech.[34] It could be in principle, but this can hardly be assumed.

[31] For the text of the speech on the tablet, see *Corpus Inscriptionum Latinarum* 13. 1668.

[32] See Syme (1958), 317–21, 703–10.

[33] Brock (1995): 'It is sometimes suggested, or at least implied in such discussions that Tacitus' readers will have known the original [sc. the tablet], and so be well aware as we of the historian's craft, but this is a dubious assumption.'

[34] This is implicit in even the most enlightening and recent discussions, including Brock (1995); Moles (1993), 105 n. 20 also refers to the text on the tablet as 'the original text of the speech'; again Woodman (1988), 13 and 54 n. 67 identifies the text of the tablet *with what Claudius said*; even Bers (1997), 151 n. 58 does not challenge this assumption. Tony Woodman has argued to me that the idiosyncratic self-address in the text of Claudius' speech rendered on the tablet represents what Claudius actually said—on the basis that it would otherwise have been edited out. In response to this specific observation I would invoke the dictum in Barthes (1982), 16 that a specific detail like this signifies 'the category of the real' and not its various contents (cf. Riffaterre (1990), 21). Overall, I would argue that even if the tablet were to be a lexically or thematically precise transcription—the burden of

4.4 DIRECT DISCOURSE AND NARRATIVE
AUTHORITY: ANCIENT CONCEPTIONS

The grammarians' distinction between direct and indirect discourse may well have had some influence on the original composition of Roman historiography. But its influence on Roman historians was rather different from its effect on those who write about them now. The selection of direct or indirect discourse was significant because of its effect on the rhetoric and presentation of internal truth in the narrative in which these modes of discourse were deployed. This use of angled narration of dialogue in Livy is a striking example:

'minime' inquit; 'quid enim salvi est mulieri amissa pudicitia? vestigia viri alieni, Collatine, in lecto sunt tuo; ceterum corpus est tantum violatum, animus insons; mors testis erit. sed date dexteras fidemque haud impune adultero fore. Sex. est Tarquinius qui hostis pro hospite priore nocte vi armatus mihi sibique, si vos viri estis, pestiferum hinc abstulit gaudium.' dant ordine omnes fidem; consolantur aegram animi avertendo noxam ab coacta in auctorem delicti: mentem peccare, non corpus, et unde consilium afuerit culpam abesse. 'vos' inquit 'videritis quid illi debeatur; ego me etsi peccato absolvo, supplicio non libero; nec ulla deinde impudica Lucretiae exemplo vivet.'

(*Ab Urbe Condita* 1. 58. 7–11)

'Not at all well' she said, 'What can be well with a woman who has lost her honour? The traces of another man, Collatinus, are in your bed; but only my body has been raped, my soul is unharmed. Death will be my witness. But give your right hands and pledge that the adulterer will not go unpunished. It is Sextus Tarquin who came last night, an enemy in the guise of a guest, and took his pleasure to my ruin—and to his—if you are men.' They all gave their promise; and consoled her in her distraction by trying to turn the harm done from the victim to the perpetrator of the deed: they said it was the mind that sinned not the body, and that there could be no guilt if there was no intention. 'You will see through whatever is due to him—as for me, even if I do absolve myself from any fault, I do not free myself from punishment. Let no unchaste woman remain alive after Lucretia's example.'

proof lies with all those who hold that it is—it is important to remember that a transcription is not the *same* as the speech it reports. At the very least we should not take the text of the tablet as the ideal 'control' for Tacitus' text in *Annals* 11. 24—though I cannot deny that degrees of closeness to whatever Claudius may have said are possible.

The modes of reporting discourse in narrating a legendary story like this patently have nothing to do with the questions of evidential reliability: they really serve to enhance Lucretia's stature in relation to those around her.

Achieving poetic truth is quite a distinct matter from telling the truth about what may actually have occurred. Recent studies of ancient conceptions of historiography suggest that definitions and purposes of history writing with regard to telling the truth were very different from our own. One could easily devise a syllogism to demonstrate that if this is so, the same must apply to the definitions and purposes of direct discourse which is incorporated as an element of that history writing. But in case this seems too sophistic, it would be helpful to have some ancient evidence to indicate that the distinction between direct and indirect discourse in Roman historiography was conceived as a matter of stylistic technique and not based on degrees of veracity.

There are not many testimonies to go on—although we do have an enigmatic remark by an Augustan historian, Pompeius Trogus, (which is preserved in Justinus' epitome of his *Historiae Philippicae*):

quam [orationem] obliquam Pompeius Trogus exposuit, quoniam in Livio et in Sallustio reprehendit, quod contiones directas pro sua oratione operi suo inserendo historiae modum excesserint.

(Justinus 38. 3. 11)

Trogus set out this speech in indirect discourse, since he reproves in Livy and Sallust the fact that by inserting direct addresses in place of their own discourse in their works, they went beyond the bounds of history/historical research.

If he singled out Livy and Sallust in this way, it is likely that Trogus was appealing to a practice of history writing (as well as his own) which did not employ direct discourse: possibly the annalists' accounts.[35]

Modern readers, given the popular presupposition that direct discourse ought to be veridical, will probably assume that Trogus opposed it in historiography because whatever the historian quotes might lack sufficient truth status. Polybius suggests that a historian

[35] Wiseman (1982a) gives some discussion of the annalistic sources for Livy filtered through Antias and Macer; see also Horsfall (1990). Brock (1995), 9 suggests that 'ancient historians as a general rule avoided treating in direct speech those orations which were accessible to the reading public'.

who represents speeches risks writing fictitiously.[36] If the phrase
historiae modum is taken to mean 'the bounds of historical research',
Trogus' position would be more sceptical about the truth-value of
speeches in historiography. The implication would be that a
historian lacks sufficient evidence for what he might quote. But
some Roman historians have passages of indirect discourse which
are so extensive or mimetic that our own impression of hearing the
precise words of an original speaker could be almost as strong as
those produced by direct discourse. This rather suggests that
preoccupation with the truth status of reported discourse was *not*
Trogus' preoccupation in making this prescription.

There is another possibility. Trogus could have been suggesting
that the decorum of historical style is offended by the use of direct
discourse. This could be indicated by taking the phrase *historiae
modum* to mean 'the bounds of *history*'—where *historia* denotes
history as a genre of writing. Style, and speech presentation as a
feature of style, is part and parcel of genre. A contrast made in
Cicero's *Brutus* could provide a parallel for this interpretation:

Demochares, autem, qui fuit Demonstheni sororis filius, et orationes
scripsit aliquot et earum rerum historiam quae erant Athenis ipsius
aetate gestae non tam historico quam oratorio genere, perscripsit.

(*Brutus* 286)

Demochares (who was the son of Demosthenes' sister) also wrote a number
of speeches and he also composed a history of things that had been done in
Athens in his own lifetime, in a genre which was more oratorical than
historical.

Perhaps the implication here is that Demochares, who wrote
speeches as an occupation, put a large number of speeches in his
history, and thus would have made it look more like a work of
oratory.[37] Genre also has a bearing on performance: it is feasible

---

[36] Polybius 2. 56. 10, cf. n. 23 above. See Walbank (1960), 216 f., and Walbank
(1985), 242–61. On history and tragedy, and the criticism of ψυχαγωγία in history
see Ullmann (1947), 25 f. Brink (1960) modifies Walbank's arguments—'tragic
history' did exist, and was prominent enough to be criticized by Polybius. See R. G.
Austin (1971) on *Aeneid* 2. 486 which has an affinity with Livy 1. 29 (the fall of
Alba). Norden (1912), 155 f. suggests that Livy's early sources were influenced by
early epic or Hellenistic tragic history, or that Virgil was influenced by Ennius.

[37] Here I follow the discussion of this passage in Woodman (1988), 115 n. 149.
Woodman compares Diodorus 20. 1. 1–3 which is roughly contemporary: '[Dio-
dorus] complains that some other historians put too many (and too long) speeches
into their histories, thus almost turning them into works of pure oratory.'

that Trogus, rather like Socrates in the *Republic*, simply prefers narrative without direct discourse, possibly because in his view it is a more appropriate stylistic register of historiography.[38] Although I find that second interpretation of Trogus' remark preferable, I have to concede that it cannot be proven. Moreover, no single and decisive conjecture can be made in general about the views of Roman historians on direct and indirect discourse in factual narrative. However their actual practice is enough to indicate that Roman attitudes, though they varied, were very different from the views held currently.

4.5 THE ROLE OF DIRECT DISCOURSE IN FACTUAL NARRATIVE: A NEW MODEL

The flaws of views currently held have been discussed in 4.3. The remaining part of this discussion will present a way of looking at reported discourse in Roman historiography which can supersede the perspectives we have considered so far. Whilst I acknowledge there is much we have yet to establish about ancient theory, I allow for the possibility that the ancients do not always give the best accounts of their own procedures. Both the Romans and ourselves see the possible ways of presenting spoken or thought discourse in narrative in terms of syntactic forms (as direct discourse or as various forms of indirect discourse). The identification of these syntactic forms was and still is useful for the purposes of rhetorical and stylistic criticism. But theorists of discourse from Plato onwards have imbued those syntactic forms with degrees of perceived veracity—there is supposed to be an ascendance in veracity or attemped veracity as a narrator moves from indirect to direct discourse. I hope I have shown that any application of this scale to degrees of historical truth is deeply misconceived.

[38] Ancient writers show little interest in genre *qua* genre (contrary to many modern assumptions): feasibly the change of style could affect the tone of the formal *recitation* of historical texts, if it occurred. Sources for the recitation of historical texts in Rome by Trogus' time include the Elder Seneca, *Controversiae* 4. *praef.* 2—Asinius Pollio was the first to read out his work, to select groups—and Cicero, *De Finibus*, which provides specific evidence for historical *akroases*. Compare Wiseman (1982*a*), 35: ' The pleasure [of history] . . . applies to eveyone, even poor people and *opifices* "artisans". Here too we must not think of books being read; historians are even wordier than epic poets, and the man in the street could hardly buy twenty volumes of Sempronius Asellio or Claudius Quadrigarius, much less 140 volumes of Livy. He must have heard his history, not read it.' On *recitatio*, see Ch. 3 n. 74.

That scale can be replaced with a new one which classifies the presentation of historical personages' spoken or thought discourse according to levels of *presence* or 'intrusion'. Both scales can be set out as in Table 4.1. At the top of the new scale come direct discourse *and* standard indirect discourse. Direct and indirect discourse are to be understood here, not in terms of reproduction or representation, but as the maximum possible presence of an alien speaker in a monologic utterance. Even so, the elevation of indirect discourse to a position of relative equivalence with direct discourse will appear controversial.

TABLE 4.1: *Two models for understanding the reporting of discourse*

1. Traditional Syntactic Model (functions as epistemological scale)

Degrees of '*knowledge*' of reporter/narrator:

(a) *Oratio recta*
Direct discourse—impression of hearing 'actual' words. Full 'revelation' (e.g. Tac. *Annals* 15. 67)
Free direct discourse—impression that these are 'actual' words may be doubtful. Full 'revelation' though reliability may be questioned (e.g. Tac. *Ann.* 11. 24)

(b) *Oratio obliqua*
Free indirect discourse. Partial 'revelation' (Tac. *Ann.* 15. 62)
Standard indirect discourse—impression that reporter is obscuring 'actual' words of utterance. Partial 'revelation'

(c) *Oratio memorata*
Minimal report of speech act . No 'revelation'

2. New Pragmatic Model (functions as scale of presence)

Degrees of '*intrusion*' into narrator's discourse

(a) *Direct discourse and standard indirect discourse*
Maximum possible 'intrusion' of other speakers into narrator's discourse

(b) *Free indirect discourse and focalization*
Synthesis of narrator's discourse with that of other personages.

(c) *Intertextuality*
Minimum form of 'intrusion'
'Transposition of one or more systems of signs into another, accompanied by a new articulation of the enunciative and denotative position'.

(Kristeva 1981)

By way of justification, it is important to emphasize that, in this
new scheme, only standard indirect discourse can enjoy this
elevation—that is, indirect discourse governed, or 'understood' to
be governed, by a declarative verb of saying or thinking which is
evident in the narrative. I acknowledge that it has been customary
to regard the narrator as mediating, even owning, the words which
are rendered in indirect discourse. However, the very existence of a
declarative verb is a clear signal that whatever message it governs is
not the narrator's property. The formal difference between direct
and indirect discourse is conspicuous in Latinate languages—and
especially so in Latin itself. This has led to an overestimation of the
semantic and pragmatic differences between the two modes. The
semantic and pragmatic differences are relevant in some fields (in
distinguishing fiction from drama for instance). But for the study of
something like historical narrative, these differences are largely
significant only as a matter of style and syntax.

The middle range of the scale includes forms of expression in
which the narrator's discourse is blended or hybridized with that of
another personage or personages. These forms of expression are
conventionally classified as either embedded focalization or as free
indirect discourse. Narratology has insisted on keeping free indirect discourse and focalization apart. Genette hammered home the
distinction between 'who speaks?' and 'who sees?': free indirect
discourse is a form of speech presentation whilst focalization is
what used to be called 'point of view'.[39] As a rule of thumb, I would
say that focalization is an intrusion on a lexical level, affecting one or
two words; free indirect discourse is an intrusion which affects a
whole phrase or group of phrases. The distinction between 'who
speaks' and 'who sees' is not easily made for certain passages.
Consider for instance this sentence describing Agrippina's situation just before her death:

cubiculo modicum lumen inerat et ancillarum una, magis ac magis anxia
Agrippina quod nemo a filio ac ne Agerinus quidem: aliam fore laetae rei
faciem; nunc solitudinem ac repentinos strepitus et extremi mali indicia.

(Tacitus, *Annals* 14. 8. 3)

There was a dim light in the chamber and just one of the maids. Agrippina
was more and more alarmed because no one came from her son, not even

[39] See 3.3.2*b* for an account of focalization.

Agerinus: a happy state of affairs would have had a different complexion; now the isolation and the sudden uproar were indeed signs of something very wrong.

But in this new schema, free indirect discourse and focalization can be conflated. Both represent an equivalent level of intrusion in the narrator's discourse. The intrusion is evident: the rhetorical force of *ne Agerinus quidem* ('not even Agerinus') and the opposition of *laetae rei* ('a happy state of affairs') and *extremi mali* ('something very wrong') diagnose the situation in Agrippina's terms; the use of the *nunc* ('now')—rather than *tunc* ('at that point')—certainly presents Agrippina's view or expression of the crisis and not the narrator's. But this intrusion is not heralded by a declarative verb which would decisively individuate it from the narrator's discourse.

At the far range of this scale comes intertextuality. This is the faintest form of intrusion: the most remote way in which a narrator's discourse can be modified by an alien voice. Not only is it the case that there is no declarative verb—there is no clue to the identity of the intruding personage. Kristeva defines intertextuality as the 'transposition of one or more systems of signs into another, accompanied by a new articulation of the enunciative and denotative position'.[40] This is of course related to what happens when the words of a specific personage are reported in a narrative. It should now be clear that even the use of direct discourse changes many aspects and objects of the utterance which it seeks to reproduce. Notwithstanding appropriations of the term by classicists, intertextuality can be understood as being akin to speech presentation or quotation in a text or utterance.[41]

When intertextuality is discernible in a particular text, we cannot derive indications of the presence of an alien text or speaker from that text alone. Tacitus, *Annals* 15. 63 yields an example of this most attenuated form of intrusion:

complectitur uxorem et paululum adversus praesentem fortitudinem mollitus rogat oratque temperaret dolori neu aeternum susciperet, sed in

[40] Kristeva (1981), 15. Compare Kristeva (1974), 59–60.
[41] Some of these (mis?)appropriations, in the context of Latin poetry, were considered in Ch. 1. The infelicitous definition of 'intertextuality' in Hornblower (1994), 1—heralding discussion of Greek historiography—is different again, and might better serve as an account of allusion: 'the awareness shown by one writer of another's work, and the difficulties of assuming direct influences'.

contemplatione vitae per virtutem actae desiderium mariti *solaciis honestis* toleraret.

(Tacitus, Annals 15. 63. 1–2)

He embraced his wife, and, softening up a bit in a way rather contrary to his timely courage, Seneca asked and begged his wife to temper her grief and not to indulge it for ever, but to bear the memory of her husband with the *honourable consolation* of the virtuous life he led.

It has been noted that the words *honesta solacia* are in fact to be found in an epistle of Seneca.[42] The *Annals* provides other examples of stylistic registers of authors on the specific occasions those authors feature in his narrative.[43]

Those concerned with historiography *qua* history may not deem this relevant. But I have brought intertextuality into this discussion for three reasons. First and foremost, it is a crucial part of my pragmatic model for understanding reported discourse in historiography. The sense of the scheme would not be so clear if I had left intertextuality out of it. Second, it is important to emphasize that intertextuality is not a feature exclusive to poetic language (even though Kristeva who invented the term occasionally gives that impression): intertextuality belongs to all discourse in all situations. Third—and this follows on from the previous point— intertextuality is more consistently palpable in historiography than in any other kind of writing. This is because, in a sense, every work of history is entirely constituted by reported discourse on one level or another. An intertextual relation may be seen to obtain between the discourse of a historian and the discourse of his eyewitnesses, of his documentary sources, of his predecessors, of his rivals and of the occasional inscription.

My account of both these models for understanding reported discourse is of more than theoretical interest. The presentation of the traditional model shows just how much the quest for mythical

---

[42] Seneca, *Epistulae Morales* 78. 3. 3: *quae mihi tunc fuerint solacio dicam, si prius hoc dixero, haec ipsa quibus adquiescebam medicinae vim habuisse; in remedium cedunt honesta solacia, et quidquid animum erexit etiam corpori prodest.* ('I shall say what consoled me at that time, stating this at the outset: that these very things by which I claimed myself had the potency of medicine. *Honourable consolation* results in a cure, and whatever has uplifted the soul is also good for the body.') Tony Woodman drew my attention to this passage.

[43] The account of the deaths of Lucan and Petronius in *Annals* 16. 17–20, which I shall discuss on another occasion, is rich in parody, stylization, and intertextuality.

Fictions of Authority

ipsa verba has been tangled up in categories which are really only of grammatical interest. These categories are of particular relevance to the Latin language. Latin makes a stronger syntactic differentiation between direct discourse and indirect discourse. But this syntactic differentiation does not necessarily entail pragmatic or semantic differences. Nor does it apply analogously to Greek and many other non-Latinate languages. Hebrew speakers for instance—it is interesting that Sternberg happens to be one—are far more prone to regard direct discourse and indirect discourse as practically interchangeable. Roman writers were unlikely to have been clear about this because these grammatical categories were of course current and influential. However, perhaps they were not as preoccupied by the problem of direct discourse in historiography as we are. The legacy of Platonic poetics which attaches so much significance to direct discourse has further confused us.

My presentation of a new model at least offers a scheme for understanding reported discourse in historiography which is not index-linked to notions of veracity. It also points to the partiality of the historical narrator as a speaker himself. It becomes clearer that the historical narrator is as much characterized and constituted by the discourse he reports as those to whom he ascribes it. In these respects I hope to have shown that the problem of reported speech in history is to a major extent a linguistic one. Once we acknowledge this, we may even aspire to understand certain presuppositions held by Roman historians.

4.6 HISTORY VERSUS FICTION: THE SPEECHES IN THUCYDIDES' *HISTORY*

The relevance of these conclusions to the actual study of the distinction between fictional narrative and historical narrative might need further underlining. In this section, the insights reached above will be brought to bear on some problems raised by readings of a famous Greek text. The 'preface' to Thucydides' *History of the Peloponnesian War*, spans most of the first book. But it is at 1. 22 that the historian outlines his aims and methods—specifically stating the criteria on which he has recorded speeches and events. The historian's comments on how he records speeches have aroused a great deal of controversy and argument:

As for all the things each side said in speech (λόγῳ εἶπον) either when they were about to begin the war or when they were already in it, it was hard for me to remember the precise content of what was said, both of the things I heard myself and for those who reported to me from various places. But as each speaker, in my view, would say the things most necessary (τὰ δέοντα) in the circumstances, so I have rendered the speeches (οὕτως εἴρηται—literally 'so it has been said') keeping as closely as possible to the general purport (ξυμπάσης γνώμης) of what truly was said.

(Thucydides 1. 22. 1–2)

It should be noted that those who discuss Thucydides' 'speeches' are referring to passages of *direct discourse* attributed to personages in the *History*. It is also worth noting that—in spite of the universal practice of English translators—Thucydides' Greek here does not have a noun 'speeches'. The use of that noun carries the misleading implication for English readers that in this passage Thucydides is making reference to 'set piece' speeches (*rheseis*) in direct discourse.[44] In fact no actual reference is made at all in the original passage to any specific mode of speech to be employed in Thucydides' work. We are simply being informed of the principles on which he renders spoken discourse in general.

However, this statement of method has traditionally been interpreted in one of these three ways:[45]

1. The speeches in direct discourse are entirely the invention of Thucydides. Although they present different points of view, this is only for the purposes of characterization.
2. The speeches given in the *History* are an endeavour to present the kind of thing a particular speaker might have said in a particular situation.
3. The speeches are supposed to set out what (Thucydides knew or believed) was actually said.

[44] Steup (1881–6) is right not to regard ἐν λόγῳ as simply pleonastic (i.e. telling us no more than that everything was said in words). However Steup, like many commentators in his wake, goes too far if he is suggesting that the expression refers to the actual *rheseis* (i.e. set speeches in direct discourse) instead of meaning 'in debate' or 'in argument' in the more general sense. It is my contention that Thucydides is making no specific mention of direct discourse (as opposed to other speech modes) in this passage.

[45] These alternative interpretations are presented by Gomme (1945–81) on 1. 143–8 and (1937), usefully summarized by Walbank (1985), 244–5. Walbank's summary is being glossed here.

Walbank rightly argues that Thucydides' use of the phrase 'what truly was said' (τῶν ἀληθῶς λεχθέντων) is hard to reconcile with any theory that the speeches were composed without any reference to the original words. Overall we might imagine that Thucydides was faithful to the gist, but it would be too much to expect that Thucydides or his informants were able to render at all closely the actual words people said. This would seem to be a sensible conclusion to draw. However, Walbank is not satisfied with it. He still sees a fundamental problem with this passage, which has continued to fox its interpreters:

There is a contradiction between the two ideas of recording what was actually said and what the historian would have thought the speakers would have said (ὡς . . . ἂν ἐδόκουν μάλιστ' εἰπεῖν) on the various occasions. The criterion of the one is quite simply the truth, the criterion of the other is suitability, τὸ πρέπον, πιθανότης, a concept which was frequently to arise in the rhetorical theory about speeches in history. In the ambiguous formulation of 1. 22. 2 Thucydides calls for truth and then confuses it with something quite other. Thus his theory contains a residual contradiction, never fully surmounted and an unfortunate legacy to his successors.[46]

Hornblower's commentary on the first book of Thucydides' *History* expresses a similar view:

I agree with those who believe the two halves of the sentence to be incompatible: the criterion of the first half is subjective appropriateness, that of the second half is fact, 'what was actually said'.[47]

Attempts made by specialists to get around this perceived contradiction generally involve inventive or subtly qualified translations of Greek words in the passage. For instance, Wilson effectively insists that *ta deonta* should be translated not as 'the things said which [Thucydides considered] were most necessary in the circumstances', but as 'the things which actually were necessary in the circumstances among other things which were said'. De Ste Croix, on the other hand, has argued that *xumpasa gnome* should be taken to mean the 'main thesis' of a speech which could be completely invented by Thucydides.[48] These kinds of solutions

---

[46] Walbank (1985), 245.
[47] Hornblower (1991), 60 ad loc.
[48] De Ste Croix (1972), 7–16

have suppporters and opponents: a proliferation of writing on this
problem has lead to an involved criss-crossing of opinions.[49]

Scholars will, no doubt, continue to minutely analyse this
passage for a long time to come, in the hope that the text itself
will throw up a solution. However, this problem is really about
historiography in general, not about Thucydides. No amount of
reading or rereading of this particular passage will solve it, unless
we think about the presuppositions which underlie those readings.
Scholars who work diligently on the interpretation of ancient texts
do not always appreciate the extent to which examination and
questioning of our own categories can directly assist such interpretation. As we should expect, those treating this passage who do
sense the broader issues involved are concerned with the differences between (i) literary and historical approaches, between (ii)
'literature' and 'history' in general; and between (iii) our conceptions of both literature and historiography in relation to those
which can be attributed to the ancients.[50]

However, our understanding of this passage can be enhanced by
bringing to bear the critical consideration of the categories of direct
and indirect discourse undertaken in the earlier sections of this
chapter. As I hinted in the previous section, such a consideration
has a role to play in more general speculations about the difference
between history and literature. If all (or even nearly all) the spoken
discourse presented in Thucydides' *History* had been rendered by
indirect speech modes, it would be extremely unlikely that any
modern reader would be able to discern a contradiction in what is
said in 1. 22. If we read or hear (e.g. in a factual, journalistic
account) a rendering of somebody's spoken words in indirect
discourse, we automatically take on board the understanding that
some elements of the message belong to the original speaker, and
that others belong to the current speaker. In normal circumstances
we are not cynical enough to assume that a factual reporter of an

[49] In addition to treatments already cited see Brunt (1993), 150–3, 402–3; the
essays in Stadter (1972); Woodman (1988), 11–15; Moles (1993).

[50] For (i) see Hornblower (1987), 45–6: 'Historians (rather than students of
literature) have tended instinctively to put more weight on the phrase "what was
really said" and less on "what was appropriate". They claim for instance that
Thucydides does his best to remain anchored to *ta alethos lechthenta* . . . But those
whose interests are literary more than historical tend to emphasize *ta deonta* "what
is appropriate", sometimes leaving "what was really said" out of account
altogether.' For (ii) see Moles (1993); for (iii), Woodman (1988), 11–15.

utterance who uses indirect speech is making *everything* up.[51] Nor are we generous enough to believe we are getting a precise *verbatim* rendering of what was originally said (altered only by the lexical shifts which occur when an original utterance in direct discourse is rendered in indirect discourse). We are inclined to think that we are getting a *version* of what was said. It is manifestly a version because the presented utterance is transformed by the reporter's manner of framing it. The transformation is taken for granted as inevitable rather than regarded as detrimental. In other words, the successive speaker is both conveying accurately what was said and at the same time offering (inevitably) an opinion of what was said.

Our assessment of speech in direct discourse in accounts purported to be factual (like Thucydides') should be made on exactly the same basis, if the contention entertained in the previous chapter—that all direct discourse outside of literature is effectively FDD—is allowed. Any rendering of something once uttered which is ever given in direct discourse can only be a version of what was said. The reporter's interventions are no less involved and no less inevitable than they are in renderings of utterances given in indirect discourse. This case has already been made with regard to Thucydides by John Wilson. The fact that no attention has been paid to his argument by subsequent commentators may be due to the fact that Wilson himself does not give it much prominence in his discussion of Thucydides' speeches. The relevant remarks are well worth quoting in full:

If Thucydides did not report the substance of what was actually said (rather than what ought to have been said, or 'what the situation called for') even in the brief *obliqua* passages, then he is guilty of very grave inaccuracy indeed. For the words in the passage, we might reasonably feel, are much more like deeds, than are the words of the lengthy set speeches: they are themselves facts in a much stronger sense. Either (for instance) the Corcyraeans hinted at bringing in Athens as an ally, or they did not (1. 28. 3): either Nicostratus agreed to a Corcyraean proposal to exchange five of his ships, or there was no such proposal and agreement (3. 75. 2–3).

---

[51] It is feasible however that a whole utterance can be 'invented' with the general truth still being told. RSA is most likely to cause this by implying a speech act occurred when it did not: The proposition 'Mr Clark committed himself to a system of state funded education' could hold when all Mr Clark may have done was to nod or twitch at an inopportune moment. The converse can also occur: 'He did not reply to this' could record an original statement along the lines of 'There is little to add' or 'I have nothing more to say'.

All such reportage—threats, demands, agreements, suggestions, formal edicts and so on—comes under ὅσα λόγῳ εἶπον: and if Thucydides got these wrong by deliberately putting down what he thought the speakers ought to have said (in effect, ought to have done), he can hardly be trusted at all. But nobody, as I say, seriously entertains this view—despite the fact that he must have omitted and abbreviated a great deal, exercised some selectivity, and made no attempt to reproduce the speakers' individual styles. Why then—one might ask—should these facts be held against him in the *recta* speeches? My suspicion is that we tend to be bewitched by the idea that everything in this format (anything in inverted commas or 'quotes,' as it were) must set out to reproduce photographically, rather than to give the general sense. That may be a modern convention, but (like inverted commas themselves) not an ancient one . . .[52]

Wilson touches on another important point here which deserves further consideration: in real life an utterance is equivalent to a deed. To claim an utterance occurred when it did not occur is tantamount to claiming a deed occurred when it did not occur. It is notable (and natural enough when you think about it) that most of the speeches in Thucydides' *History of the Peloponnesian War* are also *speech acts*: encouragements, commands, promises, threats. The dilemma of whether these should be rendered by direct discourse (as they usually are), indirect discourse, or simply by speech-act verbs ('Nikias gave an order') is trivial compared to the question of whether to excise speech acts (which are events) from a narrative or not, and whether or not to make them up. This all throws some new light on the problem of Thucydides' speeches. In historiography, the words of personages in direct discourse present no more and no less of a dilemma than words presented in indirect discourse.[53]

4.7 DIRECT DISCOURSE IN HISTORIOGRAPHY AND ITS IMPLICATIONS

It is not surprising that the kind of questions which have been raised by the use of direct discourse in Thucydides have cropped up

---

[52] Wilson (1982), 101–2.

[53] I am not claiming my discussion solves everything. There will still be a problem with the extensive passages of analysis some of Thucydides' speeches contain, regardless of whether they are rendered in DD or ID. It is partly because of this that scholars focus on the problem of *ta deonta* (see the references in nn. 47–51 above).

in discussions of other historians. Hornblower sees a parallel with the problem of speech (i.e. direct discourse) in medieval chroniclers and directs us to a footnote in Runciman's *History of the Crusades*. This is a valid parallel, but only in the sense that there is a parallel between Thucydides' 'speeches' and direct discourse in all history books everywhere. Runciman's note explains the difficulties involved in using sources to ascertain what Pope Urban said in his announcement to the Council of Clermont in 1095:

Urban's speech is given in five of the chroniclers . . . All the versions vary considerably. Munro analyses the differences between the versions and hopes to find the actual text by collecting the points on which they agree. But it is clear that each author wrote the speech that he thought the Pope ought to have made and added his own favourite rhetorical tricks.[54]

However, this particular comment in its context is more interesting than it first appears to be. There is a delicious irony in that last sentence of the footnote if we look at the main text to see how Runciman himself renders the speech. Runciman has taken a leaf from the chroniclers, himself writing the speech he thinks Pope Urban ought to have made and adding his own favourite rhetorical tricks. Runciman's most conspicuous rhetorical trick is to slide from recording speech acts, more or less soberly, into the reputedly poetical mode of free indirect discourse:

It seems that he began his speech by telling his hearers of the necessity for aiding their brethren in the East. Eastern Christendom had appealed for help; for the Turks were advancing into the heart of Christian lands, maltreating the inhabitants and desecrating their shrines. But it was not only of Romania (which is Byzantium) that he spoke. He stressed the special holiness of Jerusalem and described the sufferings of the pilgrims that journeyed there. Having painted the sombre picture, he made his great appeal. Let western Christendom march to the rescue of the East. Rich and poor alike should go. They should leave off slaying each other and fight instead a righteous war, doing the work of God; and God would lead them. For those that died in battle there would be absolution and the remission of sins. Life was miserable and evil here, with men wearing themselves out to the ruin of their bodies and their souls.[55]

Runciman's footnote shows that he does not mean to claim any authority for his own version of what Urban said. As he does not aspire to reproduce the Ur-text of Urban's utterance, he eschews a

---

[54] Runciman (1951), 108 n. 1.   [55] Runciman (1951), 107–8.

direct rendering. But the FID Runciman ends up adopting is almost as dramatic as direct discourse, and surreptitiously fuses his own words with those attributed to Pope Urban. This runs the risk of guiding the reader to certain interpretations of what the Pope might have said. In some ways the use of free *direct* discourse, such as we get in classical or medieval chronicles, might have been healthier: the provisional nature of the words rendered would have been automatically signalled.

Two conclusions may be drawn about speech in historiography, one firm and one speculative. Both might lead us to worry about the status of historical representation in general and the degree to which it might be deemed inventive in nature. First the firm conclusion. Utterances and events have an equal existential status in the world of objective reality. Utterances are indeed a kind of event, a subset of 'events'. Thus an utterance is as open as an 'event' is to manipulation by a historian. Hayden White has clarified the relation of *events* to history writing:[56] 'In short, it is events that belong to objective reality: facts are constructions created by the subjection of events to the protocols of different discursive characterizations.' Events are of course abstractions from facts—no event can be directly apprehended. But there is an analogy between White's observation and the relation between utterances and speech presentation. In short, it is *utterances* that belong to objective reality: instances of presented speech (whether direct, indirect, or free indirect) are constructions created by the subjection of utterances to the constraints of narrative. In this scheme of things, utterances correspond to, are at one with events, out there in the past or in the field. Utterances and events are irrecoverable. Speeches are in the text, on a level with facts. Both the narration of facts and the narration of speech are constructions of the historical narrator.[57]

The second, more speculative conclusion is this. Although speech in narrative and facts are on a level in historical narrative, they do not coexist in a simple parallel. There is a complex relationship between speech and the 'facts' we encounter in a historical narrative. Virtually all the facts we ever read in historical narratives derive from utterances, or from spoken and written

[56] H. White (1986), 109–10.
[57] This is not to deny that quotation from a document *verbatim* is a construction of a rather different sort.

texts.[58] An event becomes a fact when it is constructed in discourse.[59] That could be why Thucydides explains the manner in which he presents what was said *before* he explains the manner in which he presents what was done. This is not because, as positivist interpreters think, 'speech precedes, and issues in actions and deeds'.[60] It is because what was done can only be apprehended through what was said. In my view, Thucydides himself makes this perfectly clear:[61]

> But as to the facts of the occurrences of the war, I have thought it my duty to give them, not as ascertained from any chance informant nor as seemed to me probable, but only after investigating with the greatest possible accuracy each detail, in the case both of the events in which I myself participated and of those regarding which I got my information from others. And the endeavour to ascertain these facts was a laborious task, because those who were eye-witnesses of the several events did not give the same reports about the same things, but reports varying according to their championing of one side or the other, or according to their recollection.
>
> (Thucydides 1. 22. 2–4)

Once Thucydides discusses the problem of ascertaining facts and actions, he is actually dealing with the problem of how to assess, select and, by implication, *render* verbal testimonies. In a very strong sense, all historiography is presented discourse. It is not always easy to appreciate this because the interaction between speech and fact is mostly going on off the page, out of sight.

The suggestion that quotation in history can only be provisional may well give the impression that historiography and other kinds of factual reportage (ethnography, journalism) are, after all, a kind

[58] The case of historical narratives which purport to be derived from autopsy is not the threatening exception that it may seem. The practical status of eyewitness accounts as self-contained examples of historiography in the conventional sense is not secure (see e.g. Woodman (1988), 18–20). In theory there are problems too: the conversion of events or scenes into narrative discourse involves the problem of 'linearization'—see Levelt (1981), epitomized by D. P. Fowler (1991), 29. On the incorporation of eyewitness accounts by a historian, see Thucydides 1. 22. 2–4 and my discussion of this passage below.

[59] Schafer (1981) and De Certeau (1978) in different ways consider the implications for narrative of the construction of the event in psychoanalysis. Crapanzano (1992) is a full study of the implications of psychoanalysis for ethnology and other forms of discourse.

[60] Moles (1993), 104.

[61] I accept that the informants Thucydides refers to here are not speakers whose words he claims to reproduce: the point of my reading is that the speakers (from whose testimonies the facts and actions are constructed) are not explicitly *identified*.

of invention—especially if it is maintained that factual narratives
are *entirely* made up of discourse presented from somebody somewhere. In that no live utterance can ever be reproduced in a
narrative, historiography must be regarded, if not as invention,
then at least as a kind of improvisation. However, this assertion
does not provide sufficient grounds for the contemporary application of words like 'fictive', 'fictional', 'imaginary', or 'creative' to
historical and ethnographic writing which I discussed at the
opening of this chapter.

Even if such terms are only applied in a weak sense, they can have
a detrimental effect on historical and ethnographic practice: the
stronger senses of the terms can be smuggled in all too easily. It is
useful—and liberating—to regard historiography and other kinds
of factual narrative as partial, rhetorical and provisional. But to
regard descriptive discourses of witness as fiction could paradoxically give them a more powerful status. If read as fiction, such
narratives will acquire the role fiction has come to enjoy of
conveying symbolic truth. Narrative genres like history and ethnography would be read and written for the sake of the moral of the
story, the higher truth to which the material gathered would be
excessively subordinated.[62]

The observations of this chapter have actually highlighted a
fundamental difference between factual and fictional representation. The difference between the status of direct discourse in factual
narrative and the status of direct discourse in fictional narrative is
tantamount to the difference between historical and fictional
narrative in general. Factual narrative—like any direct discourse
it may contain—is rhetorical and provisional. Fictional narrative—
like any direct discourse it may contain—is authoritative and
absolute.[63]

[62] On notions of higher truth in ancient historiography, the discussions in Moles
(1988), 35–6 and Moles (1993), 118–21 are enlightening.
[63] My conclusion here tallies, to some extent, with Aristotle's influential expression of the distinction between poetry and history in *Poetics* 9 (1451[b]) although
I came to it without (consciously at any rate) relying on Aristotle's formulation:
'The difference between the historian and the poet is not merely that one writes
verse and the other prose—one could turn Herodotus' work into verse and it would
be just as much history as before; the essential difference is that the one tells us
what happened and the other the sort of thing that would happen. That is why
poetry is at once more like philosophy and more worthwhile than history, since
poetry tends to make general statements while those of history are particular.' (This
is Margaret Hubbard's translation of the passage, in Russell and Winterbottom
(1972), 102.)

5

The Rhetoric of Epic: Speech Presentation in Virgil's *Aeneid*

Virgil would not have been a Roman if he had not valued practical effect above any theoretical insight.

(Richard Heinze, *Virgil's Epic Technique*)

As soon as it was produced, the *Aeneid* became the canonical work of Latin literature. The history of reception ensured Virgil's poem continued to be the paradigm for the epic genre in western Europe and beyond.[1] However, it is easy to overlook the extent to which Virgil's epic differed radically—in form as well as content—from its Greek and Roman predecessors.[2] This chapter will show how techniques of speech presentation are responsible for some of the poem's major formal innovations. It will also show how the important themes of the *Aeneid* are constituted, and not just conveyed, by these innovations of form. The relationship between the discourse of the poem's narrative and the discourse of its characters—Virgil's 'rhetoric of epic'—has a significant role in engineering the distinctive pathos and disturbing political message of the *Aeneid*.

All major ancient epics contain a large proportion of quoted speech. In this repect, the *Aeneid* is no exception—almost half of the text is taken up with the presentation of characters' words in

[1] Ch. 7 will help illustrate this by reviewing the transformation of the celestial messenger motif in epic. Comparetti (1908) describes the early responses to the *Aeneid* as well as its medieval reception. P. Hardie (1993) treats the Roman epic tradition after Virgil; the essays in Martindale (1997), esp. at 1–103, and in Horsfall (1995), 249–311, provide an overview of Virgil's *Nachleben* in European culture. See also Martindale (1993).

[2] The stylistic analysis of Virgil in Goerler (1978) shows this; Jocelyn (1979) is also important. Kleywegt (1995) is a newer treatment of Virgil's adventurous linguistic innovations, mostly in the *Aeneid*; see also Conte (1986), 36–9 and *passim*. Quint (1993), 9 (and elsewhere) shows the bearing of epic form on the message of the *Aeneid*: 'the *Aeneid* ascribes to political power the capacity to fashion human history into narrative . . . drawing on the two narrative models offered to it by the *Iliad* and the *Odyssey*, Virgil's poem attached political meaning to narrative form itself'. O'Hara (1997), Goerler (1985), and Horsfall (1995), 217–48 treat Virgil's style.

direct discourse.³ But the narrator also uses a number of indirect modes to present the speech and thought of characters.⁴ Even a discussion confined to the effects of indirect discourse would be too extensive for the scope of this chapter.⁵ So this treatment of speech presentation in the *Aeneid* does not claim to be comprehensive. It will concentrate on some specific features: the association of speech with power, the use of silence for dramatic ends, the role of speech presentation in achieving realism, and the employment of free indirect discourse (FID).

These issues can be closely connected with each other. All of them allow us to focus on the relation between the narrator and his characters which we saw scrutinized by Plato in Chapter 2: a study of the discourse of characters better enables us to understand the discourse of the narrator himself. Examination of these various features also shows, in different ways, how extensively silence is used in the *Aeneid*—as a narrative tactic to surprise or exclude the reader, as a sign of subordination on the level of story, and—in the

³ In Homer two-thirds of the *Iliad* is given over to DD, and half the *Odyssey* (if we include Odysseus' account in 9–12 to Alcinous). De Jong (1987a), 115 gives a more detailed breakdown for the *Iliad*: 'there are 677 speeches as against 88 cases of indirect speech (rarely longer than two verses) and 39 of speech act mention.' Figures for other epics are: 29 per cent in Apollonius' *Argonautica*, 47 per cent in the *Aeneid* including Aeneas' narrative, 32 per cent in Lucan, 31 per cent in Silius Italicus. Further information is to be found in Avery (1936), Hentze (1904), Highet (1972), Lipscomb (1909), Loesch (1927), Offermann (1968), and Sangmeister (1978). Hunter (1993), 138–51 is a particularly useful discussion of DD and ID in the *Argonautica* of Apollonius. The most recent study of DD in Roman epic is Helzle (1996)—the introductory section, 11–48, treats *recitatio* and *ethopoiie* in particular; Lefèvre (1987) briefly surveys monologues in Virgil. The importance of DD in epic was noted in antiquity. In addition to Plato, *Rep.* 392–5 and Aristotle, *Poetics* 1460ª5, discussed in Ch. 2, see Plato, *Ion* 535 and Murray (1996), 122 on this passage.

⁴ *All* such speech modes in an epic should be taken into account for any proper assessment of discourse in its narrative—though existing treatments have tended to concentrate on direct discourse to the exclusion of the other modes. In Highet (1972), for example, the treatment of speeches and thoughts rendered indirectly in the *Aeneid* is confined to a list in an appendix, where Highet claims: 'It is possible that during his revision, Vergil would have turned at least some of these passages into direct speech.' Study of DD does at least allow more scope for consideration of the role of rhetoric in poetry, one of Highet's preoccupations. Recent literatures have been better served: there are a variety of speech modes employed in the modern novel and the number of works treating this aspect of the genre is vast. See especially Cohn (1978) for extensive treatment and bibliography, and Page (1988). Haig (1986) treats speech in Flaubert; S. Ullman (1957) is also useful. Bakhtin (1973) on Dostoevsky, and Genette (1980) on Proust have very general applications.

⁵ A fuller account of direct and indirect discourse in Virgil was given in Laird (1992), ch. 1.

case of FID—to generate a realm between spoken and thought discourse. Viewed together, these features of speech presentation reveal some rhetorical strategies which are central to the epic narrative of the *Aeneid*.

5.1 SPEECH PRESENTATION AND REALISM IN VIRGIL

In contemporary treatments of ancient rhetoric and literary theory, the term 'realism' tends to apply specifically to vivid physical detail, particularly of a visual nature, in passages of description.[6] Ancient notions like *enargeia* ('vividness'), *phantasia* ('visualization'), and *subjectio sub oculos* ('putting before the eyes [of reader or audience]') correspond to what is called 'the reality effect' in modern critical idiom.[7] Thus:

1. Realism can be understood as concrete detail.

However, in broader discussions of literary representation (bearing on literature of all periods) the word 'realism' is frequently used, but seldom so neatly defined. From the usages which are most prevalent, two further definitions can be distilled:

2. Realism consists in attention to mundane or even vulgar subject matter, as opposed to elevated or noble themes (when such themes are regarded as the standard subject matter of literary representation).[8]
3. Realism is discernible as verisimilitude, achieved by narrative techniques which induce most awareness of the content or story, and least awareness of form or narrative itself.[9]

All three definitions of realism offered here bear on speech presentation. Indeed the endeavour 'to reproduce actual speech'

[6] Zanker (1987) is useful; G. Kennedy (1989), p. xiii offers a convenient overview. Conte (1997) provides an excellent account of theory and practice of realism in literature, ancient and modern. Debates about *philosophical* realism (see introd. to Ch. 4 and accompanying n. 12) are not relevant to this discussion.

[7] The term *'l'effet du réel'* was coined in Barthes (1982). This essay provides a history of the evolution of the use of concrete detail as 'referential illusion'.

[8] Consider the importance of 'good' or 'serious' (πράξεως σπουδαίας) action for the definition of tragedy in Aristotle's *Poetics* 1449[b].

[9] Consider e.g. the discussions of realism in European literature in Boyle and Swales (1986).

has been seen as the sole defining element of realistic poetry.[10] The use of direct discourse can also be regarded as analogous to the first of the definitions given here—that realism is the generation of concrete detail, and of visual detail in particular. I have already considered the drawbacks involved in what I call 'visualist' conceptions of direct discourse in Chapter 3. We saw that direct discourse cannot offer a perfect correspondence between imitation (the presented discourse) and reality (what we postulate as the actual utterance): it *constructs* speech rather than reports it. Yet in providing this construction of speech, direct discourse engineers the illusion of absolute referentiality. There is then a clear analogue between the function of direct discourse in a narrative and the function of concrete physical detail or 'reality effect': 'Flaubert's barometer, Michelet's little door, say, in the last analysis: *we are the real*. It is the category of the real and not its various contents, which is being signified.'[11] Something similar applies where direct discourse is concerned: although the content of a direct speech is obviously important, there is a sense in which the *category* of the utterance is what direct discourse really signifies.

My second definition of realism—attention to vulgar or mundane themes—is relevant to certain cases of speech presentation. These may involve the inclusion of colloquial styles of speech presented in a variety of modes (compare my earlier discussion of *skaz* in Chapter 3), or they may contain elements which may appear to be of incidental importance to a particular perception of the plot. Since this form of realism is constructed by audience response, it can be understood in ideological terms.[12] The third definition of realism— as instances of verisimilitude in which the content or story seems far more salient than the form of the text—is of especial interest in relation to speech presentation. Of course this effect of verisimilitude is still achieved by features of form, or narrative.

It is important to exercise caution in applying contemporary categories of realism to the reading of ancient epic.[13] Even ancient

[10] See Weinreich's definition of realism in Preminger (1974), 685.
[11] Barthes (1982), 16.
[12] The following chapter on Petronius will throw further light on the relationship between this aspect of realism and presented discourse in the discussion of speech and the social world.
[13] However, see Kroll (1924), 52 for the ancient notion of πιθανὸν πλάσμα ('plausible fiction') which Feeney (1991), 50 n. 183 argues, corresponds to the 'reality effect'.

authorities do not tend to regard epic as either veridical or even as possessing verisimilitude. It is manifestly obvious to us as modern readers that epic, particularly Roman epic, devotes little attention to the lower strata of society; that epic verse can hardly ever approximate to the patterns of actual speech or prose rhythms; and that it often relies on far-fetched images, metaphors, and descriptions of a miraculous or fantastic nature. However, these deficencies in realism are most conspicuous, to both ancient and modern critics, when the epic genre is considered in relation to other forms of narrative expression, such as historiography, prose fiction, or comedy. Every genre of discourse can be seen to present reality in its own way.[14] Epic may not only be seen as a type of discourse, but also as a way of configuring the world: I shall return to this question at the close of this chapter.

In my view, Virgil's *Aeneid* does engineer a specific kind of realism in the presentation of discourse. Consideration of uses of speech presentation in relation to the poem's narrative design reveals the rhetorical strategies which help to achieve this. In the rest of this section I shall consider the use of speech presentation on a relatively broad scale over two extensive parts of the poem.

5.1.1 Aeneid 1: The Beginning of an Epic

In his *Ars Poetica* ('Art of Poetry'), Horace, a contemporary of Virgil, criticizes narrative poets who induce great expectations for their subject matter—expectations which cannot be fulfilled:

> nec sic incipies ut cyclicus olim:
> 'fortunam Priami cantabo et nobile bellum.'
> quid dignum tanto feret hic promissor hiatu?
> parturient montes, nascetur ridiculus mus.
>
> (*Ars Poetica* 136–9)

Avoid a beginning like the cyclic poet—
I will sing of Priam's fortune, and a reputed war.
How can the promiser bring forth anything worthwhile if he opens his mouth as wide as that? The mountains will go into labour, and there shall be born—a ridiculous mouse.

Horace goes on to praise the way Homer's *Odyssey* begins:

[14] Compare Conte (1994), 132 quoted in Nightingale (1995), 3.

> quanto rectius hic qui nil molitur inepte:
> 'dic mihi Musa, virum, captae post tempora Troiae
> qui mores hominum multorum vidit et urbis.'
> non fumum ex fulgore, sed ex fumo dare lucem
> cogitat, ut speciosa dehinc miracula promat.
>
> (*Ars Poetica* 140–3)

How much more on the right lines is the poet who toils at nothing in vain:
> Tell me, Muse, of the man who after the time of Troy's fall
> looked upon the manners and cities of many men.
In no way does he consider turning fire to smoke—rather he turns smoke to light, so that after this point he can work magnificent wonders.

Other testimonies from Virgil's time, however ironic they may be, indicate that the business of embarking on an epic was not taken lightly.[15] Horace's comments on the integration of a proem with the rest of the work are actually in the context of a general discussion of verisimilitude in epic. He advocates the invention of a consistent fiction (*Ars Poetica* 119) and praises Homer for mixing truth with falsehood so that the beginning, middle, and end of his narrative are all consistent (*Ars* 152). This intimates that the manner of opening an epic does have some importance for the capacity of what follows to be convincing. But the intertextuality of the first verse of Virgil's *Aeneid* with the *Odyssey* and the cyclic *Little Iliad* could suggest that this opening is not particularly modest:[16]

> Arma virum cano, Troiae qui primus ab oris . . .
> (*Aeneid* 1. 1)

I sing of arms and the man, who first from the shores of Troy . . .

Yet the narrative that follows never seems to strike readers as unconvincing (at least not in relation to the opening) or as an anti-climax to the proem which heralds it.

My own explanation for this lies in the way speech presentation is

---

[15] I am thinking of the convention of *recusatio* in Roman love elegy, in which the poet affects not to be capable of treating epic themes, e.g. Virgil, *Eclogues* 6. 3–5; Horace, *Odes* 4. 15. 1–4; Propertius 3. 3. 1–26; Ovid, *Amores* 1. 1. For further discussion of *recusatio* and comparisons, see Nisbet and Hubbard (1970), 81–8 (on Horace, *Odes* 1. 6) and Wimmel (1960). However Brink (1982), 259 points out that Horace's own use of *recusent* 'scarcely justifies the modern use of recusatio as a descriptive term'.

[16] Compare *Odyssey* 1. 1 and the first line of the 'Little Iliad' (*Ilias Parva* F1) in Davies (1988), 53: 'I sing of Troy and the Dardanian city abounding in horses, over which the Greeks, servants of Ares suffered much.' Horace's referral to the latter in *Ars Poetica* 137 (quoted above) is challenged by Brink (1971) ad loc. at 214.

deployed in the first book of the poem. We are led very gradually into the sequence of events the poem purports to present. It is a cliché that the *Aeneid* starts *in medias res*.[17] As we have seen, the poem begins by following diction and style customary for programmatic openings to epics. The narrative then proceeds to the central stages of the poem: first the divine arena, and then the mortal one. This is a complex accomplishment, yet we hardly notice the transition from the relatively timeless and spaceless plane of the narrator to the plane of the events tracked in his story.[18] I will show how this transition works, and draw attention to the important part played by speech presentation in the opening of Virgil's epic narrative.

The first seven verses of the poem outline the narrator's brief of the story to be told. Then an 'epic question' is put to the Muse: verses 8–11 seek an an account of the causes of the story and an explanation for Juno's resentment of the Trojans. A summary account of Carthage's history and Juno's grudge follows (1. 12–33): this resumé answers the question just posed. The next verses mark the slowing of the narrative time:

> Vix e conspectu Siculae telluris in altum
> vela dabant laeti et spumas salis aere ruebant,
> cum Iuno aeternum servans sub pectore vulnus
> haec secum: 'mene incepto desistere victam
> nec posse Italia Teucrorum avertere regem! . . .'
> (*Aeneid* 1. 34–8)

They had happily set sail for the deep sea and were hardly out of the sight of the Sicilian coastline, churning the salty foam with their bronze prows, when Juno, nursing a longstanding wound in her breast, brooded as follows: 'To stop what I've begun, defeated in my ability to keep the king of the Trojans from Italy! . . .'

We are brought closer to the temporal pace of the story. But this progress is checked by the characterization of Juno's wound as something which is longstanding (*aeternum*). We are still not quite

---

[17] Compare Austin on 1. 1 f. and 34–49. The coining of *in medias res* was of course made by Horace in the *Ars Poetica* 147–9: *nec gemino bellum Troianum orditur ab ovo:* | *semper ad eventum festinat et in medias res* | *non secus ac notas auditorem rapit* ('He doesn't begin relating the Trojan war from the egg; he always hurries on to the outcome and snatches his listener into the very middle of things— just as if they were already known.'

[18] Indexicals given here and elsewhere in the *Aeneid* were discussed in Ch. 1, pp. 25–34.

in the realm of action—even of divine action. Then comes a soliloquy from Juno (1. 37–49). Direct discourse normally indicates that the pace of the narrative and the pace of the story are converging. However, the first two words of this very speech mark yet another 'beginning' (*incepto*), stalling the progress of Virgil's narrative, as they contain a sonic echo of the first word of the *Iliad*.[19] Moreover, not all the sentiments in Juno's speech appear to belong exclusively to this context in the story. She complains first that Athene has the power to scatter the Argive fleet while she has not beeen able to turn the Trojans back from Italy, and second that her own worship is being neglected. Finally (1. 50 ff.), the real narrative gets underway, perhaps most securely indicated by the use of the perfect *venit* ('[the goddess] came'):

> Talia flammato secum dea corde volutans
> nimborum in patriam, loca feta furentibus Austris,
> Aeoliam venit. hic vasto rex Aeolus antro . . .
> *(Aeneid* 1. 50–2)

Turning these things over in her inflamed heart, the goddess came to Aeolia, the country of clouds, a place teeming with the raging winds of the south. Here king Aeolus was in his deep cavern . . .

At last we sense that we have got into the story; something is happening which is neither just a resumé nor a description which sets the scene for something else. We can be more sure Juno's next (spoken) words, to Aeolus, were uttered there and then in a specific spatial and temporal context. Indeed her words here are in fact what show us that such a context has been reached.

The description of the effects of Aeolus' winds (1. 84 f.) and the introduction of Aeneas' speech bring us nearer to the present state of affairs on the mortal plane. Aeneas' words—the first to be uttered by a mortal in the poem—are prompted by the storm:

> ingemit et duplicis tendens ad sidera palmas
> talia voce refert: 'o terque quaterque beati,
> quis ante ora patrum Troiae sub moenibus altis
> contigit oppetere! O Danaum fortissime gentis
> Tydide! mene Iliacis occumbere campis
> non potuisse tuaque animam hanc effundere dextra,

---

[19] Levitan (1993) argues that the first word of the *Iliad*, Μῆνιν, can be heard in *mene incepto* (1. 37).

> saevus ubi Aeacidae telo iacet Hector, ubi ingens
> Sarpedon, ubi tot Simois correpta sub undis
> scuta virum galeasque et fortia corpora volvit!'
> Talia iactanti stridens Aquilone procella
> velum adversa ferit, fluctusque ad sidera tollit.

(1. 93–103)

He groaned and, stretching out both his palms up to the stars, uttered these words:
'O three, four times fortunate are those who happened to fall under the high walls of Troy in front of their fathers! O son of Tydeus, bravest of the Greek race, it was not possible for me to fall at your hand and breathe my last on the Trojan plains, where raging Hector was thrown down by Achilles' weapon, where great Sarpedon lies, where the river Simois churns so many shields, helmets and strong bodies of men!'

As he hurled out these words, the shrieking blast of the north wind struck against the sail and raised the waves to the stars.

The description of the elements which encloses this speech gives it a peculiar kind of stature; that description also reflects Aeneas' image of the Trojan river churning the arms and bodies of men in its waves.[20] That image presents Aeneas' immediate predicament as a paradigm of a more longstanding one—the hardship of leading the scattered remnants of a war-torn people.[21] The mention of the Trojan heroes for the first time in the poem is also significant: we see the type of men with whom Aeneas is to be associated. But could Aeneas articulate all this in such circumstances as these? In themselves, his words are more conventional than realistic: they must be classified in the speech mode of free direct discourse (FDD).[22]

[20] This relation is corroborated by an image of the effects of the storm in 1. 118–19: *apparent rari nantes in gurgite vasto,* | *arma virum tabulaeque et Troia gaza per undas.* The collocation of *arma virum* recalls 1. 1. If these verses are focalized through Aeneas, this evocation would be all the more poignant: we see, and Aeneas himself sees, everything he stands for being churned through the waves.

[21] The symbolism of the storm in *Aeneid* 1 is discussed by P. Hardie (1986), 93 n. 24: Virgil associates storm-forces with theological and moral evil.

[22] For FDD, see Ch. 3, pp. 90–4. Austin (1971) ad loc. lists speeches in storms from other poems as parallels. *Odyssey* 5. 299–312 has Odysseus making a similar speech: the context would suggest this too is FDD. Compare especially Lucan 5. 578 f.; Valerius Flaccus 1. 627–32. The convention of oratory in seastorms can be paralleled to Greek lyric poetry on storms (see H. Fraenkel (1975), 190 f.). The patent lack of realism of poetic speeches in such circumstances is parodied in *Satyricon* 115: Giton and Encolpius having avowed their love for each other in the storm (114), seek to rescue Eumolpus who insists on completing a poem he has

Nonetheless, in their context, they contribute to what could be perceived as a larger realistic design. Aeneas' words facilitate the transition from the presentation of discourse on the divine plane to the presentation of discourse on the human plane. Like Juno's soliloquy, Aeneas' speech draws us further into the action of the poem. His words offer a mortal and, more specifically, a Trojan perspective on events. The fact that the speech begins with a prayer is also significant for the bridging role it has: the primary addressees here are the gods, or even the poem's audience, not Aeneas' comrades. We are brought finally and firmly to events on the mortal plane and to the main action of the story by a further passage of direct discourse—addressed by a mortal to other mortals. This is the speech in which Aeneas seeks to encourage his dispirited comrades (1. 198–207).

By this point in the narrative, these words from Aeneas seem to be completely appropriate. Nothing about this instance of direct discourse seems awkward or implausible in the framework in which it has been presented. Thus, the *Aeneid* eases us into its story and into the presentation of characters' speeches, in a series of gradual stages:

Verses	*Speaker*	*Mode used*	*Status of speaker*
(*Focalization of Juno* 1. 24 f.)			
First speech 1. 37–49	Juno	Soliloquy: FDD	Immortal
Second speech 1. 65–75	Juno	Standard DD	Immortal
Third speech 1. 76–80	Aeolus	Standard DD	Immortal
Fourth speech 1. 94–101	Aeneas	Soliloquy: FDD	Mortal
Fifth speech 1. 132–41	Neptune	Standard DD	Immortal
Sixth speech 1. 198–207	Aeneas	Standard DD	Mortal

The speeches illustrate (and help to effect) a transition from the general to the specific, first on the immortal plane, and then on the mortal plane. We have seen that direct discourse can be regarded as the kernel of literary *mimesis*: when verbal expression of the narrative appears to be identical to verbal expression issued in the world of the story, as narrative time appears equal to story time. Had, say, Aeneas' direct discourse been rendered immediately after the proem, its effect would have been very different. The generation of a story world would have been much more abrupt, and as a consequence, its credibility would have been weaker.

been composing during the story. Paul's speech during a storm in *Acts* 27. 21–6, which gives the impression of being more functional, makes an interesting contrast.

The narrative strategy employed in the opening of the *Aeneid* conforms to Horace's recommendations in *Ars Poetica* 119–52. There verisimilitude is connected with the relation between the beginning of a poem and the material to follow. What Horace says of Homer's *Odyssey* at the end of that discussion could equally apply to Virgil's narrative technique here:

> atque ita mentitur, sic veris falsa remiscet,
> primo ne medium, medio ne discrepet imum.
>
> (*Ars Poetica* 151–2)

He tells his fables and mixes truth with falsehood in such a way that the middle squares with the beginning and the end with the middle.

The transition from the immortal world to the world of mortal events and speech in Homer's *Odyssey* is comparably subtle: the link is made by having Athene descend to Ithaca so that Telemachus can address her (*Od.* 1. 123–4). Virgil's manner of homing into his story certainly resembles the opening of the *Odyssey* more closely than the openings of other epics we have.[23] The subject of the poem is outlined in the first ten verses of the *Odyssey*; verses 11–21 swiftly narrate the situation the story has reached so far; from 22 onwards we are told that, while Poseidon has gone to Ethiopia, the other gods are assembled in the halls of Zeus. Zeus is first to speak. He is prompted to do so by his recollection of Orestes' killing of Aegisthus, and begins his words with the general reflection that mortals cannot blame the gods for all their problems. What he says appears at first to have a timeless, universal quality, though it soon leads to a specific discussion about the fate of Odysseus. But whilst these opening speeches of Homer's Zeus and Virgil's Juno have a comparable function, Juno's soliloquy does not form any part of a conversation. Thus her oration might best be classed as FDD: it

---

[23] The *Iliad* begins by announcing the subject of the poem (1. 1–7). A direct question is posed (as in Virgil) to ask which god was responsible for the strife. The answer—Apollo—leads straight into the story: Chryses' speech comes at 1. 17–21. Apollonius' *Argonautica* opens with an apostrophe to Apollo and summary of the poem's matter. The cause of the voyage is given 1. 5–19, followed by a catalogue for over 200 verses before the story gets underway (234 f.). The first speech, remarkably, is still in FDD which represents the sentiments of those watching the heroes setting off on their voyage (1. 242–6). Even the next speech, from one weeping woman to another, has the quality of FDD. A declarative phrase closing the speech at 1. 260 indicates this: 'in this way they were talking'. See De Jong (1987*b*), 177–8 on τις- speeches in the *Iliad*.

conveys her general state of mind more than it is likely to correspond to a speech we might imagine her to have uttered at any given moment.[24]

Another intertextual aspect of Juno's first soliloquy bears on the accomplishment of realism in the opening of the *Aeneid*. Speeches of Olympian deities open some comedies, and also a number of tragedies by Euripides.[25] Euripides' gods, like Juno here, tend to announce a grievance and their chosen way of settling it.[26] Gods in Euripides' prologues generate a certain kind of dramatic illusion. At the beginning of a tragedy, a theatre audience is likely to be all too aware that it is regarding an enactment. But if the first dramatic personage to speak appears in some way to acknowledge the audience as addressees before engaging with other characters, a connection will be forged between the character–audience relation on the one hand and the relations between characters within the story on the other.

The prologue speaker thus helps to establish the reality of the story in which he or she is about to be involved. This principle need not be confined to drama. Regardless of whether the *Aeneid* was recited before an audience or read silently, Juno's speech can be seen to perform this bridging function. The poem's audience or readers are her first addressees: this enables Juno's character and its credibility to be established before any sustained narration gets underway.

---

[24] This speech at least satisfies conditions 4 and 5 for FDD, given earlier in 3.4.1*b*, pp. 93–4.

[25] For comic openings, see Stoessl (1957; 1959), and Handley (1965) on Pan in Menander, *Dyskolos* 1–49. The most celebrated speeches from Euripides' plays are by Apollo in *Alcestis*, Dionysus in *Bacchae*, Aphrodite in *Hippolytus*, and Hermes in *Ion*. Apparitions of deities at the beginnings of Euripides' tragedies are discussed by Nestle (1930) including those in the lost plays; see also Jens (1971). Compare Iris' speech in Eur. *Herakles* 822–42. Virgil's paralleling of Juno with Dido, who resembles a Euripidean heroine, might be significant. Dido's harsh speeches to Aeneas (4. 305–30, 4. 365–87) recall Medea's words to Jason in *Medea* 465–626. Fenik (1960) and Muecke (1983) treat connections between Virgil and Euripides. For Virgil's reception in Roman drama, see Wigodsky (1972).

[26] In her prologue speech in *Hippolytus*, Aphrodite says she favours those who revere her power and that she destroys the proud—Hippolytus has shown more favour to Artemis than to her. Her explanation of her revenge outlines the action of play. Juno does not outline any plan: instead we see her go straight into action as she seeks out Aeolus—but her speech to him might have the role of a 'prologue'.

5.1.2 Aeneid *6 and* Georgic *4: Speech Presentation and* katabasis

The Greek term *katabasis* ('descent') is applied by scholars to ancient literary accounts of journeys to the underworld. Such accounts may belong to traditions of wisdom or vision literature, or they may form part of a more general poetic endeavour. Since antiquity, the account of the underworld in the sixth book of the *Aeneid* has enjoyed a particular authority and influence.

Katabases are generally recounted by an involved narrator who has gone down, or across, to the world of the dead and offers an account of what has been seen. Such a speaker may be the first-person narrator of the whole text. This is the case for the narrator of the biblical book of Revelation, as it is for two of its major sources—Ezekiel and Zecheriah. Dante's *Commedia* uses the same device, following the form of medieval vision literature. Alternatively, there is an identifiable character-narrator who recounts his journey to a characterized addressee or set of addressees in the story. In *Odyssey* Book 11, Odysseus himself relates his experience of the underworld to the Phaeacians; in Plato's *Republic*, Socrates relays to his friends the myth of Er as an embedded narrative, presented largely as a speech from Er in indirect discourse.[27] Or again, as in some Orphic texts and in Apuleius' story of Psyche, directions are given by an authority to an initiate who must follow them.[28]

In the *Aeneid*, the technique used is strikingly different. This *katabasis* seems, at least *prima facie*, to come right out of the mouth of the principal narrator ('Virgil') himself. Perhaps it is unsurprising, then, that Virgil, identified as he has been with the principal narrator of the *Aeneid*, soon began to acquire the status of a seer.[29] The employment of third-person narrative for a *katabasis* has a powerful rhetorical effect. It is a device which does not appear to have been used previously in this context, and which may help to

[27] *Republic* 614c–621b. See p. 76 above. Socrates specifically contrasts this account with Odysseus' to Alcinous—perhaps to indicate that the one he offers is more truthful. However see Lucian, *Verae Historiae* 3–4 and the *Scholia in Lucianum*: Rabe (1906), 18.

[28] Apuleius, *Metamorphoses* 6. 17–19. The narrative of Psyche's performance of these instructions is briefly given in 6. 20. See Kenney (1990), 212 on 6. 17. 2.

[29] See Céard (1976). Comparetti (1908) offers a full treatment of Virgil's reputation in the Middle Ages. The account in Carver (forthcoming) of the history of the perceived relationship between Apuleius the author and Apuleius' persona from antiquity to the present time has relevant implications.

explain the authority and priority this account of the underworld came to have in later periods.[30]

However Virgil's innovation of having the principal narrator appear to present a description of the underworld is cunningly and cautiously engineered. There are more instances of direct discourse in the sixth book of the *Aeneid* than in any other. A total of 36 speeches takes up more than half the text of this book. At the same time there is a smaller number of personages who speak than we find in any other book in the poem.[31] The Sibyl and Anchises have the lion's share of the direct speech—about 160 verses each. It is they who supply most of the information given to Aeneas, and thus to the audience, about the underworld. The narrator has actually passed the real burden of responsibility on to these characters for presenting this *katabasis*. Thus the Virgilian account of the underworld secures a certain kind of credibility, even realism: the principal narrative is not directly responsible for the descriptions provided by his characters and is therefore not directly subject to refutation.

Speech presentation contributes to the overall rhetorical effect of one other Virgilian *katabasis*. The final part of the fourth *Georgic* (315–566) consists of a narrative about Aristaeus. In a manner typical of epyllion (a small scale epic), the outer narrative contains an embedded narrative (452–527), which is recounted by Proteus, the seer whom Aristaeus consults. Proteus recounts to Aristaeus the story of Orpheus' attempt to recover Eurydice from the underworld. A full range of available speech modes is only to be found in Proteus' narrative, and not in the account which encloses it. As a narrator, Proteus makes use of apostrophe (465–6) and simile (511–15) as well as FID (491, 504–6, and possibly 526). None of these devices are to be found in the outer narrative; thus Proteus' narrative possesses a peculiar richness and complexity.

The attribution of more vivid and dramatic narration to a creature as protean as Proteus is very appropriate: the seer can transform himself physically into 'all manners of wonderful things'

---

[30] 'Servius' remarks on *Aeneid* 6: 'Though all of Virgil is full of knowledge, it is predominant in this book, of which the greater part is from Homer. Many things are simply said, many from history, many from the deep wisdom of philosophers, theologians, Egyptians; so that several have written whole treatises about specific passages of this book.' The Christian commentator Fulgentius devotes more attention to *Aeneid* 6 than he does to the rest of the poem as a whole. The importance of Virgil's *katabasis* for Dante is well known.

[31] For tabular presentations of speeches by speaker in the *Aeneid*, see the appendices in Highet (1972).

(*omnia transformat sese in miracula rerum* 441). The use of FID has the effect of 'transforming' Proteus the narrator into Orpheus, his character:

> quid faceret? quo se rapta bis coniuge ferret?
> quo fletu Manis, quae numina voce moveret?
> illa quidem Stygia nabat iam frigida cumba.
>
> (*Georgic* 4. 504–6)

What was he to do? Where could he go now his wife was snatched away a second time? With what lament could he move the Shades and what divine powers could he move with his voice? Indeed already cold Eurydice was drifting away in a Stygian bark.

This final sentence could either be a thought attributable to Orpheus or it could be Proteus' discourse entirely. In fact Proteus provides the only example of an embedded narrative in Virgil, given by one character, which uses FID to present the words and thoughts of another character.[32] Thus Proteus himself is characterized by his own style of narration and speech presentation.[33] As a consequence, his character is considerably more developed than is often thought. In this respect, Proteus' *katabasis* narrative appears to be more salient and plausible than the narrative in which it is enclosed. And the mere fact that we can detect different levels of verisimilitude in these verse narratives allow us to apply the category of realism to epic.

5.2 FREE INDIRECT DISCOURSE IN THE *AENEID*

In one sense, the occurences of FID in the *Aeneid* could expose the illusory quality of epic narrative because they call attention to the presence of the narrator. However, as has often been recognized, FID can, perhaps paradoxically, enhance the reality effect in narrative. There are no decisive and unambiguous forms of FID in Latin poetry before Virgil.[34] But remarkably, FID is only

---

[32] This effect is found on several occasions in Ovid, *Metamorphoses*: nearly all the narratives in this poem are spoken by characters who can use FID to present the words or thoughts of others.

[33] The title of the treatment of speech presentation in Sternberg (1982a): 'Proteus in quotation-land' is more suitable than many would realize.

[34] Compare Perutelli (1979), 80–1. There are certainly no clear examples of FID in Ennius, Naevius, and Livius Andronicus (the epic poets prior to Virgil) from extant fragments. Catullus 64. 58–9 provides a possible instance.

slightly less common in Virgilian narrative than the soliloquy in direct discourse. The first occcasion on which FID is used by the principal narrator of the *Aeneid* (at 4. 283–4 and 291–4) is particularly memorable.[35] The relevant verses convey Aeneas' complex reactions to the apparition of the god Mercury, who has instructed him to leave Carthage:[36]

> At vero Aeneas aspectu obmutuit amens,
> arrectaeque horrore comae et vox faucibus haesit.
> ardet abire fuga dulcisque relinquere terras,
> attonitus tanto monitu imperioque deorum.
> *heu quid agat? quo nunc reginam ambire furentem*
> *audeat adfatu? quae prima exordia sumat?*
> atque animum nunc huc celerem nunc dividit illuc
> in partisque rapit varias perque omnia versat.
> haec alternanti potior sententia visa est:
> Mnesthea Sergestumque vocat fortemque Serestum,
> classem aptent taciti sociosque ad litora cogant,
> arma parent et quae rebus sit causa novandis
> dissimulent; *sese interea, quando optima Dido*
> *nesciat et tantos rumpi non speret amores,*
> *temptaturum aditus et quae mollissima fandi*
> *tempora, quis rebus dexter modus.* ocius omnes
> imperio laeti parent et iussa facessunt.
>
>   (4. 279–95)

But Aeneas was dumbstruck and aghast at the apparition. His hair bristled with horror and his voice stuck in his throat. He burns to flee away and leave the sweet lands, overwhelmed both by so mighty a warning and the gods' command. *Oh what should he do? With what words is he to dare now to approach the queen in her rage? What beginning should he choose?* His thoughts swiftly moved now this way now that way—he rushes them in various directions and turns them through all the possibilities. This seeemed to him to be the best course of action as he wavered: he calls Mnestheus, Sergestus and brave Serestus: let them make ready the fleet in silence, marshall the crews down to the shore, prepare their arms and keep secret the reason for altering their plans. *Meanwhile he, since the noble Dido neither knows nor expects so great a love to be shattered, would try an approach and to find the most tactful time to speak to her and the right way to handle the matter.* At once all the men, happy at the command, carry out the orders.

[35] FID is employed in Aeneas' narrative in Books 2–3: 3. 39 will be considered briefly at the end of this section.

[36] Mercury's delivery of Jupiter's message to Aeneas (4. 219–85) will be treated in Ch. 7, pp. 264–74.

For the first time in Book 4, the narrative directly provides a psychological portrait of Aeneas.[37] 279–82 show the effect of Mercury's apparition and speech. Aeneas is dumbstruck (*obmutuit amens* 279, *vox faucibus haesit* 280): so it is inconceivable that any of his *spoken* discourse is being rendered by the deliberative questions in 283–4. The questions are expressed in the third person—we need not imagine Aeneas formulating these questions to himself in these words. Yet at the same time there is a vivid impression of Aeneas' quandary: he is troubled by a number of conflicting demands. The use of present tenses for these deliberative questions perhaps contributes to this impression[38]—it contrasts with the aorists which have been used in the narrative since the close of Mercury's speech at 276. The FID in 283–4 helps reinforce the more anatomical description of Aeneas' feelings (in the narrator's discourse) which precedes these verses. At the same time we are slightly prepared for the intrusion of his voice by the sympathetic focalization of *dulcis* ('sweet').[39] Had 283–4 been expressed in direct discourse ('Alas what am *I* to do?' etc.), the sentiments would have seemed absurdly mannered or melodramatic—and the complete change of voice would have sounded awkward and uncomfortable.

The examination of Aeneas proceeds, as the narration of subsequent events continues. First we have another description (exclusively in the narrator's voice) of Aeneas' hesitation (285–6) until (at 287) he comes to a conclusion (*haec alternanti potior sententia visa est* 'This seeemed to him to be the best course of action'). The nature of that conclusion is revealed as Aeneas promptly acts on it in 288 f.: the action itself offers some other sorts of speech presentation. Aeneas summons his officers to arrange the departure of the fleet in secret. The actual summoning (288) is given as RSA; ID is employed for the content of the orders given. However the construction for the account of Aeneas' musing on how he should explain his decision to Dido (291–94) is technically awkward.[40] The

---

[37] See R. G. Austin (1955), 92 on 279–85.

[38] The present subjunctive is not necessary for FID: the imperfect is also found: cf. *Georgic* 4. 504–5 discussed at the end of the previous section. See Leumann, Hoffmann, and Szantyr (1965–79), ii. 338, on subjunctive tenses in these contexts. Regula (1951) discusses the use of the present subjunctive in deliberative questions, and remarks on the FID in *Aen.* 2. 27 f.. See also R. L. Fowler (1987).

[39] See 3.4.2*b* pp. 98–9 for an account of focalization, and 5.3 pp. 184–8 on *Aeneid* 6. 455–74.

[40] Conington (1884), on verse 289 describes it thus: 'a sort of *oratio obliqua* depending on the sense rather than on the expression of the previous line'.

syntactic modification makes it look more like standard ID. On the other hand, the absence of an obvious declarative verb makes this resemble FID. It is not until we reach the singular form *temptaturum* ('he . . . would try') at 293 that we can establish that the speech made employed here is FID.

This FID construction in 291 f. (*sese interea*) shows that Aeneas and his feelings are still the subject of the narrative. His worries about Dido are expressed in the same sentence as that in which he gives orders to his men, and have equal priority. Again, as in 283–4, any direct discourse from Aeneas at this point would perhaps unwelcomely sunder an expression which conveys the conflict of Aeneas' wants. In both instances of FID quoted in this excerpt, Aeneas is preoccupied with how he is to express himself to Dido, and with what words he is going to use. In other authors of Latin narrative (as well as elsewhere in Virgil), the mode of FID can similarly be found in contexts where the character is presented as being lost for words.[41]

Other instances of FID in the *Aeneid* offer striking parallels to this passage from the fourth book. The narrator conveys Turnus' psychological state as he is trying to find a way to enter the enclosure into which the Trojans have retreated:

> ignescunt irae, duris dolor ossibus ardet.
> qua temptet ratione aditus, et quae via clausos
> excutiat Teucros vallo atque effundat in aequum?
>
> (9. 66–8)

He blazes with rage and the pain of it burns through his hard bones. How could he try an approach? What device could shake out the Trojans, as they were enclosed in their rampart, and pour them out on to the plain?

Like Aeneas in 4. 288, Turnus is in a state of high emotion—he has just been compared to a fierce wolf (9. 59 f.) howling around a sheep pen, tormented with hunger and frustration. The phrase *temptet aditus* ('try an approach') here used literally, is only found elsewhere in Virgil at 4. 293—in the previous passage of FID noted. It is even harder to imagine Turnus issuing these rhetorical questions vocally, given the state he is in. However these questions in the

---

[41] Compare e.g. Apuleius, *Met.* 3. 9 where the narrator Lucius uses FID to illustrate his account of events which rendered him speechless with astonishment. In Ovid, *Metamorphoses* 6. 572–4, FID is used poignantly to render the thought discourse of Philomela who is physically dumbstruck because her tongue has been removed (cf. Ovid, *Fasti* 2. 800–4).

narrative clearly present his preoccupations at this point in the story. It is less easy to establish whether the sentiments in the verses which follow should be attributed to Turnus:

> classem, quae lateri castrorum adiuncta latebat,
> aggeribus saeptam circum et fluvialibus undis,
> invadit sociosque incendia poscit ovantis
> atque manum pinu flagranti fervidus implet.
>
> (9. 69–72)

The fleet!—which was out of sight moored along the side of the camp, protected by ramparts at one end and the tide of the river at the other—he attacks the fleet and demands fire from his cheering comrades; and still burning inwardly he fills his hand with a blazing pine.

Classem ('The fleet') is significantly the first word. We seem to be shown Turnus' answer just as it strikes him, or at least an instant after. But then verses 69–70—which provide more detail about the location of the fleet—seem to be in the voice of the narrator. In 71 the verb *invadit* ('he attacks') appears to be in the narrator's voice entirely: it recounts Turnus already acting on his realization. However, a remark in 'Servius' could imply that this verse might be in some way mimetic of Turnus' utterance:

> hysteroproteron ut aviditatem iuvenis ostenderet.[42]

A reversal of customary word order (i.e. *hysteroproteron*) [is used] to show the young man's zealous enthusiasm.

Thus Turnus can almost be heard ordering his comrades to attack the fleet and to provide him with fire. We might compare the general effect of 9. 69–72 here to that of *Haec alternanti potior sententia visa est* ('This seemed to him to be the best course of action as he wavered') at 4. 287 f. Aeneas' realization there, as we saw, was also followed by the presentation of a command to troops in ID.

The second passage of FID in Book 9 comes in an account of Nisus' extreme agitation when his lover Euryalus is dragged off by the enemy. The verses in FID (9. 399–401) come in this immediate context:

---

[42] See the entry for *hysteroproteron* in Lausberg (1973) and Bell (1923), 271. Other examples of *hysteroproteron* being used in this way in the *Aeneid* are 7. 150 and 7. 287 f. E. Fraenkel (1950), 29–30 (on Aeschylus, *Agamemnon* 48) comments on the ancient practice of adapting the content of a cry or exclamation to the construction of the sentence that narrates it.

> audit equos, audit strepitus et signa sequentum;
> nec longum in medio tempus, cum clamor ad auris
> pervenit ac videt Euryalum, quem iam manus omnis
> fraude loci et noctis, subito turbante tumultu,
> oppressum rapit et conantem plurima frustra.
> *quid faciat? qua vi iuvenem, quibus audeat armis*
> *eripere? an sese medios moriturus in enses*
> *inferat et pulchram properet per vulnera mortem?*
> ocius adducto torquet hastile lacerto
> suspiciens altam Lunam et sic voce precatur . . .
>
> (9. 394–403)

He hears horses, he hears the clatter and the signals of the pursuers; in no time shouting reaches his ears and he sees Euryalus. Already the whole band carries Euryalus off, overwhelmed as he is by the treachery of the place at night and the sudden uproar, yet he makes every effort against the odds. *What is Nisus to do? By what force or what arms is he to dare to rescue his young friend? Or should he be ready to die and hurl himself into the midst of their swords and rush through wound after wound to a glorious death?* In that moment he draws back his arm and brandishes a spear—looking right up to the Moon he makes this prayer . . .

Again, given how little story time is available in such a moment, the deliberative questions posed in this way convey anxious confusion and indecision more convincingly than would any self-address in direct discourse. This means that the prayer to Diana which takes up six verses has far more impact: we understand Nisus' need for divine assistance, but this speech increases our sense of tension as we are only too aware that it takes up part of the precious time in which he has to act.[43]

There is a final example of FID in which the narrator appears to express the deliberative questions which the character has neither time nor composure to utter (or formulate) in 12. 486. Aeneas is pursuing Turnus' chariot which continues to elude him as a result of Juturna's endeavours. Again Aeneas' discourse is presented in FID when he is in a state of high anxiety and confusion:

> *heu, quid agat?* vario nequiquam fluctuat aestu,
> diversaeque vocant animum in contraria curae.
>
> (12. 486–7)

---

[43] Alternatively, this slowing of the narrative pace for deliberation could be conveying a 'real time' description of Nisus' consciousness: for the subject of an experience like this, time could slow down at such a moment.

Alas what is he to do? Fruitlessly he courses over a tide of impulses, and competing passions pull him in different directions.

It is worth noting that deliberative questions of similar import are expressed in *direct* discourse by Dido and Turnus when they face crucial turning points or moral crises. Dido during a sleepless night 'courses over a tide of anger' (*irarum fluctuat aestu* 4. 532—compare 12. 486 just quoted) and begins a soliloquy as follows:

> en, quid ago? rursusne procos inrisa priores
> experiar, Nomadumque petam conubia supplex,
> quos ego sim totiens iam dedignata maritos?
>
> (4. 534–6)

So then, what am I to do? Shall I go back to my former suitors as a laughing stock and seek in supplication a match from the Numidians, whose marriages I so often scorned?

Turnus expresses his aporia in a very similar way when he begins to confront the prospect of defeat in a speech to his sister Juturna:

> nam quid ago? aut quae iam spondet Fortuna salutem?[44]
>
> (12. 637)

What am I to do then? What Fortune assures my safety now?

The contrast between these externalized speeches and the use of FID to present Aeneas' thoughts in analogous situations gives Aeneas more dignity. The implication might be that he has more self-control than Dido or Turnus because he does not actually give voice to his doubts and anxieties, yet we are still meant to see that he suffers them.[45]

---

[44] Similar deliberations are obviously found in Homer, e.g. *Odyssey* 20. 17. Again see R. L. Fowler (1987) and n. 38 above. Perutelli (1979) notes these passages in the *Aeneid* and points out that this self-questioning, and the considering of possible options recalls the τί δράσω ('What shall I do?') topos of Greek tragedy.

[45] Compare Perutelli (1979), 78 who remarks that the narrator's use of FID inclines the reader to be more sympathetic to Aeneas by integrating the sentiments Aeneas feels with the overall design of the poem. Mackie (1988), 81–2 has a rather different interpretation: 'Aeneas' dilemmas . . . are conveyed by means of the indirect deliberative. The narrator asks the questions whilst Aeneas himself acts out the dilemmas. Thus the reader's direct involvement in these dilemmas is with the narrator rather than with the character. Unlike the cases of Dido and Turnus, Aeneas is placed in the dramatic background.' In my view, the posing of such questions by the narrator allows us to share the dilemma more intimately with the character. Even so, Mackie's reaction shows that there is a paradox here in the effect of the FID. Incidentally, FID is often found in the locality of a sympathetic apostrophe—see the discussion of Macrobius' remarks to follow.

In all these passages of FID there are deliberative questions of some kind, expressed in the present rather than the imperfect subjunctive. They are usually in contexts where the narrative present tense abounds. The questions in FID thus have a vivid, urgent quality about them. At the same time as highlighting a character's plight, they hold the audience in suspense about the course of action the character will take. After the pause in narration of actual events achieved by these passages of FID, we see promptly what happens next: in 4. 296–305 it is actually Dido who confronts Aeneas; Turnus decides to set the Trojan camp on fire in 9. 71; Nisus resolves upon a prayer at 9. 404; and Aeneas in 12. 488, hit by Messapus, embarks upon a series of killings, or *aristeiae*.

Another common feature of these passages of FID is more curious. They tend to be followed by apostrophic questions in the narrative. These apostrophic questions seem to be of an order quite different from that of the deliberative questions in the actual passages of FID. For example, after the FID used to present Aeneas' thoughts about Dido in 4. 291–94, the narrator asks entirely in *his own* voice:

> quis fallere possit amantem?
> (4. 296)

Who could ever deceive someone in love?

And after Turnus has settled and acted on the strategy of burning the Trojan ships (9. 69–76), the narrator asks:

> Quis deus, o Musae, tam saeva incendia Teucris
> avertit? tantos ratibus quis depulit ignis?
> (9. 77–8)

What god, o Muses, turns these cruel fires from the Trojans? Who drove the great flames away from their ships?

Apostrophic questions from the narrator at 12. 500–4 also follow Aeneas' FID (already quoted) at 12. 486: they are related to it in so far as they reflect on the extent of Aeneas' *aristeiae*). Again, an apostrophic exclamation to Euryalus and Nisus comes right at the end of the account of their tragic adventure:

> Fortunati ambo! si quid mea carmina possunt,
> nulla dies umquam memori vos eximet aevo,

dum domus Aeneae Capitoli immobile saxum
accolet imperiumque pater Romanus habebit.
(9. 446–9)

You fortunate pair! If my poetry has any power, no day will ever erase
you from the memory of future ages, while the house of Aeneas occupies
the immovable rock of the Capitol and the Father of Rome holds his
empire.

It is feasible that the deliberative questions in the preceding
passages of FID serve to draw attention to the presence of the
narrator's voice and thus make an appropriate context for the
apostrophes which follow each of them. I remarked above that
one issue often raised in these passages of FID was the character's
preoccupation with how he is to express himself. This preoccupation is also one for the poet-narrator in two of the instances of
apostrophe just quoted.

   There is another argument to suggest that these instances of FID
and narratorial apostrophe are not juxtaposed out of mere coincidence: FID, apostrophe and related figures, such as exclamations
to an imagined audience, are perhaps not such different orders of
narrative discourse as they may first seem. Take for instance the
observation about the suicides in the sixth book of the *Aeneid*:

   quam vellent aethere in alto
nunc et pauperiem et duros perferre labores!
fas obstat, tristisque palus inamabilis undae
alligat et novies Styx interfusa coercet.
(6. 436–9)

Now how they would wish to endure both poverty and hard toils in the air
above! But that is forbidden, and the hateful swamp of the gloomy waters
binds them, and the ninefold currents of the Styx intertwine to keep
[them] in.

The first sentence (436–7) may well just be read as a concerned
exclamation from the narrator, followed by the grim details in the
second (438–9) which explain how securely the sad souls are
confined. Yet the verses could also be read as the discourse of the
sad souls. Indirect speech is often used to express the shared
sentiments, spoken or thought, of a group. In that way we could
imagine this as a reported utterance. The present tense in 438–9
need not then only be read as a narrative present—it could be the
present tense of a more live utterance. 438–9 might also be read as

woeful free *direct* discourse.[46] In Lucan there are several passages
which are similarly indeterminate: they may first appear to be in the
narrator's voice, but they could also be instances of FID presenting
discourse which is partly attributable to characters.[47]

The distinction I had made between deliberative questions in
FID on the one hand, and apostrophic questions (which are wholly
in the voice of the narrator) on the other, may not have been
apparent to ancient audiences.[48] The device of FID—now generally recognized as a speech mode—was never specifically identified
or discussed by ancient grammarians. Macrobius (who was writing
in the fifth century AD) considers some of the passages of FID I have
discussed in his treatment of *addubitatio* ('hesitation'):

facit apud oratores pathos etiam addubitatio quam Graeci ἀπόρησιν vocant.
est enim vel dolentis vel irascentis dubitare quid agas.
     en quid ago? rursusne procos inrisa priores
     experiar? . . .
et illud de Orpheo:
     quid faceret? quo se rapta bis coniuge ferret?
et de Niso:
     quid faciat? qua vi iuvenem quibus audeat armis
     eripere?
et Anna permoventer:
     quid primum deserta querar? comitemne sororem
     sprevisti moriens?
                          (*Saturnalia* 4. 6. 11–12)

A rhetorical figure which the Greeks call *aporesis* generates pathos: this is
addubitatio (hesitation). For it is characteristic of someone in a state of grief
or anger to hesitate about what to do:

[46] It is interesting that *palus* and *Styx* which govern the verbs *alligat* and *coercet*
do not have a stated object like *illos* in the Latin, although translators are naturally
bound to insert 'them' in their English versions. This lack of an object increases the
possibility of ambiguity: the fact that the clear precedent to these verses in Homer,
noted by commentators since 'Servius', is itself part of a speech in DD helps my
case for relative indeterminacy here. The speech is made by Achilles in *Odyssey*
11. 489–51: βουλοίμην κ' ἐπάρουρος ἐὼν θητευέμεν ἄλλῳ | ἀνδρὶ παρ' ἀκλήρῳ, ᾧ μὴ βίοτος
πολὺς εἴη, | ἢ πᾶσιν νεκύεσσι καταφθιμένοισιν ἀνάσσειν. ('I would rather be bound as a
thrall to another, even a poor man, with no land to his portion than be king over all
the dead.')
[47] Lucan, *De Bello Civili* 1. 479–80; 3. 56–8; 4. 399–400; 6. 586–7; 9. 46–7.
[48] The condemnation of Lucan's apostrophe in the wake of Haskins (1887)
might be tempered by consideration of the positive dramatic effect of this device in
the context of a recitation. Endt (1905) has interesting observations on apostrophe
in Latin epic.

So then, what am I to do? Shall I go back to my former suitors as a laughing stock . . .? [*Aen.* 4. 534–5]

Again concerning Orpheus:

What was he to do? Where could he go now his wife was snatched away a second time? [*Georgic* 4. 504]

And concerning Nisus:

What is he to do? By what force or what arms is he to dare to rescue his young friend? [*Aen.* 9. 399–400]

And Anna emotionally cries:

What shall I lament first as I am left deserted? Have you died to spurn your sister and friend? [*Aen.* 4. 677–8]

Macrobius uses the word *de* ('concerning') in relation to the characters Orpheus and Nisus in his second and third examples. This implies a presupposition that the deliberative questions in these two examples are primarily in the voice of the poet: questions are posed *by* the poet *about* the characters. But Macrobius' remark that *addubitatio* 'is characteristic of someone in a state of grief or anger' reveals awareness that the figure in some way represents the utterance of a character.

Macrobius' classification of third-person deliberative questions (along with those in the first person) as *addubitatio* is also instructive in showing how they have an affective impact on the audience. By posing these questions in the third person, the poet is also giving a strident declamation of his own. An observation by 'Longinus' on self-questioning is pertinent here:

Emotion carries us away more easily when it seems to be generated by the occasion rather than deliberately assumed by the speaker, and the self-directed question and its answer represent precisely the momentary quality of emotion. Just as people who are unexpectedly plied with questions become annoyed and reply to the point with vigour and exact truth, so the figure of question and answer arrests the hearer and cheats him into believing that all the points were raised and are being put into words on the spur of the moment.

(*On the Sublime* 18. 2[49])

Even if the standard mode of reception of the *Aeneid* in antiquity was by individual reading, awareness of the possibility of recitation could still colour attitudes to the main narrator. The narrator's voice could still be identified with a hypothetical *recitator*: ancient

---

[49] This translation is taken from Russell and Winterbottom (1972), 482.

critics would tend to see the third-person deliberative questions
(which we regard as FID) in rhetorical terms, as a technique used
by a storyteller to draw attention to his own discourse.

Other passages in the *Aeneid* can be classified as examples of
FID. However, these further passages could be understood as
forms of apostrophe, but they do not contain deliberative questions. It is impossible to establish decisively whether they present
characters' discourse directly or indirectly. This passage, for example, conveys the laments and complaints of the Trojan women
after the funeral of Anchises:[50]

> at procul in sola secretae Troades acta
> amissum Anchisen flebant, cunctaeque profundum
> pontum aspectabant flentes. *heu tot vada fessis*
> *et tantum superesse maris*, vox omnibus una;
> urbem orant, taedet pelagi perferre laborem.
>
> (5. 613–17)

But the Trojan women had withdrawn far off to an isolated beach and were
weeping for the loss of Anchises, and all of them were looking out at the
deep sea as they wept. *Alas so many waves and so great a sea for the weary to
overcome*—one voice common to all: they pray for a city, it is grievous to
endure the toil of the ocean.

Some texts place *heu . . . maris* ('Alas . . . overcome') within
quotation marks, others do not. If these words are to be regarded
as direct discourse, the infinitive construction—normally indicative of the indirect mode—could be explained as an accusative and
infinitive of exclamation.[51] If *vox* is translated as 'utterance'[52] ('one
utterance common to them all'), we can have the idea of the Trojan
women saying the same thing in choric unison.[53] Direct discourse is

---

[50] Nugent (1992) offers a thorough and fascinating discussion of the political role
of the 'voice of the women' in *Aeneid* 5, with a particular bearing on this passage at
267–84.

[51] See R. D. Williams (1960) ad loc., and R. G. Austin (1971) on 1. 37.

[52] *Vox* is elsewhere found in the context of utterances in DD in the *Aeneid*, e.g.
2. 119, after the oracle of Phoebus to the Trojans has been quoted; 3. 40–1, cf. 3. 93–
4 (another oracle); 6. 686 (of Aeneas' utterance to Anchises); 7. 95 (oracle to
Latinus); 7. 117 (Iulus' utterance); 9. 112. See also p. 238 n. 63.

[53] Given the Euripidean feel here, there may be a poignancy in Virgil's use of the
word *Troades*, the title of a play which of course has a chorus of Trojan women—
the word occurs only here in the *Aeneid*. (Ennius might have written a *Troades*, see
Fantham (1982), 4–5). If there is some kind of generic absorption going on, it might
be appropriate for a group of women to give forth a direct utterance in chorus. And,
more speculatively, might it be significant that it is at this point Iris enters *acting a
part*—that of Beroe—and speaks, 620 f.? On *Virgil*'s 'ventriloquism' here, again see
Nugent (1992), 277–84.

not usually ascribed to groups of speakers in the *Aeneid*, but one
exception to Virgil's standard practice would offer a fascinating
parallel for this passage in Book 5. When the Latin citizens rush to
the walls to watch the conflict on the plains, their women, led by
Amata, utter a prayer which is presented chorically in free direct
discourse:

> et maestas alto fundunt de limine voces:
> 'armipotens, praeses belli, Tritonia virgo,
> frange manu telum Phrygii praedonis, et ipsum
> pronum sterne solo portisque effunde sub altis.'
>
> (11. 482–5)

And they pour out sad cries from the high temple portal: 'Mighty in arms,
ruler of the battle, Tritonian maiden, with your hand break the spear of the
Phrygian bandit, and lay him flat on your soil and fell him under your high
gates.'

The sentiments of these shared cries (*voces*) of the Latin women, like
the utterance (*vox*) of the Trojan women, also resist the course of
fate. Alternatively, the phrase in 5. 615–16 could be in some form of
indirect discourse. This would be likely given its brevity, and the
nature of its context—as the distillation of several utterances made
by a group. So it is best regarded as another example of FID.[54] The
word *heu* ('alas') could equally signal either the reaction of the
narrator as he interjects, or the merging of his voice with that of
the women.[55] The question of who is speaking could remain open.[56]
This indeterminacy would be more prominent in an ancient
unpunctuated text.

A second example also comes at a point in the story when the
character whose discourse is reported is in a state of high agitation.
This is the description of Amata's raving after she has failed to

---

[54] For standard ID, the Latin would read rather awkwardly: there is the problem
of this infinitive construction being dependent either on *flentes* or on a declarative
verb that has to be understood.

[55] Compare the function of *eheu* in Catullus 64. 61 (mentioned in the next
chapter). Ariadne is also woefully looking out to sea: *saxea ut effigies bacchantis,
prospicit, eheu | prospicit* and the *heu* in the storm simile in *Aen.* 12. 452–3 (*miseris,
heu, praescia longe | horrescunt corda agricolis*). On the difference between *eheu* and
heu see Lyne (1978), 212–3 on *Ciris* 264.

[56] Ennius, *Annales* 163 might provide some kind of precedent for a passage like
5. 615–6: *Inde sibi memorat unum superesse laborem. Memorare* can be a declarative
verb for direct or indirect speech: it would not be impossible for this to be in DD
too: *inde sibi memorat: 'unum superesse laborem!'*

convince Latinus by argument that it is Turnus whom Lavinia
should marry. Driven to a frenzy by Allecto's serpent, she is
compared to a spinning top as she rages through the city, pretending to be driven by Bacchus' presence. The possible rendering of
Amata's discourse follows this comparison:

> quin etiam in silvas simulato numine Bacchi
> maius adorta nefas maioremque orsa furorem
> evolat et natam frondosis montibus abdit,
> quo thalamum eripiat Teucris taedasque moretur,
> euhoe Bacche fremens, solum te virgine dignum
> vociferans: etenim mollis tibi sumere thyrsos,
> te lustrare choro, sacrum tibi pascere crinem.
>
> (7. 385–91)

What is more, Amata flew out to the woods feigning that she was possessed
by the god Bacchus, and rising to greater evil and greater madness, she
hides her daughter in the leafy mountains in order to wrest the bride from
the Trojans and delay the wedding, shrieking euhoe o Bacchus, and
pronouncing that you alone are worthy of the maiden: indeed for you she
takes up the soft leaved thyrsus, it is you she honours in the ritual dance,
and as a consecration to you she grows her hair.

As with nearly all other sentences where the narrator's voice in the
third person seems to merge with that of the speaker(s) described,
the narrative present is used. Here a second person apostrophe to
Bacchus appears to sprout out of the presentation of Amata's
discourse: the god is addressed in the vocative, and the pronoun
forms *te* ('you') and *tibi* ('to you') are used twice each in three
successive verses. The fact that Amata's invocation to Bacchus is
not given straightforwardly in direct discourse could reinforce what
was indicated by *simulato numine Bacchi* (385); her frenzy is not a
genuinely religious one.[57]

---

[57] *Euhoe Bacche fremens* ('shrieking euhoe o Bacchus') echoes Catullus 64. 255:
euhoe there could either be the rendering of the Bacchantes' discourse or an
exclamation by the narrator. We can also compare the technique of speech
presentation here to that in the hymn to Hercules (*Aen.* 8. 287–302) which is in
indirect discourse, and contains an apostrophe to Hercules in the second person.
Amata's hymn here must also be worth considering as a precedent to the hymn to
Bacchus in Ovid's *Metamorphoses* 4. 11 f.; surprisingly Danielewicz (1990) does not
include this among the models he lists for Ovid's practice in that passage. See also
Georgics 2. 2 and esp. 2. 385–9. The quotation of 7. 385–91 given on this page and
its whole context recall the *Bacchae* heavily. 7. 385 echoes *Bacc.* 218; 7. 405
(*reginam Allecto stimulis agit undique Bacchi*): *Bacc.* 119.

The preceding review of these passages provides some useful insights on the *Aeneid*'s narrative strategy. These insights call into question contemporary assumptions about what FID actually is—or at least the applicability of those assumptions to ancient epic.

1. The passages I have classified as FID are frequently surrounded by verbs in the narrative present. This is not such a common feature of FID in modern fictional narrative.[58] However the use of the narrative present in Virgil certainly contributes to an effect of vividness which is in keeping with the common conception of FID as a means of representing 'streams of consciousness'. The narrative present facilitates reproduction of characters' physical perceptions (for instance) in the narrator's voice.

2. In the *Aeneid* and *Georgics*, FID occurs when the characters whose discourse is being presented are in a state of extreme anxiety or even frenzy. Whilst this is the case in other Latin authors, the trend is not so evident in modern fiction—FID or 'indirect interior monologue' is often the norm for expressing a principal character's thoughts and feelings about anything, however incidental or trivial.[59] Indeed, many modern novels are narrated wholly or almost wholly in FID. This suggests that FID in Virgil functions principally as a rhetorical resource for a narrator at crucial points in a story; its role is not to confer idiolects on characters, but to signal traumatic experience in a dramatic and recognizable way.[60]

3. Thus in Virgil, FID can be seen to render narratorial comment as much as the sentiments of a character. Our confusion about what is unequivocally narratorial intrusion or apostrophe shows the extent to which this is so.

4. It is not always clear whether FID serves to present spoken words or silent thoughts. The last two instances considered (the Trojan women complaining and Amata's prayer at 7. 389) definitely seem to be speeches; the previous passages largely seem to be

[58] Rimmon-Kenan (1983), 111–13 identifying the linguistic features of FID in contemporary fiction notes, 'FID retains the "back-shift" of tenses characterisitic of ID.'

[59] For examples of FID applied in other Latin authors (after Virgil) for situations in which characters are in a state of high agitation, see references in the notes above. The device is most conspicuous in Ovid, e.g. *Fasti* 2. 771–5, 2. 800–4; *Metamorphoses* (also in a first-person form in the *Heroides*, e.g. 10. 11–12: see Ch. 3 n. 65). It also occurs in the epic narratives of Statius and Valerius Flaccus.

[60] Pasolini (1988) lays great emphasis on the role of ideolect and ideology in modern uses of FID.

renderings of thought. In this respect, one element of the passage of
FID, already examined, which presented Aeneas' thoughts at
4. 279 f. should be noted. Aeneas deliberates about what he
should say to Dido, and what words he should use:

> At vero Aeneas aspectu obmutuit amens,
> arrectaeque horrore comae et vox faucibus haesit.
> ardet abire fuga dulcisque relinquere terras,
> attonitus tanto monitu imperioque deorum.
> heu quid agat? quo nunc reginam ambire furentem
> audeat adfatu? quae prima exordia sumat?
> atque animum nunc huc celerem nunc dividit illuc
> in partisque rapit varias perque omnia versat.
>
> (4. 279–95)

But Aeneas was dumbstruck and aghast at the apparition. His hair bristled
with horror and his voice stuck in his throat. He burns to flee away and
leave the sweet lands, overwhelmed both by so mighty a warning and the
gods' command. Oh what should he do? With what words is he to dare now
to approach the queen in her rage? What beginning should he choose? His
thoughts swiftly moved now this way now that way—he rushes them in
various directions and turns them through all the possibilities.

This is a clear example of the reflexive quality of this form. The
character is speechless, in part because he does not know what he is
going to say—the narrator cannot then let his audience hear such a
dilemma expressed in direct discourse. It is worth comparing a
possible earlier use of FID, in a part of Aeneas' first-person
narrative of his experiences to Dido. Aeneas has related a horrific
portent—how blood flowed from the roots of the saplings he was
pulling up to cover an altar:

> tertia sed postquam maiore hastilia nisu
> adgredior genibusque adversae obluctor harenae,
> (eloquar an sileam?) gemitus lacrimabilis imo
> auditur tumulo . . .
>
> (3. 37–40)

But after I set about the third set of spearlike shrubs with a still greater
effort and on my knees strain against the resisting sand, (should I speak or
be silent?) a tearful groan sounds from deep in the mound . . .

If they do not mark a pause in narration by Aeneas before Dido and
company, the words *eloquar an sileam* ('should I speak or be silent?')
could be FID conveying his own doubt and hesitation at the time of

the incident he is describing. Part of the riddle of FID is whether it presents speech or silence.[61]

5.3 SPEECH AND SILENCE IN THE *AENEID*

The next two sections of this chapter will consider further aspects of speech and silence in the *Aeneid*. Relationships between speech and silence play an important part in the overall rhetorical strategy of the poem. Consideration of a curious feature in the narrative of the *Aeneid* sheds important light on that strategy. The curious feature is this: on the majority (approximately three-quarters) of the occasions in which the narrator presents the speech of his characters in direct discourse, just one single speech is given. Such a speech receives no verbal response at all from the person addressed. The shortage of replies has often been remarked upon by scholars, though it has never been satisfactorily explained.[62] The apparent deficiency is especially noticeable in scenes modelled on episodes in Homer, where exchanges of speeches between speakers can be quite sustained.[63] In contrast, there are very few occasions in the *Aeneid* on which two or more speakers exchange a speech each, and fewer still in which more than two speeches are exchanged.[64]

---

[61] On *Aen.* 3. 39, the Servian corpus has: *ELOQUAR AN SILEAM parenthesis ad miracula posita; qua magnitudinem monstri ostendit. et bene auditorem attentum vult facere.* Compare Euripides *Iphigenia in Tauris* 939–40: λέγοιμ' ἄν· ἀρχαὶ δ' αἰδε μοι πολλῶν πόνων | ἐπαὶ τὰ μητρὸς ταῦθ' ἃ σιγῶμεν κακὰ . . . On related devices of *aposiopesis* see Lausberg (1973) §§887–888 and Aphthonius 1. 258–9.

[62] Lyne (1987), 145 in introducing his notion of the 'cut-off' technique comments on the lack of 'conversation' in Virgil: 'V. does appear to pass up the chance. His normal practice (there are some exceptions) is to restrict conversation to two characters, and on each occasion to permit no more than a speech, a reply and then perhaps a further retort by the first speaker.' Compare Feeney (1983), 213 f. and accompanying notes.

[63] Heinze (1993), 315–21 = (1915), 404–14.

[64] The passages in which two or more speakers exchange speeches are: 1. 65–80; 1. 229–96; 1. 522–78; 1. 595–630; 1. 753–3. 715 (Dido's request for Aeneas' story, and the story itself. That 2. 1–3. 715 should be counted as an exchange of *rheseis* will be argued below). Within Aeneas' account, exchanges of speech occur at: 2. 69–194 (Sinon and the Trojans); 2. 281–95; 2. 322–35; 2. 535–50; 3. 359–462. Then: 4. 9–53; 5. 348–56; 5. 724–42; 5. 781–815; 5. 843–51; 6. 318–30; 6. 388–407; 6. 560–627; 6. 669–76; 7. 116–34; 7. 545–60; 8. 36–78; 8. 127–74; 8. 374–404; 9. 6–22; 9. 83–103; 10. 524–34; 11. 108–31; 11. 502–19; 11. 705–17; 12. 889–95; 12. 931–49. I concur with Highet (1972) in giving this maximum estimate of 32 altogether. In addition H. counts six cases in which there are two speakers who make a speech each, but in which the first speaker is not directly addressed in response by the second, but the second speech is made as a consequence of the first e.g. Latinus makes a prayer at 12. 197–211, just after Aeneas has done the same (12. 176–94)

The fact that the majority of occasions in which direct discourse is presented in the *Aeneid* involve only one (unanswered) speech is positively significant. Here I will offer two different sorts of reason for the lack of replying in Virgil. The first, set out in the rest of this section, pertains to the *Aeneid* specifically, and concerns the way speech and silence are used for dramatic effect. The second, pursued in section 5.4, has general implications which go beyond the realm of Roman poetry.

Dramatic effect can account for the absence of a reply to a single speech in direct discourse, but it applies only in very exceptional cases. These occur at points in the story where the poem's audience might expect an addressee to make a speech in reply and feel disconcerted when this does not happen. A celebrated example is Dido's cold silence after Aeneas' words to her when he sees her in the Plains of Mourning in the Underworld (*Aeneid* 6. 450 f.). Even after her death, Dido cannot forgive Aeneas for leaving her. There is a precedent for this in the eleventh book of Homer's *Odyssey*. When Odysseus speaks to the shade of the dead Ajax, he does not reply. In contrast to what we shall see in Virgil, the audience are not really led by Odysseus' closing plea to expect any words in response:

> ἀλλ' ἄγε δεῦρο, ἄναξ, ἵν' ἔπος καὶ μῦθον ἀκούσῃς
> ἡμέτερον· δάμασον δὲ μένος καὶ ἀγήνορα θυμόν.
> (*Odyssey* 11. 561–2)

'Come to me now, Lord [Ajax], and hear my words and speech; subdue your spirit and proud heart.'

Ajax's stubborn silence is then brought home by Odysseus (who is Homer's narrator at this point):

> Ὣς ἐφάμην, ὁ δέ μ' οὐδὲν ἀμείβετο, βῆ δὲ μετ' ἄλλας
> ψυχὰς εἰς Ἔρεβος νεκύων κατατεθνηώτων.
> (*Odyssey* 11. 563–4)

So I spoke, *but he made no reply to me*, and only followed to Erebus the other souls of the dead and deceased.

---

when they strike their truce. There are 17 occasions on which 3 to 8 speeches are exchanged. Most of these involve the exchange of 3 or 4 set speeches (*rheseis*) which are spoken by personages of effectively equal status.

That silence had a great impact on Homer's early readers. 'Longinus' said this silence was more sublime than any speech.[65]

The effect of Dido's dramatic silence is rather different. The passage in which it occurs must be quoted in full to show exactly how it is achieved:

> demisit lacrimas dulcique adfatus amore est:
> 'infelix Dido, verus mihi nuntius ergo
> venerat exstinctam ferroque extrema secutam?
> funeris heu tibi causa fui? per sidera iuro,
> per superos et si qua fides tellure sub ima est,
> invitus, regina, tuo de litore cessi.
> sed me iussa deum, quae nunc has ire per umbras,
> per loca senta situ cogunt noctemque profundam,
> imperiis egere suis; nec credere quivi
> hunc tantum tibi me discessu ferre dolorem.
> siste gradum teque aspectu ne subtrahe nostro.
> quem fugis? extremum fato quod te adloquor hoc est.'
> talibus Aeneas ardentem et torva tuentem
> lenibat dictis animum lacrimasque ciebat.
> illa solo fixos oculos aversa tenebat
> nec magis incepto vultum sermone movetur
> quam si dura silex aut stet Marpesia cautes.
> tandem corripuit sese atque inimica refugit
> in nemus umbriferum, coniunx ubi pristinus illi
> respondet curis aequatque Sychaeus amorem.
>
> (6. 455–74)

Aeneas wept and addressed her with sweet love: 'Unhappy Dido, so was the message they brought me true, that you were dead and had ended your life with the sword? Alas! Was I the cause of your dying? I swear by the stars, by the gods above, by whatever there is to swear by in the depths of the earth, it was against my will, O Queen, that I left your shore. It was the orders of the gods, that drove me on, as they now drive me through these shades, through this desolate place and deep night. I could not have believed that my leaving would have caused you such sorrow. Do not move away and leave my sight. Whom are you fleeing? Fate has decreed that I shall not speak to you again.'

---

[65] *On the Sublime* 9. 2. Russell (1964) ad loc. compares a similar judgement to that of 'Longinus' in the scholia on *Od.* 11. 563. Ajax's silence prompted an interpolation in Homer's text (11. 565–7) which softens its effect: in those verses Odysseus is made to maintain that nonetheless Ajax would have spoken to him, and he to Ajax, were it not that he was keen to see the other souls of the dead. See Heubeck and Hoekstra (1989) ad loc.

With these words Aeneas, shedding tears, was trying to comfort that burning spirit. But staring grimly, she turned away and kept her eyes fixed on the ground. Her face showed she was no more moved at his opening words than if she had been hard flint or a crag of marble from Mount Marpessus. So, finally, she rushed away, still hostile, into the shadows of the wood, where Sychaeus her former husband responds to her cares and equals her love.

Even if the questions which open Aeneas' speech require no answers from Dido, the strength of his oath and declaration that he left Carthage unwillingly, failing to predict the extent of her grief, ought to get some kind of response. But as Aeneas speaks, Dido starts walking away, as *siste gradum etc.* ('Do not move away . . .') at 465 indicates. *Quem fugis?* ('Whom are you fleeing?') in the following verse shows that Dido is still in retreat. Aeneas' speech ends with an urgent plea: this is the last time fate will allow him to speak to her.

However the diction following Aeneas' direct discourse, in my view, leads the audience to expect that Dido *is* going to speak. The narrative strategy which induces this expectation—only to frustrate it—is what proves that this silence is pointedly dramatic. That frustrated expectation is partly engineered by the imagery in 469–71. These verses give the misleading impression that Dido stops moving away *after* she has heard the speech. Verse 469—*illa solo fixos oculos aversa tenebat* ('she turned away and kept her eyes fixed on the ground') briefly gives us the wrong idea—that Dido is still present after Aeneas has spoken. Moreover, the phrases *fixos oculos . . . tenebat* ('she kept her eyes fixed'), *nec magis . . . movetur* ('she was no more moved') and the comparison with hard flint and the crag from Mount Marpesssus, give the impression of Dido being immobile far more powerfully than the exact conception of *when* this is. Properly the phrases only convey that Dido was motionless at the point in the story when Aeneas *began* speaking (*incepto . . . sermone* 470).[66] This is simply because the description of her earlier immobility is positioned in the *narrative* after the presentation of Aeneas' words: in fact the description applies to the moment in the *story* when Aeneas is speaking. This has been noted by one modern commentator, but the fact that he is obliged to emphasize this demonstrates that it is not made immediately clear by the verses

[66] Here I draw support from 'Servius' who glosses *incepto . . . sermone* as *a principio orationis* ('from the beginning of his speech').

themselves.[67] My point is that the narrative actively tricks the audience into temporarily thinking that Dido is still standing there, when she has already gone.

The frustrated expectation of a reply from Dido is also engineered by another means. The diction of 6. 469–70 here echoes an earlier exchange between Aeneas and Dido, in the fourth book. The verses echoed run as follows:

> Talia dicentem iamdudum aversa tuetur
> huc illuc volvens oculos totumque pererrat
> luminibus tacitis et sic accensa profatur:
> 'nec tibi diva parens generis nec Dardanus auctor,
> perfide, sed duris genuit te cautibus horrens
> Caucasus . . .'

> (4. 362–7)

For some time Dido had turned away as she regarded Aeneas whilst he said these things. Turning her gaze here and there, she surveys everything with silent eyes. Then, on fire with rage, she speaks:

'It was no goddess that brought forth your lineage nor was Dardanus your ancestor, you traitor, but the freezing Caucasus with its hard crags spawned you . . .'

Those verses in book 4 *were* followed by a speech from Dido, while 6. 469–71 are not.[68] Yet we are tempted into expecting one: after *tandem* in 6. 472, we might well expect *dixit* ('she spoke') or some other declarative verb. Instead there is the abrupt *corripuit sese* ('she rushed away'). I am not grounding this argument for there being a frustrated expectation purely on the contrast made by the comparable diction of these two passages. At numerous earlier points, the narrator has described the countenance of characters, particularly

---

[67] R. G. Austin (1977) on 6. 468: 'Virgil is in fact restating the situation as Aeneas was speaking: this line looks back to 455, with *lenibat* here corresponding to *dulci adfatus amore* there, *demisit lacrimas* picked up in *lacrimas ciebat* here, a chiastic arrangement. Similarly, what follows describes first Dido's reaction to the opening of Aeneas' speech (*incepto sermone*, 470) then her convulsive movement (472) at the point where Aeneas cries *siste gradum* (465).' D. P. Fowler (1990) offers various ways of interpreting this passage.

[68] Dido's speech there (4. 365–87) ends with her abrupt departure. Aeneas again wants to address her, but cannot in 4. 388–91: *his medium dictis sermonem abrumpit et auras | aegra fugit seque ex oculis avertit et aufert, | linquens multa metu cunctantem et multa parantem | dicere.* The situation is not quite the same as in 6. 455 f. Aeneas' lack of opportunity to speak may be pathetic (the narrator makes it clear that Aeneas would have plenty to say if he could), but we are not tricked into expecting a speech when nothing follows. The tableau here is more similar to that of Evander's farewell to Pallas which I shall treat next.

making mention of their eyes, immediately before their speech is presented.[69] The impact of Dido's silence after the narration of Aeneas' speech has not been fully understood. The narrative devices employed in this scene serve to surprise the audience. Aeneas himself, though saddened by Dido's silence, is not so surprised by it, because he must have been aware of Dido's departure from the point at which he began addressing her.[70] An elaborate narrative strategy contributes to the disconcerting effect of this episode. Readers of Virgil have long been aware of the force of Dido's refusal to reply—even though unanswered speeches are a routine feature in the *Aeneid*.[71]

---

[69] The instances preceding this one in 6, apart from 4. 362–3, are: 1. 227–9 *atque illum talis iactantem pectore curas | tristior et lacrimis oculos suffusa nitentis | adloquitur Venus: 'o qui res hominumque . . .'*; 2. 68–9 *constitit atque oculis Phrygia agmina circumspexit, | 'heu, quae nunc tellus . . .'*; 2. 687–9 *at pater Anchises oculos ad sidera laetus | extulit et caelo palmas cum voce tetendit: | 'Iuppiter omnipotens . . .'*; 4. 220–2 *audiit Omnipotens, oculosque ad moenia torsit | regia et oblitos famae melioris amantis | tum sic Mercurium adloquitur ac talia mandat . . .* There are of course other examples later in the poem e.g. 7. 249 f. and 8. 152–4. Especially notable are the mentions at the climax of the poem of the eyes of Turnus before he begs Aeneas for his life (12. 930) and of Aeneas' eye movements (*volvens oculos* 12. 939) which eventually catch sight of the swordbelt prior to his harsh reply. See Heuzé (1985), 540–81 for a full treatment of '*regards*' in Virgil: especially 563 f. on *volvere oculos*. As eyes were regarded as a 'mirror of the soul', H. suggests eyes provide extra information (even if it is not always easy to decode). This can complement whatever insight we may glean from the speeches.

[70] This seems to be the case even if we consider the possibility that 469–71 are focalized through Aeneas. At the close of this episode (6. 475–6) Aeneas is described as being horror-struck, probably more at Dido's grim fortune than at her refusal to answer him (cf. 'Servius' ad loc.): *nec minus* [i.e. no less than Sychaeus, cf. *respondet curis* 474] *Aeneas casu percussus iniquo | prosequitur lacrimis longe et miseratur euntem*.

[71] Two parodies bear witness to the general force of this episode. In Ovid, *Fasti* 3. 601 Aeneas and Achates stumble upon Anna on the Lavinian shore: *aspicit errantem* (cf. *errabat, Aen.* 6. 451) *nec credere sustinet Annam*. Aeneas' hailing of Anna echoes his oath to Dido (6. 458 f.): *Anna, per hanc iuro, quam quondam audire solebas | tellurem fato prosperiore dari, | perque deos comites . . .* (*Fasti* 3. 613 f.). Anna does reply, but her response is presented in RSA (*errores exposuitque suos* 626): we do not hear her words. The second parody, in Scarron's 17th-cent. *Le Virgile Travesti* (ed. Serroy 1988) plays more directly on Dido's response at 6. 1756 f. : *Mais elle, d'une mine grise, | Paya ce joli compliment, | Sans s'ébranler aucunement | Des beaux endroits de sa harangue, | Et, lui tirant un pied de langue, | Rendant son visage vilain, | Faisant les cornes d'une main, | Et de pétarade, | Et sur le tout une gambade, | Le laissa pleurer tout son soûl. | Quelque auteur (il faut qu'il soit fou) | Écrit que cette âme damnée | Dit au révérend maître Énée: | <Allez vous faire tout à droit . . .* The editor supplies the following comment on this last verse: 'Terme qui sert à couvrir une parole qu'on ne veut pas prononcer'.

Another example of this kind of dramatic effect occurs when
Evander sees off his son, Pallas, who is joining the Trojan forces.
Fama, the personification of rumour, who has propagated fear and
foreboding through Evander's city (8. 554–7), has a role in generating the grim effect of this farewell scene—she will return later to
spread the word of Pallas' death (11. 139–41). But several features
of Evander's farewell speech themselves induce a sense of unease:

> tum pater Evandrus *dextram complexus* euntis
> haeret inexpletus lacrimans ac talia fatur:
> 'o mihi praeteritos referat si Iuppiter annos,
> qualis eram cum primam aciem Praeneste sub ipsa
> stravi scutorumque incendi victor acervos
> et regem *hac* Erulum *dextra* sub Tartara misi,
> nascenti cui tris animas Feronia mater
> (horrendum dictu) dederat, terna arma movenda—
> ter leto sternendus erat; cui tunc tamen omnis
> abstulit *haec* animas *dextra* et totidem exuit armis:
> non ego nunc *dulci amplexu divellerer usquam,*
> *nate, tuo,* neque finitimo Mezentius umquam
> *huic capiti* insultans tot ferro saeva dedisset
> funera, tam multis viduasset civibus urbem.
> at vos, o superi, et divum tu maxime rector
> Iuppiter, Arcadii, quaeso, miserescite regis
> et patrias audite preces. si numina vestra
> incolumem Pallanta mihi, si fata reservant,
> si visurus eum vivo et venturus in unum,
> vitam oro, patior quemvis durare laborem.
> sin aliquem infandum casum, Fortuna, minaris,
> nunc, nunc o liceat crudelem abrumpere vitam,
> dum curae ambiguae, dum spes incerta futuri,
> dum *te,* care puer, mea sola et sera voluptas,
> *complexu teneo,* gravior neu nuntius auris
> vulneret.' haec genitor *digressu* dicta *supremo*
> fundebat; famuli conlapsum in tecta ferebant.
>
> (8. 558–84)

Then the father Evander, as his son was departing, *clung on to his right arm*
in an embrace. He wept uncontrollably, and spoke words like these:
  'If only Jupiter would give me back the years that are past, when, as I
was, I laid low the front rank of the enemy's battle line under the very walls
of Praeneste, heaping up their shields and burning them to celebrate my
victory; when *with this right hand* I sent down to Tartarus the king Erulus,
whose mother Feronia had given him three lives at birth—horrible to

recall—three sets of armour to carry into battle, and three times I had to lay him dead on the ground, when in those days, *this one right hand* was able to take his lives and strip him of so many sets of armour, then *I would never now be torn from this sweet embrace with you my son*, and Mezentius would never have been able to trample upon his neighbour, putting so many to the sword and widowing the city of so many people.

O gods in heaven, and you, Jupiter, greatest ruler of the gods, pity, please, an Arcadian king and hear a father's prayers. If your divine powers and the fates preserve Pallas for me unharmed, if I am to live to see him and be together with him again, then I pray for life and will prepare to endure any trial. But if, Fortune, you threaten an unspeakable disaster, now at this moment allow me to break off this cruel life, whilst my sorrows are still unclear, whilst my expectation of the future is still uncertain, whilst *I still hold you in this embrace*, dear child, my sole and late found source of joy, and let no grim news wound my ears.'

The father was pouring these words out at their *final parting*. He had collapsed and his attendants were carrying him into the house.

Evander holds Pallas in an embrace throughout the time he makes this speech. We are constantly reminded of the posture of the speaker and his addressee while this speech is being made, by indexicals such as *hac dextra* ('with this right hand'), *dulci amplexu . . . tuo* ('this sweet embrace with you') emphasized in the excerpts above. It is also clear that Pallas departs—or tries to depart—as Evander is still speaking: the expression *digressu . . . supremo* ('at their final parting' 583) actually conveys the physical sundering of their embrace.[72] The imperfect tenses in Latin (*fundebat, ferebant*

---

[72] Belfiore (1984*b*) treats embraces in Virgil. On 8. 583, 'Servius' notes: *SUPREMO hoc ex persona poetae, quia periturus est Pallas*: a narratival *prolepsis*—see Genette (1980), 40—signalling Pallas' death, while very much in the Virgilian manner, is one possibility. On the poetics of 'Servius' in relation to modern theory, see Lazzarini (1989). *Supremo* may also indicate the grim foreboding tone of Evander's speech. *Digressu . . . supremo* might be a comment on the quality of Evander's discourse here and previously. The structure of this speech accomodates Nestorean digressions and reminiscences (Fordyce (1977) on 560 f. lists speeches in the *Iliad* recalled by this one): 8. 561–7 contain an anecdote to illustrate what E.'s past years were like; the comment about Mezentius and the prayers to the gods also have narrative elements. *Digressu . . . supremo* might have an additional meta-literary significance: this is Evander's last speech to contain digressions: his final speech (11. 152–81) has no recollections of the more distant past and only expresses wishes that recent events had gone differently. Quintilian (10. 5. 17; 4. 3. 14; 10. 1. 49) provides instances of *digressus* having a figurative sense of 'deviating in speech' or 'digression'. Possibly *digressus* was used colloquially instead of *digressio* for the figurative as well as the literal sense of the latter word (compare the interchangeability of *accessio* and *accessus*).

584) also suggest Evander is carried away as he is still speaking.[73] In spite of all this, and in spite of being apostrophized emphatically in his father's speech (*nate* 569, *te, care puer* 581), Pallas says nothing in response.

The heavenly gods, including Jupiter (572–3) and Fortuna (578), are also addressed by Evander. Whilst gods do not generally make verbal replies to prayers in ancient epic, the lack of any divine sign here seems more significant because Evander's previous speech (8. 470–519) did obtain a response from the gods. Then there was a clap of thunder and Aeneas' arms appeared in the sky. Much later, in his final speech in the poem, Evander remarks on the gods' indifference to his prayers for his son's life (11. 157–8). No other character speaks in this scene to reassure Evander: the grim effect recalls premonitory scenes of mourning in the *Iliad*.[74] This scene can also be compared to Juturna's display of grief in anticipation of Turnus' death (12. 885–6) following her prior soliloquy.

Poignantly significant silences are found elsewhere, in ancient genres other than epic: in the tragic drama of Aeschylus, in the comedy of Menander, and, very frequently, in a notable contemporary of Virgil—the historian Livy.[75] But these two scenes from the *Aeneid* share a couple of distinctive features. The fact that replies in the Homeric models for these scenes do exist induces the

---

[73] Conington and Nettleship (1883) ad loc. compare 4. 391–2, but remark that the imperfects show 'that the old man fails and is carried away while he is yet speaking'.

[74] Andromache and the women symbolically mourn for Hector who is still living (*Iliad* 6. 498–502) and for Priam (*Iliad* 24. 328). Thetis' grief for Achilles at *Iliad* 24. 94—which does not quite amount to mourning—provides the prototype for Juturna.

[75] See Taplin (1972) and Thalmann (1985*a*) and (1985*b*) on silences in Aeschylus; Bardon (1943–4) considers the role of silence in Menander's drama. In Livy, significant silences take two distinct forms: (i) the hush is explicitly mentioned as an event in the story (e.g. 1. 13. 4 *silentium et repentina fit quies*) which adds suspense. Ogilvie (1965) on Livy 3. 47. 6 lists instances with bibliography; (ii) silence is used for purposes of characterization. For example in Tarquin's interview with Attus Navius (1. 36. 4), the seer is shown to be reticent and modest by the presentation in ID of his respone to Tarquin's impertinent question in DD. On hearing Tarquin's second command to cut the whetstone, Attius Navius says nothing but simply acts. Similar narrative techniques present Coriolanus as the strong silent type in 2. 40: the second time envoys approach his camp, they are sent away with no reply at all. C.'s response to the news that a group of women is approaching the camp is behavioural not verbal (*multo obstinatior adversus lacrimas muliebres erat*). Even when Coriolanus comes to embrace his mother, the only words we hear are hers: no speech from him is hinted at throughout the narration of this incident.

sensation that replies in these Virgilian scenes are missing. Internal features of Virgil's narrative in these passages also raise the audience's expectation of a speech in response—an expectation which is not fulfilled.

5.4 POWER RELATIONS BETWEEN SPEAKERS AND ADDRESSEES

Instances like those just considered, in which the lack of reply to a speech is an obviously significant response, are very much the exception in the poem. The superior positions of speakers in the poem, and their power over their addressees account for the 125 remaining unanswered speeches. Altogether, 88 of the total of 127 speeches which receive no answer are made by a speaker who is of a superior standing to his addressee(s) in political, military, divine, gender, or family status or, occasionally, in knowledge or expertise.[76]

In the *Aeneid*, far more than in previous epics, it seems to be for those in authority to speak and the inclination or the duty of those with less power to remain silent. This is conveniently illustrated by the behaviour of Aeneas' son, Ascanius. His role as an agent and speaker varies in different situations, which require him to be dominant on some occasions and subordinate on others. As a child, generally in the presence of his father, he is normally seen and not heard.[77] For example, by way of saying farewell to Ascanius before he goes into the final battle, Aeneas advises him to follow the examples of his elders:

---

[76] For a finer examination of silence in the *Aeneid* in relation to the politics of gender, see Nugent (1992).

[77] Compare Highet (1972), 28: 'Young people in the *Aeneid* say very little. The high-spirited Nisus talks most, with fifty-seven lines; but Pallas has only twenty-four, Camilla less than seventeen. Lavinia and Lausus, in spite of their importance in the plot, never speak at all. The voice of Ascanius is heard for the first time briefly in the fifth book, where he sounds like a young prince (5. 670–673). During his father's absence, he speaks four times uttering forty-one lines in all. Thereafter we see him weeping (12. 399) and in the farewell embrace of his father (12. 433–434), but he speaks no more. He is no Telemachus.' However conclusions drawn from a limited analysis like Highet's can be misleading. For a start, there is no discernible category of 'young people' in the *Aeneid* which corresponds to Highet's: Camilla and Lavinia, for example, as young women are very different in terms of function and status. Nor need 'importance in the plot' ever necessarily require detailed portrayal or, as part of this, a large number of words to say.

Ascanium fusis circum complectitur armis
summaque per galeam delibans oscula fatur:
'*disce, puer*, virtutem ex me verumque laborem,
fortunam ex aliis. nunc te mea dextera bello
defensum dabit et magna inter praemia ducet.
tu, facito, mox *cum matura adoleverit aetas*,
sis memor et te animo repetentem exempla tuorum
et *pater Aeneas* et avunculus excitet Hector.'
Haec ubi dicta dedit, portis sese extulit ingens
telum immane manu quatiens.

(12. 433–42)

He takes Ascanius in an armed embrace, and kissing him lightly through
his helmet, says: '*Learn, boy*, the nature of virtue and true toil from me, of
fortune from others. Now my right hand will defend you in combat and
lead you to great rewards. Make sure you are mindful *when you come of age*,
let your *father Aeneas* and uncle Hector inspire you as you reflect on the
examples of your kinsmen.' When he had said this, he went out of the gates,
brandishing a huge missile in his hands.

Ascanius is not given the opportunity of any verbal response at all
here, not even just to say that he has heard and will obey. Nor are we
told anything of Ascanius' disposition at this stage or of his
reactions to this speech—the narrator follows it by immediately
describing Aeneas' progress into battle. So many indications of the
power relation between father and son are given in Aeneas' few
words that this lack of narratorial attention to Ascanius can hardly
seem inappropriate. The son's youth and subordinate position are
emphasized: Aeneas addresses him as *puer* ('boy') and makes
reference to his future coming of age. Aeneas' paternal authority
is underlined not only by the commands and exhortations he
pronounces, but also by his use of his own name and title in his
words at 440 (*et pater Aeneas*). In this speech, Aeneas' paternity is
presented only as a matter of status. Aeneas' emotional attachment
is demonstrated not by what he says but by his action of embracing
and kissing his son through his helmet.

The detail of the helmet has led commentators to see this episode
as an echo of the scene in the *Iliad* when Hector takes his leave of
Andromache and his son Astyanax. There, Andromache is actually
the first to speak (*Il*. 6. 407–38), and Hector's words (*Il*. 6. 441–65)
are in reply to her lament. It is Astyanax's crying at the sight of his
helmet that prompts Hector's next speech (*Il*. 6. 467–81) which is

actually a prayer addressed to Zeus and the other gods for his son to be as valiant and pre-eminent as he is. Andromache laughs through her tears, but her grief prompts Hector to come out with one more speech of consolation and instruction (*Il.* 6. 486–93). After Hector leaves, Andromache and her handmaidens break into weeping.

So, overall, the tone of the Homeric farewell scene is quite different from Virgil's. This is in part down to the different quality of speech presentation. There is more direct speech in the scene from the *Iliad*, and two speakers. Even though Andromache speaks only once and Hector thrice, it is first her words and then the child's behaviour, and finally her weeping which provide cues for Hector's words. That is why this scene conveys more emotion than Aeneas' farewell: Aeneas seems by contrast to be pronouncing a set of instructions which almost seem to have been rehearsed for the moment, rather than spontaneously evoked. His mention of Hector may achieve some pathos as we think of the Iliadic farewell, but even that occurs in a line which is a formal and precise echo of Andromache's words to him about Ascanius earlier, in *Aeneid* 3. 343. Critics assess the tone of Aeneas' farewell by considering the Homeric precedent. Yet they fail to make the obvious point: Hector's kin have the right to reply and respond; Ascanius does not. The nature of the transformation of this scene in the *Aeneid* gives the impression of a world unlike Homer's—a world in which authority has the last word, and in which the emotions of subordinate characters are denied expression.

However, Ascanius can come into his own as a speaker and personage at other points in the poem when his father is absent. Ascanius is the first to approach and address the Trojan women after the fire they have caused has been reported:

> 'quis furor iste novus? quo nunc, quo tenditis' inquit
> 'heu miserae cives? non hostem inimicaque castra
> Argivum, vestras spes uritis. en, ego vester
> Ascanius!'—galcam ante pedes proiecit inanem,
> qua ludo indutus belli simulacra ciebat.
> accelerat simul Aeneas, simul agmina Teucrum.
> ast illae diversa metu per litora passim
> diffugiunt . . .
>
> (5. 670–7)

'What is this new frenzy? What now?' he says 'What are you trying to achieve—alas you poor women citizens? It is not the enemy and the hostile

The Rhetoric of Epic

>*The Rhetoric of Epic* 195

Rhetoric of Epic* 195

```

camps of the Argives you are burning, but your own hopes. Behold I am your Ascanius'—he threw before their feet an empty helmet, the one he wore for his war games. At the same moment Aeneas came rushing up, and the columns of the Trojans with him. The women scattered in fear, far and wide over the shores . . .

Ascanius speaks to the women from a superior position. Even if there are no actual commands or exhortations here, the rhetorical questions clearly convey that he is reprimanding the women. He reproves them for being no good as citizens, and is in a position to inform his addressees of their error and its implications. Finally Ascanius, like Aeneas in 12. 440, uses his own name to set a seal on his claim to authority.[78] The women make no reply, but scatter in all directions. Overall, the style of this speech is remarkably similar in form and content to another speech Aeneas makes at 12. 313–17, when he rebukes the soldiers for not keeping to the terms of the pact made with Latinus.[79] Later on, in Book 9, we again see Ascanius in a position of authority. Nisus and Euryalus seek his audience in order to volunteer to be the messengers who will find Aeneas (230–3). Ascanius speaks twice in the scene that follows—to propose his rewards for Nisus and Euryalus' venture (257–80), and (296–302) to agree to Euryalus' request to look after his mother.

The only time Ascanius does speak in his father's presence is the exception which proves the rule. Ascanius' words fulfil an important prophecy:

> 'heus, etiam mensas consumimus?' inquit Iulus,
> nec plura, adludens. ea vox audita laborum
> prima tulit finem, primaque loquentis ab ore
> eripuit pater ac stupefactus numine pressit.
>
> (7. 116–19)

---

[78] 'Servius' on 5. 670 interprets this rather differently—Ascanius announces his name because the women, possessed by *furor* do not initially recognize him: *QUIS FUROR ISTE NOVUS quasi ad furentes loquitur: unde ne tum quidem agnitus, cum dixisset 'en ego vester Ascanius: galeam proiecit inanem'.*

[79] '*quo ruitis? quaeve ista repens discordia surgit? | o cohibete iras! ictum iam foedus et omnes | compositae leges. mihi ius concurrere soli; | me sinite atque auferte metus. ego foedera faxo | firma manu; Turnum debent haec iam mihi sacra.*' (*Aen.* 12. 313–17) Note how similar the pattern of this speech is to Ascanius' at 5. 670 f. Two rhetorical questions are followed by an appeal for the Trojans to restrain their anger (*iras*): Ascanius had commented on the Troades' *furor*. Here too the speaker brings his utterance to a close by considering himself and his status in the situation. *Ego* is forcefully used in both cases. Compare also Laocoon's speech in *Aen.* 2. 42–9 which is in a similar vein. There are parallels in other authors e.g. Lucan 1. 8 f.
```

'So we're eating our tables then?' said Iulus,—no more: he was joking. The
hearing of that utterance first marked the end of their toils. His father
seized upon that first utterance as he spoke it, and stunned by the omen,
silenced him.

The traditional explanation for Aeneas' action goes back to the
fourth century: Ascanius is prevented from saying more to ensure
that the favourable omen given in the few words he has uttered is
not jeopardized.[80] But nonetheless, it can hardly be a complete
coincidence that Ascanius is silenced the one time he does speak in
the company of his father. This seems to be the only occasion in the
Aeneid in which any character speaks out of turn: the transgressive
quality of this utterance as well as respect for the omen might
explain why Ascanius is silenced.

The relation between Ascanius as speaker and Ascanius' social
status is sustained throughout the story. In theory, we might
question how far we can always discern in this way the social
superiority of one personage or group in the *Aeneid* over another.
In practice, this is quite easy. If a number of quoted speeches are
exchanged between two characters, it is because they are level
pegging: the extended conversations between Aeneas and Dido in
Book 4 or between Aeneas and Anchises in Book 6 can occur
because the characters have an equivalent rank.[81] Otherwise,
prayers provide instances of subordinates petitioning their super-
iors: gods who do not utter replies but who may act on the requests
(e.g. Jupiter's reactions to prayers at 4. 219 f. and 9. 630 f.; Faunus
at 12. 777–83).

In this way, a full list of speakers and their addressees, according
to the number of speeches exchanged, can be used to survey the
relative status of speaker and addressee, within hierarchies of both
mortals and gods in the poem. Hierarchy provides the principal
explanation for the frequent occurrence of single unanswered
speeches in contexts where direct discourse is presented. A power
relation obtains between those who have the right to speak in the
first place, those who have the right to reply, and those who have no

---

[80] 'Servius' comments *'pressit' autem vocem Ascanii, quo possit ipse numina
deprecari*. See also Fordyce (1977) ad loc.

[81] One could query whether Virgil's original audience could ever see Anchises
and Aeneas being of equal status given the importance of paternal authority (*patris
potestas*). The famous story of Fabius Maximus in Livy 24. 44 provides one
precedent for authority passing to the son.

right to reply at all. This principle definitely holds, but there is no actual remark upon it in the text of the *Aeneid*. There is a practical relation between speech and power, but no explicit statement about this from the narrator or any of the characters.

The relation between speech and power in the Homeric poems is comparable, but it is presented rather differently. Exchanges of speech are frequently sustained in scenes which are precedents for episodes in the *Aeneid* where characters are more laconic. We also find numerous speeches from personages far lower in status than their interlocutors. As far as Homer's *audience* is concerned, characters low in status are able to speak first and answer back. Yet this is not the way *characters* seem to want it. We need only think of the passages discussed in the first chapter of this book: Odysseus' suppression of Thersites' speech in *Iliad* 2, or Telemachus telling Penelope that it is not for her to speak because she is a woman. Thus in Homer, explicit statements of the relation between speech and power are made by characters, but that relation does not always obtain practically in the narratives we hear.[82]

So why, in the *Aeneid*, is it more exclusively the privilege of those in authority to speak, and the inclination or obligation of the subordinate to remain silent? Is this merely a feature of Virgil's more austere narrative technique or is the poem telling us something about the way the things are (or should be) in the world beyond it? In the opening chapter I remarked that some social scientists have been concerned with the relation between speech and authority in the world today and with 'muted groups' (e.g. women, children) whose symbolic weight in a society cannot easily be assessed by the ethnographer because such groups 'do not speak'. The readings of the passages from Horace's *Satires* 1. 5 and Suetonius' biography of Augustus in Chapter 1 show how these observations about the *Aeneid* might be considered in the light of

---

[82] It is less easy to make comparisons in these respects with the *Argonautica* of Apollonius of Rhodes—in spite of the extensive influences this Hellenistic poem has on the *Aeneid*, the narrative style diverges from that of both Homer and Virgil. Whilst general investigation of speech presentation in the *Argonautica* yields a great deal, there is no clearly discernible relationship between speech and power in the poem. On speech in the *Argonautica*, see Hunter (1989), 35–40 and (1993), 138–51. The fabulous nature of Apollonius' subject matter makes it harder to establish precisely (on other criteria) the nature of social hierarchy on the mortal plane. Feeney (1991), 57–98 considers the problematic role of divine authority in Apollonius' *Argonautica*.

historical evidence about speech and silence in political, military, legal, and domestic contexts in Virgil's time.

There is also potential comparative evidence on another level: the relations between speech, silence, and power in the formal construction of other texts in other genres. If a text is a product of a particular society, it follows logically that its style, narrative techniques, and any other formal features are a product of that society, just as much as its themes. Critics regularly fail to take into serious consideration this way in which the form of a specific text is determined by society that produces it. Bakhtin and Voloshinov have been exemplary in this regard: their claims only look eccentric because they remain to be fleshed out with evidence and examples.[83] The *form* of narrative and the potency of its rhetoric has become a prominent issue in the theory of ethnography and the social sciences.

Much modern ethnography, in aspiring to tell impersonally and impartially the stories of peoples, in fact reveals a great deal about the situation of the ethnographer. It is significant that the modern 'science' of ethnography developed in the wake of imperialism, as accounts of some cultures, such as those in the 'third world', by specialists from dominant nations, play into the political and economic subjugation of such cultures. Anxieties about the ideological effect of the 'poetics' of ethnographic writing could equally—and quite appropriately—be expressed about ancient epic. Like much modern ethnography, ancient epic, with a comparable affectation of impersonality, sought to recount the 'histories' of peoples in the historical or mythological past. Yet in this process, epic poets perhaps unwittingly recorded the preoccupations and mores of their own contemporary culture. And like modern ethnography, much ancient epic seems to have evolved in the shadow of imperialism.[84] Consider Bakhtin's definition of epic:

The epic as a genre in its own right may, for our purposes, be characterized by three constitutive features: (1) a national epic past—in Goethe's and Schiller's terminology 'the absolute past'—serves as the subject for the

[83] e.g. Bakhtin (1973; 1981); Bakhtin and Medvedev (1978); Voloshinov (1973). See also R. Fowler (1981). Quint (1993) scrutinizes the relationship between power and epic form in Virgil and later poets.
[84] On the relation between ethnography and imperialism, see Balandier (1955) and Asad (1973).

epic; (2) national tradition (and not personal experience and the free thought that grows out of it) serves as the source for the epic; (3) an absolute epic distance separates the epic world from contemporary reality, that is from the time in which the singer (the author and his audience) lives.[85]

On this passage, Todorov remarks: ' "epic" the term under definition here, appears twice in the definition itself ("epic past", "epic distance"); in sum, the category is an anthropological one before it becomes literary.'[86] At the time of its production, an epic poem like Virgil's *Aeneid* probably had a range of functions and significations beyond those of mere 'literature': it could be read not only as poetry, but also as political propaganda, history, aetiology, cosmology, and philosophy. As well as illustrating a certain sort of relationship between discourse and power in its narrative, the *Aeneid* itself could be regarded as a discourse of authority. The epic is a form of speech which, by exerting power over its 'silent' audience or readers, renders them submissive, turning them into a kind of 'muted group'.[87]

One more example from the *Aeneid* may help illustrate this. The longest speech in the *Aeneid* is made by the most powerful human individual in the poem.[88] It is Aeneas' account to Dido's court of the fall of Troy and his subsequent wanderings. This is introduced by the principal narrator in the following way:

[85] Bakhtin (1981), 3–40 at 13. Subsequent parts of Bakhtin's important essay 'Epic and Novel' develop this crucial definition.

[86] Bakhtin's definition of epic is discussed in Todorov (1984), 88.

[87] The notion of 'muted groups' was introduced in 1.2, p. 13; ideas of narrative as being akin to speech were presented in Chs. 1 and 2. The concluding parts of this chapter consider Virgil's narrative as a form of speech.

[88] The fact that this narrative also functions as a speech seems to have been widely ignored, e.g. Highet (1972), 305 omits this speech from his list of speeches categorised as 'Narratives, Explanations and Descriptions'. Feeney (1983) opens thus: 'Aeneas' speech of defence before Dido is the longest and most controversial he delivers.' Throughout, Feeney refers to 4. 333–61 as his longest speech in the poem: a consideration of books 2–3 might make Aeneas less taciturn. Otis (1963) does not discuss Aeneas' narrative as speech, or consider its implications for his characterization. Contrast R. G. Austin (1964), p. xvi on book 2; Warde Fowler (1920), 184; and D. P. Fowler (1990), 49–50: 'It is easy to forget in Aeneas' long narration that he speaks, not Vergil the narrator, and this narrative amnesia is inescapable: when Austin comments on 2. 427 *dis aliter visum*, "The comment comes from Virgil's private world of thought to move each reader in his own private way", the elision of the distinction between Aeneas and Vergil is unfortunate but invited by the text.'

> Conticuere omnes intentique ora tenebant;
> inde toro pater Aeneas sic orsus ab alto . . .
>
> (*Aeneid* 2. 1–2)

All were silent and held an attentive gaze. Then father Aeneas began to speak from his high couch as follows . . .

The detail that 'all were silent' (*conticuere omnes*) for Aeneas' speech, though not an untypical audience reaction in epic, is interesting in the light of the observations above.[89] Moreover, this detail—along with other diction in 2. 1–3—is echoed when the principal narrator formally closes Aeneas' speech, at the end of the next book:[90]

> Sic pater Aeneas intentis omnibus unus
> fata renarrabat divum cursusque docebat.
> conticuit tandem . . .
>
> (*Aeneid* 3. 716–8)

Thus did father Aeneas alone recount the fates of the gods and teach his wanderings to all the attentive company. At last he was silent . . .

The repetition of the epithet *Pater Aeneas* enhances the stature of Aeneas relative to the company he addresses. His words in Books 2 and 3 come to the length of an ancient tragedy—and, unlike Odysseus during his performance in the *Odyssey*, Aeneas is not once interrupted.

However, this long speech is not only an emblem or affirmation of Aeneas' status within the world of the story. Too little attention has been paid to the aesthetic quality of his speech as a *mise-en-abyme* narrative.[91] The verses which immediately precede *conticuere omnes* (2. 1) give a better impression of how Aeneas' account fits into its context. These verses describe what happens just after the applause for Iopas' cosmological poem:

---

[89] *Iliad* 3 95; 7. 92; 7. 398; and Apollonius *Argonautica* 1. 512–4 (Orpheus' cosmological poem) provide examples of attentive audiences in epics prior to the *Aeneid*.

[90] 'Servius' notes part of this resemblance and the 'ring composition' effect produced by it in his note on 3. 718: *CONTICUIT TANDEM ut <II 1> conticuere omnes. sane in secundi principio duo poetae sunt versus, sicut hic tres et similis est finis initio: 'conticuit' et 'intenti'.*

[91] On the *mise-en-abyme* or 'embedded narrative', see Ricardou (1967) and Dällenbach (1978).

nec non et vario noctem sermone trahebat
infelix Dido longumque bibebat amorem,
multa super Priamo rogitans, super Hectore multa;
nunc quibus Aurorae venisset filius armis,
nunc quales Diomedis equi, nunc quantus Achilles.
'immo age et a prima dic, hospes, origine nobis
insidias' inquit 'Danaum casusque tuorum
erroresque tuos; nam te iam septima portat
omnibus errantem terris et fluctibus aestas.'

(1. 748–56)

Unhappy Dido was indeed dragging out the night with all sorts of conversation and drinking a long draught of love, as she kept on asking many things about Priam and many things about Hector—at one moment in what arms the son of Aurora had come to battle, and at another what the horses of Diomedes were like, at another how great Achilles was. 'But rather, stranger', she said, 'tell us from the very beginning about the plots of the Greeks, the misfortunes of your kin, and your own wanderings, for this is now the seventh summer to carry you as a wanderer over land and sea.'

Hector, Priam, Diomedes, and Achilles are major figures in the *Iliad*; Dido is asking Aeneas to relate events that are on the whole more 'Iliadic' than those which we are to hear in Books 2 and 3.[92] The range of material Dido wants Aeneas to cover happens to be the stuff of poetry. Perhaps Aeneas had already complied before granting her request, presented in direct discourse, that he relate from the beginning the fall of Troy and his subsequent wanderings (*Danaum casusque tuorum | erroresque tuos*, 753–4).[93] Those phrases supply a kind of programmatic design for the account which follows, and could hint at its literary status.[94] Aeneas' own opening words introduce his story both dramatically and poetically:

[92] *Aurorae . . . filius* (751) is Memnon, who was the main subject of Arctinus' *Aethiopis*, a Greek epic poem possibly dating from the 8th cent. BC. Memnon is only mentioned fleetingly by Homer (*Od.* 4. 188, 11. 522). See R. G. Austin (1971) on *Aen.* 1. 489 and 1. 751 for further details.
[93] 'Servius' on *RENARRABAT* (3. 717) considers an alternative possibility—he thinks 2 and 3 consist of Aeneas recounting in the right order what he has told Dido already: *aut apparet Aenean ante de suis casibus cum Didone confuse locutum. et ideo hic addidit 'renarrabat', quasi quae dixerat antea, ex ordine referebat, quod notat in primo* (753) *immo age et a prima dic hospes origine nobis.* This interpretation is explained in greater detail by 'Servius' on 1. 753.
[94] Crump (1920) and Berres (1982) have argued that the story (or at least part of it), which comes out of Aeneas' mouth, may originally have been conceived for presentation in the third person by the poet's principal narrator.

'Infandum, regina, iubes renovare dolorem,
Troianas ut opes et lamentabile regnum
eruerint Danai, quaeque ipse miserrima vidi
et quorum pars magna fui.'

(*Aeneid* 2. 3–6)

'Unspeakable, O Queen, is the grief you bid me to renew, how the Greeks
destroyed the wealth of Troy and a kingdom which is always to be mourned
and the most pitiful events which I myself witnessed, and in which I played
a great part.'

Whilst Aeneas' situation plainly recalls Odysseus' narration to the
Phaeacians in Books 9–12 of the *Odyssey*, his diction here recalls the
opening of the most famous account of the Trojan war—Homer's
Iliad:

Μῆνιν ἄειδε, θεά, Πηλϊάδεω Ἀχιλῆος
οὐλομένην, ἣ μυρί᾿ Ἀχαιοῖς ἄλγε᾿ ἔθηκε . . .

(*Iliad* 1. 1–2)

Sing of the baneful wrath, goddess, of Achilles son of Peleus, which laid
countless agonies on the Achaeans . . .

The juxtaposition of adjective and noun *infandum . . . dolorem*
('unspeakable grief') corresponds approximately to that of Μῆνιν . . .
οὐλομένην ('baneful wrath'); Aeneas' address to Dido (*regina*
'queen'), who has prompted his story matches Homer's invocation
of the Muse (θεά 'goddess') who inspires his discourse.[95] Aeneas'
words in 2. 3 f. signal a kind of poetic status for this embedded
narrative—which, again like Odysseus', follows that of a professional poet: in this case Iopas.[96] At the same time, in tension with
that literary self-consciousness, the diction at the opening and

---

[95] Compare the heralding of Hypsipyle's long narrative of the murder of the
Lemnian men in Statius, *Thebaid* (5. 49–498): *immania vulnera, rector, | integrare
iubes*, 5. 29–30.

[96] Cf. 10. 159–62. Even Aeneas' emphasis on his role as a participant in events he
describes (*quaeque ipse miserrima vidi | et quorum pars magna fui*, 5–6) could serve to
enhance the idea that his account is a kind of literary creation in itself, if we recall
the praise of Demodocus in *Odyssey* 8. 477 f.: 'Either the Muse taught you, the
daughter of Zeus, or else Apollo. Very beautifully you sing the fate of the Achaeans,
their deeds, sufferings and toils *as if you were there yourself* or had heard them from
someone else. But change your tune now and sing of the making of the Wooden
Horse.' Here, the Wooden Horse is of course exactly Aeneas' subject and he was
there himself. On the parallel of *Virgil* with Iopas, see P. Hardie (1986), 52 and
Duke (1950), 191–3 who makes a case for Iopas being an essay in the poet's 'self-
portraiture'.

closing of Aeneas' narrative clearly links it with the story situation in which it is being told.[97]

One final point should be made about the introduction to Aeneas' account. Aeneas is reluctant to give this account. The iterative RSA ascribed to Dido at 1. 750 f. shows that she has had to press him. There is a silence before Aeneas speaks (2. 1) and when he does so, the first word he says is *Infandum* ('unspeakable'). He says that no one can talk of the Myrmidons, of the Dolopes, or of tough Ulysses without shedding tears (6–7). He indicates that his tale of Troy's final trials will be short:

> sed si tantus amor casus cognoscere nostros
> et breviter Troiae supremum audire laborem . . .
>
> (*Aeneid* 2. 10–11)

But if you have so great a love to be acquainted with our sufferings and to hear briefly about the final suffering of Troy . . .

This use of *breviter* ('briefly') seems curious in a preface to such a long speech: the implication must be that Aeneas' sufferings are so great that any account of them will be too short.[98] Perhaps Aeneas

---

[97] Note the link between 2. 1 and 3. 716–8 discussed below. Other connections are: (i) The theme of knowledge that began with the didactic poet Iopas who gave a recitation to the court, sustained delicately by Dido in 1. 755–6 and taken up by Aeneas at 2. 8–9 (*et iam nox umida caelo | praecipitat suadentque cadentia sidera somnos*) is recalled at the end of Aeneas' account 3. 716–7 (*fata renarrabat divum cursusque docebat*; cf. the RSA presentation of Aeneas' words at 12. 110–11 (*tum socios maestique metum solatur Iuli | fata docens, regique iubet responsa Latino*).

(ii) Aeneas' use of *amor* ('love') in his opening words at 2. 10 (*sed si tantus amor casus cognoscere nostros*) as well as his echoing Dido's use of *casus* from 1. 754). This has an irony beyond Aeneas' ken: Dido was previously described as 'drinking long draughts of love' (749).

[98] It is worth noting that Aeneas prefaces his *second* longest speech in the poem (4. 333–61) with the words *pro re pauca loquar* ('I shall say only a few things') (4. 337). The quotation of Conington's remarks (4. 337 ad loc.) in Feeney (1983) on the use of *pauca* ('a few things') may be helpful for a consideration of *breviter* in this passage: '*"pauca"* . . . seems to express Virgil's feeling *that the words come slowly and with effort*, and bear no comparison to what the lover would have said had he given way to his emotion.' An explanation in 'Servius' is different again. It is first supplied on 1. 753 (*Et a prima dic hospes origine nobis*): *id est a raptu Helenae: quod quidem Dido cupit, sed excusat Aeneas. et dicit ruinam se Troiae* breviter *esse dicturum, habita ratione temporis ut suadentque cadentia sidera somnos* [!] This is emphasized again on 2. 11: *ET BREVITER praescribit, quia Dido dixerat* [1. 753 quoted again] *ergo non ad Didonis voluntatem, sed narrantis officium. et quibusdam hic hysterologia videtur; prius enim est, ut Troiae laborem, post Aeneae casus agnoscat.* *Breviter* is used elsewhere in the poem to describe characters' manner of speaking by the poet before their speeches are quoted. The other contexts are 1. 561 (to describe Dido's reply to Ilioneus 1. 562–78—quite a long speech), 4. 632 (for

gets more carried away in his narration than he imagines he will. Or perhaps the word is used because there is much more to be told that Aeneas decides not to disclose: the story is always bigger than the narrative. It is clear anyway that this is a tale that the hero finds hard to tell. He continues:

> quamquam animus meminisse horret luctuque refugit,
> incipiam.
>
> *(Aeneid* 2. 12–13)

Although my mind shudders to remember, and recoils from this grief, I shall begin.

Even before this point Aeneas has not found it easy to speak. The majority of his utterances so far have been accompanied with moans, groans and anguish.[99]

All in all, Aeneas' spoken text rather undermines the often convenient distinction theorists have made between 'discourse' and 'narrative'.[100] The first line of Aeneas' personal epic has the opening of the *Iliad* as an intertext, just as the opening line of the *Aeneid* itself is intertextual with the *Odyssey*. The story of Aeneas, then, serves simultaneously as a *discursive* speech and as an epic *narrative*. Both Virgil's text and Aeneas' text alike leave no room for reply. This meta-literary observation has important implications.

The idea that epic is a discourse of power in some ways comparable to a state decree or military command may seem far fetched. But aestheticized narratives of many kinds can be instruments and

---

Dido's speech to Barce the nurse), 6. 321, 6. 398 and 6. 538—all to describe the Sibyl's speeches to Aeneas (2 speeches of 8 lines; 1 of 5); 9. 353 for Nisus' order to Euryalus 355–6; 10. 251 describing Aeneas' prayer in the four ensuing verses; 10. 621 followed by Jupiter's words 622–7. These are not by any means the shortest speeches in the poem. 'Servius' has routine comments on the word at 4. 632 and 6. 538, but some of a note on 1. 561 might be applicable here too: *TUM BREVITER DIDO atqui non breviter loquitur, sed breve et longum, parvum et magnum perfectum nihil habent, sed per conparationem intelleguntur* [tr. '"brief" and "lengthy", "small" and "great" are not absolute, but are to be understood relatively']. If Virgil can describe a speech in DD as brief, when—compared to other passages of DD presented—it is not, we might again be sceptical about how far DD in the poem is supposed to present what was said.

[99] The instances are 1. 93–4; 1. 208–9; 1. 221–2; 1. 371–2; 1. 459.

[100] See the opening part of Ch. 1. The classic exposition of the distinction is Benveniste (1971), discussed in Genette (1982a), 138–40. See also Jakobson in Sebeok (1960) and H. White (1981). For an account of the distinction, and some of its implications for Latin narrative literature, see Laird (1990). Calame (1986) applies Benveniste's insights to the study of narrative and narration in Greek literature.

emblems of authority. A contemporary example can be found in the following excerpt from a description, by a social anthropologist, of a visit made by a powerful sheikh to a Lebanese village. Like Aeneas, the sheikh provides a domineering narrative re-enactment of his feats to a subordinate audience late at night:

People who act as minor *dramatis personae*, kin in a subordinate position but sharing in some reflected glory, attendants who were there when it happened, may set the situation up for him to embark on his performance. They begin by evoking that story-everyone-has-heard of what Abu Ahmad did that day in that place. They perform their socially conventional role. The hero sits quiet, unspeaking in the silence of the truly fearful, leaving mere words to subalterns as heroes do. But he is urged on. Expectation grows. The tellers cannot do it justice, they have not the style, they cannot act the form that is integral to what was done, only one person can do that. Abu Ahmad begins to speak in a dark, harsh voice, abrupt cadences, piercing looks suddenly switched from one hearer to another, cutting and precise gestures, everything apparently pared down to its absolute, iconic rightness. . . . It is the force of his being . . . which animates the rhetorics of the performance in which we are privileged to participate.

Such is the display of *marajul*, of manly performance. It is difficult in the sober columns of learned journals to convey the impact. To this outsider it was oppressive, grotesque, horrifying, impressive, riveting, frightening and yet unwillingly admired.[101]

The re-enactment described has general parallels with heroic narration inside epic—and this account has some disturbingly particular parallels with the lead-up to Aeneas' narration: the storyteller is himself the protagonist; his tale is already well known; yet his audience nonetheless urge him to tell it. But the sheikh's framed narrative has an affinity with epic discourse itself,which is just as disquieting. Epic discourse also functions in the world of lived experience. If Virgil's epic can so discreetly encode a social hierarchy in its narrative, then such a form of expression should be carefully interrogated as well as enjoyed.

5.5 RHETORIC AND REPRESENTATION IN EPIC DISCOURSE

The aim of the final part of this chapter has been to demonstrate that the formal techniques of speech presentation in the *Aeneid*

[101] Gilsenan (1989), 197.

help constitute power relations between groups and characters in the story of the poem. These techniques of speech presentation accomplish this extremely systematically—we saw that the right to speak and reply operates as an index of social status far more thoroughly in Virgil than it does in Homer. However, this demonstration may not appear to marry well with the claims made at the beginning of this chapter for the *Aeneid* possessing the quality of realism. Presentations of relations between speech and power in the contemporary world tend to be far more complex, whether we encounter them in social scientific writing, in the media, or even in literature. Is it possible for an epic to be realistic, if its narrative rhetoric portrays division of power in such a tidy and systematic way?

It certainly is possible both in principle and in practice. The observations made in the first part of this chapter serve to show that realism in narrative is itself engineered by rhetoric. Since, in principle, the generation of realism will always be ideological, representations of divisions of power are more properly judged in terms of their effectiveness rather than their truth value. In practice, epic can be seen as a type of discourse which configures the world—and therefore the power relations obtaining within it—in its own legitimate way.[102] The potential presence of instances of FID in the *Aeneid* adds further weight to the claim that epic can be regarded as realistic. I argued in the previous chapter that the fusion of a narrator's and character's voice generated by FID frequently occurs in non-fictional and non-literary contexts. However it is undoubtedly the case that there is a heavier distribution of this speech mode in fictional narrative which can be classed as realistic by any of the three definitions offered earlier. In particular, FID exemplifies the kind of verisimilitude achieved by complex features of form which direct attention to the content or story of a text.

FID also has an ideological dimension which bears on the relation between speech and power in the *Aeneid*. The narrator's discourse is itself partial: if Virgil's narrator does occasionally fuse a character's discourse with his own, there could be important political implications. For example, the presentation of Aeneas'

---

[102] Compare 1.2 'Speech as an Index of Power' for consideration of how different genres of discourse are bound to present speech/power relations in different ways; the 'anthropological' quality of Bakhtin's definition of epic (quoted above) is obviously relevant.

discourse in FID at 4. 283 f. could suggest that Aeneas' words enjoy a higher status, as they are fused with the authoritative voice of the narrator, than they would if they had been presented in some other speech mode. Alternatively (and perhaps simultaneously) this fusion could modulate our impression of the characterization and ideology of the narrator: his discourse is 'shared' by Aeneas and Turnus for instance, but it is not shared by many other major characters including, for example, Dido. In this respect, it is worth noting that the words and thoughts of the most powerful agents in the poem—the gods—are never presented by the narrator in FID.[103]

Émile Zola's novel *Thérèse Raquin* (1868) is an outstanding example of literary realism, as it is now understood. Consideration of one of this novel's most memorable episodes will provide a useful coda to my discussion of speech presentation in Virgil's *Aeneid*. The episode occurs in the seventh chapter: Thérèse, the heroine, makes a speech to Laurent, just after they have become lovers. Thérèse gives vent to all her frustrations in direct discourse which runs over several pages. She describes her loveless marriage to the invalid Camille and recalls her miserable childhood with him under the tyranny of her aunt, Camille's mother. Her speech is striking because, until this point, the narrator has constantly emphasized Thérèse's silent and passive nature. And the speech is all the more arresting, because, until this point in the seventh chapter, none of Thérèse's spoken discourse has been presented in *any* form at all— even though she has been present in the story from very early on. Such a rhetorical strategy in the narrator's discourse makes the rhetoric of Thérèse's own discourse all the more forceful. Thus, the full significance of her opening words has a potent effect on the reader:

Oh! si tu savais, disait-elle, combien j'ai suffert!
'Oh if you knew', she said, 'how much I've suffered!'

This significance must be lost on Laurent, to whom those words are primarily addressed.

This illustration shows clearly how the presentation—or

---

[103] It is a remarkable contrast that there is at least one instance of *focalization* through a god in the poem: Juno in 1. 23 f. D. P. Fowler (1990) discusses this and emphasizes the ideological aspects of focalization, cf. Rimmon-Kenan (1983), 81–5.

suppression—of a character's discourse can function for dramatic effect. It shows that the rhetorical use of speech and silence in the *Aeneid* is by no means confined to epic or to ancient literature. This is something which pervades all genres and periods. So too does the association between speech and power: the transformation of Thérèse's role, from that of passive victim to manipulative and eventually murderous instigator of events, coincides with the first presentation of her discourse. *Thérèse Raquin* provoked a great deal of hostile criticism—but never on the grounds that this endeavour in '*naturalisme*' was unrealistic.

6

Ideology and Taste: Narrative and Discourse in Petronius' *Satyricon*

One who creates a direct word—whether epic, tragic or lyric—
deals only with the subject whose praises he sings, or represents or expresses, and he does so in his language which is
perceived as the sole and fully adequate tool of realizing the
word's direct, objectivized meaning . . . The position of the
parodic-travestying consciousness is, however, completely
different: it too is oriented towards the object—but towards
another's word as well, a parodied word about the object that
in the process becomes *itself* an image.

(Mikhail Bakhtin, *The Dialogic Imagination*)

The study of Greek and Roman literature has long depended, with
varying degrees of explicitness, on *taste* as a fundamental point of
orientation. The very notion of 'classics' belongs to a connoisseurish rhetoric which canonizes certain texts, and attaches aesthetic
properties to them.[1] Multiculturalist critiques, in challenging the
hegemony of the western tradition, have done something to unmask
the frequently 'Eurocentric' nature of this aestheticization.[2] At the
same time, the study of Greek and Roman culture has also long
depended on its illusory claim to objectivity. It is easy to believe
that the ancient world can be safely detached from our own, and

---

[1] Luck (1958), 157–8 defined the 'classical' neither as what is ancient, nor as the
canon, but as 'elements in the mind that survive and transcend great stretches of
time and bridge every distance of environment and race'. Accounts of all kinds
exhibit unhelpful circularities of this sort—compare Eliot (1944), Wellek (1965),
Fleischmann (1974), Calvino (1987), 125–34. However, the treatment of taste in
Bourdieu (1984) has some salutary insights.

[2] Robbins (1991) gives an account of the 'sensationalist demagogy' that erupted in
the United States following attempts in universities to broaden civilization courses
and establish a multicultural etiquette. Whilst Eurocentrism in works like Jenkyns
(1991) is an easy target, the cultural chauvinism of classical scholarship is more
pernicious where it is less easily detected. Consider e.g. the sentiments in Griffin
(1982), 176–8; examples from scholarship on Petronius will be considered below.

that our approach to it can therefore claim to be reasonably neutral. We are prone to think that antiquity and its discourses can be impartially, even scientifically, surveyed because we assume that we must be disinterested observers.[3]

Both of these two points of orientation—taste and the illusory sense of objectivity—are ideological. Both have long been the *preconditions* for the study of classical literature (along with some other fields in the humanities). They still provide the framework for the studies of classical languages, literature, and history, even in their most progressive forms. The study of Petronius' *Satyricon* is particularly remarkable for revealing the indispensability of these ideological positions for contemporary scholars. This is because, first, much of the story of the *Satyricon* is seen to be about the very issue of taste: Encolpius the principal narrator, Trimalchio, and Eumolpus the poet are characters who are preoccupied in different ways with ideas of refinement. Indeed, Petronius the author will always be associated with Tacitus' Petronius: Nero's 'arbiter of elegance'.[4] Second, a preoccupation with objectivity has been held by literary critics of the *Satyricon*, as well as by historians who regard it as discourse of evidence. It is probably no coincidence that modern interpreters who try to throw light on the *Satyricon* end up being themselves illuminated and uncomfortably exposed. Perhaps the *Satyricon* is bound to prompt self-conscious readings because it is anomalous: it is perceived as an anti-classical classic.

A very large proportion of the *Satyricon*, as we have it, is taken up with the speech of various characters. Study of speech presentation in this text will highlight significant variations in narrative style in different parts of the work. This study will also facilitate exploration of the polarities the *Satyricon* appears to establish—between the literary discourse of poetry and the non-literary language of 'standard' discourse, and between classical Latin and vulgar Latin, for which the *Cena* (the account of Trimalchio's dinner) is especially celebrated. The perception of these polarities actually depends on the two fundamental positions which still interfere

---

[3] This is what Voloshinov (1973), 73 calls 'philologism': 'The philologist-linguist tears the monument out of the real domain and views it as if it were a self-sufficient isolated entity. He brings to bear on it not an active ideological understanding but a completely passive understanding in which there is not a flicker of response, as there would be in any authentic kind of understanding.'

[4] The biography of C. or T. Petronius, Nero's *arbiter elegantiae*, is given in *Annals* 16. 17–20.

with the reading of Greek and Latin texts: taste and the illusory sense of objectivity.

6.1 FIRST-PERSON NARRATION

The consideration of speech and first-person narration is particularly appropriate for a study of the *Satyricon*. Scholars have been very preoccupied with the relation between the narrator Encolpius and the author of this text—albeit Petronius as an historical author—and the presentation of Encolpius as a character.

6.1.1 *Distinction between 'Author' and 'Narrator'*

The Life of Lazarillo de Tormes, published in 1554, is the earliest Spanish picaresque novel. The name of the first-person narrator 'Lazarillo' has also come to designate the author of the work, about whom no facts are known. Nonetheless, certain passages of this book allow us to say some things about the *author* as opposed to the *narrator*. The closing chapter provides an example of one such passage:

> We got married and I've never been sorry because, besides her being a good and attentive girl, the priest is always very kind to me. Every year I get a whole load of corn; I get my meat at Christmas and Easter and now and again a couple of votive loaves or a pair of old stockings. He arranged for us to rent a house next to his . . . But evil tongues, that we're never short of and never will be, make life impossible for us, saying this and that and the other; that my wife goes and makes his bed and cooks his dinner. I hope God forgives their lies.[5]

> (*Lazarillo* 7. 32–43)

Lazarillo's account of the priest's generosity and of the malevolent gossip he has to endure carries a fairly clear implication that his wife is having an affair with the priest. Lazarillo himself is either naïvely unaware of this possibility, or, he *is* aware of it, and is trying to put his addressee off the scent. Whichever is the case, the *author* uses the irony of omission or understatement to convey that Lazarillo the *narrator* is being cuckolded. Though our awareness of these machinations does not yield any historical information about the enigmatic author of *The Life of Lazarillo de Tormes*, it does give an impression of the author's character which is distinct

---

[5] This translation is from Alpert (1969), 78.

from that of the speaking narrator.[6] Thus, in first-person narratives, authors can send up their narrators and establish a complicity between themselves and their readers—who are their 'superaddressees'.[7] This complicity occurs even though authors only speak through their narrators and even though the discourse of author and discourse of the narrator are co-extensive. This complicity is something which an ironized narrator (and any addressee the *narrator* configures or hopes for) cannot share. The distinction between the narrator and our impression of the author may be of fundamental importance for interpretation. In literary texts, it is most conspicuous in novels which have a number of first-person narrators who write letters or entries in journals. The author is perceptible as the invisible hand which presents these narrations and arranges them in a series.

A third-person narrative, on the other hand, makes it very difficult to demonstrate any distinction between the voice of the principal narrator and the voice of the author. Virgil's *Aeneid* is a good case in point. Narratorial indexicals (considered in my first chapter) which locate the narrator, as a speaker who belongs to a certain place and time, tend to encourage identification of the *Aeneid*'s narrator with Virgil the historical personage. The only indexical which might incline us to conceive of a distinction between author and narrator is an interesting exception, *Aeneid* I. I: 'Arma virumque cano' (I sing of arms and the man). These words constitute a speech act. In giving the utterance 'I sing of arms and the man' the speaker is already supposed to be performing the action he describes. This pronouncement could signal the moment at which the author (standing 'outside' the narrative) gives way to the narrator (who is 'inside' the narrative, as a constituent of it).[8] The word *cano* ('I sing') distances the author from the narrator even more: Virgil the author is *writing* the poem which the narrator is supposed to sing. Author and narrator part

---

[6] Unsurprisingly, an inadequate grasp of what is recounted is a common feature of first-person narrative in children's literature: in S. E. Hinton's *Rumblefish* (1975), the first-person narrator, Rusty-James is unaware of the irony—discerned by his companions—of his claim not to believe another character whose name is 'Cassandra'.

[7] For the 'superaddressee', see 1.2.

[8] My discussion of the Prologue to Apuleius' *Metamorphoses* and the opening of C. S. Lewis' *The Magician's Nephew* (1955) in Laird (1993a), treats transitions of this kind which are a standard feature of literary and fictional narrative.

company here: a typically 'third person' narrator is speaking in the first person.[9]

The distinction that obtains between the narrator and our impression of the author is not just a feature of fictional narrative. An analogous distinction obtains when we assess veridical accounts in real life. The distinction emerges when we test discourses of evidence against our impression of what actually happened. Our impression of what actually happened corresponds to the impression of the author's design we derive from fictional texts; our treatment of the autobiographer or journalist actually corresponds to our treatment of first person narrators when we read fiction. Some examples should clarify this. When Ian Paisley gives an account of an event in real life, we assess it by setting it against our own apprehension of the event itself, or of others' accounts of it. When a fictional narrator like Lazarillo gives an account, again we can set it against the apprehension of the state of affairs that we ourselves construct from the narrative before us. The state of affairs Lazarillo describes, whether truthfully or not, leads us to the 'author' who is to be understood as a rationalization engineered by the reader.[10]

6.1.2 *The Content of First-Person Narratives*

The distinction (in fictional narrative) between narrator and author obtains because of a second fundamental feature of all first-person narrative which is often overlooked. This was introduced earlier in Chapter 2. There it was shown that a first-person narrative and a third-person narrative of the same story differ on more than a cosmetic, stylistic level. The example of testimonies about an air crash demonstrated that a first-person account by a survivor differs substantially in *content* from a third-person account of the same event. That was because the survivor's presence (and *ergo* her

---

[9] Genette (1980), 244 cited this use of the first-person form in *Aeneid* 1. 1 to challenge the customary opposition of 'first person narrative' and 'third person narrative'. The two categories are not in fact mutually exclusive.

[10] For the construction of the 'author' derived from a narrative, compare Riffaterre (1983), 5 quoted in Ch. 2 n. 55. Such a construction perhaps has more in common with the story world or *diegèse* than the flesh and blood author—who cannot know everything about the fictional worlds he creates. For instance, Raymond Chandler could not identify all the culprits in *The Big Sleep* (1939) to William Faulkner who adapted the novel for Howard Hawks's 1946 film. D. Thomson (1997) recounts the making of the film.

survival) would be an inescapable element of the story from the very beginning. Thus, a first-person narrative is not a transparent medium. As it recounts events, it cumulatively characterizes a narrator, not only as a protagonist in the story told, but also in his or her telling of the story. Third-person narrators (like those of historians or of Virgil in the *Aeneid*) are inevitably characterized as speakers, but probably not to the extent of interested first-person narrators.

By an 'interested' narrator I mean simply a narrator who is also a character in the story he recounts. It has been argued that a narrator's involvement in the story is a more important considera-tion than whether he speaks in the third or first person.[11] In some respects this is true. However, the observations immediately below suffice to show why, for the purposes of this study at least, a division between first and third person narration is worth preserving.

6.1.3 *Presented Spoken and Thought Discourse in First-Person Narrative*

The difference between first-person and third-person narrators not only affects our response to their narrations as discourse. The issue of whether a narrative is given in the first person or the third person also has consequences for the discourse of characters contained within it. These consequences may seem trivial at first sight: a first-person narrator has the linguistic competence to employ all the modes of presenting spoken or thought discourse available to a third-person narrator: DD, FDD, all forms of ID including (controversially) FID, and RSA. However that competence is not always fulfilled. For instance, first-person narrators are unlikely to use forms of direct discourse or FID to render the thoughts of characters other than themselves. This is for the simple reason that an involved narrator (assuming he is an ordinary human being) can only realistically render the thought processes of others as infer-ences about their mental processes from their outward behaviour.

Where the presentation of spoken discourse is concerned, first-person narrators are able to exploit all the linguistic facilities available to third-person narrators. Yet it is arguable that DD, at

---

[11] Genette (1980), 244 f. pointed this out: a first-person characterized narrator need not, and often does not, have any more involvement in the story than a third-person one. For Genette's terms 'homodiegetic' and 'heterodiegetic', I employ 'interested' and 'disinterested' respectively.

least, has overall quite a different effect in first-person narrative from the effect it has in third-person narrative. Most third-person narrators, particularly those in the major ancient genres of epic and historiography, do not often draw attention to the process of narration, or to their presence as narrators. Thus, third-person narrative seems to be a window looking into the world of the story; and spoken direct discourse of characters, especially, seems to possess literal fidelity—an attribute we saw challenged earlier.[12]

Direct discourse in first-person narrative may give a rather different impression. An interested first-person character-narrator (who is or was involved in the events described) constantly reminds us of his presence as he mediates events. We may question his infallibility and his impartiality. Such questioning must extend to a narrator's 'reproduction' of direct discourse in conversations he recounts. In everyday life, speakers who affect to report their own words and the words of others have been shown to 'construct' dialogue.[13] Poetic license may be granted to fictional narrators. For instance we are inclined to regard the dialogue relayed by Holden Caulfield (in J. D. Salinger's *Catcher in the Rye*) as 'reliable'. Conscious as we are of Caulfield's poor intellect, moral defects and pitiful command of the English language, we are quite happy to accept that whatever he presents as what was said in direct discourse *is* what was said.

Even so, the assumption that most first-person narrators are like human individuals with ordinary human attributes might give us some cause to worry about their ability to 'recollect' accurately. Furthermore, interested first-person narrators (like Petronius' Encolpius and Apuleius' Lucius in the *Metamorphoses*) are principal agents: their accounts are angled as speeches or discourses in a far more evident way than those given by disinterested third-person narrators. How far do fictional first-person narrators 'construct' the discourse they present (as real people do) rather than faithfully report it? This issue will emerge towards the end of this chapter which considers some aspects of the narrator's presentation of social divisions in the *Satyricon*.

---

[12] At 3.6 and 4.3.
[13] Tannen (1989).

6.2 CHARACTERIZATION OF THE NARRATOR IN THE *SATYRICON*

The text of the *Satyricon* starts *in medias res*: in the midst of a debate about the current state of oratory in Rome. Whatever may have preceded this has not survived in our manuscripts. Even the first speech with which our text opens does not appear to begin at the beginning. It is an attack on declamation and the speaker turns out to be our narrator (3). The reply he receives from Agamemnon (3–6) turns out to be even lengthier. This exchange might well give the initial impression that text to come will be entirely devoted to a discussion of oratory—rather like Tacitus' *Dialogus*. The first indication that a story is being told comes after Encolpius has reported Agamemnon's speech:

Dum hunc diligentius audio, non notavi mihi Ascylti fugam. (6. 1)

As I was listening to him so attentively, I failed to notice Ascyltus fleeing away.

The opening of our text balances the attention given to each of the two speakers. This is felicitous in exemplifying the way that Encolpius, though he is an interested narrator, is presented from a number of angles. Encolpius is always surrounded by companions: his personality is largely determined by the way he conducts himself in various exchanges of speech.

Auerbach's term 'two-fold mirroring' has been used to describe the way in which Petronius uses the testimonies of different characters to cast a variety of perspectives on events and on each other.[14] Developing this observation for Encolpius, Paul Veyne distinguished between Encolpius' role as Petronius' 'porte-parole' in the *Cena* and as his 'alibi' in the rest of the work.[15] Notwith-

---

[14] Auerbach (1953), 27: 'The presentation explicit though it be, is entirely subjective, for what is set before us is not Trimalchio's circle as objective reality, but a subjective image, as it exists in the mind of the speaker who himself belongs to the circle. Petronius does not say: This is so. Instead he lets an "I" who is identical neither with himself nor yet with the feigned narrator Encolpius turn the spotlight of his perception on the company at table—a highly artful procedure in perspective, a sort of twofold mirroring which I dare not say is unique in ancient literature as it has come down to us, but which is most unusual there . . . This procedure leads to a more meaningful and more concrete illusion of life.'

[15] Veyne (1964): 'Dans tout le reste du roman, c'est à dire dans les épisodes burlesques, l'auteur cesse d'utiliser Encolpe comme porte-parole et la fausse

standing its apparent injection of the historical author into Encolpius' character, the nature of this distinction is useful. I shall apply less misleading labels: the Encolpius recounting the *Cena* might be called a 'transparent narrator' and the Encolpius recounting the other episodes an 'agent narrator'. These labels are subdivisions of the 'interested narrator' already defined: the transparent narrator records in detail what he witnesses; the agent narrator records his participation (speaking, acting) in events.

Veyne also noted the way in which the first-person narrator is ironized—Encolpius seems to see what he recounts and to see himself 'with the eyes of the reader'. The following study of the presentation of Encolpius' spoken and thought discourse seeks to show how this effect is achieved.

6.2.1 *The Presentation of Encolpius' Speech*

Encolpius the principal narrator frequently presents his own spoken words, employing a full range of speech modes. The frequent use of direct discourse for his words naturally gives a vivid impression of Encolpius, both as a speaker and as a character. The passages of Encolpius' direct discourse are nearly all to be found in scenes other than the *Cena*.[16] Such passages allow the narrator's audience to hear and assess the spoken discourse of his character as they can hear and assess the spoken discourse of any other personage presented in the narrative.

However, there are certain passages where Encolpius' presence as a speaker seems to be diminished in relation to that of his interlocutors. This impression is induced by a specific use of the device of speech presentation which I called the *angled narration of dialogue* (AND). This specific use has Encolpius presenting his own words by using ID or RSA, whilst those of his interlocutors are presented in DD. The pattern is established from early on in our

---

naïveté fait place à l'auto-ironie. Pétrone continue à s'identifier à Encolpe mais c'est pour trouver un alibi.' In his development of Auerbach's observation, it is not clear that Veyne realizes that the 'I' Auerbach was here referring to is not Encolpius, but the person sitting next to him, whom Encolpius has asked for details about Fortunata.

[16] Passages in which this occurs are : 1–3, 7, 8, 9, 10, 20, 24 before the *Cena*; 79, 80, 81, 90, 91, 92, 94, 97, 98, 99, 100, 101, 102, 114, 115, 125, 126, 127, 130 (a quoted letter), 132 (in verse), 133 (a prayer to Priapus in verse), and 140 after the *Cena*. For the three instances of Encolpius' DD in the *Cena*, see n. 20 below.

text. In this example, Encolpius the narrator recounts how he tried to find out what was upsetting Giton. Giton is the boy Encolpius was in love with, whom he calls his *frater* ('brother'):

Cum quaererem numquid nobis in prandium frater parasset, consedit puer super lectum et manantes lacrimas pollice extersit. perturbatus ego habitu fratris, quid accidisset, quaesivi. at ille tarde quidem et invitus, sed postquam precibus etiam iracundiam miscui, 'tuus' inquit 'iste frater seu comes paulo ante in conductum accucurrit coepitque mihi velle pudorem extorquere. cum ego proclamarem, gladium strinxit et "Si Lucretia es" inquit "Tarquinium invenisti." '

(9. 2–5)

When I asked my brother whether he had prepared anything for a meal, the boy sat down on the bed and wiped away his flowing tears with his thumb. As I was anxious about the demeanour of my brother, I asked him what had happened. He said, rather slowly and reluctantly—and after I combined a show of anger with my pleas—'That brother or companion of yours ran into our lodging a little while ago and started trying to extract my modesty. When I shouted out, he drew his sword and said "If you're Lucretia, you have found your Tarquin." '

It is worth noting here that Giton, in his response to Encolpius' question, uses exactly the same manner of speech presentation to reproduce his exchange with Ascyltus (*Cum* + imperfect subjunctive, perfect indicative describing an action in main clause, followed by eventual reply in DD). The effect of this is to put far more emphasis on the dramatic force of the replies given by Giton and Ascyltus than on the utterances prompting them (of Encolpius and Giton respectively).

This passage is interesting for another reason. Giton's trauma recalls consciously and explicitly the rape of Lucretia. This resemblance is discerned in the *story* by Ascyltus who brazenly compares himself with Tarquin, the notorious rapist portrayed by the historian Livy and the poet Ovid. But there are more specific resemblances, on the level of Encolpius' *narrative*, to both of the classic Roman accounts. Giton's speech echoes both the diction of the narratives of the rape of Lucretia in Livy and Ovid, and the pattern of speech attribution employed in those texts. Neither Livy nor Ovid quote Lucretia's objections in direct discourse. Livy and Ovid both ascribe direct discourse to Tarquin.[17] Here though,

[17] Tarquin's words to his victim in Livy 1. 58. 2: '*Tace, Lucretia,*' *inquit, '*Sex. Tarquinius sum; ferrum in manu est; moriere, si emiseris vocem*' ('Be quiet, Lucretia,'

Giton's speech is relayed to us through Encolpius' discourse as narrator.

An important observation follows from this. In a sense, Giton's deployment of speech modes is *really* Encolpius'. The fact that the pattern of speech modes selected for Giton is the same as the pattern Encolpius has selected for himself corroborates this. The intimate connections with the Lucretia narratives are in the end made by Encolpius. His moulding of the presentation of his own speech, Giton's speech and Ascyltus' speech establishes these connections. Encolpius is then not so much reporting discourse as overtly constructing it. It is worth bearing this conclusion in mind for all the occasions in which discourse is presented in the *Satyricon*.

Intricacies like this could be commandeered—possibly rightly—to support claims for the highly involved literary artistry of the *Satyricon*.[18] However, we should also recognize that parallels for this sort of intricacy are also to be found in non-literary texts. Consider again, for example, Ian Paisley's account of his meeting with the British Prime Minister discussed in the Introduction:

When we entered the room Mr Major said to me: 'Except you now give me a categorical assurance that you believe me, I will not talk with you.'
I told Mr Major: 'When you hear my submission, you will know what my position is.'
Mr Major: 'I will not listen to your submission, except you right now give me a categorical assurance that you believe my word.'
Mr Paisley: 'You are the first Prime Minister that ever asked a political opponent in this room, or outside this room, that if he doesn't swear he believe in your truthfulness, then you will not listen to him.'

he said, 'I am Sextus Tarquin, there's a sword in my hand and you will die if you say anything'); and in Ovid, *Fasti* 2. 795–6: *'ferrum, Lucretia, mecum est. | natus' ait 'regis Tarquiniusque loquor'* ('I have a sword, Lucretia,' he said, 'and it is Tarquin the king's son speaking to you.')

[18] This is a view frequently expressed in Conte (1997). Laird (1998) reviews this, offering slightly different opinions on the distinction between author and narrator in the *Satyricon*: (i) First-person narrators in texts are frequently, perhaps inevitably, ironized by an author whom we rationalize from our readings of texts. (ii) The construction of the narrator's character in the *Satyricon* in particular is even more dependent on the reader than Conte allows: he effectively demonstrates a distinction between narrator and author in the *Satyricon*, but his configuration of Petronius and Encolpius can only be ideological, because it is readers' varying determinations of intertextuality that really construct Encolpius.

He said: 'Get out of this room and never come back until you are prepared to say that I speak the truth and do not tell lies.'

The expression 'Except you now' is an Irish idiom—in English 'unless' would be used instead of 'except'. Yet Paisley, who is Irish, twice attributes the use of this Irish idiom to Major, who is English.[19] We might be tempted to say that Paisley is constructing rather than truthfully reporting discourse in his *narrative*. There is a twist: all this is ironized on the level of the *story*, which is about truthfulness. Major insists on his own truthfulness whilst we may discern implications that in certain ways his opponent, the narrator, is 'lying'. And there is a further twist: Paisley, though he is the narrator here, is no more the author of this piece than Encolpius is the author of the *Satyricon*. If Petronius had been the journalist, we would doubtless praise the literary artistry of this newspaper dialogue.

Encolpius' specific type of AND is virtually a rule in the narration of the *Cena*.[20] There, examples abound of the narrator rendering his own discourse in ID (sometimes conflated with that of his friends after a first person plural verb form) and the discourse of his interlocutors in DD.[21] This technique is really what constitutes the celebrated division of the narrator in the *Satyricon*. In the *Cena* Encolpius is very much a 'transparent narrator': he diminishes as a portrayed character in order to spotlight the

---

[19] Another feature of Paisley's rendering of Major's discourse is the opening of Major's final sentence 'Get out of this room'. Paisley's utterance immediately prior to this used the words 'in this room, or outside this room' for rhetorical emphasis. Tannen (1989) treats instances of verbal repetition like these in her account of 'involvement strategy' in everyday spoken discourse.

[20] The three occasions on which the narrator reports his own speech in DD in the *Cena* have a formulaic similarity: at 49 everyone present cries out to defend a slave from a whipping, while Encolpius whispers his private opinion on the matter to Agamemnon; at 69 Encolpius again addresses Agamemnon. The DD in 69 has similar diction and structure to that in 49. Both passages begin with a construction governed by a participle, the subject of which is Encolpius; Agamemnon is actually named as Encolpius' addressee; and the declarative verb is *inquam*. Both utterances consist of two sentences and are followed by a sudden cut to Trimalchio who interrupts. Trimalchio's words stand in an ironic relief after Encolpius' remarks which lead in to them. This could explain why our narrator has availed himself of DD in these two passages. The third instance (72) is another aside, but to Ascyltos: it is interesting for the quick exchange of DD between speakers: this does not happen often in the *Satyricon*.

[21] e.g. 27, 30 (two instances), 34 (two instances), 36 (two instances), 41, 48, 49, 55 (two instances) and 72. Before the *Cena* 7–8, 9, 12, 13–14, 16, 18 and 21; after the *Cena*, further instances are to be found in 81, 86, 88, 99 and 108.

words and deeds of others. In the other surviving parts of the *Satyricon* the narrative is carried by the words and deeds of the character of Encolpius, presented and portrayed by Encolpius the involved narrator.

6.2.2 *The Presentation of Encolpius' Thoughts*

Encolpius' descriptions of thoughts he had at the time of the events he is recounting do not take up a very large proportion of the surviving text of the *Satyricon*. The presentation of Encolpius' thought discourse, like that of his spoken discourse, mainly occurs in sections other than the *Cena*. However, all these instances are important in contributing to our understanding of the character-ization of the narrator: in the *Satyricon* as a whole, a variety of speech modes are used by Encolpius to construct the propositional thoughts he formulates as a character in the story. Direct discourse is used for this purpose on occasions after the *Cena* episode. In particular, soliloquy is a suitable medium to convey Encolpius' loneliness after Giton has rejected him. The pair of soliloquies given by Encolpius at this point merits a detailed treatment. This is the first—in its immediate context:

collegi sarcinulas locumque secretum et proximum litori maestus conduxi. ibi triduo inclusus redeunte in animum solitudine atque contemptu verberabam aegrum planctibus pectus | et inter tot altissimos gemitus frequenter etiam proclamabam: 'ergo me non ruina terra potuit haurire? non iratum etiam innocentibus mare? effugi iudicium, harenae imposui, hospitem occidi, ut inter ⟨tot⟩ audaciae nomina mendicus, exul in deversorio Graecae urbis iacerem desertus? et quis hanc mihi solitudinem imposuit? adulescens omni libidine impurus et sua quoque confessione dignus exilio, stupro liber, stupro ingenuus, cuius anni ad tesseram venierunt, quem tamquam puellam conduxit etiam qui virum putavit. quid ille alter? qui [tamquam] die togae virilis stolam sumpsit, qui ne vir esset, a matre persuasus est, qui opus muliebre in ergastulo fecit, qui postquam conturbavit et libidinis suae solum vertit, reliquit veteris amicitiae nomen et, pro pudor, tamquam mulier secutuleia unius noctis tactu omnia vendidit. iacent nunc amatores adligati noctibus totis, et forsitan mutuis libidinibus attriti derident solitudinem meam. sed non impune. nam aut vir ego non liberque sum, aut noxio sanguine parentabo iniuriae meae.'
82 haec locutus gladio latus cingor, et ne infirmitas militiam perderet, largioribus cibis excito vires.

(81. 1–82. 1)

I collected my little bags, and sadly went off to rent a secret place near to the beach. There, as I shut myself in for three days, the loneliness and scorn I suffered was running through my mind; I was beating my breast worn with blows, and between so many deep groans, I was also crying out these words again and again:

'So the earth has not been able to swallow and close over me? Nor has the sea which is so harsh, even to the innocent? Have I fled justice, have I cheated the arena, have I killed my host only, after so many titles for bravery, to lie abandoned as a beggar and an exile in lodgings in a Greek town? And who has forced this solitude on me? A young man tainted by every kind of lust and deserving of banishment even by his own admission, who is emancipated by his vices, given freedom by his vices, whose years were sold at the throw of a dice, whom one hired as a girl even if one realized he was a man. And what about the other one? Who on the day he was supposed to put on an adult male toga took a skirt, who was persuaded by his mother not to become a man, who did the woman's work in a slaves' prison, who after he bankrupted and changed over the area of his desires, discarded the bond of a longstanding relationship and—oh the shame of it—like a loose woman sold everything on the basis of one night. Now pledged as lovers they lie together all night long, and quite probably when they have ground away their lust for each other they laugh at my loneliness. But not without punishment. For I am not a free man, if I do not avenge this injustice done to me by shedding some guilty blood.'

Saying this I put on my sword and, to prevent weakness from sabotaging my campaign, I summon my manly strength with an ample meal.

Encolpius' soliloquy is a clear example of iterative free direct discourse: the narrator says the speech was uttered out loud many times over the course of three days.[22] The location of an isolated seashore for this soliloquy is significant, as many have noted. Critics have long argued that we are meant to see Encolpius here as a 'second Achilles'.[23] When Agamemnon took his mistress Briseis, Achilles went to lament alone on the seashore.[24]

But Achilles' sorrow is not the only one appropriate here.[25]

---

[22] That detail becomes more significant: compare Catullus 64. 124 f.: *saepe fudisse e pectore voces* ('often . . . she poured these words forth from her heart'). The presence of Catullus 64 in this text will be considered below.

[23] Walsh (1970), 36; Conte (1997), 1–2 pursues this comparison in a different way. See also Labate (1995; 1996).

[24] *Iliad* 1. 348 f.

[25] The tableau recalls two further passages, which are themselves intertextual with the *Iliad* case: the predicament of Odysseus in *Od.* 5. 156–9 (although no speech is ascribed to him) and that of the Trojan Women in *Aeneid* 5. 615: the context of the latter was discussed earlier in Ch. 5.2.

Achilles' speech is not a soliloquy but a prayer to his mother. And, as
Walsh acknowledges, Thetis replies, initiating a longer account of
events and a request from her son to which she gives another reply
before departing. Achilles, notoriously, is more preoccupied with
his loss of honour than with Briseis herself. Encolpius is simply
lovelorn and bitter. It may be nearer the mark to compare this
soliloquy to those in Roman comedy, such as Palaestra's speech in
Plautus' *Rudens*.[26] We should also look to a topos derived from
comedy which is common enough in extant Latin literary narrative:
the lament of a grief-stricken woman abandoned by her intended
husband, often on a seashore. There are numerous celebrated
examples which pre-date Petronius: the speeches of Catullus'
Ariadne, Virgil's Dido, Ovid's Scylla, and Ovid's Ariadne in the
Fasti and the *Heroides*.[27] The angry speeches of Juno in *Aeneid* 1. 37–
49 and especially 7. 293–322 also merit consideration, because they
are intertextual with the laments of these deserted women. Encolpius' speech recalls passages of this kind, in theme and diction.

Like Catullus' Ariadne, Dido, and Scylla, Encolpius opens his
words with a series of rhetorical questions.[28] Like Catullus'
Ariadne, Dido, and Scylla, Encolpius complains that his own
behaviour has ruled out any means of escape from utter desertion:
'I have fled justice, I have cheated the arena, I have killed my
host.'[29] And like these heroines, Encolpius turns to consider who is
responsible for his predicament: 'And who has forced this solitude
on me?' (*et quis hanc mihi solitudinem imposuit?*). He does not have to
invent any extravagant bestial lineages for Ascyltus and Giton, or
say that they have hearts of stone or flint. Encolpius merely describes
them as they are.[30] This portrayal of his former companions presents

[26] *Rudens* 185–201. See F. Marx (1959), 89–90 ad loc.

[27] Catullus 64. 132–201; Virgil, *Aeneid* 4. 305–30, 365–87; Ovid, *Met.* 8. 108;
Ovid, *Fasti* 3. 459 f.; Ovid, *Heroides* 10. Lyne (1978) (on the *Ciris* which offers a
later portrayal of Scylla) treats the heroine's lament as a feature of epyllion at 34,
167 and 283–5; see also Ehlers (1954).

[28] Ariadne has a succession of rhetorical questions in *Fasti* 3. 479–86 and 495–6,
after the expression of shock in 471–8, suitably enough, at the *déjà-vu*: Bacchus
seems to be forsaking her in the way Theseus did before.

[29] (*Effugi iudicium, harenae imposui, hospitem occidi* . . .) On the 'epigraphic'
perfect in Latin literature—found in Dido's speech in *Aeneid* 4. 651–8—see
E. Fraenkel (1964). Lattimore (1942) treats the content and language of actual
Greek and Latin epitaphs.

[30] Compare Catullus 64. 154 f. and Dido at *Aen.* 4. 365: *nec tibi diva parens
generis nec Dardanus auctor* ('You have no goddess as a mother, nor a Trojan
father'). Pease (1935) on this *Aeneid* passage has a huge list of comparisons.

the two men in very sordid colours, without recourse to any purple analogies. Indeed Ascyltus and Giton are shown to be far more ignoble than Theseus, Aeneas, or Minos could ever be. The effect is amusing because the *Satyricon*'s narrative has shown that Encolpius, unlike the heroines, is not exaggerating.

Encolpius then dwells on the contentment of Ascyltus and Giton. The prospect of their gloating over him is what turns his thoughts to vengeance. Ariadne and Dido utter prayers and curses against their former lovers and Juno makes dark threats against the Trojans in *Aeneid* 7. 309–22. Correspondingly, Encolpius, rather like Scylla, declares (however ineffectually) that he will act on the situation himself by threatening bloodshed and putting on a sword.[31] If this speech is supposed to recall and parody the heroines' laments, there is a strong irony in the words *non aut vir ego*—'I would not be a man'. It is conceivable that the juxtaposition of *vir* and *ego* effect a pun on *virago* or *virgo*.[32] *This speech—in which he strikes a feminine posture—closes with the avowal that he is no man unless he avenges himself. Encolpius hardly stands out as a manly figure at any point in the Satyricon.* Needless to say, his vengeance is aborted—in spite of his hearty eating to stimulate his *vires* ('manly strength'). A soldier, or else a thief who outdoes him in pretending to be a soldier, confiscates (or steals) his weapon (82). Encolpius the narrator admits that this was a relief to him.

In addition to the suggestion of Encolpius' literary echoes and the remote location in which his thoughts are expressed, the repetitions of *solum, solitudine, mihi solitudinem, solitudinem meam* emphasize the status of this piece of direct discourse as soliloquy—the first in our text of the *Satyricon*. A similar emphasis on Encolpius' isolation frames the next presentation of his thoughts—again in the form of a soliloquy in direct discourse. Encolpius has been inspecting some paintings in a picture gallery:

inter quos [etiam] pictorum amantium vultus tamquam in solitudine exclamavi: 'ergo amor etiam deos tangit. Iuppiter in caelo suo non invenit

---

[31] Scylla says in Ovid, *Metamorphoses* 8. 76–8: *ire per ignes | et gladios ausim; nec in hoc tamen ignibus | aut gladiis opus est* ('I would dare to go through fire—and swords. But in this situation there is no need for any fire or swords'). Dido kills herself with a sword in *Aeneid* 4. 664.

[32] See Maltby (1991), 647 on ancient etymologies of *virago*. He quotes e.g. 'Servius' on *Aeneid* 12. 468: *virago dicitur mulier, quae virile implet officium* ('*virago* is what a woman who performs a man's role is called').

quod diligeret, sed peccaturus in terris nemini tamen iniuriam fecit. Hylan
Nympha praedata imperasset amori suo, si venturum Herculem ad inter-
dictum credidisset. Apollo pueri umbram revocavit in florem; [et] omnes
fabulae quoque sine aemulo habuerunt complexus. at ego in societatem
recepi hospitem Lycurgo crudeliorem.' ecce autem, ego dum cum ventis
litigo, intravit pinacothecam senex canus, exercitati vultus et qui videretur
nescio quid magnum promittere, sed cultu non proinde speciosus, ut facile
appareret eum ⟨ex⟩ hac nota litteratum esse, quos odisse divites solent. is
ergo ad latus constitit meum.

(83. 4–8)

Among those countenances even though they were of painted lovers, as if in
solitude I cried out: 'So love even touches the gods. Jupiter did not find
what he cared about in his heaven, but he was ready to sin on earth and in
fact did harm to no one. The Nymph who ravished Hylas would have
curbed her love had she realized Hercules would come to prohibit it. Apollo
recalled the ghost of a boy into a flower. All these fabulous figures enjoyed
love's embraces without a rival. But I have welcomed into friendship
someone even more cruel than Lycurgus.' Just then, as I was quarrelling
with the winds, a white haired old man entered the picture gallery. His face
was care-worn, but he seemed to promise something great, and though he
was not well turned out, it was easy to tell by that very feature he was a man
of letters, one of those whom rich people tend to dislike. So it was this man
who came to stand by my side.

Some features of this soliloquy resemble the previous one. First,
the words which introduce it (*inter quos etiam pictorum amantium
vultus tamquam in solitudine exclamavi*) echo those which heralded
the previous soliloquy (*inter tot altissimos gemitus frequenter etiam*).
Both speeches open with the word *ergo*; both close with adversa-
tives: *at ego in societatem recepi hospitem* could be seen to correspond
to *sed non impune* earlier.

These formal resemblances underline a deeper affinity between
these two speeches. The abandoned Ariadne in Catullus 64 (whose
predicament seems to have been parodied just before in 81) was
depicted on a tapestry. In this second speech, Encolpius is actually
identifying himself with depicted figures: all the gods he uses in his
mythological analogies are in the set of paintings by Apelles which
he has just seen.[33] As narrator, Encolpius describes his second

---

[33] In this respect, Encolpius is obviously comparable with Virgil's Aeneas as he
gazes at the representations of the sack of Troy in Book 1 of the *Aeneid*: Aeneas
literally sees himself as one of the heroes depicted. His response is to cry out at
1. 462: *sunt lacrimae rerum et mentem mortalia tangunt* ('there are tears for such

lament as 'litigating with the winds'. It is worth comparing the following verses in Ariadne's complaint:

> sed conubia laeta, sed optatos hymenaeos,
> quae cuncta aerii discerpunt irrita venti.
> (Catullus 64. 141–2)

But the happy marriage, the anticipated wedding, all this the airy winds plucked away as a vanity.

> sed quid ego ignaris nequiquam conquerar auris,
> externata malo, quae nullis sensibus auctae
> nec missas audire queunt nec reddere voces?
> (Catullus 64. 164–6)

But why should I, exiled by my evil deed, complain in vain to the ignorant breezes, which are not endowed with sensations, which can neither hear nor reply to my utterances?

The sudden appearance of Eumolpus when Encolpius finishes speaking yet again recalls Catullus 64—as well as other models.[34] The old man can be seen as a mischievous parallel to Bacchus who comes to the rescue of Ariadne. This is how Bacchus' epiphany is described by Catullus:

> at parte ex alia florens volitabat Iacchus
> cum thiaso Satyrorum et Nysigenis Silenis
> (Catullus 64. 251–2)

But from the other side the youthful Iacchus was flying about, with a band of Satyrs and Sileni born with Bacchus

Eumolpus' nature and behaviour, as it is subsequently portrayed,

events and mortal affairs touch the heart'). Conte (1997), 15–16 considers *Aeneid* 1. 455 f. in relation to this passage of Petronius. Juno's complaint (*Aeneid* 7. 304–10) about her limited powers compared to those of the other gods could also be recalled by Encolpius here.

[34] The entrance of Philosophy, personified as a woman, in Boethius, *Consolatio* 1. 1 could suggest a conventional type of scene accessible to both Petronius and Boethius. In Longus, *Daphnis and Chloe*, the figure of Philetas, an old sage who explains the nature of Eros, has some community with Eumolpus here. The fact that *Daphnis and Chloe* opens with a description of a picture dedicated in part to Eros, of which the ensuing narrative is an exposition (see Conte (1997), 18–19) underlines this particular connection. Bowie (1985), 72–80 suggests that the poet Philetas wrote pastoral poetry before Theocritus. As well as explaining Longus' nomenclature, this would strengthen the link between Longus' Philetas and Petronius' Eumolpus: both characters are then associated with poetry.

certainly recalls that of a Satyr if not a Silenus.[35] He gets drunk and satirizes bald men and criminals before attempting two sets of verses on hair (109). His account of his seduction of the boy in Pergamon (85) shows that, for an old man, Eumolpus is potent as well as lecherous. He soon exhibits this strong sexual appetite (for Philomela's daughter at Croton (140) as well as for Giton and possibly Encolpius himself). So the entry of Eumolpus offers a parodic contrast to the story in Catullus: Ariadne's deliverer was a youthful or 'flowering' god; Encolpius' 'rescuer' is an impecunious old man.[36] There is another even more pointed contrast between Eumolpus and Bacchus. In Catullus 64. 260 we are told, on Bacchus' entry, that the profane would love to approach and hear the music of Bacchus' rites. But here in the *Satyricon*, the aesthetically profane neglect and spurn Eumolpus, as he himself admits (83. 9–84).

Encolpius presents his thought discourse in soliloquies on several other occasions: and there are also significant links made between other soliloquies similar to the one I have identified here.[37] Only one rendition of a thought ascribed to Encolpius alone is given in the *Cena*. This is a brief proposition in the form of an indirect

[35] Eumolpus-as-Satyr might have some bearing on the title of the work as it has come down to us. Coffey (1976), 181, amidst other observations on the title, remarks: '*Satyrica* properly means things concerning satyrs, as in the title of a Greek work on the Marsyas story. The work of Petronius has nothing to do with the satyrs of Greek mythology, but the title is appropriate for a tale about lecherous rogues.' The grammarian Diomedes mentions sources which suggest the word *satura* takes its name from satyrs: *satura autem dicta sive a Satyris, quod similiter in hoc carmine ridiculae res pudendaeque dicuntur* 1. 485, Keil (1855–1923). ('Satire is so called from the Satyrs, because this sort of poetry talks about things which are ridiculous and shameful'). This is not wholly true of the genre of Roman satire as we know it, but it could apply to the *Satyricon* of Petronius.

[36] Slater (1990), 92 n. 10 'Encolpius' *ergo* at 83. 8 seems ironic: "clearly he [Eumolpus] was a literary man, the sort the rich hate—so *of course* he came over to me."

[37] 100, 115, 125, and 126. At 100 he tries unsuccessfully to reconcile himself to the fact that Eumolpus is making successful advances on Giton. 115 provides a rather different reflection (again he shouts it out, as he did in 81—*proclamo*), when he sees the body of a shipwrecked sailor he does not yet recognize. Later in 115, a second speech of a similar gloomy and philosophical nature is prompted when he recognizes the body of Lichas. This kind of expression has its origin in Greek sepulchral epigram in which dead men were addressed in their graves (see Nisbet and Hubbard (1970) on Horace, *Odes* 1. 28; Fedeli (1980) on Propertius 1. 21). See n. 29 above. There are also recurrences of diction between the soliloquies in 115 and 125. At 125. 4 Encolpius wonders about Eumolpus' scheme of tricking legacy hunters being rumbled: *dii deaeque, quam male est extra legem viventibus* . . . Compare: *Dii deaeque quam longe a destinatione sua iacet* at 115. 15.

question. Encolpius is describing his reaction to one of the extravagant dishes presented at the banquet (41.1):

interim ego, qui privatum habebam secessum, in multas cogitationes
diductus sum, quare aper pilleatus intrasset.

Meanwhile, I was occupying a quiet private space and was distracted by a
number of reflections about why the boar had made its entrance wearing
the cap of a freedman.

But the relative suppression of Encolpius' narrated thoughts in
the *Cena*, in comparison with the rest of the work, does seem to bear
out the distinction critics have made between two styles of narration in the *Satyricon*. The Encolpius of the *Cena*, as this paucity of
inner revelation shows, is more a channel for the presentation of
other characters than an object of scrutiny himself. Of course, these
differences of technique between the *Cena* and the rest of the
Satyricon are shown by prominent tendencies rather than absolute
rules. Nonethless the lack of Encolpius' words (in DD) and of his
thoughts (in any mode) in the *Cena* is positively striking. Were the
discrepancies to be any more emphasized, Petronius' division of the
functions of the principal narrator would lose its subtlety.

It remains to make an important concluding remark about
Encolpius' soliloquies. These monologues express certain sentiments in certain situations which naturally lead us to conceive of
them as Encolpius' thoughts, or as presentations of his thought
discourse. But the narrator often says they are uttered or even cried
out by his character. These soliloquies have a baroque, poetical
quality. They are not the stuff of realistic literature, even when we
consider the norms of ancient narrative, which are fairly different
from our own. A parodic tone in these speeches is indicated by the
kinds of intertexts we discern in them: elevated narrative poetry and
drama provide the vehicles for Encolpius' expression of his psychological condition.[38] The fact that actual passages of verse are used to
present Encolpius' discourse in the *Satyricon* further supports this
conclusion.

---

[38] Conte (1997) explores the implications of poetic intertexts in Encolpius'
discourse.

6.3 VERSE AND DISCOURSE IN THE *SATYRICON*

In many parts of the *Satyricon* there are passages in which prose gives way to verse: a reputed characteristic of Menippean satire.[39] Their overall role in the narrative is bound to be a matter of opinion rather than fact. However, the Bakhtinian tenor of Catherine Connors's conclusion is very persuasive: 'by producing verse within his fictional prose, Petronius sets his novel in a self-consciously agonistic relationship with the literary genres which he has repudiated'.[40] The study of these verse passages to follow will be considered in relation to the broader issue of speech presentation in the *Satyricon*. The verses fall into two major types:

1. They may, like Eumolpus' poetry (to be discussed in the next section) present, within a character's speech, compositions or celebrated quotations from other texts for consideration by other characters present—and by Petronius' audience.[41]

2. Alternatively, original verse can function as characters' speeches either in part or in whole. Verse can be used both to repeat sentiments which have already been expressed in prose and to constitute a character's entire speech. In these cases speakers do not appear to be self-concious about their use of verse.[42]

Of course, these two types are not necessarily mutually exclusive: any distinctions drawn by Petronius' readers between original verse and celebrated quotations are, again, doomed to be subjective. In general these verse passages offer a kind of interlude. They can express what has been going on in a different way—rather like the

---

[39] Buecheler (1862) assembles a complete list of the *carmina* in the *Sat.* to be found at the end of his edition which are also discussed in Courtney (1991). Connors (1998) is a full treatment.

[40] Connors (1998), 147.

[41] Verses quoted from other texts are *Aeneid* 5. 1 (by Trimalchio's slave) in 68; *Aen.* 4. 34 in Eumolpus' Milesian tale at 111; a medley of Virgilian verses in 132 indicate the response of Encolpius' member to his speech (*Aen.* 6. 469, *Eclogue* 5. 16, *Aen.* 9. 436); possibly the *senarii* which Trimalchio quotes in 56 are by Syrus. Verses produced by the characters themselves are Trimalchio's hexameter and pentameter efforts in 34 and 55, and Eumolpus' compositions on objects of desire (93) and hair (109).

[42] Agamemnon in 5, Ascyltus at 14, Quartilla in 18, Eumolpus in 83 are reiterations in verse; the *cinaedus*'s verses (23) and Tryphaena's hexameters (108), uttered to reconcile Lichas with Eumolpus' party, exemplify speeches entirely constituted by verses.

lyric recapitulation of trimeters in Greek tragedy.[43] Their role is thus comparable to songs in modern 'musicals', or longer blocks of sung verses which succeed shorter alternations of one or two lines in opera.[44] Thus Petronius' verses can either amplify words already spoken, or else they can give an intimation of what is to happen next. This sort of function is rather different from the way in which Seneca's narrative in the *Apocolocyntosis* uses verse: there it often seems to signal an additional voice or mode, with which the prose narrator is in a kind of dialogue.[45]

The technique is used principally by Encolpius and it provides the most frequent occasion for snatches of verse in the *Satyricon*. As we might expect, Encolpius' verses come in the sections we have either side of the *Cena*. Most of them seem to be placed temporally at the point of narration rather than in the story. The use of past tenses alone is enough to demonstrate this.[46] Encolpius' verses in the comical sotadean metre (132) are an interesting example. He describes how, after impotence marred his encounter with Circe, he attempted to cut off the offending part of his body. The verses carry the narrative along, actually supplying new information about what happened rather than the more typical comment on events. The way the sotadean verses are connected to the prose that surrounds them shows this:

quod solum igitur salvo pudore poteram, contingere languorem simulavi, conditusque lectulo totum ignem furoris in eam converti, quae mihi omnium malorum causa fuerat:

[43] See e.g. Bond (1981), 288 on Euripides, *Herakles* 855.

[44] For example in Monteverdi's adaptation of Busenello's libretto in *Coronation of Poppaea* (1642), Act 1 Scene 9, the stichomythia of Nero and Seneca (based on ps.-Seneca, *Octavia* 437–585) climax in a block of six verses sung by Nero and then eleven by Seneca which reformulate earlier themes of their exchange. See Tomlinson (1987), 215–39.

[45] Seneca, *Apocolocyntosis* 2 is the first example. A euphuistic verse account of autumn (2. 1–6) is succeeded by these words (in prose): *puto magis intellegi si dixero: mensis erat October* ('I think this will be better understood if I say: the month was October').

[46] In addition to the passage quoted: 15; 79 (where the sentiment recalls outbursts conventional in erotic poetry e.g. Propertius 2. 14. 9–10: *quanta ego praeterita collegi gaudia nocte | immortalis ero, si altera talis erit*); the hexameters at 127, prompted by Encolpius' dallying on the lawn with Circe; the description of the *dignus amore locus* (131); the poetic description of the temple (135) and the verses on the killing of the goose (136). The distichs on friendship (80) could be produced by Encolpius at the time of his betrayal (cf. the distichs on Tantalus in 82), but again they seem to indicate a narrator's subsequent reflection.

ter corripui terribilem manu bipennem,
ter languidior coliculi repente thyrso
ferrum timui, quod trepido male dabat usum.
nec iam poteram, quod modo conficere libebat;
namque illa metu frigidior rigente bruma
confugerat in viscera mille operta rugis.
ita non potui supplicio caput aperire,
sed furciferae mortifero timore lusus
ad verba, magis quae poterant nocere, fugi.

erectus igitur in cubitum hac fere oratione contumacem vexavi: 'quid dicis'
inquam 'omnium hominum deorumque pudor?' . . .

(*Satyricon* 132. 7–9)

Therefore I did the only thing I could to keep my pride intact: I pretended I
had contracted some sickness, and thus confined to bed, I turned the whole
fire of my fury against the one who had been the cause of all my
misfortunes:

Thrice I snatched up a fearsome two bladed axe
Thrice, suddenly fainter than the stalk of a cabbage,
I dreaded the steel which served me badly in my panic.
Now I was unable to do what I had just wanted to accomplish:
For colder with fear than frozen winter,
It had fled into my insides covered by a thousand wrinkles.
So I couldn't bare its head for execution:
Mocked as I was with my deadly fear of that prick,
I resorted to words which could do more harm.

Therefore erect on my couch I scolded the stubborn organ with a speech
rather like this: 'What can you say?' I asked 'you are the shame of all gods
and men . . .'

The *igitur* ('therefore') of the prose sentence succeeding these
verses suggests that the direct discourse which follows is a consequence of the actions those verses describe. We can draw no other
conclusion: Encolpius' attack on his member and its cowardly
retreat, thus narrated, are on the same level of reality as the
speech and other events that follow. This use of verse for pure
narration, however, is certainly unusual in the text we have: the
bawdy metre and echoes of Virgil comically heighten the account.[47]
   The speech which commences at the end of this excerpt is in

[47] See Sullivan (1968), 217–8, Slater (1990), 184–5. For discussion of the Virgil
echoes, see Zeitlin (1971).

FDD. This is signalled by the way it is introduced (*hac fere oratione* 'with a speech rather like this'). His mute organ cannot of course reply: thus the effect of opening the speech with the question (*Quid dicis?*)—which may recall Ovid's poem on impotence—is amusing more than realistic.[48] Besides, there is an obvious irony in the mention of Encolpius' 'erect' posture as he utters it.[49] The proximity of this passage of FDD in prose to these verses raises the question of the status of verse in relation to other discourse presented in the *Satyricon*. Discussions in my earlier chapters have shown that discourse presented in verse could be considered a sufficient condition of FDD.[50] FDD (like DD in general) can usually be regarded as the character's discourse rather than the narrator's discourse: the semantics and syntax of a passage of direct discourse do not usually bear directly on the semantics and syntax of the discourse enclosing it.[51]

But it is harder to determine the significance of these verse passages as presented discourse and their exact relation to the *Satyricon*'s narrative. Whilst I have noted that most of the passages seem to be in the voice of the narrator, the subject matter of this majority often seems relevant to the thoughts or speech of Encolpius the character. The verse passages often seem to open up a new mode of expression which falls somewhere between presented discourse and the narrator's voice. The celebrated passage of four distichs in 132 which has often been read as a statement of the historical author's poetic intent is a useful example. These verses seem to express a preoccupation Encolpius would have had at the time of the story, as well as at the point of narration. Encolpius the character has been arguing with himself about whether or not it was

[48] Compare Ovid, *Amores* 3. 7. 69–70: *quin istic pudibunda iaces, pars pessima nostri?* | *sic sum pollicitis captus et ante tuis* ('why don't you lie down, you shameful thing, the worst part of me? I have been taken in before by your promises of this sort').

[49] The same kind of joke is made earlier (88) when Encolpius uses the word to describe the effect upon him of Eumolpus' anecdote about the boy from Pergamon whom he tutored—an anecdote which is basically pornographic: *erectus his sermonibus consulere prudentiorem coepi . . .*

[50] At 2.2 and 3.4.2b.

[51] However instances of temporal telescoping in FDD like those discussed in Ch. 3 show how direct discourse *can* interfere with the narrative which encloses it: the time taken for direct discourse to be presented is too short for the time the actual utterance would take to be articulated. Thus FDD can show the narrator at work as he accelerates the pace of his narrative on the level of the story.

right for him to scold his penis. His subsequent justification for reproaching a part of his anatomy, which begins in prose, drifts into a verse attack on Stoic moralists:

nec minus ego tam foeda obiurgatione finita paenitentiam agere sermonis mei coepi secretoque rubore perfundi, quod oblitus verecundiae meae cum ea parte corporis verba contulerim, quam ne ad cognitionem quidem admittere severioris notae homines solerent. mox perfricata diutius fronte 'quid autem ego' inquam 'mali feci, si dolorem meum naturali convicio exoneravi? aut quid est quod in corpore humani ventri male dicere solemus aut gulae capitique etiam, cum saepius dolet? quid? non et Ulixes cum corde litigat suo, et quidam tragici oculos suos tamquam audientes castigant? Podagrici pedibus suis male dicunt, chiragrici mani-bus, lippi oculis, et qui offenderunt saepe digitos, quicquid doloris habent, in pedes deferunt:

> quid me constricta spectatis fronte Catones
> damnatisque novae simplicitatis opus?
> sermonis puri non tristis gratia ridet,
> quodque facit populus candida lingua refert.
> nam quis concubitus, Veneris quis gaudia nescit?
> quis vetat in tepido membra calere toro?
> ipse pater veri doctos Epicurus amare
> iussit, et hoc vitam dixit habere τέλος.

> (*Sat.* 132. 12–15)

And as soon as I had finished a rant as disgusting as this, I began to feel remorse for making this speech and to blush secretly because, forgetful of any propriety, I had had words with that part of my body to which men of a severer character are not inclined to devote their thoughts. After rubbing my forehead for a long while, I said ' But what wrong have I done if I have eased my suffering with a tirade which is quite natural? Why else is it that we tend to curse a part of our body: the stomach, throat, even the head on the frequent occasions it aches. Did not even Ulysses quarrel with his own heart, and some tragic figures castigate their own eyes as if they could hear? Gouty people curse their feet, those with chalk stones curse their hands, the dim-sighted their eyes, and those who have often hurt their toes, put down whatever pain they have in metrical feet:

> Why do you look at me with frowning brows, you Cato types
> and condemn a work of new simplicity?
> The grace of my pure speech laughs happily,
> my clear tongue reports what people do.
> For who does not know of concupiscence, of Venus' joys?
> Who would stop limbs glowing in a warm bed?

> Epicurus the father of truth himself bade wise men
> to love, and to hold this as the *telos* of life.

Encolpius excuses himself for having just addressed his penis with
an argument by analogy in the prose part of his speech: people
address parts of their body in literature as well as everyday life. In
the verses, Encolpius continues the justification: the reprimand is
an artistic innovation, it is amusing, it describes what people do;
finally, the importance he attaches to sex is not abnormal and is
endorsed by Epicurean teaching. Encolpius is addressing these
remarks in verse to Stoic thinkers (*Catones*). A little earlier he
himself had been ashamed of his speech because 'men of a severer
character'—perhaps Stoics?—are not inclined to devote their
thoughts to this part of the body.

But the verses are not entirely sealed into their context in the
story. As I remarked, critics have treated these verses as a defence
by *Petronius* of the poetical and thematic preoccupations in the
Satyricon as a whole. The diction which heralds them might
indicate that some reflexive comment is afoot: the expression *in
pedes deferunt* 'they pass their suffering down to their feet' is
immediately followed by the appearance of metrical *pedes*
('feet').[52] The phrase *novae simplicitatis opus* ('work of new simpli-
city') suggests something else, in addition to the morally dubious
speech Encolpius made earlier. The line *sermonis puri non tristis
gratia ridet* ('The grace of my pure speech laughs happily') makes
the strongest case for this verse passage having more than a local
function in the story. These words do more than just characterize
the mournful indignation of Encolpius' earlier harangue.

Whether or not they are placed inside or outside monologues,
whether they are attributable to Encolpius the narrator or Encolpius the character, the verse passages in the *Satyricon* often have the
effect of expanding and enriching the principle narrator's powers of
expression.[53] They can present his thoughts, words and experiences, as well as his reflections upon them. The verse passages can
make up part of what was originally uttered in the story, they may
constitute the narrator's present discourse, or interrupt it. Moreover, passages of verse in a text which is largely in prose lay claim to

---

[52] Compare Laird (1996), 82–3 on a similar wordplay in the final couplet of
Propertius 2. 12.
[53] The flexible role of the chorus in Greek tragedy could provide a kind of
parallel for the way verse passages are used in the *Sat.*

a kind of literary status, which the audience or reader will transfer to the *Satyricon* as a whole. The use of verse signals that Encolpius is more than a realistic imitation of an individual speaker telling his story in everyday speech. By occasionally using poetry Encolpius becomes a *literary* figure in two senses: he himself speaks to his addressee as a man of letters and, secondly, as a literary creation, he mediates to the reader of the *Satyricon* the discourse of another artist, Petronius the author.

6.4 EMBEDDED NARRATIVE AND PRESENTED DISCOURSE

A great deal of what we have of the *Satyricon* is given over to quite extensive stories within the major story. Of course embedded narratives feature elsewhere—in Latin literature they are a common feature of narrative poetry. However, the embedded narratives of the *Satyricon* have a rather distinctive relation to the narrative which, we believe, ultimately encloses them.[54] Our examination of the verse passages well illustrates how the *Satyricon*, like the form of literary dialogue, is able to include excerpts and instances of 'texts' of various poetic genres. The prose 'texts' included can be, and are, just as varied. Such a level of inclusion is not possible in, say, hexameter epics like the *Aeneid* or Ovid's *Metamorphoses*. Whilst we can often discern the influence and inclusion of other genres in poems like these, formal differences are smoothed out—at the very least, prose and alien metres are converted into hexameters. But the discourse of texts like the *Apocolocyntosis* and the *Satyricon* can literally exchange one generic voice for another. Thus embedded narratives within a text like the

---

[54] In martial epic poetry the embedded narratives usually have some causal connection with the principal narrative: they are told by involved narrators recounting their own lived experience to account for a present situation (e.g. *Aeneid* 2 and 3 in which Aeneas explains to Dido how he got to Carthage.) In epyllion, they can affect the mood and significance of the outer story: Ariadne's desertion darkens the marriage of Peleus and Thetis in Catullus 64. Ovid's *Metamorphoses* renders stories that characters use to entertain those around them in the outer story. Often embedded narrations in the *Met.* accomplish an end in the outer story: Vertumnus uses the tale of Iphis and Anaxarete as a *narratio* to seduce Pomona (14. 697–764). As our text of Petronius is not complete, we cannot be sure that Encolpius' whole story as we have it is the definitive outer narrative. Compare the flexibility of the frame in Antonius Diogenes, *The Wonders beyond Thule* discussed in Morgan (1985).

Satyricon can differ greatly. For instance, Eumolpus' civil war poem is located both in a poetic realm and in a historical past—Eumolpus himself gives short shrift to historical accuracy.[55] Trimalchio's and Niceros' ghost stories, on the other hand are supposed to be located in the world of experience of their narrators.[56]

The techniques of speech presentation in the *Satyricon*'s embedded narratives can reveal a great deal about the nature of these stories and their narrators, as well as about the characters in their stories. Eumolpus is responsible for the longest and most conspicuous intrusions of embedded narratives into the text we have. This section will consider aspects of speech presentation which bear on interpretation of two of his narratives: the epic verses he recites on the civil war, and his tale of the widow of Ephesus.

6.4.1 *Eumolpus' Civil War Poem*

Eumolpus' epic verses (119–24) are meant to serve as a demonstration of his literary skill: they follow his exposition of ideas about how a civil war poem should be written (118). Critics have been very much concerned with the extent to which these verses parody the epic poet Lucan (with whom Petronius is thought to have been contemporary).[57] Eumolpus' verses evidently share the subject matter of Lucan's poem on the civil war, and numerous specific passsages have content and diction similar to the *De Bello Civili*. Consideration of aspects of speech presentation, even in such a short piece, reveals further points of resemblance between Lucan and this part of our text of Petronius.

It is a conspicuous feature of Lucan's work that the employment of indirect discourse is unusually rare—even for an epic poem. Long declamatory speeches in DD or FDD are by far the most

---

[55] *Sat.* 118. 6: *potius furentis animi vaticinatio appareat quam religiosae orationis sub testibus fides* ('it should rather appear as the prophecy of a raging spirit than as the witnessed testimony of a solemn speech').

[56] This is an important point. The ghost stories are subject to refutation, as their narrators indicate when they end their accounts. Eumolpus, on the other hand, does not ask that his story about the Widow of Ephesus be believed (though he says it is a *rem sua memoria factam*)—it is really supposed to entertain. This kind of distinction between embedded narratives is not typical of epic poetry (see n. 54 above), but Pirithous and Lelex discuss the credibility of the stories they hear in Ovid, *Met.* 8. The significance of this is explored in Feeney (1991), 229–39.

[57] Studies of the question include Baldwin (1911), Walsh (1968), Luck (1972), George (1974), Grimal (1977), and Zeitlin (1971) 67 f. Slater (1990) and Connors (1998), 100–46 are more recent accounts.

frequent way of presenting the discourse of characters.[58] There are no unequivocal instances of FID in Lucan.[59] On the rare occasions in which thoughts of characters are mentioned in ID type constructions, Lucan, unlike Virgil, only renders thoughts which could anyway be imputed to characters from their words and behaviour.[60] Protracted propositional thoughts are expressed in DD soliloquy.

Discourse which is specifically spoken in Eumolpus' poem is presented in the same fashion as it is in Lucan. Exchanges of lengthy speeches in direct discourse are the standard pattern. Dis' words to Fortuna (79–99) are followed by Fortuna's response (103–21), again about 20 verses long, which explictly picks up the preceding speech it follows (cf. 80–3 with 107–9).[61] Both speeches culminate in gruesome references to Tisiphone. Caesar's prayer (156–76) is again of similar length. Lastly follow Discordia's words (283–94). There is no RSA in Eumolpus' poem, and only one example of ID. However, as this occurs in a message ascribed to Fama (the personification of rumour), it is an exception which proves the rule:

> interea volucer motis conterrita pinnis
> Fama volat summique petit iuga celsa Palati
> atque hoc †Romano† tonitru ferit omnia †signa†:
> iam classes fluitare mari totasque per Alpes
> fervere, Germano perfusas sanguine turmas.
> arma, cruor, caedes, incendia totaque bella
> ante oculos volitant . . .
>
> (*Satyricon* 123. 210–16)

Meanwhile swift Fama flaps her wings in terror and seeks the lofty roofs of the high Palatine, and strikes all the images with thunderous news for Rome: fleets of ships are already sailing over the sea, and cavalries soaked in German blood were seething over the Alps. Arms, gore, slaughter, fire and whole wars fly before the eyes . . .

[58] For accounts of DD in Lucan, see Basore (1904) and Tasler (1972). Laird (1992), 96–105 gives an overall account of Lucan's speech presentation.
[59] The five possible instances for *De Bello Civili* are listed in Ch. 5 n. 47.
[60] There are only six examples worth taking into account: Lucan, *De Bello Civili* 2. 527–30; 5. 499–503; 5. 526–7; 5. 653–4; 8. 10–12; 9. 1037–8
[61] Dis says (80–3): *Fors cui nulla placet nimium secura potestas,* | *quae nova semper amas et mox possessa relinquis,* | *ecquid Romano sentis te pondere victam,* | *nec posse ulterius perituram extollere molem?* Fortuna's response to this comes correspondingly early in her speech (107–9): *omnia, quae tribui Romanis arcibus, odi* | *muneribusque meis irascor. destruet istas* | *idem, qui posuit moles deus.*

Typically for Roman epic, the words of Fama are never quoted in direct discourse.[62] However, here the poet commends Fama's skill as a narrator: her account is so vivid that she achieves the rhetorical effect of *enargeia* ('vividness') as the things she recounts 'fly before the eyes' of those who hear her.

The diction used to open and close passages of DD in Eumolpus' verses is also reminiscent of Lucan and other poets.[63] It is not only previously acknowledged features of Eumolpus' poem—subject matter, tone, and literary style—which converge with Lucan's. The techniques and even the terminology of speech presentation seem to reinforce these connections. Moreover, it is the speeches in Eumolpus' poem which in themselves provide a large number of the verbal parallels it has with Lucan's *De Bello Civili*.[64] This is an important consideration in the face of recent attempts to play down Petronius' community with Lucan in particular.[65] Whilst it is true that a number of Virgilian parallels can be found in Eumolpus' poem, it is important to appreciate that all these are noted in

[62] Compare *Aeneid* 3. 121, 4. 184 f.; *Thebaid* 2. 201 etc. Baldwin (1911) cites Silius Italicus *Punica* 4. 1–9.

[63] e.g. *Tunc Fortuna levi defudit pectore voces* (*Sat.* 121. 102) ('Fortuna issued these words from her light heart') can be compared with Lucan 2. 285: *arcano sacras reddit Cato pectore voces* ('Cato returned these holy words from the shrine of his heart'). Comparable expressions in similar contexts in Eumolpus' poem are: *ac tali volucrem Fortunam voce lacessit* 78; *intentans cum voce manus ad sidera dixit* 155; *atque has erumpit furibundo pectore voces* 282. Baldwin also finds paralells for 155: *Aen.* 2. 687–8: *at pater Aeneas oculos ad sidera laetus | extulit et caelo palmas cum voce tetendit*, cf. *Aen.* 10. 667, *Iliad* 1. 450; for 282, *Aen.* 2. 129: *rumpit* and *Aen.* 3. 246: *rumpitque hanc pectore vocem*. The use of *vox* or *voces*, to be translated as 'utterance' or 'words', though found in prose authors, is far more common in poetry (*OLD* s.v. 7). In the prose sections of the *Satyricon*, *vox* or *voces* nearly always mean 'voice' in the sense of speech organ, or the facility or manner of speaking.

[64] For the speeches in Eumolpus' poem, the parallels are: Petronius 79–81, Lucan 1. 510 f., 2. 12 f.; P. 82–6, L. 1. 3, 1. 70–2, 1. 81; P. 95–9, L. 6. 718; P. 98 f., L. 1. 330–1, 7. 317, 7. 851, 865; P. 111–15, L. 1. 679–94; P. 116–21, L. 1. 522–3, 2. 1–4; P. 156–76, L. 1. 195–203, 1. 299–351, 7. 250–329, 1. 225–7; P. 160, L. 7. 473; P. 164 f., L. 1. 288 f.

[65] e.g. Slater (1990), 198: 'The whole procedure of hunting for parallels . . . is founded on the assumption, that a parodic relationship *should* exist. Without this assumption, all but a handful of the parallels softly and silently vanish away; of those remaining, most have good Vergilian parallels as well.' This 'assumption' is not too unreasonable, given Eumolpus' subject matter and the widely held view that Petronius and Lucan were contemporary. Secondly, the Virgilian parallels identified by Rose (1971), 60–8, 87–94, which Slater considers at 120, are in passages which were already identified as Lucanic parallels. Haskins and Heitland (1887) assembles references to Virgil in Lucan. Slater does not take account of Baldwin (1911)—a specific study of this part of the *Sat.* which assembles all the parallels between Petronius and Lucan here, with commentary.

passages which have themselves been identified as Lucanic parallels. Countless Virgilian 'echoes' have been seen in Lucan's poem in the first place.

6.4.2 *Eumolpus' Tale of the Widow of Ephesus.*

This famous story (111–12) is about a bereaved widow who was keeping a fatal fast in her husband's tomb.[66] A soldier, who is set to guard the bodies of some criminals gibbeted nearby, restores her will to live and then seduces her. Whilst the soldier is spending time with the widow, the relatives of one of the criminals remove his body from the cross. When the soldier tells the widow he will face a death penalty for allowing this to occur, she offers to have her dead husband's body affixed to the cross so that his negligence will not be detected.

The deployment of speech modes in this story can tell us something about the character and prejudices of its narrator, Eumolpus. The soldier's discourse is not once presented directly on any of the occasions in which his speech is reported. Yet we are told he used blandishments (*blanditiis* 112. 1) to seduce the widow, and that he struck the widow as being eloquent as well as handsome (*nec deformis aut infacundus* 112. 2—an elegant litotes which also characterizes Eumolpus, the speaker). The widow had a handmaiden who played a part in helping the soldier to win over her mistress—by inclining her first to eat and then to yield to his advances. The maid's words are, in contrast, foregrounded strongly by being quoted directly, and in entirety. We do not even hear (in DD) the soldier telling the widow that one of the criminals' bodies is missing—though her reply is quoted directly:

'nec istud' inquit 'dii sinant, ut eodem tempore duorum mihi carissimorum hominum duo funera spectem. malo mortuum impendere quam vivum occidere.' (112. 7)

'God forbid' she said 'that I should have to witness two deaths of the two men I have most cared about. I prefer to hang the dead than kill the living.'

This utterance effectively provides the punchline to the story. The widow who was earlier renowned for her chastity and for sacrificing

[66] Fedeli (1986) examines the form and structure of this story. Numerous versions of it have enjoyed a *Nachleben* independent of the rest of the *Sat.* See Ure (1956). Petronius' version has not only been of interest to classicists: Bakhtin (1981) offers an analysis of the story seeking to explain its influence at 221–4, which receives significant elaboration in Frow (1986), 130–9.

her own life to the memory of her dead husband has now become a pragmatist.

Had the speeches and pleas of the soldier in this story been rendered in DD, the soldier would have been far more conspicuous as a moral agent. Eumolpus' use of AND causes the women to be presented with more salience as the ones who take the initiative, when it is really the soldier who motivates everything. This interpretation of Eumolpus' use of speech modes seems consistent with his aim and attitude in telling this story. Implicit and explicit features in his narration indicate an inclination to exculpate the soldier and highlight flaws in the resolve of the women. He shows it was the *maid* who first succumbed to the soldier's exhortations to the widow to eat:

sed eadem exhortatione temptavit dare mulierculae cibum, donec ancilla vini certum habeo odore corrupta primum ipsa porrexit ad humanitatem invitantis victam manum, deinde refecta potione et cibo expugnare dominae pertinaciam coepit[67] ... (111. 10)

but with the same sort of encouragement he attempted to offer food to the dear little woman, until the maid—I'm sure of it—corrupted by the smell of the wine gave in to this generosity and stretched out her hand. Then restored by the food and drink she began to assail the fixed resolve of her mistress ...

The use of the diminutive *muliercula* ('poor little woman') also suggests Eumolpus the narrator is sharing the soldier's point of view. Indeed he has earlier used the soldier's focalization to describe his sequence of realizations:

descendit igitur in conditorium, visaque pulcherrima muliere primo quasi quodam monstro infernis imaginibus turbatus substitit. deinde ut et corpus iacentis conspexit et lacrimas consideravit faciemque unguibus sectam, ratus scilicet id quod erat, desiderium extincti non posse feminam pati ... (111. 7–8)

He then went down into the tomb and, catching sight of a very beautiful woman, at first he stopped, terrified as if by the hellish image of a ghost. But once he also made out the body of a man lying there and took account of the woman's tears and her face clawed by her fingernails, he naturally saw what was going on: the woman could not bear her loss of the dead man ...

---

[67] *certum habeo* may not be the correct reading; perhaps these words should be omitted altogether as they are in the *l* MS and the *Florilegia*; but the phrase *vini odore corrupta* is incriminating enough.

These things are only visible to the soldier: we are privy to his conjecture about the nature of the situation which is endorsed by the narrator.

The soldier could hardly be faulted for giving the woman food, but his audacity in proceeding to seduce her is more controversial.[68] Yet Eumolpus is explicitly indulgent: here he discreetly shifts any disapprobation his hearers might feel away from either the soldier or the woman:

ceterum scitis, quid plerumque soleat temptare humanam satietatem.

(112. 1)

Well you all know the sort of feelings that are likely to tempt people who have a full stomach.[69]

Such appeals to common knowledge and expressions of common opinion are a feature throughout this story and offer further occasions for the presentation of discourse in this tale. However, when the rest of these expressions are reviewed in sequence, a rather different message emerges—one that is possibly outside the frame of the story:

matrona quaedam Ephesi tam notae erat pudicitiae, ut vicinarum quoque gentium feminas ad spectaculum sui evocaret. (111. 1)

There was a certain lady from Ephesus whose reputation for chastity was such that it drew women from all the nearby regions to gaze at her.

una igitur in tota civitate fabula erat, solum illud affulsisse verum pudicitiae amorisque exemplum omnis ordinis homines confitebantur . . .

(111. 5)

So the talk (*fabula*) of the whole city took one form: men of every class professed that there was only one real shining example of love and chastity . . .

nemo invitus audit, cum cogitur aut cibum sumere aut vivere. (111. 13)

No one is reluctant to heed the order to eat something or the order to live.

praeclusis videlicet conditorii foribus, ut quisquis ex notis ignotisque ad monumentum venisset, putaret expirasse super corpus viri pudicissimam uxorem. (112. 3)

[68] Again, Frow (1986), 130–9 expands Bakhtin's interpretation.

[69] A formally similar, though perhaps more creditable, appeal to common knowledge was made to Encolpius by Eumolpus when he justified his false promise to the boy from Pergamon in 86. 6: *scis quanto facilius sit, columbas gallosque gallinaceos emere quam asturconem.*

They naturally shut the doors of the tomb so that anyone they knew or did not know would think that this chastest of women had expired over the body of her husband.

posteroque die populus miratus est qua ratione mortuus isset in crucem. (112. 8)

On the next day people wondered by what means a dead man had got onto the cross.

The first two expressions of general opinion commend the widow's conduct by giving it a public dimension. However, the latter three show up all these opinions as inadequate, uninformed, and far short of the truth. By yielding to the general judgements invoked by the soldier to seduce her (and by Eumolpus to account for her seduction), the change in the widow's behaviour shows the limitations of all the judgements made about her. She ends up outsmarting everybody. The rhetoric of conventional opinion which carries this story forward is in fact turned in on itself.

   This reporting of sententious discourse also bears heavily on the literary and generic status of Eumolpus' tale. Renderings of common opinions which are highly similar to those quoted above feature in the story of Cupid and Psyche, an embedded narrative in a later work of Latin prose fiction: Apuleius' *Metamorphoses*. Indeed it is the expressions of common opinion about Psyche's prodigious beauty which actually set that story into motion: the goddess Venus was upstaged and set out to punish Psyche.[70] These two embedded accounts have other similarities. Both narratives also function as speeches made by characters who are attempting to reassure those around them: in Apuleius an old woman tells the story to calm down Charite who has been kidnapped and suffered a bad dream. Eumolpus' narration is introduced thus:

ceterum Eumolpus, et periclitantium advocatus et prasentis concordiae auctor, ne sileret sine fabulis hilaritas, multa in mulicbrcm lcvitatcm coepit iactare: quam facile adamarent, quam cito etiam filiorum obliviscerentur, nullamque esse feminam tam pudicam, quae non peregrina libidine usque ad furorem averteretur. nec se tragoedias veteres curare aut nomina

---

[70] See esp. Apuleius, *Met.* 4. 28–9. There are even lexical and structural resemblances to some of the sentences quoted from Eumolpus' tale: *at vero puellae iunioris tam praecipua, tam praeclara pulchritudo . . . multi denique civium et advenae copiosi, quos eximii spectaculi rumor studiosa celebritate congregabat.*

saeculis nota, sed rem sua memoria factam, quam expositurum se esse, si vellemus audire. conversis igitur omnium in se vultibus auribusque sic orsus est . . . (110. 6–8)

Meanwhile Eumolpus, our spokesman whilst we were in danger and the author of the present peace between us, so that our merriment should not fall silent for want of stories (*fabulis*), began to rail against the fickleness of women: how easily they fall in love, how quickly they forget even their own children; he maintained that no woman was so chaste that she could not be distracted to the point of madness by passion for a stranger. Nor was he thinking of old tragedies or of famous names from past ages, but of something that occurred in his own lifetime, which he would relate to us, if we were willing to hear. Then when the eyes and ears of all present were turned in his direction he began as follows . . .

Eumolpus' story then begins with the customary formula quoted above (*matrona quaedam Ephesi tam notae erat pudicitiae* . . .). This brings to mind the beginning of the embedded story in Apuleius' *Metamorphoses*: *Erant in quadam civitate rex et regina* . . . ('There were in a certain country, a king and a queen . . .').[71] Both accounts are labelled as *fabulae* by their narrators. The word *fabula* is apposite in each case: it can mean both 'conversation' or 'talk' (cf. 'talk of the town' in 111. 5 above) and 'story'.[72] Both narratives can further be classed by their *readers* (if not their fictional addressees) as Latinized versions of a Greek literary form of *fabula*—the Milesian tale. The Greek *Milesia* seem to have been prose erotic literature.[73]

Apuleius tells his reader explicitly that the story of Psyche is Milesian.[74] Eumolpus, on the other hand, insists that his tale of the widow does *not* belong to a literary realm. He claims that the events it contains occurred in his lifetime. Whether or not this claim is believed by his hearers in the story, it is a fact for Petronius' readers that the tale is not unique to the *Satyricon*: a different version is told

[71] Apuleius, *Metamorphoses* 4. 28: Walsh (1970), 13 n. 2 says 'The first sentence . . . sets the stage with description of the central character and the locale; the last sentence rounds off the episode. Compare Sallust *B.J.* 12, and many Livian scenes, on which see my *Livy* (Cambridge 1967), 178 ff.'

[72] See Laird (forthcoming *a*) on the use of *fabula* in Apuleius *Metamorphoses* 1. 1.

[73] Plutarch in *Crassus* 32 mentions that the Roman Roscius read this sort of literature (to Roscius' discredit).

[74] *Met.* 4. 28: *Sed Apollo, quamquam Graecus et Ionicus, propter Milesiae conditorem sic latina sorte respondit.* Moreschini (1990) argues convincingly that the principal narrative of the *Met.* is just as much a Milesian tale as the story of Psyche.

in an earlier verse fable by Phaedrus.[75] However, Eumolpus' very claim to have personal knowledge of events related was a feature of the Milesian story.[76] His telling gives the narrative a literary or sub-literary quality—for instance the insight he expresses on the soldier's sequence of realizations (111. 7–8) could only come from a fictional narrator.

Another aspect of Eumolpus' telling (which also bears on speech presentation) signals the literary nature of his story. In spite of the narrator's disclaimer that he is not 'thinking of old tragedies or of famous names from past ages', Virgil's tragedy of Dido has an important role in this story.[77] Both remarks the maid makes to her mistress contain quotations from *Aeneid* 4. The verse in the maid's first suggestion that her mistress should eat, which tallies almost exactly with *Aeneid* 4. 34, is here italicized:[78]

'quid proderit' inquit 'hoc tibi, si soluta inedia fueris, si te vivam sepelieris, si antequam fata poscant, indemnatum spiritum effuderis?
　　id cinerem aut manes credis sentire sepultos?
vis tu reviviscere? vis discusso muliebre errore, quam diu licuerit, lucis commodis frui? ipsum te iacentis corpus admonere debet ut vivas.'

　　　　　　　　　　　　　　　　　　　　(*Sat.* 111. 11–13)

'What good will it be to you' she said 'if you starve yourself away, if you bury yourself alive, if, before the fates allow it, you gasp out your last breath?
　　Do you suppose that ashes or buried shades can sense all this [sorrow]?
Will you not begin life again? Will you not get rid of this womanly failing and enjoy the advantages of living in the light, as long as it is allowed? His very body lying there ought to advise you to live.'

The maid's second utterance, encouraging her mistress to succumb to the soldier's charms, wholly consists of a quotation from Virgil (*Aeneid* 4. 38):

---

[75] *Appendix Perottina* 13 in Postgate's text of 'Phaedrus' (1919). This relation is far shorter: 31 verses of *senarii*, with fewer complexities in speech and thought presentation. There are only two occasions on which speech is explictly presented: the soldier's request for water, as RSA (indirect command) (12) and the widow's words in DD towards the close of the poem ('*Non est quod timeas' ait*, 28). Typically, Phaedrus' version makes the moral of his story very clear: *sic turpitudo laudis obsedit locum* (31). The significance of the story for Eumolpus' audience is, as Slater remarks (p. 110) more difficult to place.　　　　　　[76] Walsh (1970), 11 n. 4, 14 n. 3.
[77] Slater (1990), 109 argues that the Widow of Ephesus story is 'from the first presented in the language of theatre and role-playing'.
[78] The verse differs in only one word from *Aeneid* 4. 34: *sentire* ('feel') has replaced the original *curare* ('care for').

'placitone etiam pugnabis amori?'   (*Sat.* 112. 2)

'Will you fight love even when it is pleasing?'

Both speeches from the maid ensure the success of the soldier's
appeal. Both Virgilian passages come from Anna's speech to Dido
in *Aeneid* 4. 31–54: that speech inflames her desire for Aeneas and
releases her from her doubts and inhibitions about gratifying it.[79]
The widow is parallelled to Dido, although her destiny will follow a
very different course.[80] So this story is actually related to the
tragedies and famous names of Virgilian epic: but it is a relation
of contrast. Whilst Eumolpus' other accounts offer stylistic parodies of epic *narrative* in Virgil and Lucan—the *Halosis Troiae* (89),
and the *De Bello Civili* considered above—this prose tale parodies
epic on the level of *story*. It could be read as a burlesque foil to the
moral authority of the epic genre. But the picture can be further
complicated. In the *Aeneid* the narrative of Dido has comic
elements: traces of figures like Palaestra in Plautus' *Rudens* can be
discerned in the construction of Dido's speech and character; again
Dido's exchange with Anna (*Aeneid* 4. 9–54) recalls scenes of new
comedy as well as Euripidean tragedy.[81] Petronius' story of the
Widow of Ephesus, as a later intertext of the *Aeneid* serves to
'excavate' or bring to greater prominence the comical resonances
'buried' in Virgil's epic.

We have already seen the blending of the realm of elevated
literature with the world of the characters in the *Satyricon* in the
principal narrative of Encolpius. But perceived intertexts (e.g. the
'uses' of Livy or Catullus) and the verses in Encolpius' principal
narrative have a very different effect from the parodies of Eumolpus. The speech of Encolpius constantly transposes and absorbs
discourses from other texts, endowing those discourses with new
registers. Encolpius' discourse is as intertextual as the *Satyricon*
itself, because the discourse of Encolpius the speaking narrator *is*
the *Satyricon*.

On one level, what applies to Encolpius' discourse must apply to
Eumolpus: all of Eumolpus' words are embedded in Encolpius'

[79] *Aeneid* 4. 54–5
[80] On the contrasts between the Widow and Dido, see Frow (1986), 138–9.
Frow's whole analysis of this story is illuminating.
[81] On relationships between Virgil and his Roman predecessors, see e.g. Jocelyn
(1964; 1965) and Wigodsky (1972).

discourse and therefore constitute part of it. However, insofar as we regard Eumolpus as a *character*, the signifying range of his discourse is delimited and defined by its role in relation to other signifying components of the text. We may permit ourselves to see Eumolpus as a purveyor of good old-fashioned allusion simply because he is presented more or less explicitly as a parodist of Virgil and Lucan. The very fact that Eumolpus quotes Virgil in DD, for instance, allows us to recognize the distinction he draws in 110. 8 between real life (*rem sua memoria factam*) and literature (*tragoedias veteres*). But Eumolpus' 'real life' is of course a reality effect.[82]

The rhetorical exploitation of the distinction between literature and life has come to be a common way of engineering the reality effect in fiction. Yet Encolpius does not avail himself of it in the way Eumolpus does. Literary models are not isolated and surveyed by Encolpius' narrative; they are fused into it. Eumolpus' story of the widow when considered as *Encolpius'* discourse is a good case in point. For Eumolpus and his audience it is discourse of evidence— he can tell it convincingly; Encolpius on the other hand is absorbing into his own discourse a story which has been told in another text. Encolpius' discourse intertextually 'presents' Phaedrus' fable; Eumolpus' discourse—considered in its own right—does not.

In short, the reality effect of the principal narrative of the *Satyricon* is less powerful than that achieved by an embedded speaker in the text. To put it another way: the constructed character Eumolpus appears to have a firm grasp of the difference between life and literature; Encolpius the narrator who constructs Eumolpus does not. This is very unusual. Further specific observations about speech presentation underline stylistic differences between Encolpius as principal narrator and Eumolpus as embedded narrator.[83] The next section will consider the broader significance of style being used to mark character in Petronius.

[82] Notwithstanding the claim in Bakhtin (1981), 223: 'everything occurs on the level of real life; it is completely credible that a widow should be aroused through food and drink to new life in the presence of the legionnaire's strong young body'. Here I am developing the case made in Frow (1986).

[83] Eumolpus has a characteristic diction and manner of narration. All his embedded narratives diverge both from the outer text that encloses them and from each other in techniques of speech presentation. The number of instances of presentation of thought or speech in each one may be small, but sufficient to show an overall difference of trends. Eumolpus tells two stories in prose: an autobiographical account of his seduction of the boy from Pergamon and the tale of the Widow. There is consistency in the techniques of speech presentation used in

6.5 PRESENTED DISCOURSE AND THE SOCIAL ORDER: PROBLEMS OF APPROACH

George Eliot's *Adam Bede* provides a memorable example of a speaker who is characterized by his manner of speaking—even as he comments on styles of speech, including his own:

'I'm not this countryman, you may tell by my tongue, sir. They're curious talkers i' this country, sir; the gentry's hard work to hunderstand 'em. I was brought hup among the gentry, sir, an' got the turn o' their tongue when I was a bye. Why, what do you think the folks here say for "hev'nt you?"—the gentry, you know, says "hev'nt you"—well the people about here says "hanna yey". It's what they call the dileck as is spoke hereabout, sir. That's what I've heard Squire Donnithorne say many a time; it's the dileck, says he.'[84]

Mr Carson maintains his speech is that of the gentry: yet the forms of pronunciation, words and syntax he employs undermine this claim. It is interesting to compare Echion's speech about his style of speech in the *Cena*. The English translation below seeks to convey the apparent irregularities of the Latin here:

videris mihi, Agamemnon, dicere: 'quid iste argutat molestus?' quia tu, qui potes loquere non loquis. non es nostrae fasciae, et ideo pauperorum verba derides. scimus te prae litteras fatuum esse. quid ergo est?

(*Sat.* 46. 1–2)

Agamemnon, you seem to me to be saying 'What is this here nuisance chattering of?' Because you who's able to speak doesn't speak. You're not of our cut and that's why you mock the words of the poors. We know that you are mad along of your learning. So what?

Commentators have noted that Echion's Latin becomes more conspicuously 'incorrect' as he addresses Agamemnon the

---

both. But the first story was 'autobiographical', told by an involved first person narrator, while the second involves events in which Eumolpus himself has played no part. In the first story, Eumolpus presents his own discourse in DD; in both stories Eumolpus tends to favour ID, reserving DD to highlight exceptional utterances. Thus Eumolpus' first person narration uses a form of AND which is the converse of Encolpius'. Encolpius rarely uses indirect discourse to render the speeches of characters other than himself: only on exceptional occasions does he put his own words in DD.

[84] This excerpt from *Adam Bede*, ch. 2, is quoted in N. Page (1988), 135. From my own reading of that chapter, I would query Page's remark that this DD 'reveals the standpoint of one who is able to regard "the folks here" and the "gentry", as well as phenomena like the innkeeper [i.e. the quoted speaker, Mr Carson] *with equal detachment*' (my emphasis).

educated rhetorician.[85] The narrator, whose discourse appears less coloured, seems to ironize Echion from an apparently neutral standpoint (as George Eliot's narrator might ironize Mr Carson). Our impression of Encolpius' neutrality partly derives from his function as a 'transparent narrator' in the *Cena* noted earlier: there Encolpius attributes less direct discourse to his own character than in other parts of the *Satyricon*. This has the effect of spotlighting the words and deeds of others. Yet we have seen the effect of a narrator's neutrality is always illusory: narrative is focalized, and therefore ideological.

The inevitable relationship between discourse and power encoded in techniques of speech presentation can take many forms. For example, the previous chapter examined both the relationship between speech and power in the epic world of the *Aeneid* and the representation of that relationship in the discourse of the poem. In Petronius, a relationship between discourse and the social order has long been discerned in the diction or Latinity of the presented speech itself. However the representation of the social order in the *Satyricon* is far more complex than scholars have generally recognized. It reflects the complexity of linguistic exchanges in real life. Linguistic exchanges can be characterized as relations of what Bourdieu calls 'symbolic power': they actualize power relations between speakers or their respective groups.[86] 'Symbolic power' works in disguise: those on whom it is exerted can have a role in its exertion. In practical linguistic communication we may not find a neat proportional relation between an individual's social importance and the amount he speaks. Yet speech can continue to function both as an index and as a validation of the *status quo*.

In the world of the *Cena* this is demonstrated by what Echion says to Agamemnon about the relation between speech and power. This is as interesting as how Echion expresses it. He takes Agamemnon's silence as mockery of his words because he is someone who can speak but who does not speak (*quia tu, qui potes loquere, non loquis*). (Agamemnon has not spoken for some time: the narrator has not hitherto highlighted any positive significance to his silence.) Agamemnon's capacity to speak good Latin as a rhetorician perhaps prompts an expectation on Echion's part that Agamemnon should be speaking now rather than being silent. Echion's remark exposes his anxiety (however ironic) about speaking incorrectly and out of

[85] Smith (1975), 120–1; Boyce (1991), 84.   [86] Bourdieu (1991), 43

turn as a 'poor' man. However this anxiety does not stop Echion
speaking. It is interesting that he immediately follows the comments
quoted above with an invitation:

aliqua die te persuadeam, ut ad villam venias et videas casulas nostras?

(*Sat.* 46. 2)

Some day can I persuade you to come to my villa and see our house?

This speech act is assertive as well as polite: Echion seeks to rectify
the social imbalance he perceives—by seeking to fraternise with
someone of a different social order and by pointing to his status as a
homeowner.

Echion's words here operate on another level. Whenever the
relation between speech and status is addressed in the story of a text,
the relation is also significant for the effect of the narrative on the
text's audience. The nature of that effect can vary: for instance, we
saw that Suetonius' account of the senators' demand for freedom of
speech and Horace's account of his faltering words to Maecenas
could be interpreted in a number of ways. At least one critic has
noted a minor implication of Echion's aside to Agamemnon for the
reader.[87] However, there has been no attempt to investigate the role
readers have in determining the relation of speeches like Echion's to
the social order 'portrayed' in the *Satyricon*. Inevitably such an
investigation demands that we again take cognizance of ideological
issues raised by perceptions of the Latin language.[88] The investigation to follow will provide little new data, but it might find a way
through the complex of shifting categories and overlapping arguments which hamper existing discussions.[89]

Since the nineteenth century, scholars of Petronius have drawn
connections between characters' linguistic habits and the portrayal
of social life in the *Satyricon*. Yet in doing so, philologists tend to be
preoccupied with empirical details of variation in linguistic usage
without examining the presuppositions or horizons of expectation
which cause those empirical details to become visible. A distillation
of the 'received wisdom' from a standard commentary on the *Cena*
well illustrates this tendency:

[87] Slater (1990), 66
[88] Boyce (1991), 1–35 looks at problems raised by the term 'vulgar Latin' for
study of the *Cena*. A forthcoming study of the Latin language by Joseph Farrell
will bear on this question. See also Powell (forthcoming).
[89] Boyce (1991), 34: 'the intense scholarly scrutiny devoted to the vulgar Latin in
the *Cena* has produced little unanimity of opinion'.

In the *Cena* a clear distinction is made between the elegant Latin of the narrative and the speech of Trimalchio and his freedman guests. Petronius sets out not merely to reproduce colloquial speech in general but at least to give a flavour of lower class speech. The differentiation is obvious enough for the most part, but the corrupt state of the text in *H*, our only evidence for most of the *Cena*, leaves various details doubtful. When *H* credits Encolpius with an occasional Vulgarism, we are entitled to suspect it *a priori* as a scribal error . . . But even where the Vulgarisms most abound Petronius is careful not to come too close to the actual speech of lower class Italians, especially in phonology; too close an approximation would have meant boring or mystifying the sophisticated reader.[90]

Two problematic oppositions are invoked by Smith here: (i) Encolpius' 'elegant Latin' opposed to the 'flavour of lower class speech'; (ii) Petronius' Latin overall (including 'Vulgarisms') opposed to 'actual speech of lower class Italians'. This first opposition, also expressed as a distinction between *sermo urbanus* ('refined speech') and *sermo cotidianus* ('colloquial speech'), is common currency in Petronian scholarship even if it lacks full justification. Smith's argument for this first opposition is circular: whenever the 'clear distinction' he posits is threatened by Encolpius' use of a 'Vulgarism', he claims it may be suspected *a priori* as a 'scribal error'.[91] Moreover, if what Smith terms 'Vulgarisms' are linguistic usages which deviate from forms which are statistically prevalent in Latin texts, scribal error could conceivably eschew them in favour of more customary usage. Smith also ignores even the possibility of the freedmen in the *Cena* availing themselves of 'elegant Latin' of the kind he attributes to Encolpius. This can be seen to occur, but seeing it depends as much on being disposed to look for it as it does on how 'elegant Latin' is characterized.[92]

---

[90] Smith (1975), p. xxi. A comment in Smith's Appendix ii. 220 again reveals the full circularity of his argument: 'D.C. Swanson, *A Formal Analysis of Petronius' Vocabulary* . . . is not as helpful as it might have been, since he believes no distinction is possible between the language of the freedmen and that of Encolpius, and he therefore does not usually classify separately the facts for each of these categories.'

[91] However, Boyce (1991) 21 n. 72 notes on apparent 'vulgarisms' in Eumolpus' poem (*Sat.* 119), written in the high style: 'most of these readings do not look like vulgarisms anyway . . . but the majority of editors are most likely right in assuming that these forms were introduced into the manuscripts by copyists.'

[92] I mean that it is possible to detect correct Latin as well as 'incorrect' usages in the freedmen's speeches. Consider even Echion's words at 46. 8: *ideo illi cotidie clamo: 'Primigeni, crede mihi, quicquid discis, tibi discis. vides Phileronem causidicum:*

The second opposition, between Petronius' Latin and the 'actual speech' of lower-class Italians is also widely shared and easily confused with the first. It is partly supposed to rest on the fact that a much greater range of linguistic 'abnormalities' than we find in Petronius can be discovered in nigh contemporary Pompeian wall inscriptions. But if 'actual speech', however conceived, is where Vulgarisms truly reside, then the successful recognition of Vulgarisms in Petronius depends on knowledge of actual speech.[93] Since we have no real impression of actual speech in Latin, the process of recognizing Vulgar Latin is going to be a subjective business. So too, of course, is the recognition of actual speech, as those who see language itself as a social-historical phenomenon are only too aware.[94] The role of native Greek speakers in the *Satyricon* (*all* the major characters, including Encolpius, have Greek names) further problematizes the notion of actual speech when we consider Petronius.[95]

I argued in Chapter 1 that identification of an intertext, no matter how palpable, demonstrable, and well attested it may be, is in the end a matter of belief (dependent on the range of texts available to us) and not knowledge. That identification is *ideological* in the strict sense because we tend to assume any informed reader would agree with it: thus we ascribe to our beliefs the status of true knowledge.

si non didicisset, hodie famem a labris non abigeret. modo, modo collo suo circumferebat onera venalia, nunc etiam adversus Norbanum se extendit.' Of the 'deviant' usages here, *modo, modo* is paralleled in Seneca and Martial (see Smith (1975), 79 on 37. 3); the use of the possessive pronoun with a body part (*collo suo*) is found in *Encolpius'* narrative at 67. 9, 74. 11 and 74. 12. Echion's words here are further dignified by an intertext: they resemble in tone and form Demea's account of the advice he gives to his son Ctesipho along with Syrus' parody of it in Terence's *Adelphoe* 412–32.

[93] Pulgram (1950; 1958) advocated replacing the term 'vulgar Latin' with 'spoken Latin'; Boyce (1991), 2f. considers the problems with this: we cannot ever know enough about how Latin was spoken.

[94] Compare the attack on 'philologism' in Voloshinov (1973), cited in n. 3 above, and compare the views on Saussure and Chomsky in Bourdieu (1991) *passim*.

[95] Compare Slater (1990), 147. A comment in Bourdieu (1991) on 'popular language' in France is significant in this context: 'Fantasy . . . which generally turns the folk memories of nostalgic class fugitives towards the "purest" and "most authentic" representatives of the "people" excludes without a second thought all immigrants, whether Spanish or Portuguese, Algerian or Moroccan, Malian or Senegalese, who we know occupy a larger place in the population of industrial workers than they do in the proletarian imagination.' Encolpius, in spite of his Greek name, appears to resent being stranded in a '*Greek* town' (*[ego] exul in deversorio Graecae urbis iacerem desertus* (81. 3). This suggests Encolpius' sense of his own cultural identity is ambiguous or problematic.

The postulation of 'actual speech' or the detection of a 'Vulgarism' in Latin is no less ideological. Indeed, detection of Vulgarisms involves processes which are highly similar, if not identical, to those involved in the detection of quotations or intertexts. But the very notion of a Vulgarism is more nakedly political.

Consequently there is a natural timidity about investigating notions of the 'vulgar' or 'popular', even in linguistic or antiquarian contexts.[96] As Bourdieu puts it, 'any critical analysis of a notion which bears remotely on "the people" is apt to be interpreted as "symbolic aggression against the reality designated".' But, in fact, apparently tautologous or circular definitions of vulgarity and elegance can themselves be turned to the advantage of dominant speakers. This is shown by 'the *system of paired adjectives* employed by users of the legitimate language to classify others and judge their *quality* . . . in which the term designating the properties ascribed to the dominant always receives a positive value'.[97] This subtle form of symbolic domination, at large in all linguistic communities, accounts for the prevalent yet logically puzzling assessments made by critics and commentators of Encolpius' discourse: his narrative (in the *Cena*) is seen to be standard *and* elegant; it is seen to portray quite realistically *and* to parody, freedmen like Echion.[98]

These ambivalent assessments actually allow critics to affirm discreetly their supremacy in their own socio-lingustic domain. When they discuss social status and language as an index of social status in the *Cena,* there is an effective collusion with Encolpius: who frequently becomes 'Petronius' (and thus carries the clout of the 'objective' author). Even the apparently innocuous application of terms like *sermo urbanus* or 'elegance' to Encolpius' discourse plays into this fusion of author with narrator: one detects the not–so–subliminal influence of the historical Petronius' reputed status as *arbiter elegantiae* in Nero's court. More collusion: it goes without

---

[96] Callebat (1968), 15–19, in a very astute and informed account of competing definitions of *sermo cotidianus*, exhibits a kind of sqeamishness about the term *latin vulgaire*. He prefers the term *sermo cotidianus* because it is more comprehensive. Yet within it he retains a distinction between *sermo familiaris* and *sermo plebeius*. Boyce (1991), 2: 'The term vulgar Latin is somewhat infelicitous. In the first place, the word "vulgar" has a pejorative connotation in its ordinary usage; yet the expression *vulgaris sermo* has been in use at least since Cicero, and has by now acquired the consecrated status of a technical term.'

[97] On paired adjectives, see Bourdieu (1991), 92–3.

[98] In addition to Smith (1975) quoted above, compare the remarks in Sullivan (1968), 25 with those at 117 f.

saying that 'taste' is still a shibboleth of the dominant groups in our own societies; academics and teachers are still its arbiters, just as they are the arbiters of linguistic usage.[99]

Yet we have seen that a clear distinction between author and narrator is an inevitable function of first-person narrative: a complicity between author and reader is built up from which the narrator *must* be excluded. The fact that most critics go along with Sullivan in regarding Encolpius as a 'target for satire himself', makes this further remark from Sullivan look all the more irregular:

Nevertheless, just as Petronius is willing to direct our attention away from the hero to literary discussion by Agamemnon and Eumolpus, or to Trimalchio, so he is ready to speak through Encolpius *in propria persona* . . .[100]

I strongly take issue with this. Just because Encolpius is a 'transparent narrator' in the *Cena* (an effect which we have seen is engineered through a specific style of speech presentation) and perhaps in some other parts of the *Satyricon* does not mean that we can declare by *fiat* that Encolpius is only satirizing and is not being satirized. If we do so, we are not defining Petronius' moral and aesthetic stance (which cannot be verified), but our own.

This attempt to unmask the false consciousness of philologists and the allegation that they are claiming the status of 'arbiters of elegance' as they capriciously identify Petronius with Encolpius may seem extravagant. However, some of the earliest interpretations of speech and Latin in the *Cena* nowadays show their ideological colour: scholars from the south of Italy, following Ignarra's treatise *De palaestra neapolitana* (1770), endeavoured to associate some expressions with the Neapolitan dialect and even to show that Petronius himself was from Naples.[101] The point is *not* that the

---

[99] See 'The Production and Reproduction of Legitimate Language' in Bourdieu (1991) at 61–5 and compare Sullivan (1968), 148. In this light, Smith's 'flavour of lower class speech' (Smith (1975), p. xxi, quoted earlier) becomes an even more unhappy coinage. The Greek and Latin composition paper for the Ireland and Craven examination in the University of Oxford is entitled 'Taste'!

[100] Both quotations are from Sullivan (1968), 117. Veyne (1964), Smith (1975), Slater (1990) and Conte (1997) all, in different ways, see Encolpius as the object of satire in the *Sat.*

[101] Maiuri's excursus 'Il "sermo" della *Cena* ed i Graffiti Pompeiani' in Maiuri (1945), 227–30 gives an account of this trend. Maiuri's claim that aligning the Latin

categories of Latinity or even of vulgar Latin should be eschewed:
only that we should recognize the extent to which quite general
views of the world are inscribed into these terms by whoever uses
them.

It remains for me to state explicitly my own brief (and inevitably
partial) view of the relation between presented discourse and the
portrayal of the social world in the *Satyricon*. This can be inte-
grated with observations made in the earlier parts of this chapter. It
is Encolpius, Petronius' creation, and not Petronius, who mediates
characters like Agamemnon, Giton, Eumolpus, Trimalchio,
Echion, and others. The view offered of these characters, their
speech, behaviour and society is thus more *overtly* subjective than
the view that would be offered by an uninvolved third-person
narrator like the one in George Eliot's *Adam Bede*.[102] It follows
that the presentation of the diction of all these characters is no less
subjectively presented: in appraising this diction, we have to allow
for our narrator's capacity as an interested individual to forget,
fabricate, downplay, or exaggerate characteristic tendencies in his
presentation of discourse.

In Echion's mediated discourse in particular there is an extremely high density of strange idioms (*non es nostrae fasciae*),
corrupt verbal forms (*pauperorum*) and bad grammar (*te persuadeam*). Moreover at certain points, Echion's words seem to be
entirely constituted by choppy aphorisms and maxims. We have a
reflexive comment by Echion on the deficiency of his own words.
Yet in the last analysis, Echion's speech—form and content—is
attributable to Encolpius who relays it to us. We may regard
Encolpius as playing up anomalies in Echion's language. His
'portrayal' of a freedman's speech has to be a grotesque distortion:
it exposes an assertion of the superior status of speakers like
Agamemenon and himself. Such distortion is common even in
purportedly disinterested accounts and representations of popular
speech today.[103] Here though, the distortion itself is parodied—and

of the *Cena* with that of the Pompeian inscriptions is 'più ovvio e naturale' has
obvious ideological significance.

[102] The presentation of the speech patterns adopted at different social levels in
Adam Bede is of course subjective. The subjectivity is concealed rhetorically by the
employment of an uninvolved third-person narrator.

[103] By 'accounts and representations', I mean those in fiction (cf. remarks on
skaz in Ch. 3) or fictive media ('realistic' drama, film, comedy), as opposed to
technical transcriptions by linguists.

more clearly so than any such distortion of speech in a third-person narrative would be (like Mr Carson's in *Adam Bede*). This is because the discourse of Encolpius who provides it, is itself represented. If we conceive of Petronius as a 'rationalized' author, constructed by the reader from the narrative, Petronius could be more sympathetic to characters like Echion or Trimalchio than many have been prepared to accept. Encolpius is after all lampooned to the point of being rendered absurd at many points in the story of the *Satyricon*. Should he seem any less absurd when he unselfconsciously claims a social status and linguistic competence superior to those of some characters he presents to us?

Attempts to explain the relationship between presented discourse and the social order in a text like the *Satyricon* are complicated by two awkward considerations. First, the 'social order' should not be seen as something which has an existence independent of language and speech. Our very notions of hierarchy and class division are constituted by types of speech and patterns of linguistic exchange. Second (a related point), the social order, in any period or culture, is not something which is fixed and immutable. It is a kind of dynamic equilibrium: agents and speakers are constantly enforcing or undermining their perception of the status quo. Thus, even in the act of narration, Encolpius is influencing the situation he is portraying. Two limited but firm conclusions emerge which should provide a framework for analyses of this question: (i) there is a clear connection between presented discourse and the social world, but (ii) the nature of that connection will largely depend on how the relationship between text and reader is actualized.

6.6 CONCLUSION: DISCOURSE AS MANNER AND MATTER OF NARRATION IN PETRONIUS

The ideological issues just raised in the previous section show clearly enough how the narrative of the *Satyricon* is not a simple medium, but a message in itself. *Prima facie* it may appear to be a window to the discourse of the characters, but as discourse itself, it is really a surface which is open to scrutiny and various interpretations. This reflexivity is just as much of an issue for two other principal concerns of this chapter: first, the characterization of Encolpius the narrator, which is accomplished by Encolpius' presentation of his own speech and thoughts, occasionally expressed in verse; second, the embedded narratives which present spoken and thought discourse whilst constituting spoken discourse in themselves.

This feature of reflexivity is of course far from unique to the *Satyricon*—it is at work in every narrative text which presents spoken and thought discourse—and it is the real subject of this book.[104] However, this reflexivity is more conspicuous in a work like the *Satyricon* than it is in many other Latin narrative texts. There are two obvious reasons for this. The first is the nature of the spoken and thought discourse presented. The words of characters like Trimalchio and Encolpius are often far from crucial to our understanding of the *Satyricon*'s plot. This is a stark contrast to the way that the speeches of characters, even minor ones, in genres like epic are of central importance to the works in which they feature. Whilst it is true that all the speeches in *Satyricon* must logically bear on its story (in the technical sense) simply by virtue of being in the narrative, their apparent primary function is to characterize the speakers. Thus Petronius' work, at least as we have it, is markedly un-Aristotelian: there is no strictly organic plot structure in which every passage is part of a whole, and (contrary to the prescription for tragedy at least, in *Poetics* 1450ᵃ) character and dialogue seem to have priority over plot. In response to the objection that my response to Petronius here is invalidated by too specific a conception of plot, I can point to the influence on the *Satyricon* of genres which demonstrably eschew plot. Satire and dialogue achieve characterization almost entirely by speech presentation—and the importance for Petronius' *Cena* of Horace, *Satires* 2. 8 (the '*Cena Nasidieni*') and of Plato's *Symposium* has been well established.[105]

These two texts point us to a second explanation for the manifestly reflexive role of discourse, as both manner and matter of the *Satyricon*. Both of them have first-person narrators. Apollodorus, the narrator of the *Symposium*, like Encolpius, does not involve himself in the progress of events or topics of discussion in the banquet he is recounting. But this is because he was not actually

---

[104] See 1.2.

[105] See Sullivan (1968), 126–8 for the influence of this satire on the *Cena*; Sullivan at 126 n. 1 provides extra bibliography. Rodriquez (1981), 267–80 is a more recent and more thorough treatment. Cameron (1969), shows the influence of the structure and content of the *Symposium* on Petronius.

present to participate: he says everything he describes was reported to him by Aristodemus. The first-person narrator of Horace's satire did not attend his *cena* either: he is asking Fundanius for details about it. As in Petronius' *Cena*, the host is cast in strongest relief. In Fundanius' report most speech is ascribed to Nasidienus, some to Balatro, one line to Vibidius, and none to Fundanius. Speech is generally presented in DD in these texts of Plato and Horace, although Horace employs more variation.[106] Both pieces offer us precedents for the role of 'transparent narrator' which Encolpius provides in the *Cena*: neither Fundanius nor (inevitably) Apollodorus figure strongly in the accounts they give.[107] It should be remembered that in providing the first known example of sustained fictional narrative in the first person, the *Satyricon* is something of an innovation in Latin. Perhaps it is no wonder that the relation of the narrator's discourse to the discourse he presents is so conspicuous.[108]

As well as revealing further connections between speech presentation, ideology, and intertextuality, this study of Petronius has shown how ideas of literariness, Latinity, and politics can intersect. In fact, the relation of classicism to the social order is not a new discovery. It was involved in the invention of literary classicism. According to Aulus Gellius, Fronto categorized the classical author (*scriptor classicus adsiduusque*) in opposition to the popular writer (*scriptor proletarius*). This opposition in fact depends on socioeconomic categories.[109] The terms Fronto employed came from

---

[106] e.g. *Satire* 2. 8. 6. *ut aiebat cenae pater*; 2. 8. 31 (ID); 2. 8. 35 (RSA: indirect command).

[107] Both these precedent narrators are interlocutors in conversations embedding their accounts: Apollodorus with his ἑταῖρος and Fundanius with Horace's persona.

[108] Petronius' Encolpius never apostrophizes his reader, as Apuleius' first-person narrator Lucius does. Thus, the *Satyricon* could be recast in the third person without a great deal being profoundly changed. Perhaps we are seeing a display of discomfort with the first-person form in Petronius, instead of the virtuosity which is generally assumed. I discussed these defining characteristics of Petronius and the evolution of first-person narrative in much greater detail in Laird (1990), esp. 136–58.

[109] In Aulus Gellius, *Noctes Atticae* 19. 8. 15, Fronto speaks as follows: *Ite ergo nunc et, quando forte erit otium, quaerite, an 'quadrigam' et 'harenas' dixerit e cohorte illa dumtaxat antiquiore vel oratorum aliquis vel poetarum, id est classicus adsiduusque aliquis scriptor, non proletarius.* ('So go now and when by chance you have leisure, find out whether any orator or poet has used *quadriga* or *harenas* provided he is of that earlier band—that is, any high class or landowning/painstaking writer, not a proletarian one'.)

Roman tax law: a *classicus* was in the high earning bracket; *adsiduus* means 'land owning' as well as 'assiduous'; the *proletarius* had an income below the taxable minimum. This original conception of the 'classical' is partly metaphorical, but some classicists—at least those concerned with literature—may still feel uncomfortable about their disciplinary terrain being characterized in this way.[110] But that discomfort can be used constructively. Petronius' *Satyricon* is very much bound up with matters of ideology and taste. At least study of its discourse can point out the beams in our eyes, which can still impede our view of ancient literature as a whole.

[110] Fronto's distinction, with all its socio-political implications, derives from a discussion of correct Latin usage. The relation it has to the philological constructions of 'vulgar Latin' considered above cannot be coincidental, and merits further exploration.

7

Allegories of Representation:
Messengers and Angels

We should not doubt that these fine poems are not human, nor the work of humans: they are divine and the work of the gods; and the poets are nothing other than interpreters of the gods . . .

(Plato, *Ion* 534e)

Reported speech is speech within speech, utterance within utterance, and at the same time also *speech about speech, utterance about utterance.*

(Valentin Voloshinov, *Marxism and the Philosophy of Language*)

Textual criticism sets out to establish what a text originally said or meant to say. Anyone who checks a garbled message with the sender has given a faultless demonstration of it.

('Textual criticism', *Oxford Classical Dictionary*[1])

Modern technology has made the need for a human individual to act as a messenger a rarity, if not a complete anachronism. The word 'message' is now often used as a technical term in current theories of language and communication for the content of an utterance—for *what* is said. That notion of 'what is said' is far from unproblematic.[2] The nature of the relationship between the

---

[1] Plato's Greek word for 'interpreters' is ἑρμηνῆς: see Murray (1996), 121 and compare the discussion of the etymology of 'Hermes' in *Cratylus* 408a at the end of this chapter. For the contexts of the second and third epigraphs here see Voloshinov (1973), 115 and the article in *OCD*[3] (1996), 1490–1 by Michael Reeve.

[2] Consider, for an example of modern usage of the term 'message', these remarks from Eco (1976), 57: 'I am not saying that a single code can produce many messages, one after the other, for this is a mere truism; I am not saying that the contents of many messages can be conveyed by the same kind of sign-vehicle, for this too is a truism; I am saying that usually a single sign-vehicle conveys many intertwined contents and therefore what is commonly called a message is in fact a *text* whose content is multilevelled *discourse.*' See also Eco *et al.* (1992) on the problems of interpreting texts.

message (as substance) and its medium (as style) has been an issue
of intense debate for centuries among grammarians, rhetoricians,
philosophers, and theologians.³ Narrative representations of
messengers (encountered in literary and historical texts) who
receive and then deliver messages can be seen as a paradigm for
the whole process of communication with all its complexities:
telexes, facsimiles, electronic mail, and newspapers still confound
us with fundamental problems of interpretation.

The poetic convention of the messenger scene, in which a
celestial god despatches a minion to convey his words to the
world below, seems to be as old and enduring as poetic narrative
itself. It is to be found in the Hebrew scriptures, in the New
Testament, in Greek and Roman poetry, and in later European
epic.⁴ In the following discussion, I shall conceive this poetic
convention as a *mise-en-abyme* for verbal communication and for
narratival representation. Such a conception is not a mere caprice
on my part: the examples of the convention examined here
display a reflexive preoccupation with the issues of speech,
language, narration and meaning. Consider, for example, what
must be one of the oldest examples of the convention—in two
serial fragments of a Hittite prose translation of a Hurrian myth,
known as the *Song of Ullikummi*, which probably dates from the
second millenium BC:

Kumarbi spake these words to Impaluri: 'O Impaluri! To the words I speak
to thee lend thine ear! Into thy hand take a stick, unto thy feet put the swift
shoes. [Hurry and] go to the Irširra-gods! [And these] words speak before
the Irširras: '[Come!] Kumarbi, father of the gods calleth ye! [. . .] about
what matter he calleth ye, [ye know not]. Now come promptly!'
'The Irširras will take the child and they [will carry it] to the dark earth . . .'

(*Fragment d*)

³ Barthes (1971) still provides an excellent account of the problem, which
precedes a discussion of style.
⁴ J. T. Greene (1989) examines the role of messengers and angels in Hebrew
scripture and ancient Near Eastern literature; Bemrose (1983) considers angels in
pre-Christian religious literature, as well as in Dante; Leclercq (1924–53) surveys
angels in the Christian tradition. T. Greene (1963) is a comparative treatment of
the messenger scene in ancient and European epic. Feeney (1991) considers the
important general implications of the relationship between gods and mortals in
ancient epic; also Quint (1993). De Jong (1987a) 240–5 studies the messenger scene
in the *Iliad* in an Appendix entitled 'repeated speech in the *Iliad*'. De Jong (1991)
deals with the messenger speech in Euripidean drama: 103 f. and the Appendix on
direct and indirect speech at 199–203 are helpful.

Impaluri [. . .] and took the stick in his hand, put the swift shoes on his feet [. . .] he went, Impaluri and came to the Irṣirras: 'Come! Kumarbi, father of the gods calleth ye! About what matter he calleth ye, ye know not. Now hurry come!'
When the Irṣirras heard these words, [they . . .] made haste and [hurr]ied. And they *covered the distance in one* [and] came to Kumarbi. Thereupon Kumarbi spake to the Irṣirras: '[Take this child] and [make] him into a present [and] carry him to the dark earth! Make haste and hurry . . .'

(*Fragment e*[5])

The god Kumarbi dictates a message to his messenger Impaluri (*Fragment d*). This is duly delivered by Impaluri who repeats Kumarbi's words precisely to the Irṣirras (*Fragment e*).[6] The repetition nicely illustrates that a reduplication of diction does not amount to a reduplication of the 'substance' conveyed by that diction in the first instance: speaker, addressee, context and 'message' (in the technical sense of the word) have all been transformed. The message (in the non-technical sense) that Kumarbi dictates is actually about a message: it gives notice of a pronouncement Kumarbi will make to the Irṣirras, but Kumarbi and, in turn, Impaluri play on the fact that the Irṣirras do not know what they are being summoned to hear. This, of course, is a stratagem which secures power as well as a means of displaying it. Another interesting feature of these fragments is the prolifera- tion of expressions which draw attention to the activity of verbal communication: 'Kumarbi spake these words', 'To the words I speak to thee lend thine ear!', '[these] words speak before the Irṣirras', 'Kumarbi calleth ye!' The recurrence of these phrases— along with the details of the stick and the messenger's swift shoes— resembles aspects of narrative style for similar scenes in other ancient near eastern epic, as well as in Homer.

Simply because the messenger scene is an enduring feature of Greek and Roman epic, it tends to be labelled by classicists as a 'convention' and, like so many other conventions, deprived of serious critical attention. In fact conventions of this kind are never static and inert. They vary not only from author to author, but also from one occurrence to another within a single narrative text. Homer's *Iliad* contains over a dozen instances of messages

---

[5] Güterbock (1946) provides a text of these fragments; this English translation is from Güterbock (1948).
[6] Güterbock (1948), 127 notes this precise repetition.

transmitted from heaven to earth: no one particular method of narrating these instances recurs.[7]

The study of the poetic convention of the messenger scene in Latin epic alone is rewarding for a number of reasons. It can throw light on stylistic differences between authors by comparing practices of narration for similar kinds of episode in the same genre. The deployment of speech modes in certain contexts is a very useful way of determining stylistic autographs which has so far been neglected. The pattern of the messenger scene is particularly helpful for this kind of endeavour because it will always present (in some manner) both a dictation speech and a delivery speech. Thus it is extremely useful for this kind of endeavour. Variations are possible on the level of *narrative*: the narrator can use DD, ID, or RSA for narration of either the dictation speech or the delivery speech, or both. Variations are equally possible on the level of *story*: the dictator of the message can use DD, ID, or RSA to render to his messenger the text he wants delivered; likewise in his delivery speech the messenger can use any of these speech modes as he renders the tidings to his addressee.

It will be apparent that both dictation and delivery speeches are themselves forms of narrative: the dictations are anticipatory or proleptic 'flash forwards'; the delivery speeches are analeptic 'flashbacks'. As I have noted above, in certain texts the analogies between reported discourse in messenger scenes and the larger narrative discourse in which they are embedded can be explicitly signalled. It should go without saying that the messenger scene raises issues brought up by reported discourse in general: the question of the relation between a supposed 'original version' of a speech and its 'reported version' can be constructively examined—at least within the parameters of the story worlds generated by particular texts.[8]

Power and hierarchy, prominent concerns generally in the study of speech presentation, are no less prominent in the messenger

[7] In the *Iliad* there is a great deal of variation in the speech modes to present dictation and delivery speech, and *within* both kinds of speech. However, some obvious trends can be discerned. Homer presents all dictations of messages in DD except Achilles' prayer (23. 192) and Zeus' commissioning of Iris-Polites (2. 786 f.). All deliveries except Hera's to Iris and Apollo are also presented in DD. *Within* the speeches there is more variation; ID is fairly frequent. The messenger is never just a funnel through whom speeches are reproduced. On several occasions Iris, Apollo and Thetis add personal comments to their rendering of the official dictation.

[8] My notion of 'story world'—which corresponds to Genette's *diégèse*—was introduced at 2.5 (pp. 74–5).

scene. Simply to commission a messenger is to demonstrate some kind of superior status. In this chapter I have chosen to concentrate on celestial messages dictated by major deities for transmission to the mortal plane. Conclusions already reached about the relation between speech and power in Chapters 1 and 5 of this book will be corroborated—and developed—in what follows. Constraints of space have precluded me from presenting in any detail my study of the ways in which messages dictated by mortals to other mortals are narrated in Latin epic.[9] However, one important point which emerged from that study should be made clear. In different ways Virgil, Statius, and Valerius Flaccus use specific techniques of speech presentation to underline the difference between messages sent by Olympians and messages sent by humans.[10]

These distinct practices sharpen the division between mortal and divine message commissions which are already established by other narrative devices (familiar nomenclature, explicit attributions of power to divinities, reliance on mythical and poetic tradition). However, in Ovid's *Metamorphoses,* distinct practices of narration for mortal messages on the one hand, and divine messages on the other, are not apparent. This might be because there are too few examples of messenger scenes in Ovid's poem for distinct techniques of relating the two sorts of message to be evident. Or it may be due to the boundaries between god and man being less definite in the more conspicuously fabulous world of the *Metamorphoses*: in martial epics the Iliadic hierarchy of immortal over mortal is sustained.

In the survey that follows, I shall concentrate on variations of the convention of the messenger scene in four Roman epics (Virgil's *Aeneid,* Ovid's *Metamorphoses,* Statius' *Thebaid,* and Valerius Flaccus' *Argonautica*) and in two later European epic poems: Iacopo Sannazaro's *De Partu Virginis,* a narrative of the Christian nativity in Latin hexameters, and John Milton's *Paradise Lost.* Lucan's *De Bello Civili,* unlike all the other Roman epics, contains no messenger scenes. This is partly because no gods are active in the story. Curiously this martial poem has no such scenes at all—not even on the mortal level. But from all the other poems I have selected one or two exemplary passages to highlight various issues raised by the celestial messenger motif. Jupiter's message to Aeneas

---

[9] See Laird (1992).
[10] De Jong (1987a), 168 f. deals with messages sent and received on the mortal plane (as well as divinely commissioned messages) in Homer's *Iliad.*

in *Aeneid* 4 will be given particular attention because this episode
has exerted a great deal of influence on later poets and readers. Like
the *Aeneid* itself, it serves as a useful 'control' for the study of later
epic poetry.

7.1 VIRGIL, *AENEID*

There are five episodes in the poem in which a messenger (Iris or
Mercury) is sent down to earth under the specific direction of
Jupiter or Juno.[11] The longest of these is the account of the
transmission of Jupiter's message instructing Aeneas to leave
Carthage. It begins as follows:

> Talibus orantem dictis arasque tenentem
> audiit Omnipotens, oculosque ad moenia torsit
> regia et oblitos famae melioris amantis.
> tum sic Mercurium adloquitur ac talia mandat:
> (*Aeneid* 4. 219–22)

As Iarbas prayed these words and clutched the altar, the Omnipotent one
heard him and turned his eyes to the royal walls of Carthage and to the
lovers oblivious of their good reputation. At that point he summoned
Mercury and dictated this message:[12]

The emphasis here on Jupiter's omnipotence shows that he hears,
sees, and controls, but does not run errands. These verses nicely
illustrate an observation in *De Mundo* (a work attributed to
Aristotle) that God is even less prone than any of the Persian
kings (who because of their guards could see and hear everything) to
run any of his errands himself:

If it was ignoble for Xerxes to appear himself to perform and accomplish
everything he wished, and himself to be present to administer his domain,
it would be even more unfitting for God. It is more noble and appropriate
for him to reside in the highest place, as his power, penetrating the whole
cosmos, moves the sun and moon, turns all of heaven, and is responsible for
keeping everything on earth in a state of safety.[13]

> ([Aristotle] *De Mundo* 398b)

---

[11] These are: 1. 297 f., 4. 219 f. (Mercury); 4. 694 f., 5. 606 = 9. 2 (Iris).
[12] Compare Zeus' commission of Hermes as a guide in *Iliad* 24. 332 f. in
response to Priam's prayer.
[13] This is a short excerpt from a passage (397b–399a) which treats the analogy at
some length.

Jupiter's words to Mercury are given in direct discourse:

'vade age, nate, voca Zephyros et labere pennis
Dardaniumque ducem, Tyria Karthagine qui nunc
exspectat fatisque datas non respicit urbes,
adloquere et celeris defer mea dicta per auras.
non illum nobis genetrix pulcherrima talem
promisit Graiumque ideo bis vindicat armis;
sed fore qui gravidam imperiis belloque frementem
Italiam regeret, genus alto a sanguine Teucri
proderet, ac totum sub leges mitteret orbem.
si nulla accendit tantarum gloria rerum
nec super ipse sua molitur laude laborem,
Ascanione pater Romanas invidet arces?
quid struit? aut qua spe inimica in gente moratur
nec prolem Ausoniam et Lavinia respicit arva?
naviget! haec summa est, hic nostri nuntius esto.'
Dixerat.

(Aeneid 4. 223–38)

Go now, my son. Call the west winds and glide on your wings and speak to the Trojan leader who is now waiting around in Tyrian Carthage and is heedless of the cities granted to him by the Fates. Bear down my words to him through the swift breezes. Tell him that this is not the man his most beautiful mother promised us and rescued twice from the armed Greeks; he should rather rule an Italy fertile in power and bristling with war, bring forth a stock from the noble blood of Teucer, and put the whole world under the rule of law . . . What is he planning? What is he hoping for by tarrying among a hostile people? Has he no regard for his future descendants in Italy and the Lavinian fields? Let him set sail! That is the point. Let that be our message.' He had spoken.

The expression *Vade age* ('Go now') in 223 recalls the words of Zeus to Iris in Homer's *Iliad*.[14] The idea of speed is also suggested by the diction of the rest of the line and its modulation.[15] Jupiter's specification of the whereabouts of Aeneas (224–5) implicitly contains a criticism of his neglect. The content of the actual message to be delivered is in 227 ff.; Jupiter does not use any formal ID constructions identifiable by a declarative verb, but the words are certainly not given in the form in which they would be pronounced to Aeneas.[16] It is easier to take these interrogative

[14] e.g. *Iliad* 11. 186 and 24. 144: βάσκ' ἴθι Ἶρι ταχεῖα, 'Go swift Iris'.
[15] Conington (1884), 273 ad loc.
[16] On this problem of the ambivalence of FID in the *Aeneid* see 5.2 (pp. 175–8).

expressions as rhetorical questions indicating the speaker's vehe-
mence, than to construct them as instances of FID. Even so, Jupiter
could be seen to use the device of FID as a surrogate narrator: after
all 4. 219–22 (discussed above) have shown that Jupiter can be as
omniscient and omnisentient as the poet of the *Aeneid*—indeed the
sequence of the god's perceptions and actions related there certainly converges with the direction of the narrative at that point, if it
does not actually control it.

However we read these sentences, it is natural, as is the case in
Homer, for the god to speak of the recipient of the message in the
third person. It is easy to imagine similar words spoken to Aeneas, if
the second person were substituted for the third here.[17] But Jupiter
is not simply issuing a dictation. The arrangement here shows he is
irritated. The text of the actual message begins with his view of the
situation, followed by ever sharper rhetorical questions, and
culminates in an exhortation: *naviget!* ('let him set sail!'). In the
rest of the verse the god indicates that this is the substance of his
message. *Dixerat* ('He had spoken') marks the end of the speech.

The passage that follows clearly resembles this account of
Hermes in the *Odyssey*:[18]

So he spoke and the messenger Argeiphontes did not disobey. At once he
fastened his fine sandals beneath his feet, sandals of immortal gold, which
bore him swift as the wind over the sea and the boundless earth. And he
took the rod, with which he both lulls the eyes of men, of those he wishes,
and awakens others when they are asleep. Holding this in his hands, the
strong Argeiphontes flew off; having passed over Pieria he plunged from
the upper air down to the sea, and then sped over the waves like a sea bird
that hunts for fishes through the terrifying troughs of the barren sea and
soaks its dense feathers in the brine. Like that bird Hermes rode on the
numerous waves. But when he reached the distant island, he left the violet
sea for the land, until he came to a great cave, where the nymph of fair
tresses lived, and he found her inside.

(*Odyssey* 5. 43–58)

Virgil thus describes Mercury equipping himself and going on his
journey:

---

[17] Compare the structure of *Aeneid* 2. 189–94 where Sinon exploits the form of
his indirect report of Calchas' words to give a direct exhortation to the Trojans.
This speech formula occurs in spoken English. See Ch. 3 n. 57.

[18]   *Aeneid* 4. 228 here also resembles *Odyssey* 5. 43 (= *Iliad* 24. 339).

Dixerat. ille patris magni parere parabat
imperio; et primum pedibus talaria nectit
aurea, quae sublimem alis sive aequora supra
seu terram rapido pariter cum flamine portant.
tum virgam capit: hac animas ille evocat Orco
pallentis, alias sub Tartara tristia mittit
dat somnos adimitque, et lumina morte resignat.
illa fretus agit ventos et turbida tranat
nubila . . .
hic primum paribus nitens Cyllenius alis
constitit; hinc toto praeceps se corpore ad undas
misit avi similis, quae circum litora, circum
piscosos scopulos humilis volat aequora iuxta.
haud aliter terras inter caelumque volabat
litus harenosum ad Libyae, ventosque secabat
materno veniens ab avo Cyllenia proles.
ut primum alatis tetigit magalia plantis,
Aenean fundantem arces et tecta novantem
conspicit. atque illi stellatus iaspide fulva
ensis erat Tyrioque ardebat murice laena
demissa ex umeris, dives quae munera Dido
fecerat, et tenui telas discreverat auro.

(4. 238–46, 252–64)

Jupiter had spoken. Mercury set about preparing to obey the command of his great father: first he bound the golden sandals on his feet. These carry him along high on his wings with the speed of the wind—over waves and dry land alike. Then he took up his staff. With this he calls out the pale shades from Orcus, and sends others down to sad Tartarus; he bestows sleep and takes it away, and he also seals eyes in death. Using this staff, he drove the winds and soared through the turbulent clouds . . .
This [Atlas] was where the Cyllenian god halted, resplendent with his wings evenly extended. From here, he plunged headlong with all his weight down to the waves, like a bird which flies close to the water around the shore and around the rockpools searching for fish. Just like this Cyllene's son was flying between earth and heaven and cleaving the winds near the sandy shore of Libya coming from his ancestral mountain. As soon as he touched the lowly dwellings with his winged soles, he caught sight of Aeneas founding citadels and putting up new houses. His sword was studded with yellow jasper, and the cloak which hung from his shoulders glowed with Tyrian purple. These were gifts which the wealthy Dido had made, and she had woven into them a thread of fine gold.

The narration of this journey resembles Hermes' visit to Circe in the *Odyssey*. Moreover, both messenger scenes have an analogous function in the stories to which they belong. These obvious similarities have led critics to see these episodes as generally comparable.[19] But there is scant resemblance between the words of Homer's Hermes and those of Mercury here:

> continuo invadit: 'tu nunc Karthaginis altae
> fundamenta locas pulchramque uxorius urbem
> exstruis? heu, regni rerumque oblite tuarum!
> ipse deum tibi me claro demittit Olympo
> regnator, caelum et terras qui numine torquet,
> ipse haec ferre iubet celeris mandata per auras:
> quid struis? aut qua spe Libycis teris otia terris?
> si te nulla movet tantarum gloria rerum
> [nec super ipse tua moliris laude laborem,]
> Ascanium surgentem et spes heredis Iuli
> respice, cui regnum Italiae Romanaque tellus
> debetur'.

(4. 265–76)

Immediately Mercury set upon him: 'So now you are laying the foundations of lofty Carthage and designing a beautiful city as a devoted husband? How forgetful you are of your kingdom and your responsibilities. The ruler of the gods himself is sending me down to you from bright Olympus. He who controls heaven and earth with his divine authority orders me to carry this message through the swift breezes: What are you planning? What are you hoping for by idling your time away on Libyan soil? If the glory of your great responsibilities fails to move you, consider Ascanius as he grows up and the future of this Iulus your heir, to whom the rule of Italy and land of Rome is due.'

The pattern of the dictation and delivery of Jupiter's message in this scene does not follow the *Odyssey* passage so much as the episodes in the *Iliad* in which Iris is commissioned to deliver messages. (The pattern here is in fact a significant exception in the *Aeneid*.[20]) First, Mercury comes to the point of his message

---

[19] Pease (1935) on *Aeneid* 4 ad loc. lists parallel descriptions of Mercury. Conington (1884), 273 remarks on 4. 222: 'Imitated from Od. 5. 28 foll., . . . There is little or no resemblance between the two speeches.'

[20] There are three structures for divine messages in the poem: (i) RSA for both the dictator's and messenger's words (1. 297–302, 9. 803–5); (ii) RSA for the dictator and DD for the messenger (4. 694, 9. 2); (iii) DD for both dictator and messenger as in 4. 219 f. All stages of transmission of divine messages are narrated, however cursorily; this can occur for messages sent and received on the mortal plane, but it is by no means the rule. ID (as opposed to DD and RSA) does not occur in the narration of progress of divine messages, but it is preferred for human

rapidly and directly. Hermes, by contrast, in *Odyssey* 5 and *Iliad* 24 takes a long time to do this. Second, Mercury resembles the Iliadic Iris in that the content of the message he delivers resembles the one dictated fairly closely. There are only subtle variations: Jupiter's words are reformulated, and Aeneas is addressed in the second person. As is sometimes the case with Homer's Iris (*Iliad* 8. 413–14, 24. 172–3), the messenger's opening words are not derived from the text of the message actually dictated.

However the tone of the speech from 265 onwards is still very much Mercury's own, and the portrait of Mercury is much fuller than that of Iris in the *Iliad*. His personal rebuke to Aeneas (265–7) picks up Jupiter's words at 224, by setting Carthage in contrast to the cities he should look after. Yet Mercury himself is responsible for implicitly setting the *image* of the foundation of Carthage against Aeneas' real responsibilities. Mercury's words in his delivery speech employ the observations he made on his journey at 260 f.: *fundamenta locas* ('you are laying the foundations') recalls *fundantem arces . . . conspicit* ('he caught sight of Aeneas founding citadels'). Even Mercury's sighting of Aeneas with the cloak and sword Dido gave him could have prompted his snide use of the word *uxorius*: the queen's gifts could be symbolic of a dowry.[21] *Exstruis* ('you are designing') recalls Jupiter's *quid struit?*, which is again echoed specifically in Mercury's actual rendering of Jupiter's words.[22] The narrator had earlier described Aeneas and Dido as 'forgetful': here (267) the observation is Mercury's own. Lastly, Jupiter's command (226) to Mercury to bear his message through the swift breezes is echoed slightly at 270.

These details contribute to a subtle but effective characterization of Mercury. Like a messenger in the *Iliad*, Mercury then validates what is to come by saying who sent him.[23] But even with this functional seal of authenticity, there is an element of specific

---

messages and commands. The ID of Fama (see below) cannot easily be accommodated by these structures: it could function as a dictation speech; as a delivery speech it has no direct source.

[21] Lyne (1989), 43–6 reviews occurrences of the word *uxorius* (usually found in prose) and considers its significance here.

[22] This use of the compound word *exstruis* could add the sense of 'building' to the notion of scheming which is primary in the simple verb later on (compare Pease (1935) on 4. 235).

[23] Ζεύς με πατὴρ προέηκε τεῖν τάδε μυθήσασθαι, *Iliad* 11. 201; compare *Iliad* 15. 175, 24. 133, 24. 173.

characterization: in 268–70, Mercury can emphasize by the repetition of *ipse* ('himself'—an appropriate pronoun) the important fact that the command comes from Jupiter himself. This major contextual feature of the original speech could not of course be part of the content Jupiter gave to be transmitted. Jupiter's attribute of governing heaven and earth (269) is all the more meaningful to one who has just flown between them.

The rendering of the message itself at 271–6 might be meant to strike Aeneas as a direct quotation of the god's words. It does follow them reasonably closely, without having the quality of the perfectly memorized dispatch that we find in Homer. Mercury starts by rendering some of Jupiter's final words. Curiously, Mercury does not reproduce the actual order to set sail (*naviget!*) which Jupiter himself identified as the crucial brief of his speech (237). Jupiter's remark about Venus having protected him unnecessarily is also omitted. Mercury goes straight to the rhetorical questions originally posed by Jupiter. They are in a different sequence, with slight changes in diction. Mercury's whole speech ends with a mention of Ascanius and Italy, as it began with Carthage.[24] This was a feature of Jupiter's original words as they were presented by the narrator. But the omission of *naviget!* in Mercury's transmission rather characterizes Jupiter's speech as a 'message' (*mandata* 270) for Aeneas, albeit a grimly reproachful one, and not as an order. Nonetheless, there is no doubt that Aeneas himself sees the speech as a clear command: at 282 he is presented as 'overwhelmed both by so mighty a warning and the gods' *command* (*imperio*)'. Overall, then, Virgil is *affecting* Iliadic practice with some elaboration in his treatment of the message's transmission.

Both the dictation and delivery speeches in this episode are narrated in DD. This conforms to the general pattern of message transmission in the *Iliad*. Jupiter's reference to the recipient of the message in the third person, and the adaptation of this to the second person in delivery are also characteristic traits in Iliadic messenger scenes. However, this basic schema is adorned with variations which sustain attention. Impressions of Mercury's character and of Jupiter's status are induced, yet the audience

---

[24] It is interesting that in his delivery Mercury uses the phrase *spes heredis Iuli* in tandem with *Ascanium*: critics have made the point that the name 'Iulus' is meant to have a more emotional connotation for Aeneas (and the audience) which 'Ascanius' as a more official name does not.

may still have the feeling that the messenger is closely following the god's words.

In *De Laboribus Herculis* ('On the Labours of Hercules'), the Florentine humanist Coluccio Salutati (1331–1406) noted the divergent techniques of Virgil and Homer for narrating the speeches in this kind of scene and drew his own conclusion:

Orationem autem pro oratione posuit Maro. Nam cum Iupiter Mercurio precepisset quod Eneam deberet admonere, per hec verba videlicet, 'Quid struit? aut qua spe inmica in gente moratur?' Mercurium postea mandata peragentem inducit orationem hanc taliter immutare: 'Quid struis? aut qua spe Libicis teris ocia terris?' Hoc ferme nusquam fecit Homerus sed eisdem ubique verbis commissionis formulam repetebat. Sed noluit excultissimus Latinorum vates taliter Homerum servatis omnibus prosequi quod non ostenderet quam late poetica facultas valeat ampliari.

(*De Laboribus Herculis* 1. 2. 7)

Virgil put one set speech in place of another. For example when Jupiter instructed Mercury about how he should admonish Aeneas plainly in these words 'What is he planning? What is he hoping for by tarrying among a hostile people?', Virgil causes Mercury, when he subsequently delivered these instructions, to change this wording as follows: 'What are you planning? What are you hoping for by idling your time away on Libyan soil?' Homer hardly ever did this, but always repeated the formula of the commission with the same words. But the most refined poet of the Latins did not want to follow Homer by keeping everything to the degree that he would fail to show how extensively the poetic faculty could be increased.[25]

A consideration of which speech modes are employed for which personages can shed further light on Virgil's narrative techniques and characterization. There would seem to be no necessity either for the narrator to treat so fully the transmission of a message, or in doing so, to imitate the Iliadic model (as opposed to having Jupiter dictating, or Mercury delivering in ID or RSA). That model is not followed when Jupiter commissions Mercury in 1. 297 to prepare the Carthaginians for the Trojans' arrival or in the scenes when Juno sends down Iris at 4. 693 and 9. 1 f. (Neither the manifestation of Anchises at 5. 726 nor Mercury's second appearance to Aeneas in a dream at 4. 556 f. seem to be prompted by Jupiter.)

A reason for the words of both sender and messenger being presented in direct discourse in this passage may emerge when we see how Mercury and Fama (the female personification of

[25] A text of this work is in B. Ullman (1951).

rumour) are paralleled and contrasted in this part of the *Aeneid*. Fama informs Iarbas of Dido's involvement with Aeneas. Iarbas, who is a frustrated suitor of Dido, complains of this in a prayer to his father Jupiter. By giving Iarbas this information, Fama starts the chain of events which brings about Jupiter's message to Aeneas.

There are several parallels between Mercury and Fama. Mercury acts in response to Jupiter's command, as Fama swiftly responds to the prompting of events. Both go to Libya (173, 257); both fly (e.g. 176–7, 223, 226, 241, 246) and make their flight between heaven and earth (184, 256); both are compared to birds. But the two agents are also contrasted as opposite forces. Fama can spread truth and untruth on earth (188–90); Mercury is the true messenger of heaven. Fama never closes her numerous eyes to sleep (185); Mercury gives and takes away sleep, and closes the eyes of the dead. These contrasting qualities of the two agents are enumerated fully by Philip Hardie who also remarks:

> Finally the ancient allegorical tradition may help us to a full evaluation of the contrast between *Fama* and Mercury. *Fama* is a divinity of perverted speech; one of the most consistent allegorical identifications of Mercury is as *Logos*, *Ratio*, the unperverted word. More particularly, the Homeric scene of the equipping of Hermes was allegorised with reference to the descent of the divine *Logos* from heaven to earth.[26]

The discourse ascribed to Virgil's personification of rumour is presented indirectly because Fama does not have a direct source for her message. This practice is followed by most subsequent Latin poets. On the other hand it is only appropriate that the words of Mercury—who *does* have a direct source—should be given by the narrator in direct discourse. The variation in use of speech mode enhances the essential contrast between the nature of the two messengers.

A close examination of the ID ascribed to Fama indicates that this message at least might have a significance which goes beyond its function on the level of the *Aeneid*'s story. This is how Virgil's description of Fama concludes:

[26] P. Hardie (1986), 278. The best assembly of evidence for Hermes as an embodiment of λόγος or λογισμός is in Buffière (1956), 289–96; compare various ancient commentators on *Od.* 5. 45 f., *Iliad* 24. 343, etc.

. . . tam ficti pravique tenax quam nuntia veri.
haec tum multiplici populos sermone replebat
gaudens, et pariter facta atque infecta canebat:
venisse Aenean Troiano sanguine cretum,
cui se pulchra viro dignetur iungere Dido;
nunc hiemem inter se luxu, quam longa, fovere
regnorum immemores turpique cupidine captos.
(*Aeneid* 4. 188–94)

She clings on to her lies and distortions as often as she tells the truth. At that time she rejoiced in plying peoples with talk on many levels, she was singing facts and fictions mixed in equal parts: how Aeneas sprung from Trojan blood had come to Carthage and how the beautiful Dido was thinking it fit to join herself with him as husband; how they were even now indulging themselves and keeping each other warm the whole winter through, forgetting about their kingdoms and how they had become captured by foul lust.

Fama has much in common with the poet of the *Aeneid*. Like the poet, she *sings* her story. The subject matter of her rumour is the very subject matter of the fourth book of the poem. In fact, everything she reports is just as it has already been narrated. Within the world of the story, then, Fama is peddling only facts. Yet Virgil says that at that time (*tum*) she was dealing in *multiplici sermone* ('talk on many levels') and mixing fiction in equal part with fact. What is the basis for this? It can only be that if one considers Fama's report on a pragmatic level then it can be no more true than the *Aeneid* itself is true. In this respect, poetry is very much like rumour: after all Horace, Virgil's contemporary, characterized the ideal epic poet as someone who 'lies and mixes truth with falsehood' (*ita mentitur, sic veris falsa remiscet*).[27] So Fama may have a reflexive significance for the *Aeneid*: she is not only a character in the story; she is also a formal component of the narrative. The appearance of Fama in the *Aeneid* generally marks a change of scene or turning point in the actual construction of the poem.[28]

Some might challenge any parallelism between Fama and the poet in *Aeneid* 4 by appealing to the value judgements in Fama's account of the union between Aeneas and Dido. They would claim

[27] Horace, *Ars Poetica* 151–2. This passage was discussed in Ch. 5, p. 163.
[28] *Aen.* 4. 666; 7. 104; 9. 474; 11. 139. Standard divine messenger scenes also effect changes of scene: for example *Aeneid* 1. 297–302 moves the location of the story from Olympus to earth.

that the account of the couple 'indulging themselves . . . forgetting about their kingdoms and . . . captured by foul lust' conveys a singularly explicit condemnation of events so far recounted in the poem. However, even before the appearance of Fama, the narrator has been far from benign about those events.[29] It is, anyway, a general practice of epic poets to signpost the plots of their poems by naming passions, virtues, or vices which happen to be prominent in ancient discussions of ethics.[30] Indeed, Fama's message programmatically determines subsequent events in *Aeneid* 4, as much as it records what has gone before: Iarbas' prayer to Jupiter, the message Jupiter dictates to Mercury, the text Mercury delivers to Aeneas, and even Aeneas' apologetic speech to Dido can all be seen to report and reconfigure the state of affairs described by Fama. The narrative of *Aeneid* 4 is almost entirely constituted by successful or unsuccessful exchanges of communication. One might compare Jean Ricardou's celebrated interpretation of Sophocles' *Oedipus Tyrannus* as a play revolving around three conversations which are themselves *mise-en-abyme* narratives.[31]

Our insight on the reflexive role of both Fama and Mercury in the *Aeneid* can be developed by the examination of the role of the messenger scene in a very different work: the *De Partu Virginis* ('On the Virgin Birth'), a biblical epic by the Renaissance poet Iacopo Sannazaro.

7.2 IACOPO SANNAZARO, *DE PARTU VIRGINIS*

De Partu Virginis (published in 1526) is a short epic poem in three books which recounts the story of Christ's nativity.[32] This discus-

---

[29] e.g. *Aen.* 4. 169–72

[30] There are abundant examples in epic proems e.g. μῆνιν ('wrath') *Iliad* 1. 1; ἄλγεα ('woes') *Odyssey* 1. 5; *ira* ('wrath') *Aeneid* 1. 5; *furor* ('frenzy') and *licentia* ('licence') in Lucan, *De Bello Civili* 1. 8. Compare Horace's characterization of the Homeric poems in ethical terms in *Epistles* 1. 2. *Paradise Lost* of course begins: 'Of man's first *evil* . . .'.

[31] See the chapter entitled 'L'Histoire dans l'histoire' in Ricardou (1967). The most exhaustive study of *mise-en-abyme* in narrative is Dällenbach (1977).

[32] The best and most recent edition of the poem is provided by Fantazzi and Perosa (1989) which also contains texts of the author's correspondence concerning the poem. Pontano's dialogues in Latin, edited in Previtera (1963), feature Sannazaro as a speaker and offer contemporaneous perspectives on his poetry and poetics. *DPV* is discussed in Jacob (1960) as well as T. Greene (1963). Kidwell (1993) is a general treatment of Sannazaro with biography; Hathaway (1968) and Weinberg (1961) are relevant surveys of Italian humanist culture.

sion will concentrate on the first book which treats the Annunciation: God sends his angel to fly to a maiden in Judaea to inform her
that she has been chosen to give birth to a divine child. The virgin
happily accepts and conceives. Meanwhile Fama, the personification of rumour, descends to the underworld to announce
that the day is coming when the shades can leave Tartarus.

The dispatching of the angel (which is the first event to be
narrated) has an obvious reflexive significance because it provides
a rationale for all the events which are to be narrated subsequently,
as well as an epitome of them. The rationale begins where the
narrative begins at verse 33: the king of heaven has been observing
the helplessness of the human race and sees Tisiphone plundering
the earth to fill Tartarus. This prompts the king of heaven's first
soliloquy (41–54): Men will no longer die and be punished for the
crimes of their ancestors, but will be called to the empty places
that await them in heaven. Since womankind had been responsible
for all earthly evil in the first place, let her now bear help and bring
an end to all this suffering. The speaker then calls his servant to
take his commands to the chaste girl he has chosen. In this
dictation speech we find the epitome of the story to follow. This
is further enhanced by the account given of the virgin as the
messenger beholds her, before delivering his news. Indeed,
Sannazaro's poem is largely characterized by journeys and movement, with a particular prominence given to journeys from heaven
to earth.[33]

The dictation speech of Sannazaro's ruler of heaven is given in
direct discourse and ends as follows:

> 'Ergo age, nubivagos moliri per aëra gressus,
> deveniensque locum, castas haec iussus ad aures
> effare et pulcris cunctantem hortatibus imple,
> quandoquidem genus e stygiis mortale tenebris
> eripere est animus saevosque arcere labores.'

---

[33] For instance: in Book 3 Mercury's descent is picked up both by the descent of
Laetitia or 'Joy' to Bethlehem and by the descent of a dove from heaven which the
god of the river Jordan sees predicted in an urn. In Book 2, the virgin journeys to
visit Elizabeth wife of Zachariah, and to Bethlehem. In the same book, the narrator
'travels' himself as he uses rich geographical description to conjure up a journey
through the known world: the fact that, at the close of Book 3, the poet is called
back to his abode at Mergellina suggests that the narrative itself has been a kind of
excursion.

Dixerat. Ille altum Zephyris per inane vocatis
carpit iter, scindit nebulas atque aëra tranat . . .
(*DPV* 1. 77–83)

'Go then, push through the air with your cloud-coursing strides and, when
you come down to the place, as you are bidden, pronounce these things to
her chaste ears, and, as she wavers, fill her with beautiful counsels, since it is
my will to snatch the race of mortals from the Stygian darkness and keep
them from cruel toils.'

He had spoken. The messenger, after calling the west winds, picks his
way through the empty sky, parts the clouds and soars through the air . . .

Like Virgil's Jupiter, Sannazaro's deity does not give a precise
verbal formulation of the message to be delivered. This dictation
speech is also concluded in the same way: the verb *Dixerat* ('he had
spoken') is followed immediately by a new sentence beginning with
the pronoun *ille* to describe the minion's prompt response. Sannazaro's messenger corresponds to Luke's Gabriel—but Sannazaro's
characters have no proper names. The account of this messenger's
descent from heaven to earth again has conspicuous resemblances
to Mercury's in *Aeneid* 4. 238–65. Both figures are compared to
birds in similes: Mercury is likened to a low flying sea bird, whilst a
longer simile in Sannazaro's account compares the divine messenger's journey to the effortless flight of a swan. Both figures alight at
vantage points where they can catch sight of their quarries: Virgil's
conspicit atque illi (*Aeneid* 4. 261) corresponds to Sannazaro's *aspicit
atque ille* (*DPV* 1. 93). Mercury sees Aeneas helping Dido to build
Carthage whilst Sannazaro's angel is somehow able to watch the
'queen' (*regina* is the word used) whom he is to address as she
contemplates the predictions of soothsayers for generations to
come. From this point, the parallel is one of contrast: Aeneas is
offending the ordinances of fate and is immediately rebuked by
Mercury. Sannazaro's narrator, on the other hand, eulogizes the
virgin before describing the messenger's apparition and speech.
But the girl's initial reponse of speechless terror and stupefication,
comparable with Aeneas' reaction to Mercury, restores the correspondence with Virgil's account:[34]

---

[34] The beginning of Aeneas' response to Mercury's speech is described thus at
Aeneid 4. 279–80: *At vero Aeneas aspectu obmutuit amens,* | *arrectaeque horrore
comae et vox faucibus haesit* ('But Aeneas was dumbstruck and aghast at the
apparition. His hair bristled with horror and his voice stuck in his throat'). The
verses that follow these lines are quoted and discussed in 5.2, pp. 168–70, 182.

Stupuit confestim exterrita virgo,
demisitque oculos totosque expalluit artus:
non secus ac conchis siquando intenta legendis
seu Micone parva scopulis seu forte Seriphi
nuda pedem virgo, laetae nova gloria matris,
veliferam advertit vicina ad litora puppim
adventare, timet, nec iam subducere vestem
audet nec tuto ad socias se reddere cursu,
sed trepidans silet obtutuque immobilis haeret . . .

(*DPV* 1. 123–31)

The terrified maiden was immediately stunned. She lowered her eyes and all her limbs went pale. Just like a maiden in bare feet, the fresh pride of a happy mother, intent on gathering shells from the rocks on little Mykonos or perhaps on Seriphos, when she notices a sailing boat approaching neighbouring shores, is afraid, and does not now dare to hitch up her skirts and make a run for safety to her companions. But she trembles, is silent and stares, rooted to the spot . . .

There are further parallels between these accounts on an allegorical level. The descent of the celestial messenger in *De Partu Virginis* also dovetails with an account of a journey by Fama which follows (1. 225). Whilst Sannazaro is unlikely have been aware of the ancient (pre-Virgilian) allegories, he would have known Christian allegorizations of Mercury which were on very similar lines. Fulgentius, the sixth-century commentator on Virgil, offers this remark on Mercury's appearance to Aeneas in *Aeneid* 4:

In quo diu commoratus Mercurio instigante libidinis suae male praesumptum amorem relinquit; Mercurius enim deus ponitur ingenii, ergo ingenio instigante aetas amoris confinia deserit . . .

(Fulgentius, *Expositio Virgilianae Continentiae*, in Helm (1898), 94. 20)

And after he has dallied for a long time, Aeneas leaves behind his immoral love at Mercury's instigation. Mercury functions as the god of reason. This is so that at the prompting of reason maturity forsakes the bonds of lust . . .

The extent of Fulgentius' influence on the humanists and on conceptions of epic up to Tasso is well established.[35] Moreover a comment on allegory in John of Salisbury's *Entheticus De Dogmate Philosophorum* ('Insertion on the Teaching of Philosophers')

---

[35] The *Continentia*, current through the medieval period, was known to Boccaccio and printed early in the 16th cent.; Fulgentius' text was presented with editions of Virgil well into the 18th cent. See Whitbread (1971), 105–18.

reveals something about the conception of Mercury in the twelfth century:[36]

> Alterutrum vel utrumque licet proferre, sed insta,
> ut sit Mercurio Philologia comes,
> non quia numinibus falsis reverentia detur,
> sed sub verborum tegmine vera latent.
>
> (*Entheticus* 183–7)

It is permitted to promote one or the other, but insist that Philology be the companion of Mercury; not in order that reverence might be paid to false divinities, but because under the veil of words truths lie hidden.

Mercury is thus an appropriate model for the messenger in *De Partu Virginis*—a messenger who quite literally brings the divine word down to earth. On the other hand, Mercury's involvement with the underworld—indicated clearly enough by Virgil—is not inherited by Sannazaro's heavenly messenger. In the *De Partu Virginis* it is Fama who takes over this function and goes down to the realm of the shades:

> Interea Manes descendit Fama sub imos
> pallentesque domos veris rumoribus implet:
> optatum adventare diem, quo tristia linquant
> Tartara et evictis fugiant Acheronta tenebris,
> immanemque ululatum et non laetabile murmur
> tergemini canis . . .
>
> (*DPV* 1. 225–30)

Meanwhile Fama descends to the shades below and fills the pallid abodes with true rumours: that the awaited day was coming, when they may leave sad Tartarus and flee Acheron with its darkness conquered, the monstrous howling and grim growl of the dog with three sets of jaws . . .

This portrayal of Fama differs in a very important respect from Virgil's: she tells true things which are not mixed with falsity. But Sannazaro's Fama shares a narrative function with Virgil's: the two words *Interea . . . Fama* facilitate the central shift in the narrative of Book 1, from the Annunciation to the scene of the underworld. And again, as is the case in Virgil, the rumour provided by Sannazaro's *Fama* seems to share its subject matter with a general theme of the poem as a whole. Her anticipation of the day in which souls might leave the underworld answers the ruler of heaven's anxieties about

---

[36] Petersen (1843) provides a text and commentary. The twelfth century also saw Bernardus Silvestris' commentary on Martianus Capella *De nuptiis Philologiae et Mercurii*. See Westra (1986).

the descent of the human race into Tartarus which first opened the narrative of the poem (1. 33) and prompted his soliloquy.

The allegorical figure of Mercury (the Roman equivalent of the Greek Hermes) as the transmitter of the divine word to earth is a crucial model for Sannazaro's messenger. The felicitous etymological assocation between Hermes and hermeneutics may have resonances for this poem: like the Virgilian Mercury, the angelic messenger is called *interpres* at 1. 164.[37] The pride of place given to Sannazaro's Hermes in the *De Partu Virginis* might suggest the poem itself conveys divine truth. This suggestion of a claim to truth is endorsed by an intertextual relationship with the opening of Luke's gospel. Luke makes comparable use of both a proem and messenger scene to frame and validate the narrative to follow. Luke's proem in the Vulgate runs like this:

Quoniam quidem multi conati sunt ordinari narrationem, quae in nobis completae sunt rerum: sicut tradiderunt nobis, qui ab initio ipsi viderunt, et ministri fuerunt sermonis: visum est et mihi, adsecuto a principio omnibus, diligenter ex ordine tibi scribere, optime Theophile, ut cognoscas eorum verborum, de quibus eruditus es, veritatem.

(Luke 1: 1–4)

Since many have tried to put in order a narration of things which were fulfilled among us, in the way those who themselves saw from the beginning and were messengers of the news handed it down to us. I also decided, after following everything from the start, to take care to put everything in order for you, noble Theophilus, so that you may know the truth of the words about which you have been informed.

Luke's prologue foreshadows and reinforces the first messenger scene, which involves Gabriel and Zacharia:

Ego sum Gabrihel, qui adsto ante deum: et missus sum loqui ad te, et haec tibi evangelizare. Et ecce eris tacens, et non poteris loqui usque in diem quo haec fiant: pro eo quod non credidisti meis verbis, quae implebuntur in tempore suo.

(Luke 1: 19–20)

I am Gabriel who stands before God: and I have been sent to speak to you, and to announce this good message to you. And behold you will be silent,

---

[37] It is Aeneas who thus characterizes Mercury in his speech to Dido at *Aen.* 4. 356–8: *nunc etiam interpres divum Iove missus ab ipso | (testor utrumque caput) | celeris mandata per auras | detulit* ('Now even the interpreter of the gods, sent by Jupiter himself—I swear this by both our lives—has brought down his orders through the swift winds').

and you will not be able to speak until the day this message is fulfilled, because you did not believe my words which will be fulfilled in their own time.

That scene in turn frames the Annunciation, which, in turn, frames and validates the whole of Luke's narrative to follow. Thus the *De Partu Virginis* not only shares diction and content with Luke, but also the rhetorical framing devices by which his gospel lays claim to its own truth.

Now if Sannazaro's Fama, like Virgil's Fama, can be taken to be emblematic of the poem in which she appears, an observation made earlier becomes much more significant. We have seen that Sannazaro's Fama rings the changes on Virgil's by telling *true* rumours which are not mixed with falsity. We should also note the verb *implet* in this context: Fama 'fills' the pale houses of the dead with her true rumours. That verb has already been used in two very important places. First in God's dictation speech (1. 79) quoted earlier where he instructs his angel to announce his message to the virgin and '*fill* her with beautiful counsels'. The mention of redemption from the underworld in the same passage (1. 80–1) offers another link with the function of Fama. The second important occasion for the verb *implere* is the angelic messenger's elucidation to the maiden of the incarnation itself:

> excipit interpres 'foecundam spiritus alvum
> influet implebitque potenti viscera partu . . .'
>   (*DPV* 1. 164–5)

The interpreter replied 'The spirit will flow into your fertile womb and will fill your body with its powerful issue . . .'

Whilst *implere* is never used of Fama in Virgil, forms of the verb and the related compounds *complere* and *replere* are found in seven appropriate contexts in the first chapter of the vulgate Luke.

The analogies between the figures of the messengers and the message of the *De Partu Virginis* itself suggest that this poem is not supposed to be a mixture of truth and falsity. Thus it does not conform to Horace's characterization of epic in the *Ars Poetica*. Whereas Virgil's Fama peddles information which, at least within the story of the *Aeneid*, is unclear, Sannazaro's figure of Fama explicitly conveys what is true. In the fashion of Luke's gospel, the *De Partu Virginis* advertises itself as veridical—whilst seeking to present its truth in a distinctively 'epic' way. So far, this examination has shown that for Virgil and Sannazaro, messenger scenes not only have an important role in governing the action and plot of the poems in which they occur. These scenes also function, paradigmatically, as *mise-en-abymes* for the poems themselves, which say something about the nature of what these epics convey to their audiences. This connection (between interpretation of the messenger scene and the interpretation of the text containing it) also obtains—in a different way—in Ovid's *Metamorphoses*.

7.3 OVID, *METAMORPHOSES*

There are six scenes in which messengers are dispatched in the *Metamorphoses*.[38] This discussion will concentrate on two messages from Juno—one to Somnus (11. 585 ff.) and the other to Hersilia (14. 829 ff.). Juno's communication to Somnus is issued in response to a prayer from Alcyone for her husband's life. The prayer cannot be granted. Instead, the goddess acts only to stop Alcyone praying in vain. Juno's instructions to Iris are given in only four verses of direct discourse:[39]

'Iri, meae' dixit 'fidissima nuntia vocis,
vise soporiferam Somni velociter aulam

[38] Not all these count for the purpose of this analysis: no verbal messages are taken by Mercury when he is ordered to drive the cattle to the seashore in 2. 837, or by Cupid when he is requested to strike Pluto at 5. 365 f. The message sent from Byblis to Caunus (9. 530 f.), will be considered in relation to the Hersilia episode treated below. Ceres' message to Fames (8. 788 f.) is a significant example of the convention with a sequence of events triggered off in response to a prayer—comparable to that in 11. 585 f. discussed here. Ovid's manner of narrating speeches in messenger scenes is summarized in Avery (1936): '*Oratio obliqua* is not used for dispatching messages. A messenger may deliver his message either in *oratio recta* or in *oratio obliqua*, depending upon the treatment of the previous speech.' (Avery's category of '*oratio obliqua*' includes both ID and RSA.) Where the actual choice of speech modes for *narrating* these divine commissions is concerned, Ovid diverges from Virgil only in showing less variety: the techniques the narrator's voice use conform to those in the *Aeneid*. The Juno–Iris–Somnus scene is comparable to *Aeneid* 4. 218 f. in which we hear both delivery and dictation speeches in full. The Ceres–Oread–Fames scene and the Hersilia episode involve DD dictation followed by RSA delivery. The remaining Virgilian practice of a whole sequence being rendered in indirect speech is not adopted.

[39] For further examples and bibliography on 'Kurze (pathetische) Rede an entscheidender Stelle', see Bömer (1980) at 11. 207: 8. 689, 767; 9. 143 f.; 10. 230 f., 380, 640 f.; 11. 102 f., 132 f., 160, 221 f., 323, 585 f., 676, 712 f., 720 f., 725, 727 f.

exstinctique iube Ceycis imagine mittat
somnia ad Alcyonen veros narrantia casus.'
(*Met.* 11. 585–8)

'Iris' she said 'messenger most faithful to my words, go quickly to the
drowsy home of Sleep and bid him send, in the image of dead Ceyx, dreams
narrating the true state of events.'

The expression *meae fidissima nuntia vocis* ('messenger most faithful to my words') is worth noting. Earlier in the poem, in a very
similar context, Jupiter calls Mercury *fide minister* ('faithful messenger') at 2. 837.[40] The adjective *fidus* ('faithful', 'loyal') is elsewhere used in Ovid to convey the fidelity of discourse to an idea or
event.[41] Juno wants from her messenger a precise rendition of her
demands. After some preliminary liturgical courtesy, the essence of
Iris' delivery is indeed very faithful to Juno's words:[42]

'Somne, quies rerum, placidissime, Somne, deorum,
pax animi, quem cura fugit, qui corpora duris
fessa ministeriis mulces reparasque labori,
somnia, quae veras aequant imitamine formas,
Herculea Trachine iube sub imagine regis
Alcyonen adeant simulacraque naufraga fingant.
imperat hoc Iuno.'
(*Met.* 11. 623–9)

'O Sleep, rest of all things, Sleep, most placid of the gods, peace of the soul,
from whom cares flee, who calms bodies weary of their hard ministries and
refreshes them for work, bid your dreams, which equal true shapes in their
imitations, to adopt the image of the king and approach Alcyone in
Hercules' city of Trachis. Then let them forge a likeness of the shipwreck.
Juno orders this.'

This speech contains a command similar to that employed in the
dictation speech: here Iris orders Sleep to instruct his dreams; in
the dictation speech Iris herself was ordered to instruct Sleep. Of
the mild changes of diction in Iris' transmission of Juno's request,
one deserves particular attention. Iris' insistence (628) that the
dreams should forge a *likeness* of the shipwreck implies that more

---

[40] On 2. 837, again see Bömer ad loc.
[41] For example, *Tristia* 3. 7. 1 addresses a letter as 'a faithful servant of speech'
(*sermonis fida ministra mei*); *Tristia* 3. 4. 40, *Amores* 1. 11. 27 are possibly relevant
too.
[42] Again, Bömer ad loc. for parallels.

artifice is involved than Juno's hope that the dreams would narrate what really happened (588) had suggested.[43] Iris holds that a dream which tells the truth is still just a convincing deception.[44] Her other remark supports this: dreams equal true shapes in their imitations.

Iris knows this because she has actually seen and moved aside some dreams which were in her way:

hunc circa passim varias imitantia formas
somnia vana iacent totidem, quot messis aristas . . .

(Met. 11. 613–14)

Around Sleep empty dreams lie scattered which imitate various shapes—as many as there are corn grains at harvest . . .

The resemblance of diction between these verses and Iris' remark at 626 must be significant. The messenger's eventual words to the recipient are again affected by what she noticed on the course of her mission.[45] In the manner of Homer's Iris (and Virgil's Mercury in *Aeneid* 4. 268–70), Iris ends her speech by putting a seal of divine authority on her words: Juno has ordered this—something which recalls Jupiter's closing statement in *Aeneid* 4. 237, quoted earlier. True to form, Iris departs swiftly, but this time feeling the sensation of sleep.[46] However, the chain of the message is not yet complete: Somnus passes on the instruction to Morpheus (647–8), but the narrator tells us nothing of what he says. It is clear, though, that Morpheus was told to adopt the form of Ceyx, which he soon does (653 f.). The 'true events' are then presented to Alcyone in her sleep by Morpheus–Ceyx in direct discourse (658–70): her prayers have been in vain, and she should not expect her husband's return. The content of the dream is then borne out by the discovery of Ceyx's corpse (710 f.).

The structure of this messenger scene is considerably more complicated than those of the others so far examined. But, in common with them, this episode can be seen to bear on the

[43] The sense of Juno's expression *veros narrantia casus* (588) is not completely clear: as well as 'recounting true events', it could be used in a looser sense to suggest the way an *enactment* or *picture* might narrate.
[44] This paradox is ironized by Ovid in 11. 666–8 discussed below, when Morpheus posing as Ceyx claims not to be an *ambiguus auctor*. The role of the (false) dream despatched from heaven in *Iliad* as a prototype for this scene will be discussed in Laird (forthcoming *c*).
[45] Compare *Aeneid* 4. 260–4 in relation to 4. 265–7.
[46] Compare the Oread's sensation of hunger after she was despatched to Fames, the god of hunger in *Met.* 8. 811–12.

nature of epic communication—or, more precisely, on the form epic communication takes in Ovid's *Metamorphoses*. Both the dictation speech and the delivery speech refer to, or re-present what has happened in the story: the shipwreck and the death of Ceyx. Both these speeches also combine to present and re-present what will happen next in the story: how Alcyone is to know of her husband's death. Of course the informing of Alcyone is also the end to which both these speeches are given. As was the case with the prototypical messenger scene from the *Song of Ullikummi*, this message is about a message. But here the situation is more complicated.

Juno, the speaker of the dictation speech, is also a dictator of events. A god or goddess in epic who rules in the story also has power over the ultimate shape of the narrative. No less than the poet who has narrated it, Juno knows the truth about Ceyx's death: this is the epic 'content' which we have already heard. As the most faithful mouthpiece of Juno (*fidissima nuntia vocis*), it is Iris' job to ensure that this truth is translated into epic form. And in being a conventional symbol (a messenger), Iris herself embodies that epic form. The real complication lies in the extent to which the *Metamorphoses* is an epic in the first place. This has been much discussed by critics.[47] A related issue, which has received more recent attention is the variety of ways in which Ovid's composition highlights its status as fiction.[48]

The elaborate structure of this sort of messenger scene illustrates paradigmatically the way Ovid's unusual techniques of fictional construction mediate the more traditional epic realm. There may be only one truth (*veros . . . casus*) in the epic story, but there are many forms into which it can be fashioned, as Iris is well aware (see 11. 613–14 quoted above). It is Morpheus who does this fashioning. He goes about it by speaking to Alcyone in the guise of her dead husband. In doing so, Morpheus shows himself to be as accomplished at outright lying as he is at weaving appropriate fictions:

[47] Critical literature on Ovid's *Met.* has been preoccupied with its relationship to Virgil (and thus to epic) since Heinze (1919): Wilkinson (1955), Otis (1964), Galinsky (1975) are major studies which engage with this question (cf. Solodow (1988), 110–56). Hinds (1987) is an important treatment. Sceglov (1969) is a neglected study of formal aspects of the poem. Further discussions will be found in P. Hardie (forthcoming).

[48] Feeney (1993) and (1991), 188–249, esp. 227 f.

... non haec tibi nuntiat auctor
ambiguus: non ista vagis rumoribus audis:
Ipse ego fata tibi praesens mea naufragus edo.

(*Met.* 11. 666–8)

It is not a polysemous author who announces these things to you: you are not hearing them from vague rumours. I myself, the very victim of the shipwreck, am present as I utter my fate to you.

Morpheus is only pretending to be the ghost of Ceyx, yet the account of Ceyx's death which he makes up conforms precisely to what is 'true' in the world of the story. Indeed Morpheus' fictional embedded narrative appears to impact on 'real' events: it could be his words which prompt Alcyone to walk by the seashore where she can discover Ceyx's corpse. This final link in the chain of speeches by which Juno communicates to Alcyone is explicitly signalled as being false and fictional. Yet Morpheus' speech influences what happens in the story. It also *re-presents* the 'official' story of Ceyx no less convincingly (and in greater detail) than the poet's presentation and the speeches of Juno and Iris. The irony of Morpheus' specific claim is that he—as Ceyx—is 'present' (*praesens*). This nicely allegorizes the problem of the 'metaphysics of presence': Morpheus highlights the paradox inherent in notions of 're-presentation'.[49]

This must cause us to question the status of those earlier dictation and delivery speeches—the traditional components of the messenger scene—as presentations of 'what happened'. Nonetheless this story still retains a 'message' in the technical sense. Here the notion of truth in epic is, in my view, championed rather than threatened: the allegory of this scene simply draws attention to the ultimate impossibility of discovering that truth, however faithfully Iris or any other interpreter may seek to pronounce it.

Ovid's account of Juno's dispatching of Iris to Romulus' wife Hersilia is in *Metamorphoses* 14. 829 ff. It shows a stylistic divergence from the practice of narrating the transmission of messages from gods to mortals so far examined:

---

[49] The post-structuralist critique of presence has been derived principally from Heidegger's *Being and Time*. Angelo Poliziano's use of *praesens* in *Ambra* 431 highlights this very issue—discussed at the end of my *Envoi* on representation and responsibility. On a related complexity, arising from a play on *praesens* in Apuleius' *Metamorphoses*, see Laird (1993), 168.

> flebat ut amissum coniunx, cum regia Iuno
> Irin ad Hersiliam descendere limite curvo
> imperat et vacuae sua sic mandata referre:
> 'o et de Latia, o et de gente Sabina
> praecipuum, matrona, decus, dignissima tanti
> ante fuisse viri, coniunx nunc esse Quirini
> siste tuos fletus et, si tibi cura videndi
> coniugis est, duce me lucum pete, colle Quirini
> qui viret et templum Romani regis obumbrat.'
> paret, et in terram pictos delapsa per arcus
> Hersilien iussis conpellat vocibus Iris.
>
> (*Met.* 14. 829 39)

His wife was mourning for him as lost, when royal Juno ordered Iris to go down her curved path to Hersilia and to bear her commands to the widow in this manner:

'You are the outstanding glory of both the Latin race and the Sabine race. O lady most worthy of so great a husband in the past, and of being the wife of Quirinus now, stop your weeping. If it is your wish to see your husband, let me lead you to the grove which grows on the Quirinal and shades the temple of the Roman king.'

Iris obeyed and, after descending to earth on her painted rainbow, she directed Hersilia with the words she was ordered to speak.

Here the message is quoted precisely in the form in which it is to be delivered to Hersilia: she is in fact addressed in the second person *before* Iris has gone down and encountered her. In the phrase *duce me* ('let me lead you') the first person pronoun clearly refers to Iris and not to Juno, as Hersilia's response will make clear (842). Thus the actual delivery speech as it is to be given by Iris appears, at least, to be dictated word for word by Juno. The occasion of Iris' delivery is here narrated in RSA. And it is evident, as indicated, that Hersilia's reply is to the very speech we had quoted in Juno's words: Hersilia enthusiastically takes up the messenger's offer to lead her to Romulus.

This is not the first instance of this kind in the *Metamorphoses*: Byblis' message to Caunus is quoted in full (9. 530–63), exactly as he will receive it. But that was because Byblis wrote her words directly to her brother in a letter; here that narrative technique is exceptionally applied to an orally transmitted message. The political importance of this particular message could explain this irregular practice. Juno, as goddess of the State, is anxious Iris delivers her words precisely because the deification of Romulus is important, not only for Hersilia, but for the Roman people as a whole. This variation of the customary motif for the messenger scene will also have a particular effect on Ovid's audiences and readers. They have a text of the message as it was dictated which exactly corresponds to the message that was delivered. The sense of certainty engineered here stands in contrast to the doubts generated about representation by Juno's earlier indirect communication to Alcyone. This contrast could enhance the solemn function of the message to Hersilia in the story of the poem. The last messenger scene in the *Thebaid*—to which we now turn—is also of profound political importance.

7.4 STATIUS, *THEBAID*[50]

The communication I shall consider from Statius' *Thebaid*, alone of those examined in this chapter, involves only mortals. However, this example has a very significant connection with the three prior occasions in the poem when messages are sent under divine direction.[51] Those scenes follow broadly the patterns we observed in the *Aeneid* and the *Metamorphoses*; and Statius, like Virgil, adopts a specific method of narration for messages dictated by gods.[52]

The scene I want to examine in detail comes at the climax of the

---

[50] On the *Thebaid* Lewis (1936), 48–56 and especially Vessey (1973) provide interesting overviews. Feeney (1991), 338 f. looks in detail at the gods in the poem and supplies much useful bibliography. On the end of the poem, see Hershkowitz (1995) as well as Braund (1996). Håkanson (1972–3) has important observations.

[51] Jupiter sends Mercury to Pluto, to ensure Laius' shade rouses Laius' grandson Eteocles to conflict (1. 285 f.); Jupiter sends Mercury to Mars (7. 5 f.); and Juno sends Iris to Somnus (10. 81 f.).

[52] Jupiter's dictation at 1. 285–302 is in DD. In that passage there are two deviations from Ovid's narrative technique. First the only delivery speech presented in any mode at all is Laius' to Eteocles. Prior to that speech we see Mercury escorting Laius' shade; so it is clear that Mercury has spoken both to Pluto and to the shade—not even RSA summaries of his words are provided. We have to rely on Jupiter's dictation speech at 1. 292–302 for the gist of them: his message to Eteocles is embedded within a message to Laius, within a message to Pluto. The second deviation is a difference from all the previous epic messenger scenes in that the transmission of the message is broken by a long digression. This is marked at 1. 312 by *interea* ('meanwhile'). Polyneices' fortunes are described, until the resumption of the messenger scene 400 verses later (again marked by *interea*) at 2. 1. Jupiter's second dispatching of Mercury—to Mars—involves a long dictation speech (7. 6–33). Significantly Mars speaks first in DD (77–80). Mercury's delivery of his message is recounted in RSA (81).

Thebaid. Theseus, in response to an appeal from Capaneus' wife, sends Phegeus to deliver a message to Creon, requesting the burial of the Argive soldiers. His dictation speech, in direct discourse, opens with a series of angry rhetorical questions directed to Creon. Theseus then asserts his readiness to continue killing for the sake of justice, before he ends by charging Phegeus with a terse message:

> Quaenam ista novos induxit Erinys
> regnorum mores? non haec ego pectora liqui
> Graiorum abscedens, Scythiam Pontumque nivalem
> cum peterem; novus unde furor? victumne putasti
> Thesea, dire Creon? adsum, nec sanguine fessum
> crede; sitit meritos etiamnum haec hasta cruores.
> nulla mora est; verte hunc adeo, fidissime Phegeu,
> cornipedem, et Tyrias invectus protinus arces
> aut Danais edice rogos, aut proelia Thebis.
>
> (*Thebaid* 12. 590–8)

What Fury has brought in these new rules for kings? I did not leave the Greeks in this spirit, when I left to seek Scythia and snowy Pontus—where does this new madness come from? Did you think Theseus was defeated, grim Creon? I am here, and do not think me weary of blood: even now this spear thirsts for justified slaughter. There will be no delay. So, most faithful Phegeus, turn this hard-hooved horse, ride straight to the Tyrian towers, and announce that if there are not burial pyres for the Danaans, there will be fighting for Thebes.

The actual dictation of the message is in a compact construction governed by *edice* ('announce'). The narrator presents its consequent delivery by Phegeus, in a combination of ID and RSA. This is not so much a rendition of what Theseus actually said, as a heralding of a conflict which has become inevitable, since Creon has persisted in ignoring Theseus' warning:

> ille quidem ramis insontis olivae
> pacificus, sed bella ciet bellumque minatur,
> grande fremens, nimiumque memor mandantis et ipsum
> iam prope, iam medios operire cohortibus agros
> ingeminans.
>
> (*Thebaid* 12. 682–6)

Phegeus may be a peacemaker with innocent olive branches, but he urges wars, and he threatens war as he rages loudly, and well remembering Theseus' command, cries out that he himself is already on the way, and that he is already covering with his forces the countryside en route.

The transmission of Theseus' message is narrated in a markedly different way from the transmissions of messages dictated by other mortals in the *Thebaid*. Those messages all shared a uniform pattern: Eteocles in his dictation speech to Polyneices (2. 415–51), Tydeus in his to Eteocles (2. 697–703), and Parthenopaeus to Atalanta (9. 885–907), all gave the actual content of their messages in the form of direct discourse within direct discourse—a *rhesis* within a *rhesis*. These dictated speeches-within-speeches cannot of course be facsimiles of any eventual delivery speeches (whether they turn out to be narrated or implied in the story) if the dictator speaks in the first person and the second person is used for the recipient of the message. The presence of the commissioned messenger would always influence the real delivery. The effect of the technique of the embedded message in the dictation speech is interesting. The audience and readers are given the benefit of hearing, along with the messenger, something beyond a dictation. There is an illusion, however much the story shows it to be false, of the sender actually addressing the recipient of his message face to face.

The dictation of Theseus, a mortal, is more akin to those of Jupiter in the *Thebaid*. The fact that Theseus does not formulate his message in a speech within a speech is the exception which proves the rule. It is clear that the Athenian king has a sudden role at the end of the poem as peacemaker. It is not surprising that he should speak in the fashion of a god.[53] The authority of his words is enough; they do not need to be memorized and dictated in an exact form. This analogy of Theseus with the Olympian need not only rest on the mechanics of speech presentation in this messenger scene. Some time ago Tillyard noted, 'both Athens and Theseus are symbolical: Athens of civilisation, Theseus of the governor who upholds laws and nations.'[54] More recently, Theseus has been cast as a Roman emperor—principally on account of his association with Clementia ('Clemency').[55] A more theological view of that

[53] Note how the structure of Theseus' speech—opening as it does with rhetorical questions and culminating in a cursory dictation—also resembles that of other Olympian dictations which follows the paradigm of Jupiter's speech to Mercury in *Aeneid* 4. 223–37. The vocative *fidissime* (12. 596) also recalls Jupiter's form of address to Mercury in Ovid *Met.* 2. 837, and Juno's address to Iris in *Met.* 11. 585 which was examined in the previous section.

[54] Tillyard (1954), 103. See also Vessey (1973), 314–15.

[55] Braund (1996), 9–13.

association may have prompted the identification of Theseus with the Christian God in the medieval treatise *Super Thebaidem* ('On the *Thebaid*'):[56]

Uxores vero regum id est affectiones humanae quae prius his regibus succubuerunt supplicantur Theseo id est deo; Theseus quasi theos suus. Theseus pugnat cum Creonte, quando humilitate docetur a deo vinci superbia; et vincitur Creon id est superbia nesciens humilitati resistere. Reges etiam sepeliuntur, quia humilitatis adventu omnis occasio elationis suffocatur. Tanto autem vitiorum conflictu Thebe id est humana anima quassata est quidem, sed divinae benignitatis clementia subveniente liberatur.

(*Super Thebaidem*, in Helm (1898), 186. 2–11)

The widows of the kings, that is, human feelings, which had before been subject to these kings, beseech Theseus, that is, God, for Theseus is *theos suus*. Theseus fights with Creon, as God teaches that pride is conquered by humility: Creon conquered stands for pride unable to resist humility. The kings are buried, because every occasion for pride is blocked by the arrival of humility. By such a struggle with vice was Thebes, that is, the soul of man left shattered; but it is freed when the grace of the goodness of God comes to its aid.

The comparison of Theseus with Jupiter at least, which is suggested by my reading of Theseus' role in the final messenger scene of the *Thebaid*, is also supported by an earlier simile (*Thebaid* 12. 650–5), in which the Athenian is explicitly compared to the divine monarch:[57]

> qualis Hyperboreos ubi nubilus institit axis
> Iuppiter et prima tremefecit sidera bruma,
> rumpitur Aeolia et longam indignata quietem
> tollit hiems animos ventosaque sibilat Arctos;
> tunc montes undaeque fremunt, tunc proelia caecis
> nubibus et tonitrus insanaque fulmina gaudent.
>
> (*Thebaid* 12. 650–5)

---

[56] Helm (1898), pp. xiv–xv, gives good grounds for not attributing the *Super Thebaidem* to Fulgentius, the allegorist of Virgil. See also Whitbread (1971) for a translation and discussion of this text. Whitbread at 235–7 argues for composition in the twelth or thirteenth century.

[57] Hershkowitz (1996), 63–4 looks briefly at this passage. The simile here could be read as a bizarre inversion of the simile in *Aeneid* 1. 148–54 (discussed in Feeney (1991), 137) where the god Neptune in calming a storm (of Aeolus' making) is compared to an anonymous human statesman who quells a riot.

Just as when cloudbearing Jupiter pressed on the Hyperborean poles and made the stars tremble with the first frost, Aeolia is broken and the storm, indignant at its long rest rouses its rage and windy Arctos hisses; then the mountains and the waves roar, then there is battle among the blind clouds, and the thunder and insane thunderbolts rejoice.

7.5 VALERIUS FLACCUS, *ARGONAUTICA*

It can no longer be maintained that the Roman *Argonautica* of Valerius Flaccus has been ignored or unfairly dismissed by critics.[58] However, the striking originality of the poem—which is still underplayed—largely consists in its innovations of epic form and style.[59] It is perhaps unsurprising, then, that Valerius conspicuously rings the changes on the epic messenger scene. In contrast to the poets already examined here, Valerius hardly ever narrates all the stages of a message's transmission.[60] The typically Hellenistic technique of 'syncopated narration' (in which some episodes of the story are copiously narrated, whilst others are treated very briefly, or even omitted) certainly seems to be applied to the treatments of messages in this poem.[61]

[58] Summers (1894), Schetter (1959) and Strand (1972) are general studies of the poem; Feeney (1991), 313–37 and Hardie (1993) are short but useful discussions. A monograph study by Hershkowitz, (1998), is important. For Valerius' speech presentation, the study of Eigler (1988) on the monologues is helpful with good further bibliography. There is however much more to look at in Valerius' speech presentation than his monologues, as even this brief treatment should show: see the notes to follow.

[59] Some examples: the *Argonautica* has an unusually dense pattern of sonic repetition (phonemic as well as verbal) in comparison with other Latin epics, which merits investigation; Valerius' similes though they have been studied, deviate significantly in tone and content from those in earlier epic; the technique of 'psycho-narration' displayed in the account of Medea's thoughts at 7. 101–54 is unique in epic, and outstanding in ancient narrative as a whole.

[60] The transmission of messages given by mortals in the *Argonautica* is never related in full. Perses' warning to the Minyae about Aeetes' deceit (6. 17–26) is one of the longest passages of ID in the poem. Gesander's speech to Canthus (6. 323–39) is dictated for purely rhetorical effect. Canthus of course cannot pass the message on, because Gesander promptly kills him! Again Jason in his speech (7. 89–100) uses the function of the dictation rhetorically, to make the point to Aeetes that if Jason dies, it will be because of his treachery.

[61] This remark calls for some statement about the relation of the speech presentation in Valerius' *Argonautica* to that in Apollonius. Here I confine myself to comparing the openings of the two epics. Invocations to Phoebus open both, and the oracles received by Pelias involve the use of ID by both poets. (Ap. 1. 5 f.; V. 1. 27). The conversation between Jason and Alcimede is in DD in

292 Allegories of Representation

One striking example of an omission is Jason's failure to deliver to Phrixus the message Helle, the sea goddess, dictated to him (at 2. 600). Helle appears (2. 587) and speaks to Jason (2. 591–612). Like her, she says, he has been driven eastwards by the Fates and a hostile household, and she prophesies a great land and long voyage ahead, before Phasis offers a port. This prompts more specific directions, and a request for Jason to perform rites for Phrixus' remains and to deliver her message.[62] That message is dictated in the form of an embedded speech, in the latter part of Helle's oration:

> '. . . hic nemus arcanum geminaeque virentibus arae
> stant tumulis; hic prima pia sollemnia Phrixo
> ferte manu cinerique, precor, mea reddite dicta:
> "non ego per Stygiae quod rere silentia ripae,
> frater, agor; frustra vacui scrutaris Averni,
> care, vias. neque enim scopulis me et fluctibus actam
> frangit hiems; celeri extemplo subiere ruentem
> Cymothoe Glaucusque manu; pater ipse profundi
> has etiam sedes, haec numine tradidit aequo
> regna nec Inois noster sinus invidet undis." '
>
> (*Argonautica* 2. 598–607)

'. . . In that place is a hidden glade and there stands a pair of altars with mounds of greenery: there perform with your own hand the first pious rites for Phrixus and pass on these words of mine to his ashes: "Brother, I am not driven, as you think, along the silent shore of the Styx; dear one, you are searching the paths of empty Avernus in vain. No storm breaks me driven over rocks and waves: Cymothoe and Glaucus came to my aid immediately as I fell; the lord of the deep himself entrusted this abode to me with his judicious authority, and our gulf does not envy the seas of Ino." '

Ap. (1. 277–305); in V. it is summarized in RSA at 1. 297 f. An interesting divergence concerns Idmon's words (Ap. 1. 430–77; V. 1. 234–8). In V., Idmon's premonition of his death is not spoken out loud as in Ap., but expressed as his private thought (1. 238–9). Cf. the ID preceding Hercules' speech in V. 2. 375–7, which is given entirely in DD in Ap. 1. 865–74. All we know in Ap. of Hercules's unspoken feelings is that he was left ἑκών ('willing') by the ship instead of having entered the city. Apollonius uses ID far less than Valerius. There are 150 clear instances in eight small books of Valerius' *Argonautica*. This compares with 130 in the *Thebaid*—a poem twice its length—and thirty in the *Aeneid*; (the use of ID in Lucan is minimal). Thus there is considerable flexibility in the use of speech modes in Valerius. None of V's messenger scenes have direct equivalents in Apollonius.

[62] For the detail of 598–9 *hic nemus . . . hic*, cf. the fuller ekphrasis in Ceres' directions to the Oread, *Met.* 8. 788 f.

In what she dictates, Helle uses the first person of herself, and refers to her brother in the second person.[63] Her dictated words have an epitaphic quality: since Helle cannot request her own burial, she has asked Jason to perform the appropriate rites for Phrixus' ashes instead.[64] Helle's words to Jason close with the ending of the announcement to her brother. The use of the embedded speech may explain the omission of any delivery of this message when Jason later prays to the shade of Phrixus at his shrine (5. 194–209): the delivery of Helle's words has already been prefigured for the poem's audience, and a repetition of this passage would disrupt the coherence of Jason's own prayer.

Although more explicit accounts of transmission do occur when Olympian gods dictate messages, there is still considerable variation in Valerius' narrative technique. For example, the whole account of Jupiter's command to Iris, exhorting Hercules to delay his revenge on Troy and rescue Prometheus is compressed into four verses:

> 'i, Phrygas Alcides et Troiae differat arma.
> nunc' ait 'eripiat dirae Titana volucri.'
> diva volat defertque viro celeranda parentis
> imperia atque alacrem laetis hortatibus implet.'
> (*Argonautica* 4. 78–81)

'Go, let Hercules put off the Phrygians and the war of Troy' he said. 'Let him now snatch Prometheus from the grim bird.' The goddess flies down and bears to the hero his father's urgent instructions and fills his keen spirit with happy encouragement.

There is no further rendering of Jupiter's words. However that commission had been prompted by an appeal from

---

[63] Juno's dictation to Iris for Hersilia in *Met.* 14. 829 parallels this address to the recipient in the second person, but that seems to be dictated exactly as it will be performed.

[64] For examples of epitaphs, see Lattimore (1942). *Argonautica* 2. 600–6 can be compared with Propertius 2. 26A: Cynthia in Propertius' dream almost suffers a fate like Helle's: *me et fluctibus actam* here recalls *agitatam fluctibus Hellen* (2. 26. 5). Valerius' Helle describes the intervention of Glaucus and Cymothoe, which Propertius fears may affect Cynthia (1. 26. 13 f. *quod si . . . Glaucus . . . caerula Cymothoe*). The particular association of Helle with Glaucus and Cymothoe does not occur elsewhere, and the incident is not in Apollonius. Orpheus' reported poem about Phrixus and Helle at *Arg.* 1. 277 has already recalled imagery from the first twelve verses of the Propertius elegy. Summers (1894), 37 notes some minor echoes of Propertius in Valerius. On the colouring of elegy (and other genres) in Valerius' epic, see Feeney (1991), 322.

Apollo, reinforced by cries from Prometheus and Iapetus (4. 62–75).[65]

Later on, Juno's command to Iris, which is also issued after a conversation among divinities, provides yet another pattern of narration:

> volucrem tunc aspicit Irin
> festinamque iubet monitis parere Diones
> et iuvenem Aesonium praedicto sistere luco.
>
> (*Argonautica* 7. 186–8)

Then Juno sees winged Iris and orders her to swiftly obey Dione's command and bring the son of Aeson to the appointed grove.

It was Venus who, in her desire to accomplish a union between Jason and Medea, had earlier asked Juno to make Jason go to Diana's shrine (7. 179–81). So while Iris promptly goes to seek the Minyae to look for Jason, Venus looks for Medea. The *Iliad* (24. 74 f.) provides a precedent for two divine errands being transmitted simultaneously. In Valerius' poem it is clear by implication that both of these errands are completed. Venus' work on Medea is related immediately, as a *novus languor* takes over the girl. The meeting of Medea and Jason later (7. 396) shows that Iris has performed her mission, before the description of her flying away (7. 398–9).

As part of her design, Venus herself, disguised as Circe, speaks to Medea and passes on to her a fictitious message from Jason. Venus' presentation of the message itself is in direct discourse—the form in which it would have been dictated, had it really been uttered, by Jason:

> 'per tibi siquis', ait 'morituri protinus horror
> et quem non meritis videas occurrere monstris,
> haec, precor, haec dominae referas ad virginis aurem
> tu fletus ostende meos; illi has ego voces,
> qua datur, hasque manus, ut possum, a litore tendo.
> ipsae, quas mecum per mille pericula traxi,
> defecere deae. spes et via sola salutis
> quam dederit, si forte dabit. ne vota repellat,
> ne mea, totque animas, quales nec viderit ultra,
> dic, precor, auxilio iuvet atque haec nomina servet.
> ei mihi, quod nullas hic possum exsolvere grates!

---

[65] Compare Iarbas' prompt to Jupiter in *Aen.* 4. 198 f.

at tamen hoc saeva corpus de morte receptum,
hanc animam sciat esse suam. miserebitur ergo?
dic', ait 'an potius'—strictumque ruebat in ensem.
promisi; ne falle, precor cumque ipsa moverer
adloquio casuque viri, te passa rogari
sum potius: tu laude nova, tu supplice digno
dignior es; et fama meis iam parta venenis . . .

(*Argonautica* 7. 266–83)

'If you feel any fear' he said 'for someone who is about to die and whom you see is running into undeserved horrors, please take this message to the ear of the young woman who is your mistress. You present my grief to her—from this shore, as far as I can, I proffer to her these words and these outstretched hands of mine in whatever way I may. Those very goddesses whom I brought with me through a thousand dangers have failed me. My hope and only way of safety is what she will provide—if she will. Let her not reject my prayers, and tell her, please, to grant her help to all these lives she will never see, and to preserve these names. Alas—here I can pay no debt of thanks, but let her know that this body saved from a cruel death, this soul is hers. Will she feel pity then? Tell me', he said, 'or else . . .' and he was about to fall on his drawn sword. I gave my promise. Do not fail him, I beg you. And though I myself was moved by this man's appeal and plight, I preferred to have you receive his prayer: you are more deserving of new glory and a worthy suppliant, as my fame is already established by my drugs . . .

The message with all its vivid detail is meant to appear all the more credible to the girl. The speech takes the form of a suppliant's prayer. Having heard it directly, Medea can then feel empowered to grant the request after Venus–Circe has said that she chose to allow Medea to be the recipient of the prayer (281–2). The goddess not only plays on Medea's anxieties about Jason's life expressed earlier (7. 205–9), but adds further emotional spice by providing a melodramatic account of the hero's suicide attempt. The ruse will turn out to be effective: Medea in her speech to Jason (7. 437 f.) picks up the claim she believes he made in this message, that Juno and Minerva have abandoned him (271) so that she alone is left to help. Although the speech attributed to Jason is false, it might, like the embedded speeches examined above, allow the poem's audience to enjoy the 'virtual reality' effect of such an appeal from Jason to Medea.

Valerius' messenger scenes possess two stylistic features which also occur in the contemporary *Thebaid*: the embedded speech (2. 600), and a scene break in the execution of a god-sent commission

(7. 193–396). Neither feature occurs in the *Aeneid*. Embedded speeches occur only twice in Ovid's *Metamorphoses*: in those cases, as I have shown, they are demanded by the context of the story. The *Argonautica*, in common with the *Aeneid* and *Thebaid*, maintains a distinction between the way messages dictated by gods and the messages dictated by humans are narrated. This distinction is engineered simply by the presentation of all the stages of the commissions of Jupiter and Juno in full. Messages sent by mortals (and Helle), provide either a dictation or a delivery speech, but never the whole sequence.

7.6 JOHN MILTON, *PARADISE LOST*

The divine messenger scene has an especially important role in *Paradise Lost* (1667), because the relationship between God and man is a central theme of the poem.[66] Whilst the narrative of *Paradise Lost* postdates the other poems considered here, its story is set in a time supposed to precede the mythical ages evoked by Graeco-Roman epic. This allows the narrator to offer an 'aetiology', or fictional explanation, for the protocol of the messenger convention in classical poetry. That aetiology is provided by the particular transformation of the convention in Milton's vernacular epic: the three messenger scenes examined here can be read as a commentary on the examples from Latin poetry reviewed above.

The message from God to Adam in Book 5 is fundamental to the narrative structure of the poem. Here God instructs the angel Raphael to inform Adam of his position and to warn him of the evil which threatens him:

> 'Raphael,' said he, 'thou hear'st what stir on earth
> Satan from hell scaped through the darksome gulf
> Hath raised in Paradise, and how disturbed
> This night the human pair, how he designs
> In them at once to ruin all mankind.
> Go therefore, half this day as friend with friend
> Converse with Adam, in what bower or shade

[66] A. Fowler (1971) is the most useful edition, with a commentary, and bibliography at 643–50. Ferry (1963) treats the narrative of *Paradise Lost*; Norbrook (1984) and Quint (1993) consider various political and ideological dimensions of the poem. Lewis (1942; 1951), and Tillyard (1954) still contain important studies of Milton in relation to classical epic. For a study of Milton's messenger scene in its tradition, see again T. Greene (1963).

Thou find'st him from the heat of noon retired,
To respite his day-labour with repast,
Or with repose; and such discourse bring on,
As may advise him of his happy state,
Happiness in his power left free to will,
Left to his own free will, his will though free,
Yet mutable; whence warn him to beware
He swerve not too secure: tell him withal
His danger, and from whom, what enemy
Late fallen himself from heaven, is plotting now
The fall of others from like state of bliss;
By violence, no, for that shall be withstood,
But by deceit and lies; this let him know,
Lest wilfully transgressing he pretend
Surprisal, unadmonished, unforewarned.'
So spake the eternal Father . . .

(*PL* 5. 224–46[67])

This is not a 'dictation speech' in the sense that the commands issued to divine messengers have been in Virgil, Ovid, Statius, Valerius, and Sannazaro. Milton's 'eternal Father' conveys to Raphael the tenor of the message he is to deliver, rather than any text of it. Indeed, the informality of this communication is signalled by its own author: he asks Raphael to 'converse' with Adam 'half this day as friend with friend' (229–30).[68] The execution of these instructions is indeed leisurely: the half day the angel spends in conversation with Adam is sustained from 5. 361 until the end of Book 8, occupying over a quarter of the poem's narrative.

Certain formulae here recall the presentation of divine dictations in the epics reviewed so far. Raphael's journey to earth in which he is compared to a bird (this time a phoenix) also recalls the accounts in Milton's Latin models. However, the manner in which the angel's arrival in Eden is narrated is quite unprecedented in Latin literature:

Him through the spicy forest onward come
Adam discerned, as in the door he sat
Of his cool bower . . .

(*PL* 5. 298–300)

[67] The text used is that of A. Fowler (1971). (The quotation marks to punctuate the instances of DD are my own.)
[68] A. Fowler (1971), 270 cites *Exodus* 33. 11: 'The Lord spake unto Moses face to face, as a man speaketh unto his friend.'

Remarkably the narration of the final stage of the heavenly messenger's arrival is focalized through a mortal, and *not* (as is usual) through the divine messenger. The way in which the ensuing exchange of speech is presented is also without precedent in the Latin epics we have considered. For it is Adam, the intended recipient of the message, not Raphael, who is the first to come forward and speak:

> Mean while our primitive great sire, to meet
> His godlike guest, walks forth . . .
> Nearer his presence Adam though not awed,
> Yet with all submiss approach and reverence meek,
> As to a superior nature, bowing low,
> > Thus said. 'Native of heaven, for other place
> None can than heaven such glorious shape contain . . .
> > > (*PL* 5. 350–1, 358–62)

This is very unusual. In ancient poetry, as we have seen, the divine messenger is typically the first to speak. If the recipients of such messages speak at all, it is only after the delivery speech has been given. In ancient literature there is one conspicuous exception to this general practice. Milton's deviation from the standard protocol for this kind of scene could be significant because it recalls this exception. That exception is to be found in the fifth book of Homer's *Odyssey*, where Hermes delivers a message from Zeus to Calypso. Zeus' dictation speech (5. 29–42) had given quite precisely the words to be conveyed to her. But when Hermes reaches Calypso, it is she who is in fact the first to speak and it is not until he has finished his meal that Hermes replies to her question. This informality could in part be due to the fact that Hermes and Calypso are more or less level pegging: one god is speaking to another.[69]

By following this singular pattern of speech exchange between divine messenger and addressee in the *Odyssey*, the narrative of *Paradise Lost* at this point in Book 5 could be suggesting that the interaction between Raphael and Adam is of a similar kind. Whilst

---

[69] It might also be due to Hermes' need to be tactful. His DD delivery of Zeus' words is at first circumspect. He insists the mission is against his will (cf. Iris to Boreas and Zephyr, *Il.* 23. 200 f.). Zeus' request is presented in two pieces of ID (105, 112) separated by a digressive passage relating Odysseus' fortunes. Apart from the basic request there is little resembling Zeus' actual order and much that is new. There is a far looser connection between the dictation and delivery of this message than there is in the messenger scenes in the *Iliad*.

Adam's status is not as high as the angel's, he can converse with him on a basically equal footing: as Milton says, he is 'not awed'. The identification of a parallel between the relaxed nature of this celestial communication to Adam before the Fall and the communication to Calypso can be supported on independent criteria. First, the vivid account of Raphael's descent recalls that of Homer's Hermes no less than those of Virgil's Mercury or Sannazaro's Gabriel. Secondly, Raphael is specifically compared to the Olympian messenger:

> . . . Like Maia's son he stood,
> And shook his plumes, that heavenly fragrance filled
> The circuit wide.
>
> (*PL* 5. 285–7)

The second transformation of the convention in *Paradise Lost* is a reversal of it. At the end of Book 10, Adam and Eve, who are now aware of their fallen condition pray for God's forgiveness (10. 1100–4). The progress of their prayers is described at the beginning of the next book. The Son of God here acts as a messenger from earth to heaven and asks his Father to be allowed to 'interpret' for Adam (11. 33). Milton's use of this word recalls the characterization of the divine messenger in both Sannazaro and Virgil as *interpres*.[70]

However, the traditional mechanics of the messenger scene are restored in the eleventh book of the poem. The angel Michael, dispatched by God to remove Adam and Eve from Paradise, now speaks first:

> Adam bowed low, he [Michael] kingly from his state
> Inclined not, but his coming thus declared.
> 'Adam, heaven's high behest no preface needs . . .'
>
> (*PL* 11. 249–51)

Adam is deeply affected by the messenger's words:

> He added not, for Adam at the news
> Heart-shook with chilling gripe of sorrow stood,
> That all his senses bound . . .
>
> (*PL* 11. 263–5)

This response recalls Aeneas' stupefication at the apparition of Mercury (*Aeneid* 2. 279–80) which we also saw echoed in Sannazaro's account of the virgin's response to the divine message she

---

[70] See *Aen.* 4. 356–9 quoted in n. 37 above.

received. The restoration of the traditional mechanics of the epic
convention heralds, at this closing part of the poem, the establish-
ment of a new hierarchy in which humans are more markedly
subordinate to immortals. The events narrated in *Paradise Lost*
long precede the stories of the pagan epics. It is in this way that
Milton offers his aetiology of the power dynamics of the messenger
scene in ancient poetry: the circumstances of the Fall explain why it
was to become the custom for divine messengers to speak first to
their human addressees. As we have seen in other contexts,
authority is both indicated and in part constituted by the right or
disposition to speak first.

The messenger scenes in *Paradise Lost* also support another
general conclusion which was drawn from my examination of
previous examples of the convention. It was held earlier that
messenger scenes exhibit a reflexive concern with speech, language,
narration and meaning, and that—in the epic genre—these scenes
can indeed be regarded as a kind of *mise-en-abyme* for the poem in
which they appear. This is very clearly the case in *Paradise Lost*.
The discourse Raphael has with Adam which takes up the greater
part of Books 5–8 is the centrepiece of Milton's poem. Whilst it is
framed by the 'admonitions' to Adam which were the purpose of
the angel's descent from heaven, Raphael's accounts all present or
re-present themes which are of fundamental importance to the
poem as a whole.

7.7 PAN IN PLATO'S *CRATYLUS* AND VIRGIL'S FAMA

The association between appeals to Muses and the production of
poetry with the convention of the messenger scene in epic remains
to be explored in greater depth.[71] Here a brief account of what that
association might reveal will suffice. Muses are goddess; epic poets
(incarnated either as rhapsodes or literary authors) are human with
divine qualities. The audiences of epic poems are human *tout court*.
The epic genre repeatedly presents us with a paradigm for the
process of divine → mortal communication in the convention of the
divine messenger scene in which a celestial deity communicates to

[71] I will cover some of this ground in an essay on metafiction and the ontology of
the epic muse in Laird (forthcoming c).

mortals through a divine messenger or angel. These messenger scenes could be seen as a metafictional paradigm for the process of epic communication itself, according to the following correspondence:

God   →   Messenger   →   Mortal
Muse   →   Epic Poet   →   Audience

Just as the original words of the gods who dictate the messages are inaccessible to the mortals on the end of the chain of messages, so the discourse of the Muses is lost to the audience.[72] The epic text itself can be seen to function as a kind of delivery speech.

The argument in this chapter may well appear circular. Having asserted that messenger scenes exhibit a reflexive preoccupation with speech, language, narration, and meaning, it could be claimed I have interpreted the messenger scenes reviewed here in a particular way, in order to illustrate this assertion. To counter any such claim, I shall produce one more passage which helps to make an independent case for the importance of the messenger scene as an allegory of discursive representation. This is from Plato's *Cratylus*. Socrates is in conversation with Hermogenes who believes that language is a matter of convention. Socrates is trying to show that name-giving, like any other art, requires technical knowledge. Names are formed by composition from other words and were originally conferred by 'lawgivers' who had the appropriate knowledge to do this. In the passage I am concerned with, Socrates replies to Hermogenes, who, prompted by curiosity about his own name, has asked Socrates to examine the name of Hermes:

Well then this name 'Hermes' seems to me to have to do with speech; he is an interpreter (ἑρμηνέα) and a messenger, is wily and deceptive in speech, and is oratorical. All this activity is concerned with the power of speech. Now, as I said before εἴρειν denotes the use of speech; moreover, Homer

---

[72] The invocation of the Muses before the Catalogue of Ships in *Iliad* 2. 484 illustrates this: Homer addresses the Muses as being present and knowing all things, whereas mortals, he says, have heard only a report (κλέος) and know nothing. Homer's poem can only be an inadequate reproduction of what the Muses know (pointing to that knowledge, as the formulaic repetition of 2. 484 in the *Iliad* does on three separate occasions) but never a comprehensive communication of it. So the *Iliad* itself is rather like the delivery speech in a messenger scene—and hence a symbolic discourse which conveys x by means of y where x is greater than y. This is a weak definition of allegory with which most ancient and modern accounts would easily harmonise.

often uses the word ἐμήσατό, which means 'contrive'. From these two words, then, the lawgiver imposes upon us the name of the god who contrived speech and the use of speech—εἴρειν means 'speak'—and tells us: 'Ye human beings, he who *contrived speech* (εἴρειν ἐμήσατο) ought to be called Eiremes by you.' We, however, have beautified the name as we imagine, and call him Hermes. Iris also seems to have got her name from ἔιρειν, because she is a messenger.

(Cratylus 408a–b)

Thus Plato provides etymologies and allegorizations for both Hermes and Iris, who happen to be the standard messsengers of the Olympian gods in the *Iliad* and the *Odyssey*. But the fact that Homer is not explicitly mentioned at least means that nobody can accuse Socrates of attaching inappropriately alien meanings to those texts. Socrates is talking about language, not poetry. If his lawgiver imposed names prior to the usage Socrates claims to correct, then it follows that Socrates is holding that these allegorical etymologies are pre-Homeric. But what is a greater concern as we turn to Latin epic, is that these observations in the *Cratylus* have been articulated, given currency, and probably in some form mediated to Roman poets.[73] Such a view of language, though unusual in antiquity, could in particular influence the reception of Homeric messenger scenes, and it will be no surprise to find Roman epic poetry engaging with it in some way.

What Socrates goes on to say seems to touch on the nature of poetry:

Soc.: You know that speech *signifies all things* (πᾶν σημαίνει) and always makes them circulate and move about, and is twofold, true and false.

HERM.: *Certainly* (Πάνυ γε)

Soc.: Well the true part is smooth and divine and dwells aloft among the gods, but falsehood dwells below among common men, is rough and like the *tragic goat* (τραγικόν); for tales and falsehoods are most at home there *in the tragic, goatish life* (περὶ τὸν τραγικὸν βίον)

HERM.: *Certainly* (Πάνυ γε)

Soc.: Then Pan, who declares and *always moves* (ἀεὶ πολῶν) all, is rightly called *goat-herd* (αἰπόλος), being the double-natured son of Hermes,

---

[73] Peter Parsons informs me that one papyrus of Plato's *Cratylus* has emerged from Oxyrhynchus. It is difficult to make statistical conjectures about the relative popularity of a text on this basis, but the fact the *maximum* survival rate of papyri is estimated at 0.001 per cent at least suggests that this dialogue had some currency in Hellenistic culture. See Krüger (1990) for an assessment of published literary texts from Oxyrhynchus.

smooth in his upper parts, rough and goat-like in his lower parts. And
Pan, if he is the son of Hermes, is either speech or the brother of speech,
and that brother resembles brother is not at all suprising.

(*Cratylus* 408c–d)

Here speech is seen partly as a vehicle of meaning, and partly as a
mover and a shaker. It is also notable that speech is visually
characterized first simply as something vertical reaching from
heaven down to earth. But before this image is fully developed
into the figure of Pan, Socrates exploits the two senses of *tragikon* as
both 'tragic' and 'goatish' to fuse the notion of the false poetic
muthoi with the crude, misleading nature of mortal speech as a
whole.

This excerpt from the *Cratylus* points to a clear relation between
the transmission of divine messages and the business of verbal
communication in general. It is very comparable to Virgil's
description of the parentage and physical form of Fama which
has challenged commentators for a long time:

ingrediturque solo et caput inter nubila condit.
illam Terra parens ira inritata deorum
extremam, ut perhibent, Coeo Enceladoque sororem
progenuit pedibus celerem et pernicibus alis,
monstrum horrendum ingens, cui quot sunt corpore plumae,
tot vigiles oculi subter (mirabile dictu),
tot linguae, totidem ora sonant, tot subrigit auris.

(*Aeneid* 4. 177–83)

She advances on the ground and hides her head among the clouds. Mother
Earth bore her as a last daughter in rage against the gods, so they say, a
sister for Coeus and Enceladus, swift on her feet and on her quick wings, a
huge and horrible monster, and, as numerous as the feathers on her body,
are the vigilant eyes underneath her—strange to tell!—as numerous are the
tongues, so many mouths that sound and so many ears, always pricked.

For example, Page wrote in 1894, 'it is impossible to express many
abstract qualities in a physical form . . . while we can conceive
Rumour as a bird and also conceive a bird with an eye on every
feather yet the conception of a bird with an equal number of
tongues and ears becomes ludicrous.'[74] 'Servius' tries to be more
sympathetic, explaining that this description is not *narratio* but

[74] T. E. Page (1894), 358.

argumentatio. Indeed, he says, 'a monster who would be of this nature would keep busy as many eyes, tongues and ears as she has feathers'.[75] 'Servius' also says *subter* ('under') is an adverb, indicating these numerous eyes and tongues are not under the feathers specifically, but under Fama herself.[76]

These remarks have prompted an important observation by a modern scholar—that the 'eyes, tongues, mouths and ears belong, not to the underside of Fama's body, but to those who are prying and gossiping on earth as she flies above'.[77] This usefully alerts us to a subtle feature of Virgil's figure which constrictions of translation incline us to ignore. Fama walks on the ground with her head in the clouds; she also flies above the organs of perception and communication which may or may not constitute her. The figure is thus in possession of at least two kinds of physical attributes which are clearly distinct, if not contrary to each other.[78] There is a remarkable similarity between the image of Fama, (interpreted as incorporating the chattering inhabitants of earth) and Socrates' iconization of speech as Pan in the *Cratylus*. Like Virgil's Fama, Pan has a body which stretches from heaven to earth; he too moves about and blends truth with falsity. Needless to say that image of Pan, like Fama, is not consistently or easily visualizable either. The image of Pan's rough lower parts, like Fama's underside, dissolves into a symbol of false terrestrial discourses which appear to include poetry and stories. Fama too, as we have already seen, has a connection with poetry and stories: 'Servius'' remark on *ut perhibent* ('so they say') in line 179 shows at least that he sees the significance of this figure of allegory for Virgil's own discourse:

---

[75] 'Servius' on 4. 181: *et quod eam describit, non est narratio sed argumentatio. quidni monstrum quae huius naturae sit ut quot plumas, tot oculos, tot linguas, tot aures, et cetera?*

[76] 'Servius' on 4. 182: *OCVLI SUBTER adverbium est, ac si diceret 'non sub plumis, sed sub ipsa'.*

[77] Dyer (1989), 29

[78] Imagery which is not consistently or easily visualizable—what Nuttall (1967), 63 calls 'unspecified images' in a study of Shakespeare's allegory—is a general feature of Virgil's style. Furbank (1970), 16–22 counters Nuttall's position. A full modern study of Virgil's style (incorporating imagery) is still needed: O'Hara (1997), 257–8 gives useful bibliography.

quotienscumque fabulosum aliquid dicit, solet inferre 'fama est'. mire ergo modo, cum de ipsa fama loqueretur, ait 'ut perhibent'.

Whenever the poet states something of a mythical nature, he usually brings in the phrase *fama est*. So it is marvellous that just when he is talking about Fama herself, he says 'so they say'.

Both Fama and Pan underline a major argument of this chapter: the divine messengers in epic who convey information (or misinformation) to mortals and the very poems in which they appear are connected. Indeed it could be argued that messenger scenes recur so frequently in the epic genre simply *because* this motif involving dictation and delivery recalls the ways in which epic poems are composed and transmitted.

The preceding surveys of exemplary passages show significant divergences as well as similarities from one poem to another, and, as noted at the beginning, the various deployments of speech modes in these scenes can help us to form precise stylistic profiles of different poets. But the consideration of these various instances of the messenger scene has grander implications. The interactions between first speaker, messenger, and audience bring together many of the facets of speech presentation which I have attempted to present discretely in previous chapters. Messenger scenes in every case display the relationship between speech and power. They clearly illustrate the way speech presented in a narrative can itself be a form of narrative, as dictation and delivery speeches provide in themselves flashes forward and flashbacks of events in the story. By the same token, messenger scenes suggest that the narratives in which they appear also function as speeches. Messenger scenes always report the report of a report. Discourse uses discourse to present discourse. This prompts some speculation, in the concluding section to follow, on the nature of narratival 'representation' as a whole: how far does it really differ from speech presentation?

8

Conclusions and *Envoi*:
Representation and Responsibility

The value of fragments of thought is all the greater the less direct their relationship to the underlying idea, and the brilliance of the representation depends as much on this value as the brilliance of the mosaic does on the value of the glass paste. The relationship between the minute precision of the work and the proportions of the sculptural or intellectual whole demonstrates that truth-content is only to be grasped through immersion in the most minute details of subject-matter.

> (Walter Benjamin, *The Origin of German Tragic Drama*)

Guevara said to me once: 'Are we Marxists? I don't know at all.' And then he added, with a smile: 'It's not our fault if *reality* is Marxist.'

> (Jean-Paul Sartre, *The Burgos Trial*)

The conceptions of poetry and representation in Plato and Aristotle continue to influence speculations on the nature of discourse. However, the particular value Plato and his successors in antiquity attached to speech presentation has been largely ignored by modern theorists of language and literature. I have sought to respond to this oversight—to show that employment of various modes of direct and indirect discourse is by no means an isolated aspect of grammar or poetics, and to show that speech presentation has important epistemic, ethical and political dimensions.

The central conclusions to emerge from this study are as follows:

1 Study of speech presentation exposes the relations between discourse and power which are at work in all kinds of texts.
2. The very form of speech presentation is ideological (in the traditional sense of the term). The relation between a narrator and the discourse of others presented by that narrator is ideo-

logical, because that relation determines—and is determined by—the nature of the relation between a text and its reader or audience.

3. Speech presentation is comparable to, if not ultimately identifiable with, intertextuality. Both are concerned with 'quotation', or the perception of a text changing tenor, owing to the intrusion of another voice or text. Like speech presentation, intertextuality is ideological: the relation between a text and its intertext also determines, and is determined by, the nature of the relation between that text and its reader or audience.

4. The pragmatic and semantic function of specific speech modes within a text have a major bearing on the pragmatic and semantic functions of the whole text in which they appear.

5. Speech presentation contributes to the determination of the genre of a text. The simple presence or absence of speech presentation in a text—as well as the permutations and combinations of specific speech modes deployed in that text—can serve as a register of genre.

The question of the general nature of representation bears on all these conclusions. Representation is ideological. From the beginning of this enquiry it has been clear that no narrative can ever represent a state of affairs neutrally. However comprehensive or disinterested a writer or speaker sets out to be, the account produced cannot fail to be angled, selective, and partial. This is because of the inevitable determinations of omission, closure, provenance, and genre. Indeed representation can be conceived in terms of genre. Every kind of discourse presents reality its own way—for example, epic and the modern 'realist' novel are bound to configure the world in different fashions.

The relationship between representation in general and speech presentation as a specific feature of narrative texts has been lurking on the edges of this whole enquiry, and merits specific discussion. That relationship could first be seen in terms of *contiguity*: speech presentation simply occurs in the vicinity or context of narrative representation. Second, the relationship could be seen in terms of *resemblance*. A representation in the general sense, like a narrative, copies, or rather constructs, its object; speech presentation within a narrative copies or constructs its own object (the supposed or original words or thoughts of a personage) in a similar way.

Third, this relationship can also be seen in terms of *causation*: speech presentation, the presentation of somebody's discourse, is what brings about narrative representation—the narrator is always a speaker. A narrative is, *ipso facto,* a presentation of the narrator's discourse. Jakobson some time ago discerned a connection between poetic language and speech presentation.[1] Fourth, and more problematically, the relationship can be seen as one of *analogy*, if not *allegory*. There is a correlation between indirect discourse and narrative on the one hand, and between direct discourse and story on the other.[2] But direct discourse, though it may correspond with the level of story, cannot be equated with 'what was actually said'. The correspondence between direct discourse and 'story' is as theoretical as the notion of story itself. Direct discourse is also a form of narration.

Finally, one could go so far as to regard the relationship between speech presentation and discursive representation in general as one of *identity*. This possibility was raised tentatively at the very end of the last chapter and was argued for historical discourse at the end of Chapter 4. Such a position has been reached (though not always by the laborious route taken here) in contemporary theory and philosophy. Deleuze, for instance, holds that *all* discourse is indirect discourse—his sense of 'indirect discourse' seems to correspond to Bakhtin's 'dialogism', which, as we saw, was reconceived by Kristeva as 'intertextuality'.[3] Every utterance or narrative conveys traces and echoes of previous utterances and narratives. Derrida too has maintained that all language quotes other language, establishing a kind of infinite regress.[4] From these 'citationalist' perspectives, it has been remarked that all language could become, 'in operation if not in grammatical form—a kind of free indirect discourse'.[5]

---

[1] Jakobson (1960), 371: 'Virtually any poetic message is a quasi-quoted discourse with all those peculiar, intricate problems which "speech within speech" offers to the linguist.'

[2] Ch. 2 showed how Plato illustrates this analogy with the narrative techniques employed in the relation of the Myth of Er in Book 10 of the *Republic,* and at the beginning of the *Symposium.* The *Theaetetus* made it clear that there is a catch: Eucleides said he *constructed* his dialogue in direct discourse from Socrates' account. Ch. 7 showed how speech presentation (in the messenger scene at least) can function as an allegory of narratival representation.

[3] Deleuze and Guattari (1975), 95–109; Deleuze (1980) and (1983) are discussed in Maclean (1988), 150f.

[4] Derrida (1967), (1977*a*), (1977*b*).   [5] Rimmon-Kenan (1983), 115–17.

Ancient theories of poetry and discourse—or at least some of their implications—may not be so far away from positions like this. We saw that the term *mimesis* in Plato's *Republic* denoted 'imitation' in direct discourse, as well as imitation or representation in the general sense. Modern commentators all point out this dual significance of the notion of *mimesis*, which also creeps into Aristotle's *Poetics*.[6] But this apparent awkwardness in Plato's terminology has some point to it—if we accept that language can only represent or imitate the world by representing or imitating previous utterances. In this respect, the relation between representation and represented, between language and object can shift from degrees of divergence to complete identity. In a way, Plato's conception of *mimesis* in the *Cratylus* (which is curiously absent in Aristotle's *Poetics*) shows this no less effectively than modern speech act theory: a word is a vocal imitation (μίμημα φωνῇ) of the object it denotes, whether the word is a conventional symbol or whether it has an intrinsic connection with what it denotes.[7] Moreover, some playful devices in Plato's dialogues highlight ironically the problems of reflexivity that are involved when one uses discourse to talk about discourse.[8]

Later rhetorical conceptions of *mimesis* (*imitatio* in Latin) as the imitation of models became pervasive in ancient theory and practice of literary composition. Classicists tend to be reticent about the actual connections between the imitation of models and the predominantly Platonic–Aristotelian conception of *mimesis* as a semantic function.[9] It should now be clear that the study of speech

[6] In *Poetics* 1460ª8, Aristotle uses the cognate noun *mimētēs* in a way that presupposes Plato's restricted sense of *mimesis* as direct discourse. Halliwell (1987), 77–8 and (1986), 128 n. 34 looks at the precise way Aristotle's terminology differs from Plato's and his shifting conception of epic as *mimesis*.

[7] *Cratylus* 423b f. Lucas (1968), 263 n. 3 (in an Appendix on *mimesis*) compares Aristotle, *Rhetoric* 1404ª20.

[8] The most celebrated example of this reflexivity is the discussion in Plato, *Phaedrus* 274 of the inferiority of written to spoken words. This is itself presented in a written text. (Compare the first epigraph to Ch. 3). Two other examples have been excerpted in Chs. 2 and 7 respectively: Socrates' condemnation of writers who omit 'passages between speeches' in a piece of dialogue where Plato does this very thing (*Republic* 394b–c) and the mischievous punning on *pan* and *panu* in Greek, in a discussion of how speech pertains to *all* things (*Cratylus* 408c–d).

[9] See e.g. the recent article on *imitatio* in the *OCD*³, 749 where the various senses of *imitatio/mimesis* are defined, but no attempt is made to explain the connections between them. I shall explore the connections more fully in a forthcoming study of representation and transcendence in Apuleius' philosophical and literary writing.

presentation and consideration of contemporary notions of 'citationality' helps explain the connection between *mimesis* as representation and *mimesis* as copying of models. A passage from Horace's *Ars Poetica* nicely shows how the imitation of models and *mimesis* as representation come together:

> respicere exemplar vitae morumque iubebo
> doctum imitatorem et vivas hinc ducere voces.
> (*Ars Poetica* 317–18)

I will order the learned imitator to look to the model of life and morals, and draw his utterances living from there.

The phrase *doctum imitatorem* ('learned imitator') presupposes both the priority of imitating models and the necessity of the imitator being well versed in those models. But Horace is telling the imitator to look at the exemplar of life and to draw living voices from there—*vivas hinc ducere voces*. That phrase is also important: the imitation of life in poetry might come down, as Horace suggests elsewhere, to the imitation of real life utterances.[10] This provides the link between the two kinds of *mimesis* in literature.[11] Literary language may imitate life, but in order to do so it must also imitate itself. In fact language, whether literary or not, can only function by quoting, copying, echoing more language. Thus examination of the relationship between speech presentation and discursive representation in the broader sense could be seen to trap us in a kind of hermeneutic circle: seeing speech presentation as part of representation as a whole, compels us to use the part to define the whole, whose own definition determines the nature of its part. Hence the epigraph from Walter Benjamin.

Thus, the main emphasis in the preceding discussions has been on the functions and techniques of speech presentation, either as an

---

[10] Horace, *Ars Poetica* 95–8 *et tragicus plerumque dolet sermone pedestri | Telephus et Peleus, cum pauper et exsul uterque | proicit ampullas et sesquipedalia verba, | si curat cor spectantis tetigisse querela* ('Often too Telephus and Peleus in tragedy lament in prosaic language, when they are both poor and exiles and throw away their bombast and words half a yard long, if they are anxious to touch the spectator's heart with their complaint').

[11] The important treatment of *imitatio* in Russell (1979), 3–5 would appear to corroborate this interpretation of the passage. On *Ars Poetica* 134 *nec desilies imitator in artum* ('nor will you jump down as you imitate, into a hole'), Russell comments (at 4): 'it is difficult to believe that Horace did not mean us to have both senses [of *mimesis*] in mind.'

aspect or as a paradigm of narratival representation in general. However, it remains to say something about the question of the ontological status of the objects represented—utterances or events, whether they are deemed true or false. That question has not been the principal focus of this study but it can be of considerable ethical and political importance. In antiquity, representation was always bound up with moral responsibility. It still is. Hence the interest of Che Guevara's joke, rendered in the second epigraph.

Throughout this book I have been anxious to assert that the interpretation of texts—even in the most routine contexts—is profoundly ideological. For instance, it may be possible to analyse formally the relation between a narrator and a character whose discourse the narrator presents in terms of the speech modes adopted, but the nature of that relation is ultimately determined by the interaction between the *reader* and the text as a whole. At the same time however, I have also been anxious to oppose the now widely shared reluctance to postulate any external position of certainty. Clearly it is true that some words, discourses, or narratives only construct portrayals of events, but others—which have the status of speech acts—can affect events, even constitute events in the world of lived experience. Any view of how language operates which did not take account of this realization would be deeply flawed.

This realization obviously has important implications for the status of factual narrative, such as historiography. It is widely accepted that historical narratives constitute the facts which they may appear to convey. Unfortunately the events behind those facts can only be posited: for instance Faye's view that events can be conceived independently as *histoire lourde* is untenable.[12] That 'heavy history' can only have the status of another narrative construction. Thucydides, as we saw, has a better grasp of what is really involved: his celebrated discussion of the problem of ascertaining the facts of the Peloponnesian War is conceived in terms of the problem of how to assess, select and indeed to *render* verbal reports. What happened can only be approached through what is said. Hence both the theoretical and practical importance of speech presentation for historiography and other forms of factual narrative.

---

[12] Faye (1972) conceives of 'heavy history'—of power struggle, production and distribution of commodities—as somehow existing 'beyond' the narratives which may or may not present it.

312   *Conclusions and* Envoi

In contrast to 'reported discourse' in fictional narrative which can be completely authoritative, the presentation of speech in factual narrative can only be rhetorical and provisional. In the end, there are no epistemological criteria for the right sort of employment of speech presentation in the right sort of contexts. The criteria can only be generic, aesthetic or ethical. The ancient rhetorical category of *ethos* subsumed a notion of appropriateness to speaker, audience, and subject, along with the moral tenor of a discourse. This sense of *ethos,* which combines fact and value, might add a little more clout to protests that contemporary revisionist 'histories', which seek to diminish the scale or significance of the Holocaust, are unethical.[13] It is worth emphasizing again that *mimesis* or *imitatio,* however conceived in ancient thought, was never isolated from moral concerns. The moral element of *imitatio* is very much present in Horace's remark quoted earlier—it is not a neutral observation but a strongly worded exhortation: 'I will *order* the learned imitator'. Plato's insistence on investing poetic styles with moral significance has long exasperated his interpreters.[14] Whilst one may not concur with his censure, on ethical grounds, of direct speech, the political approach to speech presentation adopted here might make Plato's condemnation of a technical syntactic feature look considerably less eccentric.

My central purpose, however, both in the opening theoretical chapters and in the reviews of particular texts which followed, was to illustrate some of the ways in which the intersections between speech presentation and narratival representation as a whole can be conceived. The numerous consequences of those intersections for our understanding of both ancient and modern poetics and theories of discourse still remain to be explored. In addition, there are at least three broad areas for future research that could be conducted in the light of this enquiry.

First, there is plenty of scope for further detailed literary–historical studies of speech presentation in various literatures and cultures. Studies of transformations and innovations of usage from one author or genre to another would, in the first place, help establish a diachronic overview of the meanings and functions of

[13] The argument of Cavarero (1997) provides philosophical support for this position. Cavarero reads Hannah Arendt's 'spectacular ontology' as an ethic.

[14] See Ferrari's discussion of the *Republic* in G. Kennedy (1989), 118.

various speech modes. Furthermore, such studies would enhance historical understanding of a number of wider issues: the develop-ment—in particular contexts—of characterization, of generic typologies, of 'literary' language, of narrative as representation, and of the relations between speech and power. Patterns observed in the history of transformations of speech presentation as a literary technique could be related to existing theories of speech presenta-tion and character in any given literary tradition.

I lay particular stress on character and characterization because these categories are frequently bypassed or ignored by narratolo-gists and other formalists who regard them as the preoccupation of subjective or connoisseurish critics.[15] In showing that presentation of speech and thought (as a form of the text) is the primary technical medium of characterization in narrative, one might underpin more rigorously some conventional evaluations of characterization in specific authors. For example, ancient authors deemed 'empathetic' or 'realistic' tend to employ a preponderance of free indirect discourse or deviant focalization in their narratives.[16] Moreover, an understanding of characterization can come close to an under-standing of how the very notion of a human individual is con-stituted in language; this has some bearing on some applications of psychoanalysis, and on the recovery of the various categories of 'person' which existed at various stages in different times and cultures.[17]

However, research like this—especially if it is concerned with literatures in 'dead' languages like Latin and ancient Greek—will have a limited scope because the field of investigation is inevitably confined to written texts. A second major area with vast scope for future study would be an investigation of speech presentation in genres of oral narrative in various contemporary cultures.

[15] See Hochman (1985), Oliver (1989), 120 f. Laird (1997) attempts to rescue the study of character, reconceiving it in terms of speech presentation and inter-textuality.
[16] On 'intervention', 'sympathy', 'empathy'/*Empfindung*, etc. in Virgil, see D. P. Fowler (1990), 55. This recounts the impact of Otis (1964a) and 'point of view' on Italian narratological criticism.
[17] De Certeau (1978), Crapanzano (1992), Lacan (1966), and Schafer (1981) consider—in very different ways—the implications of psychoanalysis for discourse and identity. On ancient concepts of 'person', see Gill (1991), Momigliano (1985), Pelling (1990). Carrithers, Collins, and Lukes (1985) assemble useful discussions (including Momigliano's) which respond to Marcel Mauss's thesis that notions of the person should be seen in terms of ideology and social history.

Anecdotes, jokes, and folktales are examples of genres of (normally non-literary) oral narrative. Such spoken 'texts' will have their own distinctive forms of linguistic usage for speech presentation. Access to spoken texts can, needless to say, provide access to the identity and social status of the speakers and addressees. This makes research of a socio-linguistic nature far more feasible for study of the contemporary world than it could ever be for the study of ancient cultures.[18]

One specific line of enquiry would be to examine how speakers in particular communities habitually present the discourse of other speakers, and to relate these habits to their social situation.[19] Are certain forms of speech presentation (e.g. predilections for certain speech modes) favoured by certain sorts of speaker for presenting the discourse of certain sorts of people, or in certain sorts of context? An individual's position in a social hierarchy reflects or determines the extent to which he or she is disposed or able to speak: can this relation between speech and power also manifest itself in the particular techniques an individual uses to present the discourse of others? These issues really belong to anthropological linguistics: they would best be explored in the light of fieldwork on particular social groups and speech communities.[20] Practically, this kind of fieldwork would be most easily accomplished in smaller speech communities, where features of speech presentation could most easily be related to broader social situations.

The third general area for future research in the wake of what has been set out in this book is more theoretical, and of the greatest interdisciplinary significance. This would be a comprehensive and possibly syncretic study of the ethics, epistemology

---

[18] On socio-linguistics, see Gumperz and Hymes (1972), Trudgill (1984). Achard (1993) is a more cosmopolitan sociology of language. Karl Marx in his journalism and historiography shows evident concern with *who* is speaking—see e.g. K. Marx (1973). Marxist linguistic and literary theory has been more preoccupied with linking ideology to rhetoric in discourse and narrative e.g. Bakhtin and Medvedev (1978), R. Fowler (1981), Lukacs (1978), Macherey (1978), J. B. Thompson (1984).

[19] Tannen (1989) combines linguistic and literary analysis to survey the construction of dialogue in conversational discourse. The ideological and social importance of this subject is indicated but not explored. Conversely, Bourdieu's fieldwork which explored relations between speech and power has not considered the dimension of speech *presentation* as an arena for investigating political and ideological questions.

[20] Crystal (1985), 284 defines a speech community as 'any regionally or socially definable human group identified by a shared linguistic system'.

and semantics of speech presentation—or just of quotation
alone—across a range of discourses and subject areas. These
include: fiction and literary narrative; factual narrative (e.g.
historiography, ethnography, and journalism); law, legal discourse, and legal documentation; religion and theology—particularly exegeses of scriptures in different religious traditions;
rhetoric, linguistics, and translation theory; philosophy and
psychology; forms of everyday conversation, including 'idle
talk' (*Gerede* in Heidegger's terminology) and gossip.[21] The
previous pages should at least have demonstrated the importance
of speech presentation for the study of literature, for history, and
for ethnography. But it remains to consider how far any assumptions from poetics about the status of 'direct quotation' in relation
to various kinds of 'indirect' rendering have affinities in other
kinds of expression and theories of expression.

One might, for instance, dispense with the notion of direct
discourse possessing 'literal fidelity' or 'documentary authority'
in both fictional and factual narrative, only to find that immense
moral and epistemological authority can be ascribed to the quoted
word in certain religious traditions. And the mechanics of such
ascription of authority can be complex and varied. Western practitioners of biblical hermeneutics (in common with classicists
engaged in textual criticism) attribute most authority to the
'source' text: the earliest and most directly transmitted scripture.
Approaches to the 'synoptic problem'—debates about the primacy
of the Gospels—are grounded on this assumption. However,
interpretation of the Islamic tradition of the *haddith* appears to
work on rather different lines: something maintained by X, who
heard it from Y, who heard it from Z can hold a great deal of
authority.[22] It is anyway obvious that problems involving the
ethics, epistemology, and semantics of quotation abound in the
secular world: should a journalist 'reporting' another speaker in

---

[21] Heidegger (1962) I. I. 5. 35, 211–14. Eagleton (1983), 63 neatly epitomizes
Heidegger's conception of language: 'Language always pre-exists the individual
subject, as the very realm in which he or she unfolds; and it contains "truth" less in
the sense that it is an instrument for exchanging accurate information than in the
sense that it is the place where reality "un-conceals" itself, gives itself up to our
contemplation.'

[22] On the synoptic problem, see Sanders and Davies (1989); on the *haddith* see
Azami (1968).

indirect discourse or the speaker himself be held responsible, if the diction in this rendering is deemed libellous?

Finally, speech presentation could well provide a general heuristic tool. The examination of the newspaper article in the Preface demonstrated this on the local level of discourse analysis. On a grander scale, the theory of speech presentation might also provide useful paradigms for examining, by analogy, (re)presentations which are of quite different species. For example, the realization that speech presentation *constructs* discourse and cannot reproduce it, could help clarify notions of political representation. An observation about the latter is pertinent here: 'Perhaps Rousseau's most valuable contribution to political thinking was his critique of representation—of the idea that one will can be represented by another.'[23]

Whilst I have consistently opposed the use of visual models and metaphors to understand discursive representation, a reversal of this process could well enhance our understanding of discourses about the realm of the visual. The theory and practice of *ekphrasis* ('physical description') in ancient literature have significant connections with speech presentation which could be further explored.[24] Furthermore, the conception of verbal *mimesis*, which allows the relation between language and object to shift from degrees of divergence to complete identity, actually highlights a deficiency in the discussion of visual art in Plato's *Republic*, which does not take sculpture into account: surely a life-size sculpture of a table would simultaneously *represent* a table and *be* a table. A cult statue of a god also both resembles and embodies the image of the deity—much in the way that a speech act both portrays and constitutes a certain state of affairs.

I shall end on a humanistic note. A Latin poem of the Italian Renaissance elegantly illustrates the importance and the enigmatic nature of my subject. The poem is the *Ambra*, which was

[23] Nicholls (1989), 26. R. Williams (1988), 265–9 considers the changes that senses of the word have undergone in English usage since the 1300s. He covers both the political and the artistic uses of 'representative' and 'representation', and acknowledges (at 269) a degree of possible overlap between the two. The treatment of representation in Pitkin (1972) extends to art as well as politics.

[24] See e.g. Bartsch (1989); D. P. Fowler (1991); James and Webb (1991); Laird (1993b; 1996). Socrates presents an interesting idea of the relation between visual art and speech in Plato, *Politicus* 277.

composed in 1485 by Angelo Poliziano (or 'Politian') to celebrate
Homer's life and achievement.[25] It contains the longest ever
passage of indirect discourse in Latin verse: the narrator summarizes Homer's singing of the *Iliad* in a hundred hexameters. A
summary of the *Odyssey* follows, after the shade of Ulysses speaks
to Homer. Odysseus is after all, an important narrator in the
Odyssey. Did Poliziano get the idea of a summary of the *Iliad* in
indirect discourse from Plato's *Republic*? And did Socrates' observation about the *Odyssey*—that much of it consisted of direct
speech—inspire the way Ulysses himself addresses Homer here?

There is something else. Ulysses is a famous storyteller. He is no
less famous as a devious liar. Poliziano's Ulysses turns out to
demonstrate both these faculties. After he has urged Homer to
commemorate him, Ulysses' speech closes like this:

> Incipe namque adero: et praesens tua coepta iuvabo.
> Haec ait, et pariter somnusque Ithacusque recessit.
>
> (*Ambra* 431–2)

'Begin your poem, I will be here, and being present, I'll help you start it
off.'
He spoke these words, but at the same time the vision and the Ithacan
vanished.

So Ulysses was lying. In the story here, Homer is left high and
dry, compelled to compose the *Odyssey* without the help he was
promised. At the same time the narrative of the *Ambra* has
deceived its audience: Ulysses' speech act induced an expectation, which turns out to be illusory, that the story would go a
certain way. Of course, reported discourse within a text always
bears on the discourse of the text in which it is embedded, but
here the process is especially remarkable. A parallel is established
between the two levels of discourse: not so much because the
expectations of both Homer and Poliziano's audience are simultaneously thwarted, but because the performance of a poem is at
stake in both cases.

The protocols of speech presentation in the *Ambra* explicitly
mirror contemporary views that literary discourse, if not all

---

[25] The *Ambra* is in one of Poliziano's *Silvae* – a group of didactic poems
introducing ancient poets. The best edition and commentary is now Bausi
(1996), which virtually supersedes Del Lungo (1925); Galand (1987) offers a
commentary and French translation.

discourse, rests on a network of quotation. Moreover, the specific verses quoted above allegorize and exemplify current conceptions of the myth of representation. The function of representation is to represent something; whatever is represented can never be present. We have no access to the 'presence' which is the supposed object of re-presentation; just as we cannot reach the story without a narrative that conveys it.[26] 'Presence' is a chimera. Ideas of presence are really generated by, and have their origin in, representation. It is only natural that Ulysses, himself the subject of the *Odyssey*, should assure Homer he will be 'present', and then vanish as soon as the discourse representing him gets underway.

---

[26] Again Heidegger (1962), 189–95 provides the obvious source for preoccupations with the problem in philosophy and literary theory. As well as n. 21 above, see Ch. 7 n. 49.

References

ABBOTT, E., and MANSFIELD, E. (1963), *A Primer of Greek Grammar*, rev. (London).

ACHARD, P. (1993), *La Sociologie du langage* (Paris).

ALPERT, M. (ed./tr.) (1969), *Two Spanish Picaresque Novels: Lazarillo de Tormes; The Swindler* (Harmondsworth).

ARDENER, E. (1975), 'Belief and the Problem of Women', in S. Ardener (ed.), *Perceiving Women* (London).

—— (1989), *The Voice of Prophecy and other Essays* (Oxford).

ASAD, E. (1973), *Anthropology and the Colonial Encounter* (London).

AUERBACH, E. (1953), *Mimesis*, tr. W. Trask (Princeton).

AUSTIN, J. L. (1962), *How to do things with words* (Oxford).

—— (1971), 'Performative–Constative', in Searle (1971), 13–22.

AUSTIN, R. G. (ed.) (1955), *P. Vergili Maronis: Aeneidos Liber Quartus* (Oxford).

—— (ed.) (1964), *P. Vergili Maronis: Aeneidos Liber Secundus* (Oxford).

—— (1968), 'Ille Ego Qui Quondam', *Classical Quarterly* (18), 107–16.

—— (ed.) (1971), *P. Vergili Maronis: Aeneidos Liber Primus* (Oxford).

—— (ed.) (1977), *P. Vergili Maronis: Aeneidos Liber Sextus* (Oxford).

AVERY, M. M. (1936), *The Use of Direct Speech in Ovid's Metamorphoses* (diss., Chicago).

AZAMI, M. M. (1968), *Studies in Early Haddith Literature: with a critical edition of some early texts* (Beirut; reprinted Indianopolis, 1992).

BAKHTIN, M. M. (1973), *The Problem of Dostoyevsky's Poetics*, tr. W. Rotsel (Ann Arbor).

—— (1981), *The Dialogic Imagination*, tr. C. Emerson and M. Holquist (Austin).

—— (1986), 'The Problem of the Text', in *Speech Genres and Other Late Essays*, tr. V. McGee, (Austin).

—— and MEDVEDEV, P. (1978), *The Formal Method in Literary Scholarship: A Critical Introduction to Sociological Poetics*, tr. A. Wehrle (Johns Hopkins).

BAL, M. (1985), *Narratology: Introduction to the Theory of Narrative*, tr. C. van Boheemen (Toronto, Buffalo, London).

BALANDIER, G. (1955), *Sociologie actuelle de l'Afrique noire* (Paris).

BALDWIN, F. T. (1911), *The Bellum Civile of Petronius* (New York).

BALLY, C. (1912), 'Le Style indirect libre en français moderne', *Germanisch-romanische Monatsschrift* 4, 459–56.

BALZAC, H. (1965), *La Cousine Bette*, tr. M. Ayrton Crawford (Harmondsworth).

BANFIELD, A. (1973), 'Narrative style and the grammar of direct and indirect speech', *Foundations of Language* 10, 1–39.

—— (1982), *Unspeakable Sentences: Narration and Representation in the Language of Fiction* (Boston).

BARDON, H. (1943–4), 'La Silence, moyen d'expression' *Revue des Études Latines*, 102–20.

BARKER, A., and WARNER, M. (edd.) (1992), *The Language of the Cave* (Alberta).

BARSBY, J. (ed.) (1973), *Ovid Amores I* (Oxford).

BARTHES, R. (1967), 'Introduction à l'analyse structurale des récits', *Communications*, 8, 1–27. Issue reprinted in 1977 *Poétique du récit* (Paris).

—— (1971), 'Style and its Image', in S. Chatman (ed.) *Literary Style: A Symposium*, 3–15.

—— (1977), *Image—Music—Text* (London).

—— (1982), 'The Reality Effect', in Todorov (1982), 11–17.

—— (1986), 'The Discourse of History', in *The Rustle of Language* (London; French orig. 1967).

BARTSCH, S. (1989), *Decoding the Ancient Novel: The Reader and the Role of Description in Heliodorus and Achilles Tatius* (Princeton).

BASORE, J. W. (1904), 'Direct Speech in Lucan as an Element of Epic Technique', *Transactions of the American Philological Association* 35, 129–41.

BAUSI, F. (1996), *Sylvae/Angelo Poliziano* (Florence).

BELFIORE, E. (1984*a*), 'A Theory of Imitation in Plato's *Republic*', *Transactions of the American Philological Association* 114, 121–46.

—— (1984*b*), 'Embraces in the *Aeneid*', *Phoenix* 38, 27–30.

BELL, A. J. (1923), *The Latin Dual and Poetic Diction* (London).

BEMROSE, S. (1983), *Dante's Angelic Intelligences: Their Importance in the Cosmos and in Pre-Christian Religion* (Rome).

BENJAMIN, W. (1977), *The Origin of German Tragic Drama*, tr. J. Osborne (London; German orig. 1963).

BENVENISTE, E. (1971), *Problems in General Linguistics*, tr. M. Meek (Coral Gables, Fla.).

BERRES, T. (1982), *Die Enstehung der Aeneis* (*Hermes* Einzelschriften 45; Wiesbaden).

BERS, V. (1997), *Speech within Speech: Studies in Incorporated Oratio Recta in Attic Drama and Oratory* (Boulder, New York, London).

BIBER, D. (1988), *Variation across Speech and Writing* (Cambridge).

BINNS, J. W. (ed.) (1973), *Ovid* (London).

BLANCK, H. (1992), *Das Buch in der Antike* (Munich).

BÖMER, F. (1969–86), *Ovid: Metamorphosen* (Heidelberg).

BOND, G. (1981), *Euripides: Herakles: with Introduction and Commentary* (Oxford).

BOOTH, W. C. (1965), *The Rhetoric of Fiction* (Chicago and London).

BORGES, J. L. (1986), *Seven Nights*, tr. E. Weinburger (London).

BORNECQUE, H. (1933), *Tite-Live* (Paris).

BOURASSA, L. (1992), 'De l'espace au temps, du voir à la voix', *Poétique* 91 (September).

BOURDIEU, P. (1977), 'The Economics of Linguistic Exchange', *Social Science Information* 16. 6, 645–68.

—— (1979), *Algeria 1960*, tr. R. Nice (Cambridge).

—— (1984), *Distinction: A Social Critique of the Judgement of Taste*, tr. R. Nice (Harvard).

—— (1991), *Language and Symbolic Power*, ed. J. Thompson (Cambridge).

—— and EAGLETON, T. (1992), (In Conversation) 'Doxa and Common Life', *New Left Review* 191, 111–21.

BOWIE, E. L (1985), 'Theocritus' Seventh *Idyll*, Philetas and Longus', *Classical Quarterly* 35, 67–91.

BOYCE, B. (1991), *The Language of the Freedmen in Petronius Cena Trimalchionis*, (*Mnemosyne* Supplement 117; Leiden).

BOYLE, N., and SWALES, M. (edd.) (1986), *Realism in European Literature: Essays in Honour of J. P. Sterne* (Cambridge).

BOYS-STONES, G. (ed.) (forthcoming), *Metaphor and Allegory* (Oxford).

BRAUND, S. M. (1996), 'Ending Epic: Statius, Theseus and a merciful release', *Proceedings of the Cambridge Philological Society* 42, 1–23.

BRETHERTON, I. (ed.) (1984), *Symbolic Play: The Development of Social Understanding* (Orlando and London).

BRETT-SMITH, H. (ed.) (1972), *Peacock's Four Ages of Poetry; Shelley's Defence of Poetry; Browning's Essay on Shelley* (Oxford).

BRICKHOUSE, T. C., and SMITH, N. D. (1994), *Plato's Socrates* (Oxford).

BRINK, C. O. (1960), 'Tragic History and Aristotle's Schools', *Proceedings of the Cambridge Philological Society* 6, 14–19.

—— (1971), *Horace on Poetry: The 'Ars Poetica'* (Cambridge).

—— (1982), *Horace on Poetry—Epistles Book II: The Letters to Augustus and Florus* (Cambridge).

BROCK, R. (1995), 'Versions, "Inversions" and Evasions: Classical Historiography and the "Published" Speech', *Papers of the Leeds International Latin Seminar* 8, 209–24.

BRONZWAER, W. (1970), *Tense in the Novel* (Groningen).

BROWN, G., and YULE, G. (1983), *Discourse Analysis* (Cambridge).

BRUNT, P. (1993), *Studies in Greek History and Thought* (Oxford).

BUECHELER, F. (ed.) (1862), *Petronius: Satyricon* (Berlin).

BUFFIÈRE, F. (1956), *Les Mythes d'Homère et la pensée grecque* (Paris).

BULLOCK, A., and STALLYBRASS, O. (edd.) (1977), *The Fontana Dictionary of Modern Thought* (London).

BURCK, E. (1964), *Die Erzählungskunst des Titus Livius* (Berlin; orig. published 1934).

BURNET, J. (ed.) (1968), *Platonis Opera*, iv (Oxford).

CABROL, F., and LECLERCQ, H. (edd.) (1924–53), *Dictionnaire d'archéologie Chrétienne et de liturgie* (Paris).

CALAME, C. (1986), *Le Récit en Grèce ancienne: énonciation et représentation des poètes* (Paris).

CALLEBAT, L. (1968), *Sermo cotidianus dans les Metamorphoses* (Paris).

CALVINO, I. (1987), *The Literature Machine*, tr. P. Creagh (London).

CAMERON, A. (1969), 'Petronius and Plato', *Classical Quarterly* 19, 367–70.

CAMPBELL, L. (1883), *Theaetetus of Plato (Revised text and English notes)* (Oxford).

CARR, E. H. (1964), *What is History?* (Harmondsworth).

CARRITHERS, M., COLLINS, S., and LUKES, S. (edd.) (1985), *The Category of the Person: Anthropology, Philosophy, History* (Cambridge).

CARVER, R. (forthcoming), '*Quis ille?*: The Role of the Prologue in Apuleius' *Nachleben*' in Kahane and Laird (forthcoming).

CAVARERO, A. (1997), 'Etica dell' irripetibile', *Almanacco di Filosofia, MicroMega*, 91–9.

CÉARD, J. (1976), 'Virgile, un grand homme soupçonné de magie', in Chevallier (1978), 265–78.

CHATMAN, S. (ed.) (1971), *Literary Style: A Symposium* (Oxford).

—— (1981), 'Reply to Barbara Herrnstein Smith', in Mitchell (1981), 258–66.

CHAUSSERIE-LAPRÉE, J.-P. (1969), *L'Expression narrative chez les historiens latins* (Paris).

CHEVALLIER, R. (ed.) (1978), *La Présence de Virgile: Actes de Colloque de 9, 11 et 12 Décembre 1976* (Paris).

CLARKE, H. C. (1981), *Homer's Readers* (Newark).

CLIFFORD, J. (1986), 'Partial Truths', in Clifford and Marcus (1986), 1–26.

—— and MARCUS, G. (edd.) (1986), *Writing Culture: The Poetics and Politics of Ethnography* (Berkeley, Los Angeles, and London).

COFFEY, M. (1976), *Roman Satire* (London).

COHEN, R. (1994), 'Speech-Acts and SPRACHSPIELE: Making Peace in Plautus', in De Jong and Sullivan (1994), 172–205.

COHN, D. (1978), *Transparent Minds: Narrative Modes for Presenting Consciousness in Fiction* (Princeton).

COLE, P. (ed.) (1981), *Radical Pragmatics* (New York).

COLEMAN, R. (1977), *Virgil Eclogues* (Cambridge).

COLLINGWOOD, R. G. (1946), *The Idea of History* (Oxford).

COMPARETTI, D. (1908), *Virgil in the Middle Ages*, tr. E. Benecke (London; Italian orig. 1895).

CONINGTON, J. (1884), *P.Virgili Maronis Opera with a Commentary*, 4th edn. (London).

—— and NETTLESHIP, H. (1883), *Vergili Opera*, ii (London).

CONNORS, C. (1998), *Petronius the Poet: Verse and Literary Tradition in the Satyricon* (Cambridge).

CONTE, G. B. (1986), *The Rhetoric of Imitation: Genre and Poetic Memory in Virgil and other Roman Poets*, ed. C. Segal (Ithaca, NY).

—— (1994), *Genres and Readers* (Baltimore and London).

—— (1997), *The Hidden Author*, tr. E. Fantham (Berkeley, Los Angeles, and London).

CORLETT, J. A. (1997), 'Interpreting Plato's Dialogues', *Classical Quarterly* 47. 2, 423–37.

COULMAS, F. (ed.) (1986), *Direct and Indirect Speech* (Berlin).

COURTIVRON, I., and MARKS, E. (edd.) (1980), *New French Feminisms* (Amherst).

COURTNEY, E. (1991), *The Poems of Petronius* (Atlanta).

CRAPANZANO, V. (1986), 'Hermes' Dilemma: The Masking of Subversion in Ethnographic Description', in Clifford and Marcus (1986), 51–76.

—— (1992), *Hermes' Dilemma and Hamlet's Desire: On the Epistemology of Interpretation* (Harvard).

CROCE, B. (1893), 'La storia ridotta sotto il concetto generale dell'arte', in Croce (1951), 3–41.

—— (1951), *Primi saggi* (Bari).

CRUMP, M. M. (1920), *The Growth of the Aeneid* (Oxford).

CRYSTAL, D. (1977), 'Discourse', in Bullock and Stallybrass (1977), 175.

—— (1985), *A Dictionary of Linguistics and Phonetics* (Oxford).

CURTIUS, E. R. (1979), *European Literature and the Latin Middle Ages*, tr. W. Trask (London; German orig. 1948).

DÄLLENBACH, L. (1977), *Le Récit spéculaire* (Paris).

DANIELEWICZ, J. (1990), 'Ovid's Hymn to Bacchus (*Met*. 4. 11 ff.): Tradition and Originality', *Euphrosyne* NS 18, 73 f.

DAVIDSON, D. (1969), 'On Saying that', *Synthese* 19, 130–46.

DAVIES, M. (ed.) (1988), *Epicorum Graecorum Fragmenta* (Göttingen).

DE CERTEAU, M. (1978), *L'Écriture d'histoire: Histoire et psychoanalyse entre science et fiction* (Paris).

—— (1983), 'History: Ethic, Science and Fiction', in Hahn *et al.* (1983), 173–209.

324 References

DE JONG I. (1987a), *Narrators and Focalizers: The Presentation of the Story in the Iliad* (Amsterdam).

—— (1987b), 'The Voice of Anonymity: τις-speeches in the *Iliad*', *Eranos* 85, 69–84.

—— (1991), *Narrative in Drama: The Art of the Euripidean Messenger Scene* (Mnemosyne Supplement 116; Leiden).

—— (1994), 'Between Word and Deed', in De Jong and Sullivan (1994), 27–50.

—— and SULLIVAN, J. P. (edd.) (1994), *Modern Critical Theory and Classical Literature* (Leiden, New York, and Cologne).

DELEUZE, G. (1980), *Mille plateaux* (Paris).

—— (1983), *Cinéma I: L'image—mouvement* (Paris).

—— and GUATTARI, F. (1975), *Kafka: pour une littérature mineure* (Paris).

DEL LUNGO, I. (ed.) (1925), *Angelo Poliziano: Le Silve e la Strega: Prolusioni nello Studio Fiorentino (1482–1492)* (Florence).

DENNISTON, J. (1959), *Greek Particles*, 2nd edn. (Oxford).

DERRIDA, J. (1967), *Speech and Phenomena, and other Essays on Husserl's Theory of Signs* (Northwestern).

—— (1977a), 'Signature, Event, Context', *Glyph* 1, 172–97.

—— (1977b), 'Limited Inc.', *Glyph* 2, 162–254.

—— (1981), 'The Law of Genre', in Mitchell (1981), 51–77.

—— (1988), 'Like the sound of the sea deep within the shell: Paul de Man's War', *Critical Inquiry* 14, 590–652.

DE STE CROIX, G. (1972), *The Origins of the Peloponnesian War* (London).

DIK, S. (1978), *A Functional Grammar* (Amsterdam).

DODDS, E. R. (1973), *The Greeks and the Irrational* (Berkeley; orig. 1951).

DONNER, F. (1982), *Shabono: A True Adventure in the Remote and Magical Heart of the South American Jungle* (New York).

DOREY, T. A. (ed.) (1971), *Livy* (London).

DOVER, K. (ed.) (1980), *Plato: Symposium* (Cambridge).

DUBROW, H. (1982), *Genre* (London).

DUKE, T. (1950), 'Vergil—a bit player in the *Aeneid*?', *Classical Journal* 45, 191–3.

DUQUESNAY, I. (1984), 'Horace and Maecenas: The Propaganda Value of *Sermones* I', in Woodman and West (1984), 19–58.

DYER, R. (1989) 'Vergil's Fama: A New Interpretation of *Aeneid* 4. 173 ff.', *Greece and Rome* 26. 1, 28–32.

EAGLETON, T. (1983), *Literary Theory* (Oxford).

—— (1991), *Ideology* (London and New York).

—— (ed.) (1994), *Ideology* (London and New York).

ECO, U. (1976), *A Theory of Semiotics* (Bloomington, Ind.).

—— (1992) (with R. Rorty, J. Culler and C. Brooke-Rose): *Interpretation and Overinterpretation*, ed. S. Collini (Cambridge).

EDEN, P. T. (1984), *Seneca: Apocolocyntosis* (Cambridge).

EDWARDS, M. J. (1999), 'The Constantinian Circle and the Oration to the Saints', in M. J. Edwards *et al.* (edd.), *Apologetics in the Roman Empire* (Oxford).

EHLERS W. (1954), 'Die *Ciris* und ihr Original', *Museum Helveticum* 11, 65–88.

—— (1980), *Valerius Argonauticon* (Leipzig).

EICHENBAUM, B. (1965), 'The Theory of the "Formal Method"' in Lemon and Reis (1965), 99–139, also in Matejka and Pomorska (1978), 3–37.

—— (1963), tr. B. Paul and M. Nesbitt, 'The Structure of Gogol's "The Overcoat"', *Russian Review* 22, 377–99; tr. T. Todorov, 'Comment est fait "le Manteau" de Gogol', in Todorov (1965), 212–33.

EIGLER, U. (1988), *Monologische Redeformen bei Valerius Flaccus* (Frankfurt).

ELIOT, T. S. (1944), *What is a Classic?* (London).

ELSNER, J. (ed.) (1996), *Art and Text in Roman Culture* (Cambridge).

ENDT, J. (1905), 'Der Gebrauch der Apostrophe bei den Lateinischen Epikern', *Wiener Studien* 27, 106–29.

ENGLER, B. (1991), 'Textualisation', in Sell (1991), 179–89.

ENKVIST, N. (1991), 'On the Interpretability of Texts in General and of Literary Texts in Particular', in Sell (1991), 1–25.

ERNOUT, A., and THOMAS, F. (1951), *Syntaxe Latine* (Paris).

FANTAZZI, C., and PEROSA, A. (edd.) (1988), *Iacopo Sannazaro: De Partu Virginis* (Florence).

FANTHAM, E. (ed.) (1982), *Seneca: Troades* (Princeton).

FANTUZZI, M. (1988), *Ricerche su Apollonio Rodio: diacronie della dizione epica* (Rome).

FARRELL, J. (1991), *Vergil's Georgics and the Traditions of Ancient Epic* (Oxford).

FAYE, J. P. (1972), *Théorie de Récit* (Paris).

FEDELI, P. (ed.) (1980), *Sesto Properzio: Il Primo Libro delle Elegie* (Florence).

—— (1986), 'La Matrona di Efeso: Strutture narrative e tecnica dell'inversione', *Semiotica della novella latina. Atti del seminario interdisciplinare 'La novella latina'* (Rome).

FEENEY, D. (1983), 'The Taciturnity of Aeneas', *Classical Quarterly* 33, 204–19.

—— (1991), *The Gods in Epic* (Oxford).

—— (1993), 'Epilogue', to Gill and Wiseman (1993), 230–44.

FENIK, B. C. (1960), *The Influence of Euripides on Virgil's Aeneid* (diss. Princeton).

FERRARI, G. (1987), *Listening to the Cicadas: A Study of Plato's Phaedrus* (Cambridge).

FERRARI, G. (1989), 'Plato and Poetry', in Kennedy (1989), 92–148.

FERRY, A. (1963), *Milton's Epic Voice: The Narrator in 'Paradise Lost'* (Cambridge).

FILLMORE, C. J. (1981), 'Pragmatics and the Description of Discourse', in Cole (1981).

FISH, S. (1980), *Is there a Text in this Class?* (Cambridge, Mass.).

FITZGERALD, F. S. (1994), *The Diamond as Big as the Ritz* (London).

FLEISCHMANN, W. B. (1974), 'Classicism', in Preminger (1974), 136–41.

FORDYCE, C. J. (1977), *P. Vergili Maronis Aeneidos Libri VII–VIII* (Oxford).

FORNARA, C. W. (1983), *The Nature of History in Ancient Greece and Rome* (Berkeley, Los Angeles, and London).

FORSTER, E. M. (1964), *Aspects of the Novel* (Harmondsworth).

FOUCAULT, M. (1976), *The Archaeology of Knowledge*, tr. S. Smith (New York).

—— (1977), 'What is an Author?', in Harari (1977).

FOWLER, A. (ed.) (1971), *John Milton: Paradise Lost* (Harlow).

—— (1982), *Kinds of Literature* (Oxford).

FOWLER, D. P. (1989), 'On Closure', *Materiali and Discussione* 22, 75–122.

—— (1990), 'Deviant Focalization in Virgil's *Aeneid*', *Proceedings of the Cambridge Philological Society* 216, 42–63.

—— (1991), 'Narrate and Decribe: The Problem of Ekphrasis', *Journal of Roman Studies* 81, 25–35.

—— (1997), 'The Virgil Commentary of Servius', in Martindale (1997), 73–8.

—— (1998), 'On the Shoulders of Giants: Intertextuality and Classical Studies', *Materiali e Discussione* 39, 1–34.

—— and SPENTZOU, E. (edd.) (forthcoming), *Cultivating the Muse: Power, Desire and Inspiration* (Oxford).

FOWLER, R. (1981), *Literature as Discourse: The Practice of Linguistic Criticism* (London).

—— (1986), *Linguistic Criticism* (Oxford).

FOWLER, R. L. (1987), 'The Rhetoric of Desperation', *Harvard Studies in Classical Philology* 91, 5–38.

FRAENKEL, E. (1950), *Aeschylus: Agamemnon*, ii (Oxford).

—— (1964), 'Eine Forme Kriegsbulletinstil', in *Kleine Beiträge Zur Klassischen Philologie*, ii (Rome), 69–74 (orig. 1956 in *Eranos* 54, 189–94).

FRAENKEL, H. (1955), 'Die Zeitauffassung in der frühgriecischen Literatur', in *Wegen und Formen frühgriecischen Denkens* (Munich).

—— (1975), *Early Greek Poetry and Philosophy*, tr. M. Haddas and J. Willis (Oxford; German orig. 1951).

FREE, A. (1990), 'Written or Living Culture?', *Journal of Anthropological Society of Oxford* 21. 1, Hilary Term, 59 f.

—— (1996), 'The Anthropology of Pierre Bourdieu', *Critique of Anthropology* 16. 4, 395–416.

FRIEDMAN, N. (1967), 'Point of View in Fiction', in Stevick (1967).

FROW, J. (1986), *Marxism and Literary History* (Oxford).

FRYE, N. (1971), *Anatomy of Criticism* (Princeton).

FURBANK, P. N. (1970), *Reflections on the Word 'Image'* (London).

FURNEAUX, H. (ed.) (1907), *Annals of Tacitus*, 2nd edn. rev. Pelham and Fisher, ii (Oxford).

FUSILLO, M. (1986), ' "Mythos" aristotelico e "récit" narratologico', *Strumenti Critici* 52, 381–92.

GALAND, P. (ed./tr.) (1987), *Ange Politien: Les Silves* (Paris).

GALE, M. (forthcoming), *The Farmer Philosopher: Lucretian Intertextuality in Virgil's Georgics*.

GALINSKY, G. K. (1975), *Ovid's Metamorphoses: An Introduction to the Basic Aspects* (Berkeley and Los Angeles).

GEERTZ, C. (1973), *The Interpretation of Cultures* (New York).

—— (1988), *Works and Lives: The Anthropologist as Author* (Stanford).

GENETTE, G. (1980), *Narrative Discourse*, tr. J. Lewin (Cornell).

—— (1982a), *Figures of Literary Discourse*, tr. A. Sheridan (Oxford).

—— (1982b), *Palimpsestes* (Paris).

—— (1988) *Narrative Discourse Revisited*, tr. J. Lewin (Cornell).

—— (1991), *Fiction et Diction* (Paris).

—— (1992), *The Architext: An Introduction*, tr. J. Lewin (Berkeley and Los Angeles).

GENTILI, B. (1984–5), «Il coro tragico nella teoria degli antichi», *Dioniso* 55, 147 f.

GEORGE, P. A. (1974), 'Petronius and Lucan *De Bello Civili*', *Classical Quarterly* 24, 119–33.

GIBSON, B. (1998), 'Rumours as Causes of Events in Tacitus', *Materiali e Discussione* 40, 111–29.

GILDERSLEEVE, B. L. (1980), *Greek Syntax*, i (New York, Cincinnati, Chicago).

—— and LODGE, G. (1895), *Gildersleeve's Latin Grammar*, 3rd edn. (London).

GILL, C. (ed.) (1991), *The Person and the Human Mind: Essays in Ancient and Modern Philosophy* (Oxford).

—— and WISEMAN, T. P. (edd.) (1993), *Lies and Fiction in the Ancient World* (Exeter).

GILSENAN, M. (1989), 'Word of Honour', in Grillo (1989), 193–221.

GOERLER, W. (1978), 'Ex verbis communibus κακοζηλία: Die augusteischen

'Klassiker' und die griechischen Theoretiker des Klassizismus', *Fondation Hardt Pour l'Etude de l'Antiquité Classique Entretiens* 25, 175–202.

—— (1985), 'La Lingua', *Enciclopedia Virgiliana*, (Rome), 262–78.

GOFFMAN, E. (1969), *The Presentation of Self in Everyday Life* (Harmondsworth).

GOLD, B. (ed.) (1982), *Literary and Artistic Patronage in Ancient Rome* (Austin).

GOLD, B. (1987), *Literary Patronage in Greece and Rome* (Chapel Hill).

GOLDSCHLÄGER, A. (1982), 'Towards a Semiotics of Authoritarian Discourse', *Poetics Today* 3, 11–20.

GOMME, A. W. (1937), *Essays in Greek History and Literature* (Oxford).

——, ANDREWES, A., and DOVER, K. J. (1945–81), *Commentary on Thucydides*, 5 vols. (Oxford).

GOODMAN, N. (1978), *Ways of Worldmaking*, ed. J. Conant (Indianopolis).

GOODWIN, W. W. (1894), *A Greek Grammar* (London and New York).

GOULD, J. (1992), 'Plato and Performance', in Barker and Warner (1992), 13–26.

GRAFTON, A. T. (1983), *Joseph Scaliger: A Study in the History of Classical Scholarship*, i (Oxford).

GREENE, J. T. (1989), *The Role of the Messenger and Message in the Ancient Near East: Oral and Written Communication in the Ancient Near East and in the Hebrew Scriptures: Communications and Communiqués in Context* (Brown Judaic Studies 169; Atlanta).

GREENE, T. (1963), *The Descent from Heaven: A Study in Epic Continuity* (New Haven and London).

GRIFFIN, J. (1982), *Homer on Life and Death* (Oxford).

—— (1986), 'Words and Speakers in Homer', *Journal of Hellenic Studies* 106, 36–57.

GRILLO, R. (ed.) (1989), *Social Anthropology and the Politics of Language* (Sociological Review Monograph 36; London).

GRIMAL, P. (1977), *La Guerre civile de Pétrone dans ses rapports avec la Pharsale* (Paris).

GRUBE, G. M. (1965), *The Greek and Roman Critics* (Toronto).

GUMPERZ, J. J., and HYMES, D. (edd.) (1972), *Directions in Sociolinguistics: The Ethnography of Communication* (New York).

GÜTERBOCK, H. G. (1946), *Kumarbi. Mythen vom churritischen Kronos, aus den hethitischen Fragmenten zusammengestellt, übersetzt und erklärt* (Istanbuler Schriften 16; Zürich and New York).

—— (1948), 'The Hittite Version of the Hurrian Kumarbi Myths: Oriental Forerunners of Hesiod', *American Journal of Archaeology*, 2nd ser. 52, 123–34.

GUTHRIE, W. K. C. (1971), *A History of Greek Philosophy*, iii (Cambridge).

HÄGG, T. (1971), *Narrative Technique in the Early Greek Romances: Studies of Chariton, Xenophon Ephesius and Achilles Tatius* (Stockholm).

HAHN, N., BELLAH, R., RABINOW, P., and SULLIVAN, W. (edd.) (1983), *Social Science as Moral Inquiry* (New York).

HAIG, S. (1986), *Flaubert and the Gift of Speech* (Cambridge).

HAINSWORTH, J. B. (1991), *The Idea of Epic* (Oxford).

HÅKANSON, L. (1972–3), *Statius's Thebaid: Critical and Exegetical Remarks* (Lund).

HALLIDAY, M. (1985), *An Introduction to Functional Grammar* (London).

HALLIWELL, S. (1986), *Aristotle's Poetics* (London).

—— (1987), *The Poetics of Aristotle: Translation and Commentary* (London).

HAMON, P. (1982), 'What is a Description?', in Todorov (1982), 147–78.

HANDLEY, E. W. (1965), *Menander Dyskolos* (Oxford).

HARARI, J. (ed./tr.) (1977), *Textual Strategies: Perspectives in Post-Structural Criticism* (Cornell).

HARDIE, A. (1983), *Statius and the Silvae: Poets, Patrons and Epideixis in the Greco-Roman World* (ARCA 9: Leeds).

HARDIE, P. (1986), *Vergil's Aeneid: Cosmos and Imperium* (Oxford).

—— (1993), *The Epic Succesors of Virgil* (Cambridge).

—— (ed.) (forthcoming), *The Cambridge Companion to Ovid* (Cambridge).

HARRISON, S. (ed.) (1990), *Oxford Readings in Vergil's Aeneid* (Oxford).

HASKINS, C. E., and HEITLAND, W. (edd.) (1887), *M. Annaei Lucani Pharsalia* (London).

HATHAWAY, B. (1968), *Marvels and Commonplaces: Renaissance Literary Criticism* (Cornell).

HAVELOCK, E. (1963), *Preface to Plato* (Cambridge, Mass.).

HEIDEGGER, M. (1962), *Being and Time*, tr. Macquarrie and Robinson (Oxford).

HEINZE, R. (1919), *Ovids elegische Erzählung* (Leipzig).

—— (1993), *Virgil's Epic Technique*, tr. H. Harvey, D. Harvey, and F. Robertson (Bristol; orig. published Leipzig, 1915).

HELM, R. (1898), *Fabii Planciadis Fulgentii V.C. Opera* (Leipzig).

HELMREICH, F. (1927), *Die Reden bei Curtius* (Paderborn).

HELZLE, M. (1996), *Der Stil ist der Mensch: Redner und Reden im Römischen Epos* (Stuttgart and Leipzig).

HENTZE, C. (1904), 'Die Monologue in den homerischen Epen', *Philologus* 63, 12–30.

HERCZEG, G. (1963), *Lo stile indiretto libero in italiano* (Florence).

HERINGTON, J. (1985), *Poetry into Drama* (Berkeley).

HERRNSTEIN SMITH, B. (1981) 'Narrative Versions, Narrative Theories', in Mitchell (1981), 209–33.

HERSHKOWITZ, D. (1995), 'Patterns of Madness in Statius' Thebaid', *Journal of Roman Studies* 85, 52–64.

—— (1998), *Valerius Flaccus' Argonautica: Abbreviated Voyages in Silver Latin Epic* (Oxford).

HEUBECK A., WEST S., HAINSWORTH J., and HOEKSTRA A. (1988–92), *A Commentary on Homer's Odyssey*, 3 vols. (Oxford).

HEUZÉ, P. (1985), *L'Image du corps dans l'œuvre de Virgile* (Collection de l'École Française de Rome 36; Paris and Rome).

HICKMANN, M. (1982), *The Development of Narrative Skills: Pragmatic and Metapragmatic Aspects of Discourse Cohesion* (diss. Chicago).

HIGHET, G. (1972), *The Speeches in Vergil's Aeneid* (Princeton).

HINDS, S. (1987), *The Metamorphosis of Persephone: Ovid and the Self-Conscious Muse* (Cambridge).

HINDS, S. (1998), *Allusion and Intertext: Dynamics of Appropriation in Roman Poetry* (Cambridge).

HIRSCH, E. D. (1967), *Validity in Interpretation* (New Haven).

HIRZEL, R. (1895), *Theaetetus* (Leipzig).

HOCHMAN, B. (1985), *Character in Literature* (New York).

HOFMANN, J. B., and SZANTYR, A. (1965), *Lateinische Syntax und Stylistik* (Munich).

HORNBLOWER, S. (1987), *Thucydides* (Oxford).

—— (1991), *A Commentary on Thucydides Volume I* (Oxford).

—— (1994), 'Narratology and Narrative Techniques in Thucydides', in Hornblower and Spawforth (1994), 131 f.

—— and SPAWFORTH, A. (edd.) (1994), *Greek Historiography* (Oxford).

HORSFALL, N. (1990), 'Virgil and the Illusory Footnote', *Papers of the Leeds International Latin Seminar* 6 (*ARCA* 29), 49–63.

—— (ed.) (1995), *A Companion to the Study of Virgil*, (Mnemosyne Supplement 151; Leiden).

HUNTER, R. (ed.) (1989), *Apollonius of Rhodes: Argonautica Book III* (Cambridge).

—— (1993), *The Argonautica of Apollonius: literary studies* (Cambridge).

HYMAN, J. (1989), *The Imitation of Nature* (Oxford).

JACOB, E. F. (1960), *Italian Renaisance Studies* (London).

JAHN, O. (1867), 'Wie wurden die *Oden* des Horatius vorgetragen?', *Hermes* 2, 418–33.

JAKOBSON, R. (1960), 'Closing Statement: Linguistics and Poetics', in Sebeok (1960), 350–77.

JAMES, H. (1884), 'The Art of Fiction', in Shapira (1963) and Miller (1972).

JAMES, L., and WEBB, R. (1991), '"To understand ultimate things and enter secret places": Ekphrasis and Art in Byzantium', *Art History* 14. 1, 1–17.

JEFFERSON, A. (1986), 'Russian Formalism', in Jefferson and Robey (1986), 24–45.

—— and ROBEY, D. (edd.) (1986), *Modern Literary Theory*, 2nd edn. (London).

JENKYNS, R. (1991), 'The Legacy of Rome', in R. Jenkyns (ed.), *The Legacy of Rome* (Oxford), 1–35.

JENS W. (ed.) (1971), *Griechische Tragödie. Die Bauformen der griechischen Tragödie* (Beihefte zu Poetica 6; Munich).

JOCELYN, H. (1964), 'Ancient Scholarship and Virgil's Use of Republican Latin Poetry I', *Classical Quarterly* 14, 280–95.

—— (1965), 'Ancient Scholarship and Virgil's Use of Republican Latin Poetry II', *Classical Quarterly* 15, 126–44.

—— (1979), 'Vergilius Cacozelus', *Papers of the Liverpool Latin Seminar* 2, 67–142.

JOHNSTONE, B. (1987), 'He says . . . so I said: Verb Tense Alternation and Narrative Depictions of Authority in American English', *Linguistics* 25, 33–52.

KADARE, I. (1997), *The File on H*, tr. D. Bellos (London; Albanian orig. 1981).

KAHANE, A. (1996), 'The Prologue to Apuleius' *Metamorphoses*: A Speech Act Analysis', *Groningen Colloquia on the Novel* 7, 75–93.

KAHANE, A., and LAIRD, A. (edd.) (forthcoming), *A Companion to the Prologue of Apuleius' Metamorphoses* (Oxford).

KAYSER, J. (1906), *De veterum arte poetica quaestiones selectae* (Leipzig).

KEIL, H. (ed.) (1855–1923), *Grammatici Latini*, 8 vols. (Leipzig).

KENNEDY, D. (1992), '"Augustan" and "Anti-Augustan": Reflections on Terms of Reference', in A. Powell (1992), 26–58.

KENNEDY, G. (ed.) (1989), *Cambridge History of Literary Criticism*, i (Cambridge).

KENNEY, E. J. (ed.) (1990), *Cupid and Psyche* (Cambridge).

KIDWELL, C. (1993), *Sannazaro and Arcadia* (London).

KIRK, G. S., with R. Janko, J. B. Hainsworth, and N. Richardson (1985–93), *The Iliad: A Commentary* (Cambridge).

KLEYWEGT, A. J. (1995), '*Anne Latinum?* Vergilius en het latijn', *Lampas* 28. 1–2, 55–66.

KNAUER, G. N. (1964), *Die Aeneis und Homer* (Göttingen).

KNOX, P. E. (1986), *Ovid's Metamorphoses and the Traditions of Augustan Poetry* (Cambridge).

KOHL, O. (1872), *Uber Zweck und Bedeutung der Livianischen Reden*, (Jahresbericht über die Realschule und das Gymasium zu Barmen; Barmen).

KOSTER, S. (1988), *Ille Ego Qui: Dicter zwischen Wort und Macht* (Erlangen and Nuremberg).

KRISTEVA, J. (1969), *Σημειωτικη; Recherches pour une sémanalyse* (Paris).

—— (1974), *La Révolution du langage poétique* (Paris).

—— (1981), *Desire in Language—A Semiotic Approach to Literature and Art*, tr. T. Gora, A. Jardine, and L. S. Roudiez (ed.) (Oxford).

—— (1984), *Femmes et institutions littéraires* (Paris).

KROLL, W. (1924), *Studien zur Verständnis der römischen Literatur* (Stuttgart).

KRÜGER, J. (1990), *Oxyrhynchos in der Kaiserzeit: Studien zur Topographie und Literaturrezeption* (Frankfurt am Main).

KÜHNER-STEGMANN (1912–14), *Ausführliche Grammatik der lateinischen Sprache* (Hanover).

LABATE, M. (1995), 'Eumolpo e gli altri, ovvero lo spazio della poesia' *Materiali e Discussione* (34), 153–75.

—— (1996), 'Petronio «Satyricon» 80–81', *Materiali e Discussione* 35, 165–76.

LACAN, J. (1966), *Écrits* (Paris).

LAIRD, A. (1990), 'Person, *persona* and representation in Apuleius' *Metamorphoses*' *Materiali e Discussione* 25, 129–64.

—— (1992), *Modes of Reporting Speech in Latin Fictional Narrative* (Oxford D.Phil thesis).

—— (1993*a*), 'Fiction, Bewitchment and Story Worlds: The Implications of some Claims to Truth in Apuleius', in Gill and Wiseman (1993), 149–74.

—— (1993*b*) 'Sounding out Ecphrasis: Art and Text in Catullus 64', *Journal of Roman Studies* 83, 18–30.

—— (1996), '*Ut figura poesis*: Writing Art and the Art of Writing in Augustan poetry', in Elsner (1996), 75–102.

—— (1997), 'Approaching Characterisation in Virgil', in Martindale (1997), 282–93.

—— (1998), Review of Conte (1997), in *Journal of Roman Studies* 88, 198–9.

—— (forthcoming *a*), 'Paradox and Transcendence: The Prologue as The End', in Kahane and Laird (forthcoming).

—— (forthcoming *b*), 'Authority and Ontology of the Epic Muses in Performance and Reception', in Fowler and Spentzou (forthcoming).

—— (forthcoming *c*), 'Figures of Allegory from Homer to Latin Epic', in Boys-Stones (forthcoming).

LAMBERTON, R. (1986), *Homer the Theologian: Neoplatonist Allegorical Reading and the Growth of the Epic Tradition* (Berkeley and Los Angeles).

—— and KEANEY, J. (edd.) (1992), *Homer's Ancient Readers: The Hermeneutics of Greek Epic's Earliest Exegetes* (Princeton).

LARSON, M. L. (1978), *The Functions of Reported Speech in Discourse* (Summer Institute of Linguistics Publications in Linguistics 59; Dallas).

LATTIMORE, R. (1942), *Themes in Greek and Latin Epitaphs* (Illinois Studies in Language and Literature 28. 1–2; Urbana).

LAUSBERG, H. (1973), *Handbuch der Literarischen Rhetorik* (Munich; orig. 1960); tr. M. Bliss, A. Jansen, and D. Orton (1998), *Handbook of Literary Rhetoric* (Leiden, Boston, and Cologne).

LAZZARINI, C. (1984), 'Historia/Fabula: forma della costruzione poetica Virgiliana nel commento di Servio all'Eneide', *Materiali e Discussione* 12, 117–44.

—— (1989), 'Elementi di una poetica serviana. Osservazioni sulla costruzione del racconto nel Eneide', *Studi Italiani di Filologica Classica* 7, 56–109, 241–60.

LECLERCQ, H. (1924–53), 'Anges', in Cabrol and Leclercq (1924–53), 208 f.

LEECH, G. N., and SHORT, M. H. (1981), *Style in Fiction: A Linguistic Introduction to English Fictional Prose* (London and New York).

LEFÈVRE, E. (1987), 'Monologo', in *Enciclopedia Virgiliana III* (Rome), 568–70.

LEITH, D., and MYERSON, G. (1989), *The Power of Address: Explorations in Contemporary Rhetoric* (London).

LEJAY, P. (1911), *Œuvres d'Horace: Satires* (Paris).

LEMON, L. T., and REIS, M. J. (edd./tr.) (1965), *Russian Formalist Criticism: Four Essays* (Lincoln and London).

LEUMANN, F., HOFMANN, J., and SZANTYR, A. (1965–79), *Lateinische Grammatik* (Munich; orig. 1926–8).

LEVELT, W. J. M. (1981), 'The Speaker's Linearization Problem', in Longuet-Higgins, Lyons, and Broadbent (1981), 305–15.

LEVITAN, W. (1993), 'Give Up the Beginning? Juno's Mindful Wrath (*Aeneid* 1. 37)', *Liverpool Classical Monthly* 18, 14.

LEWIS, C. S. (1942), *A Preface to Paradise Lost* (London).

—— (1950), *The Allegory of Love* (Oxford).

LIDDELL, P. (1953), *Some Principles of Fiction* (London).

LIPS, M. (1926), *Le Style indirect libre* (Paris).

LIPSCOMB, H. C. (1909), *Aspects of the Speech in the Late Roman Epic* (diss., Baltimore).

LODGE, D. (1990), *After Bakhtin* (London).

LOESCH, W. M. (1927), *Die Einführung der direkten Rede bei den epischcen Dichtern der Römer bis zu domitianischen Zeit* (diss., Erlangen).

LONGUET-HIGGINS, H. C., LYONS, J., and BROADBENT, D. E. (edd.) (1981), *The Psychological Mechanisms of Language* (London and Great Neck, NY).

LOWRIE, E. (1991), *Thersites: A Study in Comic Shame* (London).

LUCAS, D. W. (1968), *Aristotle's Poetics* (Oxford).

LUCK, G. (1958), 'Scriptor Classicus', *Comparative Literature* 10, 157–8.

Luck, G. (1972), 'On Petronius's *bellum civile*', *American Journal of Philology* 93, 133–41.

Lukács, G. (1978), *Writer and Critic and other Essays* (London).

Lyne, R. O. A. M. (1978), *Ciris: A Poem Attributed to Vergil* (Cambridge).

—— (1987), *Further Voices in Vergil's Aeneid* (Oxford).

—— (1989), *Words and the Poet: Characteristic Techniques of Style in Vergil's Aeneid* (Oxford).

—— (1994), 'Vergil's *Aeneid*: Subversion by Intertextuality: Catullus 66. 39–40 and other examples', *Greece and Rome* 41. 2, 187–204.

Lyons, J. (1968), *Introduction to Theoretical Linguistics* (Cambridge).

—— (1977*a*), *Chomsky* (London).

—— (1977*b*), *Semantics* (Cambridge).

Macdonnell, D. (1986), *Theories of Discourse* (Oxford).

McDowell, J. (1973), *Plato: Theaetetus* (Oxford).

McGann, J. J. (1991), 'What Difference do the Circumstances of Publication Make to the Interpretation of a Literary Text?', in Sell (1991), 190–207.

MacHale, B. (1978), 'Free Indirect Discourse: A Survey of Recent Accounts', in *Poetics and Theory of Literature* 3, 235–87.

Macherey, P. (1978), *A Theory of Literary Production*, tr. G. Wall (London and New York).

Mack, P. (ed.) (1994), *Renaissance Rhetoric* (Basingstoke and London).

McKeown, J. C. (1989), *Ovid Amores*, ii, *A Commentary on Book I* (ARCA 22: Leeds).

Mackie, C. J. (1988), *The Characterisation of Aeneas* (Edinburgh).

Maclean, M. (1988), *Narrative as Performance: The Baudelairean Experiment* (London and New York).

Madvig, I. N. (1851), *A Latin Grammar* (Oxford).

Maiuri, A. (1945), *La Cena di Trimalchione di Petronio Arbitrio* (Naples).

Maltby, R. (1991), *A Lexicon of Ancient Latin Etymologies* (ARCA 25: Leeds).

Marincola, J. (1997), *Authority and Tradition in Ancient Historiography* (Cambridge).

Martin, R. (1981), *Tacitus* (London).

Martin, R. H., and Woodman, A. J. (edd.) (1989), *Tacitus Annals Book IV* (Cambridge).

Martin, R. P. (1989), *The Language of Heroes* (Cornell).

Martindale, C. (1993), *Redeeming the Text: Latin Poetry and the Hermeneutics of Reception* (Cambridge).

—— (ed.) (1997), *The Cambridge Companion to Virgil* (Cambridge).

Marx, F. (1959), *Plautus Rudens: Text und Kommentar* (Amsterdam).

Marx K. (1973), *The Revolutions of 1848*, ed. D. Fernbach (Harmondsworth; orig. 1848–50).

—— and ENGELS, F. (1986), *The German Ideology* (New York; orig. 1845–6).

MATEJKA, L., and POMORSKA, K. (edd.) (1978), *Readings in Russian Poetics* (Ann Arbor).

MATTHEWS, P. H. (1981), *Syntax* (Cambridge).

MEIJERING, R. (1987), *Literary and Rhetorical Theories in Greek Scholia* (Groningen).

MENDILOW, A. A. (1967), *Time and the Novel* (New York).

MILLER, J. (ed.) (1972), *Theory of Fiction* (Lincoln, Neb.).

MILLER, N.P. (1956), 'The Claudian Tablet and Tacitus: A Reconsideration', *Rheinische Museum* 99, 304–15.

MITCHELL, W. G. T. (ed.) (1981), *On Narrative* (Chicago).

MODIANO, J. (1992), 'Logiques de la description', *Poétique* 91.

MOI, T. (1985), *Sexual/Textual Politics: Feminist Literary Theory* (London).

—— (ed.) (1986*a*), *The Kristeva Reader* (Oxford).

—— (1986*b*), 'Feminist Literary Criticism', in Jefferson and Robey (1986), 204–21.

MOLES, J. L. (1988), *Plutarch: Cicero* (Warminster).

—— (1993), 'Truth and Untruth in Herodotus and Thucydides', in Gill and Wiseman (1993), 88–121.

MOMIGLIANO, A. (1977), *Essays in Ancient and Modern Historiography* (Oxford).

—— (1984), 'On Hayden White's Tropes', *Settimo Contributo alla storia degli studi classici e del mondo antico* (Rome), 49–59.

—— (1985), 'Marcel Mauss and the Quest for the Person in Greek Biography and Autobiography', in Carrithers, Collins, and Lukes (1985), 83–92.

MORAVCSIK, J., and TEMPO, P. (edd.) (1982), *Plato on Beauty, Wisdom and the Arts* (Totowa, New Jersey).

MORESCHINI, C. (1990), 'Le Metamorfosi di Apuleio, la «fabula Milesia» e il romanzo', *Materiali e Discussione* 25, 115–27.

MORGAN, J. R. (1985), 'Lucian's *True Histories* and the *Wonders beyond Thule* of Antonius Diogenes', *Classical Quarterly* 35, 475–90.

—— (1993), 'Make-Believe and Make Believe', in Gill and Wiseman (1993), 88–121.

MUECKE, F. (1983), 'Foreshadowing and Dramatic Irony in the Story of Dido', *American Journal of Philology* 104, 134–55.

MURGIA, C. (1975), *Prologomena to Servius 5: The Manuscripts* (Berkeley).

MURRAY, P. (1981), 'Poetic Inspiration in Early Greece', *Journal of Hellenic Studies* 101, 87–100.

—— (ed.) (1996), *Plato on Poetry* (Cambridge).

MYNORS, R. A. B. (ed.) (1969), *Vergili Opera* (Oxford).

NESTLE, W. (1930), *Die Struktur des Eingangs in der attischen Tragödie* (Hildesheim).

NICHOLLS, D. (1989), *Deity and Domination: Images of God and the State in the Nineteenth and Twentieth Centuries* (London and New York).

NIETZSCHE, F. (1980), *On the Advantage and Disadvantage of History for Life*, tr. P. Preuss (Indianapolis; orig. 1874).

NIGHTINGALE, A. (1995), *Genres in Dialogue* (Cambridge).

NISBET, R. G., and HUBBARD, M. (1970), *A Commentary on Horace Odes Book 1* (Oxford).

NORBROOK, D. (1984), *Poetry and Politics in the English Renaissance* (London).

—— (1994), 'Rhetoric, Ideology and the Elizabethan World Picture', in Mack (1994), 140–64.

NORDEN, E. (1912), *Ennius und Vergilius* (Leipzig).

—— (ed.) (1970), *Aeneis Buch VI*, 5th edn. (Stuttgart).

NOSARTI, L. (1996), *Studi sulle Georgiche di Virgilio* (Padua).

NUGENT, S. G. (1992), 'Vergil's "Voice of the Women" in *Aeneid* V', *Arethusa* 25. 2, 255–92.

NUTTALL, A. D. (1967), *Two Concepts of Allegory* (London).

O'HARA, J. (1997), 'Virgil's Style', in Martindale (1997), 241–58.

OFFERMANN, H. W. (1968), *Monologe im antiken Epos* (Munich).

OGILVIE, R. M. (1965), *A Commentary on Livy Books 1–5* (Oxford).

OHMAN, R. (1971), 'Speech Acts and the Definition of Literature', *Philosophy and Rhetoric* (4), 1–19.

OLIVER, D. (1989), *Poetry and Narrative in Performance* (Basingstoke).

OTIS, B. (1964a), *Virgil: A Study in Civilised Poetry* (Oxford).

—— (1964b), *Ovid as an Epic Poet* (Cambridge).

OTTER, H. (1914), *De soliloquiis quae in litteris Graecorum et Romanorum occurrunt observationes* (Marburg).

PADELFORD, F. M. (1905), *Selected Translations from Scaliger's Poetics* (New York).

PAGE, N. (1988), *Speech in the English Novel*, rev. edn. (London; orig. 1973).

PAGE, T. E. (ed.) (1894), *The Aeneid of Virgil: Books I-VI* (London and New York).

PARKES, M. B. (1992), *Pause and effect: An Introduction to the History of Punctuation in the West* (Scolar Press: Aldershot).

PARSONS, P. J. (ed.) (1974), *The Oxyrhyncus Papyri* (London).

PARTEE, B. H. (1973), 'The Syntax and Semantics of Quotation' in S. Anderson and P. Kiparsky (edd.), *Festschrift for Morris Halle* (New York).

PASOLINI, P. P. (1988), *Heretical Empiricism*, tr. B. Lawton and L. K. Barnett (New York; Italian orig. 1972).

PEASE, A. S. (1935), *Virgil Aeneid 4* (Cambridge, Mass.).

PELLING, C. B. R. (ed.) (1990), *Characterization and Individuality in Greek Literature* (Oxford).

PERUTELLI, A. (1979), 'Registri narrativi e il stile indiretto libero in Virgilio', *Materiali e Discussione* 3, 69–83.

PETERSEN, C. (1843), *Joannes Saresberiensis Entheticus de Dogmate Philosophorum* (Hamburg).

PETERSMANN, G. (1973), 'Die monologische Totenklage der Ilias', *Rheinische Museum* 116, 3–16.

PETREY, S. (1990), *Speech Acts and Literary Theory* (London and New York).

PINKSTER, H. (1990), *Latin Syntax and Semantics* (London and New York).

PITKIN, H. (1972), *The Concept of Representation* (Berkeley and Los Angeles).

POLANYI, L. (1985), *Telling the American Story: A Structural and Cultural Analysis of Conversational Storytelling* (Norwood, NJ).

POSTGATE, J. P. (ed.) (1919), *Phaedri Fabulae Aesopiae* (Oxford).

POSTLETHWAITE, N. (1988), 'Thersites in the *Iliad*', *Greece and Rome* 25. 2, 123–36.

POWELL, A. (ed.) (1992), *Roman Poetry and Propaganda in the Age of Augustus* (Bristol).

POWELL, J. G. F. (ed./tr.) (1990), *Cicero: On Friendship and The Dream of Scipio* (Warminster).

—— (1997), Review of S. Braund (1996) *Juvenal: Satires* Book 1, *Classical Review* NS 47. 2, 302–5.

—— (1999), 'Some Linguistic Points in the Prologue', in Kahane and Laird (forthcoming).

PRATT, M. L. (1977), *Towards a Speech Act Theory of Literary Discourse* (Bloomington, Ind.).

—— (1986), 'Fieldwork in Common Places', in Clifford and Marcus (1986), 27–50.

PREMINGER, A. (ed.) (1974), *Princeton Encyclopedia of Poetry and Poetics* (Princeton).

PREVITERA, C. (ed.) (1963), *Pontano: I Dialoghi* (Florence).

PULGRAM, E. (1950), 'Spoken and Written Latin', *Language* 26, 458–66.

—— (1958), *The Tongues of Italy: Prehistory and History* (Cambridge, Mass.).

PUTNAM, H. (1981), *Reason, Truth and History* (Cambridge).

—— (1983), *Realism and Reason* (Cambridge).

QUINE, W. V. (1960), *Word and Object* (Cambridge, Mass.).

—— (1966), 'Three Grades of Modal Involvement', in *The Ways of Paradox* (New York).

QUINN, K. (1982), 'The Poet and his Audience in the Augustan Age', *Aufstieg und Niedergang der Römischen Welt* 30. 1, 75–180.

QUINT, D. (1993), *Epic and Empire: Politics and generic form from Homer to Milton* (Princeton).

RABE, H. (ed.) (1903), *Scholia in Lucianum* (Leipzig).

RABINOW, P. (ed.) (1984), *The Foucault Reader* (New York).

—— (1986), 'Representations Are Social Facts: Modernity and Post-Modernity in Social Anthropology', in Clifford and Marcus (1986), 234–61.

RADFORD, A. (1981), *Transformational Syntax: A Student's Guide to Chomsky's Extended Standard Theory* (Cambridge).

REGULA, M. (1951), 'Strifzüge auf dem Gebiet der lateinischen Syntax und Stylistik; V. Besondere Darstellungsformen der Reproduktion', *Glotta* 31, 90–2.

REYNOLDS, L. D., and WILSON, N. G. (1974), *Scribes and Scholars: A Guide to the Transmission of Greek and Latin Literature*, 2nd edn. (Oxford).

RICARDOU, J. (1967), *Problèmes du nouveau roman* (Paris).

RICOEUR, P. (1988), *Time in Narrative*, iii (Chicago).

—— (1991), *A Ricoeur Reader: Reflection and Imagination*, ed. M. Valdes (New York and London).

RIFFATERRE, M. (1972), 'Système d'un genre descriptif', *Poétique* 9, 15–30.

—— (1983), *Text Production*, tr. T. Lyons (New York).

—— (1990), *Fictional Truth* (Johns Hopkins).

RIJKSBARON, A. (1994), *The Syntax and Semantics of the Greek Verb* (Amsterdam).

RIMMON-KENAN, S. (1983), *Narrative Fiction: Contemporary Poetics* (London).

ROBBINS, B. (1991), 'Tenured Radicals, the new McCarthyism and "P.C." ', *New Left Review* 188, 151–7.

ROBERTS, D., DUNN F., and FOWLER, D. P. (edd.) (1997), *Classical Closure* (Princeton).

ROBERTS, M. (1989), *The Jewelled Style: Poetry and Poetics in Late Antiquity* (Ithaca, NY).

RODRIQUEZ, M. T. (1981), 'La presenza di Orazio nella *Cena Trimalchionis*', *Accademia Peloritana atti* 57, 267–80.

ROHDE, E. (1914), *Der griechische Roman und seine Vorlaüfer* (Leipzig).

ROMAINE, S. (1985), 'Grammar and Style in Children's Narratives', *Linguistics* 23, 83–104.

ROMBERG, B. (1977), *Studies in the Narrative Technique of the First-Person Novel* (Lund).

ROSE, K. F. C. (1971), *The Date and Author of the Satyricon* (Leiden).

ROSENMEYER, T. G. (1969), *The Green Cabinet* (Berkeley).

—— (1985), 'Ancient Literary Genres—A Mirage', *Yearbook of Comparative and General Literature* 34.

ROSTAGNI, A. (1926), 'Il dialogo Περὶ Ποιητῶν', *Rivista Filologica* 4.

—— (ed.) (1944), *Suetonio De Poetis e Biografi Minori* (Turin).

RUBIO, L. (1982), *Introducción a la sintaxis estructural del latín* (Barcelona).

RUNCIMAN, S. (1951), *A History of the Crusades* (Cambridge).

RUSSELL, D. A. (ed.) (1964), *Longinus: On the Sublime* (Oxford).

—— (1967), 'Rhetoric and Criticism', *Greece and Rome* 14. 2, 130–44.

—— (1979), '*De Imitatione*', in Woodman and West (1979), 1–16.

—— (1981), *Criticism in Antiquity* (London).

—— and WINTERBOTTOM, M. (edd.) (1972), *Ancient Literary Criticism* (Oxford).

RUTHERFORD, R. B. (1995), *The Art of Plato* (London).

RUTHERFORD, W. G. (1905), *A Chapter in the History of Annotation; Scholia Aristophanica*, iii (London).

RYBERG, I. S. (1942), 'Tacitus' art of innuendo', *Transactions of the American Philological Association* 73, 383–404.

RYLE, G. (1965), *Plato's Progress* (Cambridge).

SALINGER, J. D. (1958), *The Catcher in the Rye* (Harmondsworth; rev edn. 1994).

SANDERS, E. P., and DAVIES, M. (1989), *Studying the Synoptic Gospels* (London and Philadelphia).

SANGMEISTER, U. (1978), *Die Ankündigungdirekten Rede im 'nationalen' Epos der Römer* (Beiträge zur Klass. Phil. Heft. 86; Meisenheim).

SARTRE, J.-P. (1978), *Sartre in the Seventies: Interviews and Essays*, tr. P. Auster and L. Davies (London; French orig. 1975).

SCEGLOV, J. K. (1969), 'Alcuni tratti struttarali delle Metamorfosi di Ovidio', in R. Faccani and U. Eco (edd./tr.), *I sistemi di segni e lo struttaralismo sovietico* (Milan), 133–50.

SCHADEWALDT, W. (1926), *Monolog und Selbstgespräch* (Neue Philologische Untersuchungen ii; Berlin).

SCHAFER, R. (1981), 'Narration in the Psychoanalytic Dialogue', in Mitchell (1981), 25–49.

SCHETTER, W. (1959), 'Die Buchzahl der Argonautica des Valerius Flaccus', *Philologus* 103, 297–308.

SCHRIJVERS, P. J. (1995), 'Slechte tijden, goede tijden: De Aeneid als Feest van het Vertellen', *Lampas* 28. 1–2, 67–81.

SEARLE, J. R. (ed.) (1971), *Philosophy of Language* (Oxford).

—— (1979), *Expression and Meaning: Studies in the Theory of Speech Acts* (Cambridge).

—— (1980), *Speech Act Theory and Pragmatics* (Oxford).

SEBEOK, T. A. (ed.) (1960), *Style in Language* (Cambridge, Mass.).

SELL, R. D. (ed.) (1991), *Literary Pragmatics* (London).

SERROY, J. (ed.) (1988), *Scarron: Le Virgile Travesti* (Paris).

SHAPIRA, M. (ed.) (1963), *Henry James: Selected Literary Criticism* (Harmondsworth).

SHARROCK, A. (1994), *Seduction and Repetition in Ars Amatoria 2* (Oxford).

SHATZMAN, I. (1974), 'Tacitean rumours', *Latomus* 33, 549–78.

SHKLOVSKY, V. (1965), 'Sterne's *Tristram Shandy*: Stylistic Commentary', in Lemon and Reis (1965), 25–57.

SILVERMAN, E. (1990), 'Geertz: Towards a More "Thick" Understanding?', in Tilley (1990), 121–59.

SIMPSON, D. (1989), 'Going on about the War without Mentioning the War: The Other Histories of the Paul de Man Affair' *Critical Quarterly* 31. 4, 58–68.

SIMPSON, V. (1975), 'The Annalistic Tradition in Vergil's *Aeneid*', *Vergilius* 21, 22–32.

SLATER, N. (1990), *Reading Petronius* (Baltimore).

SMITH, M. S. (ed.) (1975), *Petronius: Cena Trimalchionis* (Oxford).

SMOLENAARS, J. J. (1995), 'Schrivjers en Intertekstualiteit', *Lampas* 28. 3, 176–84.

SOLODOW, J. B. (1988), *The World of Ovid's Metamorphoses* (Chapel Hill).

SPENTZOU, E. (1997), *Reading Characters Read: Transgressions of Gender and Genre in Ovid's Heroides* (Oxford D.Phil. thesis).

STADTER, P. (ed.) (1972), *The Speeches in Thucydides* (Chapel Hill).

STANZEL, F. K. (1984), *A Theory of Narrative*, tr. C. Goedsche (Cambridge and New York; German orig. 1979).

STEELE, R. B. (1904), 'The Historical Attitude of Livy', *American Journal of Philology* 25, 15–44.

STEINMETZ, P. (1964), 'Gattungen und Epochen der griechischen Literatur in der Sicht Quintilians', *Hermes* 92, 454–66.

STERNBERG, M. (1981), 'Polylingualism as Reality and Translation as Mimesis', *Poetics Today* 2, 221–39.

—— (1982a), 'Proteus in Quotation-Land: Mimesis and the Forms of Reported Discourse', *Poetics Today* 3, 107–56.

—— (1982b), 'Point of View and the Indirectness of Direct Speech', *Language and Style* 15, 67–117.

—— (1985), *The Poetics of Biblical Narrative: Ideological Literature and the Drama of Reading* (Bloomington).

—— (1991), 'How Indirect Discourse Means: Syntax, Semantics, Poetics, Pragmatics', in Sell (1991), 62–93.

STERNE, L. (1980), *Tristram Shandy* (New York; orig. 1759–67).

—— (1997), *The Life and Opinions of Tristram Shandy, Gentleman*, ed. M. New: 'Florida Edition' (Harmondsworth; orig. 1759–67).

STEUP, J. (1881–6), *Thukydideische Studien* (Freiburg and Tubingen).

STEVICK, P. (ed.) (1967), *The Theory of the Novel* (New York).

STINTON, T. C. W. (1976), '*Si credere dignum est*: Some Expressions of Disbelief in Euripides and Others', *Proceedings of the Cambridge Philological Society* 22, 60–89.

STOESSL, F. E. (1957), 'Prologos' *Real-Encyclopädie der Klassischen Altertumswissenshaft* 23. 1, 632–41.

—— (1959), 'Prologos' *Real-Encyclopädie der Klassischen Altertumswissenshaft* 23. 2, 2312–440.

STRAND, J. (1972), *Notes on Valerius Flaccus' Argonautica* (Göteborg).

STRASBURGER, H. (1972), *Homer und die Geshichtsschreibung* (Heidelburg).

SULLIVAN, J. P. (1968), *The Satyricon of Petronius* (London).

SUMMERS, W. C. (1894), *A Study of the Argonautica of Valerius Flaccus* (Cambridge).

SYME, R. (1958), *Tacitus* (Oxford).

TANNEN, D. (1982), 'Oral and Literate Strategies in Spoken and Written Narratives', *Language* 58, 1–21.

—— (1986), 'Introducing Constructed Dialogue in Greek and American Conversational and Literary Narrative', in Coulmas (1986), 311–32.

—— (1989), *Talking Voices: Repetition, dialogue and imagery in conversational discourse* (Studies in Interactional Sociolinguistics 6; Cambridge).

TAPLIN, O. P. (1972), 'Aeschylean Silences and Silences in Aeschylus', *Harvard Studies in Classical Philology* 76, 57–97.

—— (1986), 'Tragedy and comedy—a *synkrisis?*', *Journal of Hellenic Studies* 106, 163–74.

—— (1996), 'Comedy and the Tragic', in M. S. Silk (ed.), *Tragedy and the Tragic* (Oxford).

TARRANT, D. (1955), 'Plato's Use of Extended Oratio Obliqua', *Classical Quarterly* 5, 222–4.

TASLER, W. (1972), *Die Reden in Lucans Pharsalia* (Bonn).

THALMANN, W. G. (1985a), 'Speech and Silence in the *Oresteia* 1: *Agamemenon* 1025–29', *Phoenix* 39, 99–118.

—— (1985b), 'Speech and Silence in the *Oresteia* 2', *Phoenix* 39, 221–37.

—— (1988), 'Thersites', *Transactions of the American Philological Association* 118, 1–28.

THILO, G., and HAGEN, H. (edd.) (1878–1902), *Servii Grammatici Qui Feruntur in Vergilii Carmina Commentarii* (Leipzig).

THOMAS, R. (ed.) (1988), *Virgil Georgics*, i: *Books I–II* (Cambridge).

THOMPSON, E. P. (1978), *The Poverty of Theory and other Essays* (London).

THOMPSON, J. B. (1984), *Studies in the Theory of Ideology* (Cambridge).

THOMSON, D. (1997), *The Big Sleep*, BFI Film Classics (London).

THOMSON, G. (1941), *Aeschylus and Athens* (London).

TILLEY, C. (ed.) (1990), *Reading Material Culture* (Oxford).

TILLYARD, E. M. W. (1954), *English Epic and its Background* (Oxford).

TODOROV, T. (ed.) (1965), *Théories de la littérature* (Paris).

—— (1969), *Grammaire du Décaméron* (The Hague).

—— (1978), *Poétiques de la Prose* (Paris).

—— (ed.) (1982), *French Literary Theory Today*, tr. R. Carter (Cambridge).

—— (1984), *Mikhail Bakhtin: The Dialogical Principle*, tr. W. Godzich (Manchester).

TOMASHEVSKY, B. (1965), 'Thematics', in Lemon and Reis (1965), 61–95.

TOMLINSON, G. (1987), *Monteverdi and the End of the Renaissance* (Oxford).

TROTSKY, L. (1960), *Literature and Revolution* (Ann Arbor; Russian orig. 1923).

TRUDGILL, P. (1984), *Sociolinguistics: An Introduction*, 2nd edn. (Harmondsworth).

ULLMAN, B. (1951), *Coluccio Salutati: De Laboribus Herculis* (Turin).

ULLMAN, S. (1957), *Style in the French Novel* (Cambridge).

ULLMANN, B. L. (1947), 'History and Tragedy', *Transactions of the American Philological Association* 73, 25–53.

ULLMANN, R. (1927), *La Technique des discours dans Salluste, Tite-Live et Tacite* (Oslo).

URE, P. (1956), 'The Widow of Ephesus: Some Reflections on an International Comic Theme', *Durham University Journal* (December).

VAN ERP TAALMAN KIP, A. (1994), 'Intertextuality and Theocritus 13', in De Jong and Sullivan (1994), 153–69.

VAN PEER, W. (1991), 'But what is Literature? Towards a Descriptive Definition of Literature' in Sell (1991), 127–41.

VEESER, H. A. (1989), *The New Historicism* (London).

—— (ed.) (1994), *The New Historicism Reader* (London).

VERDONK, P. (1991), 'Poem as Text and Discourse: The Poetics of Philip Larkin', in Sell (1991), 94–109.

VESSEY, D. (1973), *Statius and the Thebaid* (Cambridge).

VEYNE, P. (1964), 'Le "Je" dans le "Satyricon" de Pétrone', *Revue des Études Latines* 42, 301–24.

—— (1984), *Writing History: An Essay in Epistemology* (Manchester).

VICAIRE, P. (1960), *Platon: Critique Littéraire* (Paris).

VLASTOS, G. (1988), 'Socrates', *Proceeding of the British Academy* 74, 89–111.

VOGT-SPIRA, G. (1990), *Strukturen der Mundlichkeit in der römische Literatur* (Tubingen).

VOLOSHINOV, V. (1973) *Marxism and the Philosophy of Language* (Harvard; Russian orig. 1929).

WALBANK, F. W. (1960), 'History and Tragedy', *Historia* 9, 216 f.

—— (1985), *Selected Papers* (Cambridge).

WALKER, B. (1952), *The Annals of Tacitus: A Study in the Writing of History* (Manchester).

WALLACE-HADRILL, A. (ed.) (1989), *Patronage in Ancient Society* (London and New York).

WALSH, P. G. (1970), *The Roman Novel* (Cambridge).

WARDE FOWLER, W. (1920), *Roman Essays and Interpretations* (Oxford).

WEINBERG, B. (1961), *A History of Literary Criticism in the Italian Renaissance*, 2 vols. (Chicago).

WELLEK, R. (1965), 'The Concept of Classicism and the Classic in Literary Scholarship', *Proceedings of the 4th Congress, International Comparative Literature Association*.

—— and WARREN, A. (1949), *A Theory of Literature* (London).

WEST, D. A., and WOODMAN, A. J. (edd.) (1984), *Poetry and Politics in the Age of Augustus* (Cambridge).

WEST, M. L. (1966), *Hesiod: Theogony* (Oxford).

WESTRA, H. (ed.) (1986), *The Commentary on Martianus Capella's De Nuptiis Philologiae et Mercurii attributed to Bernardus Silvestris* (Toronto).

WHITBREAD, L. (1971), *Fulgentius the Mythographer* (Ohio).

WHITE, H. (1973), *Meta-History* (London).

—— (1981), 'The Value of Narrativity in the Representation of Reality' in H. White (1987), 1–25, and Mitchell (1981), 1–23.

—— (1986), Review discussion of McCullagh in *Times Literary Supplement*, 31 January 1986, 109–10.

—— (1987), *The Content of the Form: Narrative Discourse and Historical Representation* (Baltimore).

WHITE, P. (1993), *Promised Verse: Poets in the Society of Augustan Rome* (Cambridge, Mass., and London).

WIGODSKY, M. (1972), *Virgil and Early Latin Poetry* (*Hermes*, Einzelschriften 24; Wiesbaden).

WILKINSON, L. P. (1955), *Ovid Recalled* (Cambridge).

WILLIAMS, R. (1988), *Keywords: A Vocabulary of Culture and Society* (London).

WILLIAMS, R. D. (ed.) (1960), *P. Vergili Maronis Aeneidos Liber Quintus* (Oxford).

WILLS, J. (1996), *Repetition in Latin Poetry: Figures of Allusion* (Oxford).

WILSON, J. (1982), 'What does Thucydides Claim for his Speeches?', *Phoenix* 36. 2, 95–103.

WIMMEL, W. (1960), *Kallimachos in Rom* (*Hermes*, Einzelschriften 16; Wiesbaden).

WIMSATT, W. K. (1954), *The Verbal Icon* (Lexington, Ky.).

WIMSATT, W. K. and BEARDSLEY, M. C. (1949), 'The Affective Fallacy', in Wimsatt (1954), 21–39.

WINBOLT, S. E. (1903), *Latin Hexameter Verse: An Aid to Composition* (London).

WINKELMANN, F. (1975), *Eusebius: Über das Leben des Kaisers Konstantin* (Eusebius *Werke*, i), Griechischen Christlichen Schriftsteller (Leipzig).

WINKLER, J. J. (1985), *Auctor & Actor: A Narratological Reading of The Golden Ass* (Los Angeles).

WINTERBOTTOM, M. (ed.) (1970), *Quintiliani Institutio Oratoria* (Oxford).

WISEMAN, T. P. (1979), *Clio's Cosmetics* (Leicester).

—— (1982*a*), 'Acroasis: A Forgotten Feature of Roman Literature', *Latin Teaching* 36. 2, 33–7.

—— (1982*b*), 'Pete nobiles amicos: Poets and Patrons in Late Republican Rome', in Gold (1982), 28–49.

WITTGENSTEIN, L. (1961), *Tractatus Logico-Philosophicus*, tr. D. Pears and B. McGuiness (London; orig. 1921).

WOODMAN, A. J. (1988), *Rhetoric in Classical Historiography* (London).

—— (1995), 'A Death in the First Act: Tacitus, *Annals* 1. 6', *Papers of the Leeds International Latin Seminar* 8, 257–73.

—— and WEST, D. (edd.) (1979), *Creative Imitation and Latin Literature* (Cambridge).

—— and —— (edd.) (1984), *Poetry and Patronage in the Age of Augustus* (Cambridge).

WRIGHT, E. (1986), 'Modern Psychoanalytic Criticism', in Jefferson and Robey (1986), 145–65.

ZANKER, G. (1987), *Realism in Alexandrian Poetry: A Literature and its Audience* (London, Sydney, and Wolfeboro).

ZEITLIN, F. I. (1971), 'Romanus Petronius: A Study of the *Troiae Halosis* and the *Bellum Civile*', *Latomus* 30. 1, 56–82.

ZETZEL, J. (1981), *Latin Textual Criticism in Antiquity* (Salem).

ZOLA, É. (1867), *Thérèse Raquin*, tr. L. Tancock (Harmondsworth).

ZWICKY, A. (1978), 'Direct and Indirect Discourse', *Ohio State Working Papers in Linguistics* 17, 198–205.

Index of Principal Passages Cited

This Index contains references to passages cited from Greek, Latin and some European literary texts. Philosophers, theorists, and other authors will be found in the General Index.

General Index

Ancient authors are also in the Index of Principal Passages Cited.

Diomedes (grammarian) 48 n. 16, 70
n. 48, 227 n. 35
direct discourse (DD) 88, 89–90,
110–15
in fiction 152
in historiography 121–52
in literature 112–13
see also embedded direct discourse;
free direct discourse; *mimesis*;
quoting; visualism
discourse 3–6, 18–40
and narrative 64 n. 31, 204
see also speech modes
discursus 3
dithyrambs 69 n. 43, 70
Donatus, Aelius 27 n. 53, 38 n. 80, 42–3
Dostoevsky, Fyodor 104–5
drama 68, 69, 164, 191
see also Euripides, Plautus, Sophocles

Eclogues 27 n. 53, 29–34, 69 n. 43, 70
n. 48
Eco, Umberto 259 n. 2
ekphrasis 23, 53, 316
Eliot, George, *Adam Bede* 247, 254
Eliot, T. S. 72
embedded direct discourse 113, 289,
295, 317
embedded narrative 166–7, 235–46,
236 n. 56
see also *mise-en-abyme*
empathy (*Empfindung*) 313
see also focalization
enargeia (ἐναργεία) 53 n. 25, 155, 238
Encolpius 161 n. 22, 216–28
epic 81, 198–9, 259–305
content and form 153, 284
and ethnography 198
and historiography 81
and objectivity 25
epistemology 27, 74, 80, 119, 133–4,
139, 312, 314–15
Er, myth of 76–7, 165
ethics 28 n. 55, 57, 71 n. 49, 119,
311–12, 314–15
in epic proems 274
ethnography 13–14, 18, 117–19, 152,
197–9
ethos 312
etymology 85 n. 17, 224 n. 32, 279, 302
Euripides 164 n., 178 n. 53, 180 n.,
183 n. 61
Eurocentrism 209
Eusebius 33

events 45, 124, 311
and utterances 10, 150–1
evidence 13–14, 28 n. 56, 124, 210,
213, 246
exclamation 95, 126, 129, 171 n. 42
and FID 107, 175, 180 n. 57
in Virgil 174, 178
exotopic narration 99
expression 71–4
see also 'Longinus'
eyes 155, 188 n. 69
Ezekiel 165

fabula 243
and *syuzhet* 46, 64–5
facts 120 n. 16, 150–1
factual narrative 131, 138–52
and fictional narrative 19, 80, 116,
119, 152, 311–12
false consciousness 253
Fama (Rumour) 101, 189, 237–8,
271–4, 278–81, 303–5
ut fama 124 n. 21
family resemblances 81
Faye, Jean Pierre 28, 34, 311
FDD, *see* free direct discourse
feminism 5
fertur 43, 123–6
fiction 125, 158
fictional construction 284–5
fictional narrative, *see* factual narrative
FID, *see* free indirect discourse
fidus 282, 289 n. 53
Fielding, Henry, *Tom Jones* 133 n. 30
fieldwork 13 n. 30, 314
see also ethnography
first-person narration, *see* narrative
Fish, Stanley 18 n. 40, 119 n. 10
Fitzgerald, F. Scott 22–3, 25
focalization 98–9, 109, 139, 140–1
in Milton 298
in Petronius 240
in Virgil 41, 162, 169, 207 n.
form 13, 27, 82, 198
and content 16, 49–50, 55, 62–3
see also *fabula* and *syuzhet*; *lexis*;
narrative
Formalism, Russian 46, 64–5, 116
formulae, Homeric 271, 301 n. 72
Foucault, Michel 28 n. 55, 81
Fowler, Roger 71 n. 49, 120 n. 16
free direct discourse (FDD) 88, 90–4,
111, 113

reflexivity 14, 256, 309
 of FID 182
 of messenger scenes 260, 273–4, 275, 300
 in Petronius 234, 254, 255
renaissance humanists, *see* Poliziano, Salutati, Sannazaro, Veronese
repetition 29, 95, 200, 220 n. 19
 in messenger scene 261, 270
 sonic 224, 291 n. 59
 see also formulae; quotation
'reporting' of speech 86 n. 23, 99 n. 50
representation 45, 74–6, 79, 260, 301–5, 306–18
 epic 205–8, 287
 historical 150–2
 in Petronius 248, 254
 political 108, 316
 and speech presentation 87, 103, 112, 307–8
 visual 316
 see also *imitatio*; *mimesis*
Res Gestae 82
res/verba distinction 49, 55
 see also content; form; narrative
reusability 18 n. 42, 43, 81–2
revisionist histories 312
rheseis (set piece speeches) 144
 see also direct discourse; soliloquy
rhetoric 4–5, 315
 and defamiliarization 65 n. 33
 devices in 68
 in epic narrative 153–5, 205–8
 in historiography 116, 121
 mimesis in 309
 see also *ekphrasis*; *enargeia*; *ethos*, 'Longinus'; Macrobius; Quintilian; *res/verba*
Ricardou, Jean 274
Riffaterre, Michael 74 n. 55, 120 n. 14
Rousseau, Jean Jacques 108 n. 70
RSA, *see* records of speech acts
Rumour, *see* Fama
Runciman, Steven 149–50
Russian Formalists 64
 see also Bakhtin; defamiliarization; *fabula*; Shklovsky; *skaz*
Ryle, Gilbert 78 n. 67

Salinger, J.D. 83–4, 215
Sallust, G. Sallustius Crispus 123–4, 136
Salutati, Coluccio 271

Sannazaro, Iacopo (*De Partu Virginis*) 274–81
satire 227 n. 35, 256
 see also Horace
Saussure, Ferdinand de 67, 84 n. 13, 251 n. 94
Scaliger, Julius 71 n. 48
sceptre 7–8
semantics, *see* speech presentation
Seneca, Lucius Annaeus 127–9, 141–2, 230 n. 44 and n. 45
sermo cotidianus, *see* Latin
'Servius' 166 n. 30, 183 n. 61, 186 n. 66, 195 n. 78, 196 n. 80
 on etymology 224 n. 32
 on Fama 303–4
 on FID and focalization 109
 on genre 70 n.
 on narrative 190 n., 200 n. 90, 201 n. 93, 203–4 n. 98
Shklovsky, Viktor 46, 65 n. 33
showing and telling 53, 113
 see also *mimesis*; *diegesis*
silence 11, 19–20, 207–8
 in Aeschylus, Menander, and Livy 191
 in Luke 279
 in Petronius 248
 in reception 70, 103, 105, 109
 in Sannazaro 277
 in Virgil 154, 183–205
simulacrum 114 n. 81
skaz 83, 254 n. 103
social anthropology, *see* ethnography; fieldwork
 see also Ardener; Bourdieu; Clifford; Geertz; Gilsenan
social behaviour 108
social order (in *Satyricon*) 247–55
socio-linguistics 314
Socrates, *see* Plato
'Socratic Question' 73
soliloquy 97 n. 47, 100, 101
 in Lucan 237
 in Petronius 221–8
 in Sannazaro 275
 in Virgil 160–4, 168, 173, 191
Sophocles, *Oedipus Tyrannus* 274
sources 2, 14–15, 130, 131 n., 315
speech, 17
 and power 1–2, 6–18, 108, 248
 and power in *Aeneid* 192–208
 see also Bourdieu; direct discourse;

discourse; embedded direct
discourse; indirect discourse;
records of speech acts
speech act mention, *see* records of
speech acts
speech acts 7–8, 148, 249, 311, 316
and historiography 28, 148–9
in narrative 55
and performance 212
speech act verbs xiv, 100
texts as 18, 39, 82
theory of 4–5, 309
see *iubere*; records of speech acts
speech communities 314
speech modes 87–115
bibliography on 87–9
speech presentation xiii, xv, 5–6
as heuristic tool 120, 316
pragmatics and semantics of 86, 140,
143, 314–15
Statius, *Thebaid* 287–91
Sternberg, Meir 111–12, 132, 143, 167
n. 33
Sterne, Laurence 23 n. 47, 46
storms, speeches in 161 n. 22
story, *see* narrative/story distinction
story worlds 75, 79, 162, 213 n. 10
speech in 115, 262
verse in 66
structuralism 39, 67
style 62, 137–8, 260, 312
in Virgil 153 n. 2
subiectio sub oculos 155
subjunctive 169 n. 38
subter 304
Suetonius 15, 43 n., 249
Sullivan, J. P. 253
superaddressee 21–5, 27, 129 n. 25, 212
symbolic power 248
see also Bourdieu; speech
synoptic problem 315
syntax 82–3, 84–5
(literary) and direct speech modes
110–15
(literary) and indirect speech modes
102–10
and speech presentation 84–7
system of paired adjectives 252
systems of texts 39
syuzhet, see *fabula*

ta deonta 144, 145, 148 n. 53
Tacitus 121–6, 127–31, 132, 134,
140–2, 210, 216

Tannen, Deborah 35, 83 n. 11, 86
n. 23, 220 n. 19
taste 210–11, 253
tenses 85 n. 19, 95, 97, 107, 169, 230
aorist 103
imperfect 190
narrative present 174, 175–6, 181
past historic 82
present 72–3
Terence 251 n. 92
text 17–40
textual criticism 259, 315
Thersites 6–8, 197
Theseus 223 n. 28, 288–91
Thompson, E. P. 119
thoughts, presentation of 221
in first-person narrative 214–15
see also exotopic narration; free
indirect discourse; indirect
discourse, soliloquy
Thucydides 94 n. 35, 143–51, 311
time 30–2, 81
and DD 90, 131
and FDD (temporal telescoping)
92–3
and FID 172
and narration 45, 159
and narrative in *Aeneid* 1 159–62
see also chronology, indexicals
Todorov, Tzvetan 45 n. 2, 75, 101
n. 53, 199
tragikon 302–3
transformation 28–34, 43, 312–13
Trimalchio's dinner, see *Cena
Trimalchionis*
Trogus, Pompeius 136–8
Trotsky, Leon 119
truth 2, 38, 152
correspondence sense of 118
in epic 283–5
and falsehood 158, 163, 272–3, 278,
304
in historiography 117–19, 133,
135–7
language and 315 n. 21
in Luke and Sannazaro 279–81
see also epistemology;
historiography; ideology
Turnus 170–1, 173–4, 188 n. 69, 207

Ullikummi, Song of 260–1, 284
Ulysses 317–18
see also Odysseus

358 *General Index*

Urban, Pope 149–50
utterance 4, 18, 110–15
  historicity of 130, 131, 148, 150–1
  and language 90
  and narrative 66–71, 90
  ontological status of 125, 311
  and story 66, 93
  syntax of 87
  see also reusability

Valerius Flaccus (*Argonautica*) 101,
  291–6
  ID in 292 n. 61
verbatim, see *ipsa verba*; quotation
verisimilitude (*pithanon plasma*) 145,
  156 n. 13, 206
  see also realism
Veronese, Guarino 85 n. 19
verse, 10, 64–6, 94
  in *Satyricon* 229–39, 244, 245
  see also metre
Veyne, Paul 216
virago 224
Virgil 27 n. 53, 29–34, 38, 42–3, 124
  n. 21, 153, 165–6
  as author 212–13
  see *Aeneid*; *Eclogues*; *Georgics*;
  'Servius'

visual art 316
visualism 114–15, 156
  see also *ekphrasis*
vividness, see *enargeia*
Voloshinov, Valentin 12 n. 28,
  67 n. 39, 86–7, 89 n. 25, 104–5,
  108 n. 71, 198, 210 n. 3
vox, voces 238 n. 63
vulgarism, Vulgar Latin, *see* Latin
vulgarity and realism 156
Walbank, F. W. 137 n. 36, 145
Walsh, P. G. 223
White, Hayden 117–18, 150
Wittgenstein, Ludwig 81, 114
women 1 n. 1, 13, 178–9, 240, 243
words 127, 132
  in *Cratylus* 309
writing, written texts 58, 84, 111–12,
  212, 309 n. 8, 313
  and idea of 'text' 17
  and FID 103, 105, 107
  in Ovid 286
  see also words

xumpasa gnome 145

Zacharia 279
Zechariah, Book of 165
Zola, Émile 207–8